Also by Richard Moe

The Last Full Measure:
The Life and Death of the
First Minnesota Volunteers

CHANGING PLACES

REBUILDING COMMUNITY
IN THE AGE OF SPRAWL

RICHARD MOE

A N D

CARTER WILKIE

HENRY HOLT AND COMPANY · NEW YORK

For Julia
For Jane and for Curtis

Henry Holt and Company, Inc./*Publishers since 1866*
115 West 18th Street/New York, NY 10011

Henry Holt ® is a registered trademark
of Henry Holt and Company, Inc.

Published in Canada by Fitzhenry & Whiteside Ltd.,
195 Allstate Parkway, Markham, Ontario L3R 4T8.

Library of Congress Cataloging-in-Publication Data
Moe, Richard.
    Changing places : rebuilding community in the age of sprawl /
    Richard Moe and Carter Wilkie. —1st ed.
        p.   cm.
    Includes index.
    ISBN 0-8050-4368-3 (alk. paper)
    1. Urban renewal—United States.   2. Community life—
United States.   I. Wilkie, Carter.   II. Title.
    HT175.M65   1997
    307.3′416—dc21   97-19603

Henry Holt books are available for special promotions
and premiums. For details contact: Director, Special Markets.

First Edition 1997

Designed by Victoria Hartman

Printed in the United States of America
All first editions are printed on acid-free paper. ∞

        3   4   5   6   7   8   9   10

CONTENTS

ACKNOWLEDGMENTS

Preservation is a cause, and like all causes its success depends on the contributions of many, rather than a few.

This book would not have been possible without generous grants from three institutions whose leaders saw the need for such a work. We are deeply indebted to Julian Scheer and Nick Kotz of Protect Historic America, John Moyers of the Florence and John Schumann Foundation, and Marilyn Perry of the Samuel H. Kress Foundation for the confidence they have had in the project from the outset.

The stories in these chapters are really the stories of the people who were kind enough to share their observations of the places where they have lived and worked.

In Memphis: Ann Abernathy, Antonio Bologna, Eugene Bryan, Michael Cody, Daryl Cozen, Ann Dillard, John Dudas, Chris Fales, Jim Gilliland, J. B. Green, John Hopkins, Judith Johnson, Charlie Newman, Kay Newman, Larry Pelegrin, Mimi Phillips, Bill and Mary Reed, Jack Tucker, and Henry Turley.

In New Orleans: Annie Avery, Bill Borah, Patty Gay and her staff at the Preservation Resource Center, Tracey Hogan Hills, Scott Newman, Camille Strachan, and Thomas Tucker.

In Pittsburgh: Rhonda Brandon, Harry Clark, John Craig, Scott Brown, Harriet Henson, Stanley Lowe, Barbara Luderowski, Laura Magee, Amanda McQuillan, Howard Slaughter, Reggie Smith, Louise Sturgess, Albert Tannler, Glenn Worgan, and Arthur Ziegler and his staff at the Pittsburgh History and Landmarks Foundation.

In Bonaparte, Iowa: Gianna Barrow, Jacki Gunn, and Connie Meek.

In Chippewa Falls, Wisconsin: Louise Bentley, Alicia Goehring, Kathy LaPlante, Jeff Novak, Jayson Smith, and Virginia Smith.

In Franklin, Tennessee: Dara Aldridge, Jay Johnson, Rudy Jordan, Calvin Layhew, Mary Pearce, Catherine Whitley, and Mark Willoughby.

In Denver: Diane Blackman, Kathleen Brooker, Dana Crawford, Gerry Glick, Maurice Godgame, Jim Lindberg, Bill Mosher, Jennifer Moulton, Tom Noel, Frederico Pena, Lisa Purdy, and Cheryl St. Clair.

In St. Paul: Dick Broeker, Jeff Hess, Cheryl Kartes, George Latimer, Kelley Lindquist, Weiming Lu, John Manillo, and Charlene Roise.

In Portland, Oregon: Carl Abbott, Keith Bartholomew, Rich Brown, Lisa Burcham, Mike Burton, Rob DeGraff, Kelli Fields, Catherine Galbraith, Neil Goldschmidt, George McMath, Terrence O'Donnell, Rodney Ohiser, Judith Rees, Henry Richmond, Ruth Scott, and Bing Sheldon.

For the story of the Fourth Battle of Manassas, we thank everyone who participated in some way in that great debate, regardless of which side you were on. You are too numerous to mention, but your collective experiences will be remembered for many years to come. We would also like to acknowledge the staff of newspapers in the region whose journalism captured the frustrations and joys of the characters as events unfolded, namely, the *Journal Messenger,* the *Prince William Journal,* the *Potomac News,* the *Fauquier Times-Democrat,* the *Richmond Times-Dispatch,* all of Virginia; and the *Washington Post.*

We want to express our deep appreciation and respect for the work of our colleagues at the National Trust, especially former Chairman of the Board Henry Jordan and the current Chairman, Nancy Campbell, for their support of the project. Many members of the National Trust staff contributed their talents in important ways: Chris Beakey, Arnold Berke, Peter Brink, Jan Cigliano, Vin Cipolla, Greg Coble, Linda Cohen, Michael Corcoran, Dan Costello, Carol Cunningham, Allen Freeman, Jennifer Gallagher, Frank Gilbert, Audra Hicks, Pat Ironfield, Kim Keister, Sam Kilpatrick, John Leith-Tetrault, Edward Norton, Wendy Nicholas and the staff of the Northeast regional office in Boston, Barbara Pahl and the staff of the Mountains/Plains regional office in Denver, Frank Sanchis, Lori Schuman, Sally Sims Stokes and the staff of the National Trust Library, Anthony Verkamp, Scott Wagner, Liz Wainger, Matt Wagner, Margaret Welsh, and Amanda West. We are particularly grateful to Shelley Mastran, for her input on the potential impact of Disney's America on Virginia's northern Piedmont; Kennedy Lawson Smith, for her knowledge of the challenges facing America's Main Street business districts as well as for her comments on our draft; Constance Beaumont for her invaluable insight, her many thoughtful suggestions, and for everything she has done to put sprawl on the agenda of the preservation movement and at state capitals and local governments throughout the country. And we offer special appreciation to Dwight Young, who has been gracious in sharing his gift for expressing what preservation really means as well as his unparalleled knowledge of the preservation movement in America.

A number of individuals also deserve thanks for providing their ideas and assistance, from research leads to help in securing interviews with others. Among them are Steve Akey; Katherine Basye, who diligently waded through records at the National Trust Library, the Library of Congress, and the Library of the American Institute of Architects; Janet Carter of the Bruner Foundation; Clare Doyle; Steven Engelberg; Lester Fant; Mark Gelfand; Roberta Brandes Gratz; David Halberstam; William Klein of the American Planning Association; Kathy Kottaridis; David Kusnet; Jacquie Lawing; Mary Madden of the U.S. Department of Housing and Urban Development and a veteran of the Mayor's Conference on Urban Design; Marty Nolan; Donovan Rypkema, who always brings common sense and concern for the bottom line to any discussion of saving aging buildings; Andrew Robertson; Stanley Smith; and Ed Weiner and Richard F. Weingroff, both of the U.S. Department of Transportation.

Our agent, Gerry McCauley, was enthusiastic about the project from the beginning, and he worked his usual magic to move it forward. Bill Strachan, our editor at Holt, was equally supportive and, with his colleagues Darcy Tromanhauser and Mary Ellen Burd, saw it through unforeseen events to completion.

Finally, a work of this kind cannot succeed without the encouragement and support of close friends and family. We will be forever grateful for abundant quantities of both from Julian Scheer, David McCullough, Bob Boorstin, Julia Moe, Curtis Wilkie, and Allison Sweeney Wilkie, for her selfless support of this undertaking from beginning to end.

PREFACE

Americans have abused—and sometimes repaired—their built environment, the familiar, traditional neighborhoods, towns, and downtowns, as well as the all too familiar "sprawlscapes" where most now live. Many of America's places—new as well as old, suburban and rural as well as inner-city—are not working as they should. There are a number of reasons for it, of course, but at the top of the list is the fact that the leaders and residents of those communities made bad choices, allowed bad choices to be made for them, or made no choices at all. Communities can be shaped by choice or they can be shaped by chance. We can keep on accepting the kind of communities we get, or we can insist on getting the kind of communities we want.

Winston Churchill once said that we shape our buildings, and then our buildings shape us. He no doubt had in mind the multiple layers of history built one atop another in English cities and villages, and the evidence of culture and continuity that they gave to the successive generations of men and women who inhabited them. An important part of that culture, of course, was a deep respect for the accumulated architecture and landscapes and for the centuries of history that they represented.

While Americans are also shaped by the buildings that we have built, it is more accurate to say that we are shaped by the places that we have created. Buildings comprise a place, and architecture, it's been said, is the art of place making. In the last half of the twentieth century, we have not shaped our places very well. We have destroyed many of the most significant structures that once gave our downtowns their identity. We have abandoned and then neglected traditional residential neighborhoods that gave the people who lived there a sense of belonging. And we have allowed many of our smaller towns to dissolve into roadside clutter.

Many of our newer communities were essentially unplanned or minimally planned to provide the dream house on a large green lot far removed from schools, stores, and other community centers. The public spaces of these new communities more often than not are dominated by huge discount stores and/or strip malls along multilane highways. In fact the design of these communities is largely determined by highway engineers and superstore developers who have stepped into the void left by public officials who are either resigned to, if not eager for, this kind of "progress," and by citizens who are either complacent or who believe they are powerless. These communities are the result of a series of steps, each one apparently logical or innocuous in itself. But, as Jane Jacobs first observed more than three decades ago, "every place becomes more like every other place, all adding up to Noplace."[1]

The result of all of this is rampant sprawl, a phenomenon that has sucked the economic and social vitality out of traditional communities and filled millions of acres of farmland and open space with largely formless, soulless structures unconnected to one another except by their inevitable dependence on the automobile. That there is a diminished sense of connections—social as well as spatial—in these pedestrian-unfriendly places seems unarguable. Residents spend more time driving from one place to another and less time with one another. James Howard Kunstler has defined sprawl as "a degenerate urban form that is too congested to be efficient, too chaotic to be beautiful, and too dispersed to possess the diversity and vitality of a great city."[2]

Virtually every community in America—certainly every metropolitan area—has been affected by sprawl, but perhaps nowhere were its potential consequences more vividly dramatized or more bitterly fought than in the northern Virginia Piedmont in 1993–94, when the Disney Company sought to locate a theme park in the midst of one of the most historic and pristine areas of the country. The central issue in the ensuing controversy was not the theme park itself, but rather the collateral development that it would inevitably attract and that would overwhelm historic fragile villages, battlefields, and landscapes for miles in every direction. Although this was probably the largest and most significant sprawl battle to date, it nonetheless provides a picture of what has happened in many other communities in lesser ways, more often than not with different results. It also provides a cautionary tale of the kind of sprawl-inducing threats that will increasingly appear unannounced at unsuspecting places all over America.

There are two primary alternatives to sprawl as we know it: better planning of how we use our land; and using—or reusing—the capacity of older neighborhoods, towns, and downtowns to a greater extent than they are used now. Both alternatives are essential if we are to successfully manage growth (not stop it, but manage it) and thus contain sprawl before it bankrupts us socially as well as financially.

But before we get to alternatives we need to understand how we got to this point of disrepair. It is largely a story of good intentions gone awry, but there is more to it than that. There are many, sometimes complex reasons behind the disintegration of our older communities and the building of new ones that too often don't work. Crime, race, and the declining quality of public services, particularly education, have been important factors in spurring the exodus of residents from some of our center cities to their outlying areas. The financial rewards accruing to developers building cookie-cutter houses on cheap land—and the public subsidies that not only permit but encourage this kind of development—have given developers incentives to lure people there.

There are other reasons as well, often embedded deep in the American character. We are a restless people, seemingly always on the move. For most of the nineteenth century we moved west, until we inhabited the continent. For most of the twentieth century we continued to move west, but we also began to move shorter distances—from farm to city, from city to suburb. We like to move, and we like to occupy unoccupied places. But increasingly we move because the communities in which we live are destroyed, little by little, by insensitive development or by the arrival of the urban ills that caused us to flee the cities in the first place.

We also still tend to think of ourselves as a young country, without many man-made structures worth preserving. We don't readily see the opportunity that our accumulated architecture offers us to connect with our past, nor do we see often enough the opportunity that it offers us for reuse. We are for the most part a disposable society; when something is used up we discard it. New is better than old—tear down the old, build anew.

Happily, there are signs that this attitude is beginning to change. A growing respect for the limits of our resources and the fragility of our environment has caused us to begin recycling everything from newspapers and aluminum cans to automobiles and plastics. Belatedly, we are beginning to recognize that for the same reasons we must recycle our older communities as well.

But when it comes to communities, there are even more compelling reasons to recycle. First, it makes economic sense. We have invested billions of dollars in our older communities, in the buildings themselves as well as the public infrastructure—streets, water lines, sewers, etc.—and it is fiscally irresponsible to waste that investment. In a mobile society, that investment pays extra dividends wherever people seek out distinctive places in which to live, work, and spend their free time.

Second, recycling connects us with our past in a way that helps us to better understand who we are and where we are going. Losing the physical manifestations of our history—not just the great monuments but also the significant structures and entire neighborhoods that anchor our communities—leaves us, in the words of David McCullough, a historically illiterate nation.

Third, we don't make communities that work as well as they used to work, and it would be foolish to discard them when they can continue to serve us. Many people want the option of living in pleasant and walkable older communities, but, as we shall see, there are public policies in place that strongly favor the construction of new communities over the rehabilitation of older ones.

Finally, we imperil our whole society if we abandon entire neighborhoods and communities, and the people who inhabit them, because they no longer seem to work. We deceive ourselves if we fail to see the grievous consequences that will certainly follow such abandonment. Many of the ramifications are in fact already with us, not only in the inner cities of our great metropolitan centers but also in their outlying areas, where an estimated 4 million Americans, prompted largely by fear, today live within so-called gated communities. It is delusional to believe that the crime and decay in some of our inner cities is unrelated to what is happening in the suburbs. When the city "ceases to be a symbol of art and order," Lewis Mumford said, "it acts in a negative fashion: it expresses and helps to make universal the fact of disintegration."[3]

Twentieth-century America has turned its cities inside out, releasing industry, population, and commerce from the core, leaving ruinous environments behind. In the history of Western civilization, this phenomenon is unique. From the fall of the Roman Empire to the shrinking of the British Empire, "urban decline has usually been a product of national decline," according to urban historian Witold Rybczynski. And as author and photographer Camilio Jose Vergara has put it, America—leader of the free world—"leads the world in urban ruins."

This book is about ruins and rehabilitation. It is not about cities, per se, as much as it is about places within cities, in small towns, and across the countryside that have inspired residents to reclaim them. It is about places harmed and places healed. As much as anything, it is about places worth saving. Places such as historic Memphis, whose urban history could be the story of many once great American cities. Places such as troubled neighborhoods in New Orleans and Pittsburgh, where residents took matters into their own hands and transformed them into the livable places they once were. Places such as the small towns of Bonaparte, Iowa, Chippewa Falls, Wisconsin, and Franklin, Tennessee, where imaginative and determined businesspeople led efforts to revitalize deteriorated commercial districts and thereby gave their communities a new lease on life. Places such as Denver, St. Paul, and Portland, Oregon, where urban entrepreneurs combined with enlightened public officials to find new ways to strengthen core downtowns by turning buildings and whole districts that had been regarded as community liabilities into community assets.

These are largely unheralded stories, sometimes even within the communities where they occurred. They are the stories of men and women who challenged the prevailing wisdom of their fellow citizens to prove that they had within their existing structures the means of community rebirth. They are the stories of individuals who believed enough in their communities that they were prepared to risk their own resources and reputations, usually with little or no help from government. They are the stories of communities being shaped at the grass roots, and therefore they are uniquely American stories, filled with grit, determination, and optimism.

The message these stories carry is that our older neighborhoods, towns, and downtowns can be made to work again by realizing the potential of the physical resources that are already there. It may be necessary, particularly in the case of downtowns, to find new uses for some of those resources so they can serve the revised needs of the community. But imagination and "adaptive reuse" can be effective tools to make that happen. Every community is different, to be sure, and not every old building deserves to be saved, but virtually every community has within its borders many buildings and neighborhoods that do because they contain the physical seeds of community renewal.

We are beginning to realize that our communities, new as well as old, are not working as they should, and that the built environment that surrounds them has a great deal to do with it. We are beginning to see that we are indeed shaped in turn by the places that we shape, as Churchill suggested, and that we can do a much better job of shaping.

CHANGING PLACES

———————

1

THE FOURTH BATTLE OF MANASSAS

How much of historic America, how much of our national heritage, will be left for future generations? And what does it say
about us, of our values, of our regard for those who will follow, not
to say those who went before us, if we as citizens stand by while
others destroy historic America—knock it down, pave it over, blot
it out—in the name of so-called progress and corporate profits?
—David McCullough

In the fall of 1993, the Walt Disney Company stunned Virginians
with plans to build its next resort on undeveloped fields thirty-five miles west
of Washington, D.C., in the northern Virginia Piedmont. The announcement
sent shock waves through the region that reverberated across the nation, the
opening salvo for one of the most publicized preservation battles since the
Penn Central Transportation Company sued New York City over the fate of
Grand Central Terminal. That famous case became a referendum with national implications governing the protection of historic landmark buildings.
The Disney episode became a national referendum on the protection of historic places from urban sprawl.

If communities are shaped by the choices they make or by the choices
that are made for them, then the northern Virginia Piedmont is a classic case
in point—on both counts. In 1993, people far removed from the Piedmont
descended on it to formulate plans that would change it forever. Few if any
residents of the Piedmont were even aware of their plans, let alone helped
shape them. Over the course of a year, however, people who lived in this
unique corner of the country, with the help of others who believed that they,
too, had a stake in the fight, decided they wanted to make another choice. In
a matter of months, the episode became a battle joined by people across the
country, wherever communities are being transformed by careless decisions
about development and the use of land.

In the years since Disneyland opened in Anaheim in 1955, Disney's amusement park business had grown from a single eighty-five-acre park to four resorts on three continents: the original Disneyland Park; Walt Disney World, in Kissimmee, Florida, near Orlando; Disneyland Paris, operated in France by Euro Disney; and a financial stake in Tokyo Disneyland, in Japan. In 1993, the company tried to develop yet another destination in North America to complement its resorts in Florida and California, this time in northern Virginia, on the rim of the country's fourth largest metropolitan area, at the southern tip of the heavily populated northeastern United States.

Washington, D.C., is one of the top ten travel destinations in the United States. Almost 20 million people visited the area in 1993, and while some came for business and left quickly, 13 million visitors were Americans who came strictly on vacation and stayed longer, making travel and tourism a major regional industry worth $4 billion to the area's economy each year. After resolving to tap this vital market, the Disney Company decided that Dulles International Airport, in suburban northern Virginia, would be its gateway. East of the airport, near Washington, was a busy region, dense with highways, giant shopping malls, and the towering, sprawling office complexes of the new Virginia suburbs. Land to the west was still home to Old Virginia, large farms overlaid with two-lane roads that ran past colonial-era mills and homes, historic brick courthouses, and small, locally owned stores clustered along the main streets of scenic villages and towns. In choosing a site for its next major tourist destination in the United States, the Disney Company leapfrogged the New Virginia suburbs and settled on a pristine spot eight miles beyond the edge of urban sprawl, in a rural town called Haymarket, population 483.

Haymarket was a quiet place—only one intersection had a traffic light. Only one street was home to buildings in any significant number, and all of them were small. The narrow town hall, painted white, didn't look much different from a church, also painted white, down the street. The surrounding area was remote and relatively undeveloped, a virtually virgin landscape, as Anaheim had first appeared to the builders of Disneyland forty years before. The local terrain was dominated by hill farms, where people raised horses, beef, and hay on rolling pastures and a butcher advertised his services, "Custom Slaughtering," on a small sign poked in his yard. Here, the Disney Company could develop a locale from scratch.

Of the 3,000 or so acres Disney secured, 380 of them had been a farm picked up at an auction after a foreclosure. The core of the site, about 2,000 acres, was a former plantation, where an antebellum mansion built in 1826 had burned in 1973. Before Disney arrived, speculators had planned to develop the spot into a residential subdivision before a recession ended their plans. The property was put up for sale, but until Disney's agents arrived, there had been no takers. From the Disney Company's perspective, the location was ideal. Dulles International Airport was just twenty miles away. Tourists could arrive from Washington by driving west on Interstate 66. Access aside, the location is a beautiful spot of rolling fields nestled beside the Bull Run Mountains, where a creek named Little Bull Run flows toward the Manassas National Battlefield Park, site of two famous Civil War battles, only four miles away. In almost every direction the location is surrounded by the natural and historic landmarks of Virginia's northern Piedmont.

The Piedmont, a landscape of rolling hills that rise from the coastal plains of the Virginia Tidewater and stretch westward to the Blue Ridge Mountains, remains one of the most scenic and historic regions in the United States. Thirty-eight of Virginia's fifty-three scenic byways pass through the northern Piedmont. Of all the miles of rivers declared scenic in Virginia, almost half of them run through here, too. A short drive north of the Disney site on a two-lane scenic byway is Leesburg, a colonial-era town recognized by the National Register of Historic Places as "one of the best preserved, most picturesque communities in Virginia." Between Leesburg and the Disney site are other notable historic places, including Middleburg, the heart of hunt country, where wealthy landowners raised horses on well-kept fields and hounds hunted foxes on lands where a band of Confederate cavalrymen, Mosby's Rangers, once raided Federal supplies. Some of the surrounding hillsides were planted with orchards and even vineyards for a burgeoning regional wine industry.

For residents of the more densely populated coast, the Piedmont was still the gateway to the wooded mountains of the Blue Ridge and the verdant Shenandoah Valley. In his *Notes on the State of Virginia*, Thomas Jefferson described the scenery at the Piedmont's northwestern corner. "The passage of the Potomac through the Blue Ridge is one of the most stupendous scenes in nature," wrote Jefferson, who claimed that the Piedmont's mountains, rivers, and plains presented a landscape "as placid and delightful as it is wild and tremendous." Jefferson was so moved by what he saw in the Piedmont that he claimed, "This scene is worth the voyage across the Atlantic." A friend of Jefferson's in France, Pierre Samuel du Pont de Nemours, identified the region as an ideal location to settle his family as they prepared to emigrate to America. According to du Pont, the scenery was gorgeous and land could be purchased inexpensively before inevitable roads increased its value.

Historians have called the Piedmont "the Cradle of Democracy," for all of its connections to so many of the founding fathers. George Washington surveyed land here in the mid-eighteenth century and mapped out some of the

Piedmont's early settlements. Jefferson made his home here, as did other notable Virginians of his day, including Patrick Henry, the revolutionary firebrand who became Virginia's first elected governor; James Madison, father of the Constitution; President James Monroe; and John Marshall, the influential chief justice of the young Supreme Court of the United States. Today, their homes are stopping points for the hundreds of thousands of visitors attracted by the Piedmont's history.

Virginia's northern Piedmont was also the crossroads of troop movements during the Civil War. This was the strategically critical piece of land between the capital in Washington at one end and the capital of the Confederacy in Richmond at the other, and some of the most significant Civil War battles occurred on Piedmont soil. At Chancellorsville, the Wilderness, and Manassas, nearly thirty thousand Americans lost their lives. At the First Battle of Manassas, or Bull Run as it was known on the Federal side, Union forces suffered their first serious defeat of the war in 1861. Here, South Carolina general Barnard Bee saw Virginia general Thomas J. Jackson and shouted, "There stands Jackson like a stone wall. Rally around the Virginians!" Another Virginian, Robert E. Lee, solidified his reputation as a general here, too, when his troops handed the Union another humiliating defeat at the Second Battle of Manassas in the following year.

Soldiers who traversed the Piedmont in wartime could not help pausing to admire it, as their journals, letters, and diaries attest. While marching his troops toward Gettysburg in 1863, Robert E. Lee stopped near Brandy Station to view the Piedmont's open fields and hills. "The country here looks very green and pretty not withstanding the ravages of war," wrote Lee. "What a beautiful world God in His loving kindness to His creatures has given us. What a shame that men endowed with the reason and knowledge of right should mar His gifts." On the Union side, a soldier from Minnesota described his regiment's excitement when they crossed the Potomac River from Maryland and "set their unhallowed feet upon the sacred soil of 'Ole Virginny.'" Even by then, Virginia's history was legendary. When the same soldier marched through Haymarket, site of the future Disney development, en route to neighboring Thoroughfare Gap, he wrote of seeing "much magnificent scenery. If I were a free man I should enjoy a whole day's ramble in this vicinity."[1]

Historian C. Van Woodward has written about the Piedmont, "This part of northern Virginia has soaked up more of the blood, sweat and tears of American history than any other area of the country. It has bred more founding fathers, inspired more soaring hopes and ideals and witnessed more triumphs and failures, victories and lost causes than any other place in the country. If such a past can render a soil 'sacred,' this sliver is the perfect venue."

The Walt Disney Company saw this historic sliver of northern Virginia as the perfect venue for an amusement park playing up historical themes. As one Disney executive said, "The site itself is part of the show." Scott Stahley, a real estate scout from Disney's corporate headquarters, said that what impressed him most about the place was "how romantic it feels."[2] As Disney executives discovered the region's history, however, Virginians knew nothing of their plans. Site selection was a secretive process that one company executive described as "two years of painstaking analysis and exhaustive search."[3] Though Disney signed up some of the top local firms in real estate, land-use law, and public relations early, the company kept its project hidden from the public for as long as possible.

As rumors of Disney's activity in northern Virginia finally began to spread, Disney's spokesmen held off queries from reporters while company executives briefed only a handful of Virginia's elected officials in private. Some officials were never consulted beforehand. John Kapp, the mayor of Haymarket, said he hadn't heard a word.[4] John Milliken, Virginia's secretary of transportation, whose department oversaw highways that would critically affect Disney's plans, said, "We had no advance notice."[5] What little anyone knew about the project came from drops of information that leaked through the cracks of closed doors. Some sources told local papers that Disney's project in Virginia would be small, a theme park no larger than "the size of the original Disneyland in Anaheim," or about eighty-five acres. Others said it would be no larger than Kings Dominion, an amusement park operated near Richmond by Disney competitor Paramount Communications. The precise location of the enterprise remained a mystery. Realtors speculated that Disney would build in western Prince William County, in a remote area beyond the edge of urban sprawl. Jeff Griffin, president of Prince William 66 Partnership, a group formed to promote development along the Interstate 66 corridor, said, "It's a gorgeous setting out in that area," a landscape of "rolling terrain and so forth." Griffin predicted that a Disney development would be good for the area: "They do very high quality projects." And the prospects for local developers would be enormous, he speculated. "There would be normal collateral development," Griffin said, "hotels, retail, things of that sort." One source said that Disney had already gained control over enough land to build its fantasyland, expand in the future, and provide the site with a substantial buffer of green acres to isolate it from inevitable roadside development that would sprout outside its borders. "They're not shopping around," another source told the *Richmond Times Dispatch*. "They're going to do it." "Brace yourself," said Virginia's senior United States senator, John Warner, "Virginia's getting a big one."[6]

The Walt Disney Company announced its plans at a November press conference attended by the outgoing governor, Douglas Wilder, and his successor, George Allen, who had been elected only the week before. Allen, in fact, had just returned to Virginia from a postelection vacation with his family. They had gone to Florida, to Walt Disney World, where Allen spoke with Disney chairman and chief executive officer Michael Eisner about the project. The announcement was also attended by a cadre of local officials who helped the company unveil plans for a multifaceted real estate development centered around an amusement park the company called "Disney's America."

Disney officials told the audience that unlike Disneyland or Walt Disney World, major tourist destinations, the Virginia development would tap into the existing regional tourist market. A typical family outing to Disney's America would be a day trip. Disney spokesmen played down any impact the park would have on the surrounding region. They said visitors would travel together in large groups, via minivans, station wagons, and buses, limiting the extra traffic on local roads. The company said visitors would travel to Disney's America from Washington in the morning as area residents commuted to work in the other direction. The company refused to confirm attendance projections, but credible estimates put the number at thirty thousand visitors a day on average, up to 6 million visitors a year. Compared to popular attractions in Washington, that meant Disney's America would draw five times as many visitors in a single year as the Lincoln Memorial, four times as many as the Vietnam Veterans Memorial, three times as many as the Smithsonian Institution's Castle Building, and twice as many visitors as the National Zoo. But unlike Orlando or Anaheim, company officials said, Disney's America would not need an abundance of hotel rooms. The Washington region had sixty-five thousand rooms already, and most visitors, they said, would drive back to Washington at the end of the day to stay in hotels there. In the initial stages of park development, they predicted, a modest hotel with 150 rooms would do.

These first projections would seem misleading, or naive at best, after a few days of good questioning by the local press. But on the day of the initial announcement, icy skepticism about the scope of the project melted in the warmth of Disney's multimedia displays, which promoted the main attraction, the amusement park itself. The park was to be designed around themes in American history. As first announced, antique steam trains would take passengers on a ride through a simulated nineteenth-century town. A white-water raft ride would recall the Lewis and Clark expedition. "Presidents Square" would honor the nation's founding fathers. A "Civil War fort" would showcase skirmishes between troops in blue and gray, while around the "fort," replicas of the ironclad warships, the *Monitor* and the *Merrimac*, would clash in water. A miniature version of Ellis Island would interpret the tidal wave of late-nineteenth-century European immigration. A simulated depression-era "Family Farm" was planned, so "visitors may see how the land is harvested." A make-believe "State Fair" would celebrate "small town America at play with a nostalgic re-creation." A "sprawling airfield" would display vintage aircraft from the two world wars and serve as a stage for air shows and for fireworks at night. And a fabricated American Indian village would depict "a complex and sophisticated life lived in harmony with the land long before . . . European settlers pushed it to the edge of extinction."[7]

The legendary entertainment company's proposal to build an amusement park based on American history in one of the most historic regions of the country immediately triggered a confrontation that pitted the trademarks of popular culture against the landmarks of American history.

Promotional material for Disney's America contained ironies that opponents would exploit for months, particularly the simulation of authentic historic towns, farms, and battlefields that Virginia already possessed. Few states in the nation, if any, boasted of their history as much as the Commonwealth of Virginia. A visitor's map published by the Allen administration, for instance, showed a picture of the new governor and scenes of Virginia's colonial-, revolutionary-, and Civil War–era sites under the headline "Places to See." Richmond, Virginia's capital, promoted itself in a brochure as "Pure Virginia. Nothing artificial." The explanation for this was simple. Tourists contributed $9 billion to the state's economy each year. When the Division of Tourism of Virginia's Department of Economic Development conducted a study to see what drew tourists to the state, 73 percent of first-time visitors said history was the reason, more than twice the number who came for shopping centers, three times those who came for beaches, and four times the total who came for theme parks operated by Disney's competitors.[8] Visitors in search of historic sites, meanwhile, spent more than twice as much in Virginia as other tourists. Unquestionably, Virginia's historic sites were economic assets worth protecting and promoting.

In choosing historic Virginia as the location for a theme park based on history, the Disney Company saw a natural fit. If Disney officials expected any conflict at all, it was an old criticism that had haunted their productions before: blurring the lines between reality and fantasy, sentimentalizing history for popular entertainment. In a telephone interview with *Washington Post* reporters, Michael Eisner said, "We are going to be sensitive, but we will not be showing the absolute propaganda of the country." Eisner warned that some exhibits would be "painful, disturbing, and agonizing." For instance, he said, "We will show the Civil War with all its racial conflict."[9] "You will not see Mickey Mouse walking around in Civil War reenactments, because he doesn't belong there," said Bob Weis, vice president of Disney's creative division, the team of designers called "imagineers" by Disney employees. "This is not a Pollyanna view of America," he said. "We want to make you a Civil War soldier. We want to make you feel what it was like to be a slave or what it was like to escape through the underground railroad."[10]

In reply, African American opponents quickly said they didn't want to see the subject of slavery exploited in a theme park. In Thoroughfare, a tiny village next to the site where Disney intended to construct slave-life exhibitions, the grandchildren of slaves still farmed land where their ancestors had settled after gaining freedom following the Civil War. Some of these neighbors said they didn't want to see their family heritage demeaned by Disney displays or their local history bulldozed by the Disney development. Outside the area, a black history group formed to oppose the Disney project. One of the leaders said she didn't want to see "miniature slave ships" sold in the theme park's souvenir stands.

"We're not going to put anyone in chains," Eisner responded.[11] The project's manager, Mark Pacala, said Disney's America would send guests home happy and feeling good about their country. "We don't want people to come out with a dour face," he said. "It is going to be fun with a capital F."[12]

The growing flap over Disney's "imagineering" became the least of the company's worries. The more critical brewing controversy was not about *how* Disney would tell its stories, but *where*. The real debate was over the location, and Disney was stubborn about the spot. Spokesmen said the Piedmont was the company's only choice for Disney's America; the company had no contingency locations. "This is an idea that only works in this location," said Peter Rummell, president of Disney's development company. "If you take it to Kansas, it doesn't work."[13]

Disney was drawn to the Piedmont for the regional travel market and the accessible open land in a scenic spot. But the company also needed public officials who would favor a proposal of this scale. It found them in Prince William County at the fringes of the Washington suburbs, too remote to attract all of downtown's riches—its highest-paying employers and its diverse tax base—but close enough to want its fair share.

Prince William had no trouble attracting new residents. A development boom in the 1980s raised the county's population by 63 percent, from an estimated 144,703 people when the decade began to 235,766 by the end of 1993. Manassas had doubled its population from 1980 to 1992, earning a spot in a U.S. Census list of the twenty-five fastest growing places in America.[14] Over the next thirty years, the county was projected to maintain its rapid growth and nearly double its population again. Many new residents came for the abundant supply of relatively affordable new homes in one of the most expensive housing markets in America. In terms of housing costs, Prince William was a bargain, but the hidden costs were high. The county had the lowest ratio of jobs to residents of any county in northern Virginia. Over 60 percent of its residents commuted to jobs out of the county. The average commute took thirty-six minutes, or the annual equivalent of spending seven and a half work weeks traveling between home and work. Though two interstate highways linked the county to the metropolitan core, traveling on them during rush hours was stressful. Traffic was a political hot potato. Kathleen Seefeldt, who chaired the county's board of supervisors, said, "No issue is more important in my community than the ability to have a decent job that does not require spending three hours a day in an automobile."[15]

The only local issue that rivaled traffic was taxes. After the county became a sprawling bedroom community of residential subdivisions, its tax base had grown unbalanced. Five years earlier, Seefeldt had warned that "an explosion of growth" had placed "fiscal stress" on county taxpayers. She explained that each new homeowner paid only about sixty cents in property taxes for every dollar he or she got back from the county in the form of new roads, schools, and extended water and sewer services.[16] "Every time we build a house, we lose money," said County Executive James Mullen.[17] The county's fiscal headache wouldn't go away. Schools were crowded, and the only cost in the county budget growing faster than education was debt service—interest payments on money the county had to borrow to service mile after mile of houses, roads, strip malls, and parking lots spread out over wide, expensive distances.

"It is extremely important to achieve a balance between jobs and housing in any community," Seefeldt said. "Too many jobs result in sterile office parks that are abandoned at nightfall. Too many houses can result in bedroom communities without a central focus." Indeed, across the northern Virginia suburbs were plenty of half-empty places like the ones Seefeldt described: office complexes surrounded by parking lots, shopping malls with larger parking lots, and clusters of new houses that real estate marketers called "townhomes." But around these new "townhomes," there were rarely any towns to speak of, just more parking lots. In this sprawling built environment, few, if any, new communities had that healthy "balance" Seefeldt described, where neighborhoods, stores, schools, apartments, and offices were placed in proximity. Even the new state-of-the-art Bull Run Regional Library was built off a busy highway, tucked behind a strip mall.

Prince William County was responsible for its zoning regulations, which had invited the costly sprawl, but it was also an incidental victim of geography. Counties adjacent to Washington enjoyed metropolitan prosperity; counties further west enjoyed rural tranquillity. But Prince William County taxpayers, wedged in between, were squeezed. They paid the highest county property tax rate in Virginia, and, still, their county was desperate for more revenue. Most county officials, who represented the densely populated I-95 corridor in the eastern end of the county, felt that the only realistic solution to their fiscal woes was to attract high-value development and build their way out of it, even at the risk of angering residents in the county's sparsely populated western end along I-66. The largest source of county tax revenue, after all, was Potomac Mills Mall, America's largest regional outlet mall when it opened in 1985. In a single year, the number of shoppers at the mall exceeded the total number of visitors who went to Washington, making this suburban shopping center the number one visitor destination in the nation's capital region. When the Disney Company proposed its $650 million project, the company seemed to offer county officials everything they had hoped for and more, all in a single package. "I have wanted so badly for six years to land something," said County Supervisor Hilda Barg. "I can say that I really got the fish that will reduce your taxes. And we have landed a big one."[18]

Business leaders in western Prince William were no less enthusiastic. Hotel and store owners foresaw an influx of new customers. Anyone in real estate understood that a dormant market had blossomed overnight. Congressmen spoke glowingly about the benefits of tourism, a "clean industry" that attracted travelers who spent money in an area and then went home, placing few burdens on local taxpayers. Mike Vanderpool, a former president of the local chamber of commerce and an attorney for developers with interests in the region, encouraged business owners to rally behind Disney's America. This was Prince William's turn to be "the Center of It All," just as Kissimmee, Florida, had become when Walt Disney World arrived in town. Local business leaders formed a "Welcome Disney Committee." Another group called itself "Patriots for Disney." Other supporters formed yet another group and called themselves "Friends of the Mouse." The *Potomac News,* the daily paper for eastern Prince William County, responded with a huge front-page headline, "Disney YES," and an editorial entitled "Zippity Doo Dah!" Vanderpool said it was time to think about commercial flights landing at the small Manassas regional airport. The airport's manager said, "You get a lot of saliva in your mouth just thinking how good it would taste."[19] News of Disney's America lifted the morale of anyone who resented living in the shadows of high-rise development closer to Washington. "All of a sudden, people in northern Virginia don't think Haymarket and Prince William County are that far away," said local business leader Cal Hackeman.[20] Jeff Griffin, the developer promoting the I-66 corridor, said, "Prince William County isn't going to be thought of as a poor stepchild anymore."[21]

Disney executives had hoped county opinion leaders would favor their project, and to a great extent, they did. Yet, after two years and millions of dollars' worth of research and planning, the Walt Disney Company either failed to anticipate, or seriously underestimated, the greatest obstacle to its plans. The very qualities that made the Piedmont site so attractive for Disney's America—its historical associations, its tranquil natural beauty, and the ability to buffer the site from encroaching sprawl—were exactly the same qualities that made the place special to so many others. As many saw it, the Disney development threatened to erase those cherished qualities.

Similar emotions have greeted cataclysmic development proposals in almost every state in the nation. Citizens of Lancaster, Pennsylvania, and Petoskey, Michigan, have watched with dread as developers have threatened to displace their fragile historic downtowns as well as the natural landscapes at their borders. According to the American Farmland Trust, urban sprawl costs America 1 million acres of farmland each year, an area equivalent in size to the entire state of Delaware. Over ten recent years, Michigan, a state with some of the most productive orchards in the nation, lost 854,000 acres of farmland to development, an area roughly the size of Rhode Island. Author and journalist Tom Hylton has reported that since the 1950s, sprawl in Pennsylvania has consumed an area larger than Connecticut and Rhode Island combined, while the state's historic cities and towns have lost between one-quarter and one-half of their populations.[22] In all of these places, thousands of decisions are made about the development of communities each day, most of them behind closed doors. In most places, concerned citizens fail to notice the consequences of these decisions until it is too late to do anything about them.

In Virginia, the surprise of Disney's announcement and the enormity of its scope guaranteed that opposition from neighbors would be immediate and widespread. By announcing Disney's America in front of a backdrop of elected officials, Disney hoped to give its plans an aura of inevitability, to overwhelm any dissension that might arise from the grass roots. That tactic angered Virginians, who saw the character of their communities being sold away overnight. "It's going to change the whole flavor of western Prince William," said Richard Hefter, who was president of the area's citizens' association. People like Hefter felt the sudden announcement was a bombshell that would deliver a chaotic explosion of speculation, construction, and congestion.

The prospect of thousands of additional travelers on already congested roads became the first signal of a potentially diminished quality of life for local homeowners. A number of them came together to oppose Disney's America under the banner "Protect Prince William." Near Disney's site, I-66 was built to handle 47,000 vehicles a day on average. But up the road at Manassas traffic had already reached 77,000 vehicles a day during midweek. Where I-66 intersected the Capital Beltway, the vehicle count had climbed to 172,000, more than double its intended capacity. It wasn't long before bumper stickers appeared on cars stuck in northern Virginia traffic that labeled Interstate 66 "Disney's Parking Lot." The stickers were a product of the Disney Take a Second Look campaign, organized by residents of the region who wanted Disney to choose another site. The campaign's leaders argued that Disney had skipped over sites already equipped for such a massive project, places closer to Washington with enough land, existing road capacity, even subway service to many of the capital's attractions and hotels, not to mention proximity to job seekers in need of the kind of employment Disney's America would provide. They charged Disney's America would spawn a new interstate highway, a western bypass around Washington's outer suburbs, an outer beltway through the heart of northern Virginia's countryside. "We just think this thing would promote another new enormous wave of urban sprawl out west of Washington," said Robert Dennis, president of the Piedmont Environmental Council, a 2,500-member group founded in 1972 to "preserve the traditional nature of Virginia's Northern Piedmont."[23] Since its formation, the Piedmont Environmental Council had led efforts to preserve farmland, forests, and watersheds as well as historic villages and towns across twelve northern Virginia counties. The council's strongest base of support came from residents of scenic Fauquier and Loudon Counties, two rural counties on the edge of urban sprawl. Disney, in fact, planned to build within a mile or two of the Fauquier and Loudon County lines. Because Virginia had no planning authorities to consider the regional impacts of development proposals, Fauquier and Loudon residents would have little say in Prince William County deliberations over Disney's America. To correct that imbalance, the Piedmont Environmental Council became the most indefatigable opponent of Disney's America, lobbying tirelessly and mobilizing public opinion against the project at every turn.

Between those who chose sides in the debate were plenty of Virginians who remained open-minded about the impact of Disney's America. Kris Hodge, who had just opened a sandwich shop in Haymarket before Disney came to town, had mixed feelings on what the project would mean for the area. "That land is going to be developed no matter what," she said. "I just don't want all the big companies coming in, buying up all the land and putting up these non–small town type things, big hotels overpowering the little buildings of Haymarket. I'd hate to see the town destroyed by that." Still, she said, "Disney is a high class company, and I think they can do it in a tasteful manner. But until we get all the facts, we can't be sure."[24]

To help collect the facts, County Executive James Mullen went to Florida to consult public officials in Orlando about their experiences with Disney. He returned with a list of warnings. Disney's neighbors in Florida had told

Mullen that the company could be heavy-handed and could easily over-whelm the county's staff and taxpayers, if not kept in check.[25] In spite of these warnings, however, most county officials were eager to put Disney's America on a fast track toward approval. They had spent the two prior years trying to lure Lego, a Danish toy company, to build a $100 million amuse-ment park for children near I-95. But within weeks after Disney's announce-ment, Lego turned the county down, notifying county officials by a faxed letter that the company had opted instead for Carlsbad, California, near San Diego. After losing Lego, Prince William County officials bent over back-ward to accommodate the Disney Company. Sensing the friendly mood, Dis-ney executives asked the county to waive its zoning application fees, which totaled $621,000. Facing a budget deficit and countless hours of staff time needed to review Disney's massive plans, county supervisors didn't waive the fees. Instead, they reduced the fees by $400,000 on December 21, when most county taxpayers were too busy preparing for the coming Christmas holiday to object.

Though Disney's land-acquisition costs in this remote site were relatively low, the expense of extending services to undeveloped land would be high, and Disney sought to shift those costs to local taxpayers. The company had taken a loss on Euro Disney in France, and now it wanted to limit the ex-penses of building Disney's America. Though the company chose the site us-ing its own criteria to find a place that would produce the optimum profitable return, Disney wanted Prince William County taxpayers to chip in $15 million for new water and sewer lines, and Virginia's taxpayers to pitch in more than $100 million for road improvements. Only a month after the com-pany had wowed Virginians with its plans, Eisner warned Virginians that without public subsidies to cover the expenses of construction in Virginia's rural Piedmont, Disney's America would not be feasible. If public money did not come through, Eisner said, the total costs would "crater the company fi-nancially" and Disney would back out of the deal.[26] Some supporters of the project feared that Disney could withdraw its proposal at any time, just as Lego had recently done. The month before, when Disney had only good news to share about its proposal, the sitting governor, Douglas Wilder, had said, "How gratifying that Disney didn't subject us to a bidding war."[27]

Wilder was leaving the governor's office as a veteran of losing bidding wars. In addition to Lego, United Airlines had passed over Virginia as a place to build a major maintenance facility, choosing Indiana instead. And Wilder had been rebuked by the citizens of Alexandria, a suburb of Washington, who did not share his enthusiasm for constructing a new football stadium for the Redskins in their community. The incoming governor, George Allen, was aware of Virginia's habit of letting the big one get away and was determined to reverse that pattern. Allen gleefully called Disney's America the largest single development project in Virginia history, the keystone in Virginia's economic renaissance. "Virginia is open for business," Allen announced, and he promised Disney officials that "our administration will knock down any hurdles you may have." At a National Governors Association meeting in Washington, Allen defended Disney's request for public subsidies, saying any state would jump at such a deal. "If you ask the other 49 governors here, 'How would you like to have a $650 million investment in your state, with good clean industry providing jobs and revenues?' I guarantee you, they'd be very happy to do so."

Once in office, Allen appealed to the legislature to help finance the project with a package of subsidies and incentives worth roughly $160 million. The money would help cover road improvements, Disney's moving expenses, the cost of training Disney employees, and a promotional campaign aimed at potential visitors. Some scoffed at such a deal. Virginia had never given any business such breaks before, certainly not existing amusement parks like Kings Dominion and Busch Gardens, near Williamsburg. Nor had Virginia ever spent similar dollars to promote its numerous historic sites. But Allen was following the example of governors who had already lured highly visible development projects to their states using huge tax incentives as the bait. In 1992, for instance, South Carolina governor Carroll Campbell had sought and won from his legislature a $135 million subsidy to bring a BMW plant to his state, at a cost of $68,421 in tax dollars for every new BMW job created. A year later, Alabama governor Jim Folsom lured the makers of the Mercedes-Benz with a subsidy of $253 million for a factory that would employ 1,500 workers, a cost of roughly $168,000 per job. To press its case, Allen's administration commissioned a study that projected Disney's America would generate $47 million in state taxes and 19,440 jobs by 2007. Disney's own estimates were lower, $38 million in state taxes and 12,400 jobs by 2007.[28] Disney opponents conducted their own study, which estimated the project had the potential to generate 6,000 new jobs, but that study also warned that Disney's America could become a net drain on Prince William County's tax base when all the costs stemming from the new development were added up.

Allen's job estimates sounded appealing, but opponents charged that the Disney Company would import its own executives and middle managers and merely hire Virginians for the low-paying, part-time seasonal positions. Besides, they noted, northern Virginia was not so desperate for such a deal. Sure, some folks were hurting. Corporate downsizing had made many workers nervous, and it was easier to notice the large employers cutting jobs than it was to notice the smaller new companies fueling the region's economic growth. But, on the whole, Prince William was a prosperous county, with an unemployment rate of only 2.4 percent, the lowest in Virginia. The county's median family income was $52,078, placing Prince William in the twenty most affluent counties in the United States. Other parts of Virginia had unemployment levels double or much greater than Prince William's. Workers in Norfolk suffered defense cuts and a slumping shipbuilding industry. Workers in southwestern Virginia suffered a downward slide in coal mining. Portions of Richmond had some of the highest unemployment rates in the state. Northern Virginia, by contrast, didn't have a pool of labor available to meet Disney's needs. Fast-food franchises in the area couldn't find enough workers for all the low-paying jobs that existed already. Attracting a labor force to service Disney's America, opponents said, would burden local taxpayers with costs they couldn't meet: more roads, more schools, and more services for more new housing.

In Richmond, some legislators felt uneasy about providing millions of taxpayer dollars to a multibillion-dollar corporation run by the highest-paid CEO in America. Others worried about setting a precedent that would become costly the next time developers came knocking at the state treasury door. Still others found it hard to justify such a large investment in an unproven tourist attraction, rather than in a high-wage industry that would allow Virginia to compete in the rapidly changing global economy. Robert M. De Voursney, a professor at the University of Virginia's Weldon Cooper Center for Public Service, said the Disney debate revealed Virginia's lack of a statewide economic strategy as well as the lack of a regional economic plan for northern Virginia once Disney's America would be complete. The fiercest critics of Disney's America charged that the only plan in place seemed to be an open invitation to a corporation from Burbank, California, to come and plunder Virginia's historic character, countryside, and taxpayers. "Disney's proposal is part of the national and global trend toward corporate colonization," argued Richard Squires, a writer and composer who lived in the Piedmont. Disney's America, he claimed, would transform a rural section of northern Virginia into "a commercial colony whose profits will be sent far, far away from the local community in which they are made." Following Disney would be "a secondary invasion of national and global chains, to feed off the stream of tourists flowing through the park," he warned. "The profits from these companies—Sheraton, Wal-Mart, Home Depot, Pizza Hut—will be shipped back to their various home bases." Over time, local identity would disappear under an onslaught of outside forces. "It makes one think of the Native Americans, who thought the big men in white ships were gods, and gave them shells, beads and land—lots of land."[29]

"How, one wonders, could we have come to this point—so susceptible to gross exploitation?" asked urban affairs analyst and syndicated columnist

Neil Peirce. "Some say it's jobs—but Northern Virginia has scarce unemployment. To large measure it's greed—for all the new income to an area—and our ignorance of history." Similar occurrences could be found in other places on smaller scales, Peirce explained. "As such scenarios get repeated, again and again and again across the country, the time is ripe for a ferocious, populist-style counter revolt. Ordinary citizens, in league with environmentalists, preservationists, and regionalists, need to blow the whistle on corporations ready to rape our landscapes and plunder our tax bases."[30] That revolt would indeed erupt in the coming months, just as Peirce had suggested, but not before the Virginia General Assembly, after a massive barrage of coordinated corporate lobbying, approved Allen's package of benefits for Disney's America on the final day of the legislative session. Opponents noticed that the four hundred thousand dollars Disney spent on lobbying the capitol was the same amount by which Prince William County officials had reduced Disney's development application fees.

The eventual economic impact of Disney's America would be argued for months. Almost every study or statistic produced to prove an argument on one side invited a study or statistic to prove the opposite point on the other side. But if the impact of Disney's America on Virginia's economy was debatable, its impact on the Piedmont was undeniable. Both sides knew that the region would inevitably change from what it was into something else. Only two other places in America had gone through such an experience before. And as soon as news of Disney's America was spread throughout the country, calls and letters came in to local public offices, citizens groups, and newspapers from Disney's neighbors in California and Florida, warning northern Virginians what to expect.

Anaheim, in less than a generation, had gone from a land of quiet orange groves to one of California's ten largest cities, a sprawling agglomeration of highways littered with roadside strip development linked by asphalt lanes and parking lots. Californian J. J. Garden had watched the transformation after the Marine Corps brought him to Southern California from the East Coast in 1956. "This change from one of the most desirable places in the United States to one of the dirtiest and most crowded was accomplished with the constant urging of elected officials to accept 'progress' and 'development' that would enlarge the tax base and bring prosperity for all," Garden wrote to opponents of Disney's America. "No one apparently noticed that the large landowners who were selling were not staying to benefit from these 'improvements.' They were taking the money and wisely leaving the area. The smaller property owner however was stuck with the wall-to-wall development that followed, the bumper-to-bumper traffic, the dirty air, the crime, the lowering of the quality of life." Garden knew how easy it was for people to become tempted by the near-term prospect of jobs. His own father-in-law, he said, had hauled sand in Anaheim's expansion. But back then, Garden said, Disney's neighbors in Southern California had no way to judge what was happening around them until it was too late to alter the course. He likened them to a frog in a pot of water. "You know what they say—if you heat the water up slowly, the frog dies calmly as the water boils, but if you drop the frog in a pot of boiling water, the frog will try to jump out of the heat." After retiring from the military, Garden had moved to Fredericksburg, Virginia, far enough away to be unaffected by Disney's America, but close enough to recognize what was coming.

According to chronicles of the company's history, Walt Disney himself didn't like the sprawl that sprouted around his amusement park in Anaheim. It was ugly. It limited Disney's ability to expand. And it cut into his company's profits. So when he chose to expand the business, he went to central Florida. There he launched a secretive effort to buy up nearly thirty thousand acres, where he planned to raise a new city on open land, what he called an "Experimental Prototype Community of Tomorrow," or EPCOT for short. Since the opening of Walt Disney World's Magic Kingdom in 1971, the transformation of central Florida has been as dramatic as the change in Southern California. In two decades, Orlando became the most visited destination in the world, home to more hotel rooms than anywhere else in the United States. But some there wondered if the price of prosperity had been too high. "I have lived in central Florida most of my life," wrote one man to Virginians weighing the impact of Disney's America. "I have watched the peaceful, quiet, congenial American town of Orlando being first tempted, then transformed, and finally stripped of its identity," he said. "What the Disney organization would have you perceive as progress and opportunity will materialize into mass traffic jams [and] a massive influx of profiteers. . . . Please don't let the fine, proud people of Virginia, your beautiful landscape, and our genuine historical heritage fall victim to an irreversible mistake."[31]

In a matter of months, Disney officials began to acknowledge that plans for Disney's America were larger than initial hints had led people to believe. Traffic, the company admitted, would be heavier than earlier projections. In addition to thirty thousand daily tourists, new residents of Disney's development would help add seventy-seven thousand more cars to local roads each day. Projected road improvements would be more expensive than anyone had perceived. The number of hotel rooms Disney intended to build was triple the company's first estimate. The amount of commercial space Disney planned to develop had nearly doubled since the first announcement. In a rural landscape of one- and two-story buildings, or an occasional three-story barn, Disney wanted to build structures eighteen stories high, the same height as the EPCOT Center globe.[32]

Opponents seized the new details as confirmation of their early warnings that Disney's America would become larger than anyone could realize. "I've always said this is the tip of the iceberg," said Bobby McManus, a woman who lived near the Disney site and represented the area on the county's Board of Supervisors. "They were just giving us little appetizers to make this teasing and appeasing. We haven't got the big dose yet."[33] Bigger doses would come. The number of hotel rooms, for instance, would nearly triple again. Disney would ask for development limits to be waived on a portion of its parcel, saying plans had not been finalized. Critics said that an exemption from limits would allow Disney to build whatever it wanted on the parcel, up to seven thousand houses and enough commercial space to rival the downtown of a large city, without having to go through any public process for approval. Disney officials said they had no intention of building beyond what had already been proposed. But critics felt that once Disney's America began, there would be no way to prevent it from growing out of control. "It's a runaway freight train," McManus, the county supervisor, would say.

In its own defense, Disney said it was proud of its development record. In Virginia, the company repeatedly said that it intended to be a good neighbor, a steward of the environment, and sensitive to its surroundings. "The Walt Disney Company is a recognized world leader in providing the highest quality entertainment through its theme parks, theatrical film, television and consumer products," said the first words in the company's environmental policy submitted to Prince William County officials. "Because the Company has held a unique position of public confidence and trust for more than fifty years, it is keenly aware of its inherent ability to influence public opinion and inspire action."

Indeed, Disney inspired action and respect like few corporations in America. Developers worldwide admired the way the company managed its amusement parks. Disney's developments were typically clean, well landscaped, and carefully patrolled. Its theme parks were pedestrian-friendly environments, a fantastic escape from autocentric sprawl. To walk down Main Street U.S.A. at Disney's Magic Kingdom, visitors had to abandon their cars at a parking lot outside the gate. Once inside, no roadside parking lots spoiled the view. No traffic lights forced engines to idle while drivers choked on fumes. Model trains or horse-drawn streetcars carried people who chose not to walk. Inside its borders, a Disney amusement park was the very antithesis of sprawl; outside, sprawl reigned supreme.

Though Disney facilities in Florida covered only three thousand acres, the same amount of land the company sought in Virginia, sprawl stretched for another thirty thousand acres, in the form of restaurant franchises, motel chains, and asphalt. The areas around Disney's parks "reveal a history of maximum visual and social impact, intense agglomerated development and casual disregard for the character of the existing landscape," noted a review of the proposed Disney's America in *Landscape Architecture* magazine. "The same pattern seems to be emerging at the Virginia site. . . . So, while the jury might still be out on the merits of Disney's America, it's looking pretty mickey-mouse so far."[34]

In Virginia, opponents of Disney's America did not question the company's skill as a developer. They were much less concerned by what would happen inside the boundaries of Disney's America than they were by the collateral development that would surround it. No matter how careful Disney might be with the design of its own attractions, the company had no ability to control sprawl in its surroundings. Some of Disney's supporters in Virginia shared the same concern. "We do not have concerns with what Disney does themselves, because they're first class," said John M. Elkin, president of the county chamber of commerce. "It's that land around the property, making sure we get quality development. That's the tough one."[35] Even Disney's local team began to acknowledge these genuine fears. "The concern about urban sprawl is a legitimate concern," said Disney spokeswoman Mary Anne Reynolds.[36] But company officials repeatedly said that controlling sprawl in northern Virginia was not their responsibility. That job, they explained, belonged to area citizens and their elected leaders. Peter Rummell, the president of Disney's development company, said, "We're as worried as the Piedmont Environmental Council. It is an issue that involves Prince William County, the region, Disney and everybody else." In fact, the company's own concerns about sprawl had driven Disney to purchase enough land to buffer its site from potential unsightly neighbors, just as the company had done in Florida thirty years before. "The last thing we want is to have another Anaheim there, with places at our border that the local community doesn't want," Rummell said.[37] A local paper that ran editorials in support of Disney's America echoed his point in blunt terms: "Nobody wants another Orlando in Prince William."[38]

As Disney's executives in Virginia were growing more sensitive to the local mood, Eisner, Disney's strong-willed CEO, was not. In a June 2, 1994, appearance on *CBS This Morning*, Eisner was asked if Disney's America would transform Virginia's northern Piedmont into the next Orlando. "The fact that our acreage in Orlando, which is twice the size of Manhattan, is immaculate would be something that I would think would be a benefit to Virginia," Eisner said. "They should be so lucky as to have Orlando in Virginia."

If critics of Disney's America were concerned about the company's inability to control sprawl in Anaheim and Orlando, they were even more concerned when it came to Prince William County's ability to control sprawl in its own backyard. Over the previous two decades, Prince William County's government had "never met a strip mall, shoppette, or apartment complex it didn't fall in love with," said Harold Dutton, a lawyer in Manassas who had chaired the county's Planning Commission during a cycle of rampant development in the 1980s.[39] A six-mile strip of Route 234 outside the historic town of Manassas was lined with shopping plazas and parking lots, drive-through restaurants and parking lots, and large, bright signs that advertised everything from gasoline to fast food. Critics of Disney's America pointed to Route 234 as an example of the kind of sprawl that would follow in Disney's wake. After touring the area for himself, Eisner didn't help the company's case when he said Route 234 "makes Orlando look like The Plains." The Plains was a tiny historic village located a few miles west of Disney's site, the kind of fragile place opponents feared would become unrecognizable if Disney's America were built. In effect, Eisner said that if the area was already home to sprawl, there was no harm in sprawling more. "The First Amendment gives you the right to be plastic," he said.[40]

One of the most eye-opening appraisals of western Prince William's potential to sprawl beyond recognition came from Benjamin Forgey, architecture critic for the *Washington Post,* in a lengthy piece headlined "Disneyopolis." Forgey reported that the land between the Disney site and downtown Manassas was already zoned for 77 million square feet of development for commercial or industrial uses—roughly two and a half times the amount at Tyson's Corner, the prototypical "edge city" located halfway between Disney's site and Washington. "That is the rough statistical equivalent of today's downtown Boston," Forgey noted. "It's twice as much as downtown St. Louis. It's three times Miami. It's very nearly equal to downtown Washington." Prince William County's master plan, its longer-range guide for changes to the county landscape, allowed for even more commercial and industrial space, 784 million square feet—three times the amount of office space in Manhattan. Ed Risse, a planning consultant based in northern Virginia, argued there was no way development on this scale could occur in such a remote location. Roads were congested as it was. Development plans in the area had already been put on hold or canceled. The county's office space was already more than one-fifth vacant, the second highest vacancy rate in the region. But Disney's America, and the government's intent to subsidize it, Risse explained, would catalyze the urbanization of an area that was "now relatively immune from urban pressures."[41] As Risse envisioned, Disney's America would be followed by a heavy volume of traffic, new residents and more traffic, additional commercial enterprises and yet more traffic. In time, the existing transportation system would become dysfunctional, effectively isolating the area from metropolitan Washington. This situation would cause large employers to locate farther away from the metropolitan core to be closer to the homes of employees stranded in traffic. Eventually, residents of the area, discouraged by the congested roads and unsightly sprawl, would search for home sites in more remote, secluded locations, places with fewer competing vehicles on the road, further continuing the cycle of outward sprawl. These forces would spawn more leapfrog development, south and west of Disney's America into the Shenandoah Valley, into West Virginia's eastern panhandle, and north into western Maryland until spilling over into southern Pennsylvania. Based on trends in northern Virginia, Risse projected that in twenty years, "Disney's America would generate a disaggregated urban system that would expand the Washington/Baltimore region by 2,300,000 acres. This urban complex would have a population of 230,000 and an employment base of 120,000 workers." In terms of its size, "it would rank as the 141st largest urban region in the United States, behind Tallahassee, Florida, and ahead of Odessa-Midlands, Texas, and Roanoke, Virginia."[42] In other words, Disney's decision to locate in such a remote location would spawn the creation over time of a midsize city where none existed before. What Disney planned to build on its three-thousand-acre site would ultimately affect the metropolitan region and its surrounding countryside for miles in every direction.

When the Piedmont Environmental Council issued Risse's report, the group was accused of scare tactics, of using unrealistic expectations to frighten northern Virginians into believing Disney's America could be bad for the area. It was hard to imagine Haymarket, with a population under five hundred, becoming one of Virginia's largest cities. Preservationists countered that instead of a compact metropolis, the Piedmont would most likely be transformed into concentric strips of sprawling development, much like the areas that surrounded Disney's resorts in central Florida and Southern California.

The repercussions were felt far beyond the Piedmont. In February, the *New York Times* weighed in with an editorial entitled "Virginia, Say No to the Mouse." "The proposed Disneyfication of this unique countryside raises questions of national importance," the editorial declared. "Putting a theme park there degrades a scenic and historic resource for a project that can be built elsewhere. This is precisely the sort of exurban zoning issue that will proliferate in a 21st century America with more people and fewer well-preserved natural areas."[43]

That very issue—poorly planned development that drains investment from historic urban cores—was high on the agenda of the National Trust for Historic Preservation. Since the 1970s, the Trust had helped merchants on the main streets of America's small towns compete with sprawling strip malls that drained historic business districts of their economic vitality. A year before, when Vermonters faced proposals to build new "superstores" that would have overwhelmed their small towns as well as Vermont's careful land-use planning laws, the Trust placed the entire state of Vermont on its annual list of "America's 11 Most Endangered Historic Places." That designation sparked a public response greater than any designation had before. Vermont's governor, Howard Dean, labeled sprawl a threat to his state's environment and its economy's largest industry, tourism. Across the country, other communities fighting sprawl took notice in places where developers and local officials were forcing citizens to accept a false choice between the preservation of their community character and the promise of prosperity, just as Virginians were forced to do in the debate over Disney's America.

After examining Virginia's northern Piedmont, the Trust concluded there was no other region in America more thickly sown with such significant reminders of America's heritage. Within a thirty-minute drive of the Disney site were 18 Civil War battlefields, 14 historic district towns or villages, and another 60 individual sites listed in the National Register of Historic Places. Within a sixty-minute drive were another 14 Civil War battlefields, 24 historic districts, and 175 more individual National Register sites. The threat to such places became clear soon after Disney's announcement. When a historic house in Haymarket was quickly sold and scheduled for demolition to make way for new development, one local resident said it was "the first move to annihilate the town."

In early May of 1994, the Trust entered the debate by taking out a full-page ad in the *Washington Post* to deliver an open letter to the Walt Disney Company. "Disney's America, and the development that will inevitably ripple from it, will destroy one of the most historic and beautiful landscapes in the country," the letter said. "It will stand as a superscaled specimen of the leapfrog development that, year after year and acre after acre, erases the American countryside—sapping the vitality from existing cities and towns, fueling automobile dependency and its devastating impact on the region's air quality, and luring economic and social resources far away from where they are most needed." The letter praised the Disney Company for its long history of creativity and success. It appealed to Disney executives to put that tradition to work in a more responsible location, "closer to existing development, more handy to labor pools and serviced more efficiently and comprehensively by existing roads and mass transit." The ad also invited readers to help persuade the Disney Company to choose another site. Nearly four thousand people responded, all but a handful in support of the Trust's position. One of them wrote, "Disney cannot come close to offering enough economically in exchange for what it will help to destroy." The ad struck a chord. The Piedmont, more people began to say, was far too special to sacrifice for an amusement park.

To help persuade the Disney Company to find a more appropriate site for Disney's America, a large number of prominent historians and writers formed a group, Protect Historic America. Organized by Pulitzer Prize–winning journalist Nick Kotz and public relations consultant Julian Scheer, both residents of Virginia, the group was led by James McPherson, one of the nation's preeminent Civil War historians, who was also deeply involved in battlefield preservation efforts, and McPherson's fellow Pulitzer Prize–winning historian David McCullough, a dedicated preservationist and a member of the National Trust's board of trustees. "This is no longer a local issue," McCullough said at a press conference held to announce the group's formation. Roger Wilkins, a professor of history at Virginia's George Mason University and a descendant of Virginia slaves, said the matter went beyond Virginia's borders. He called the location of Disney's America "a national calamity."

Members of Protect Historic America were incensed at the thought of sacrificing the Piedmont and its authentic reminders of American history for a commercialized facsimile called Disney's America. "If one were to search for a surviving segment of historic America worth protecting, worth fighting for, worth keeping as it is for future generations, one could hardly do better," McCullough would say later. "This is the home ground of our Founding Fathers, the hallowed ground of those who died in our country's greatest, most costly struggle. . . . Just as Virginia would protest an amusement park at Omaha Beach or at the rim of the Grand Canyon, we speak out now for Virginia."

The prominence of Disney's critics gave opposition to Disney's America national visibility and credibility. Millions knew McCullough as the author of *Truman,* the best-selling biography of the thirty-third president. Some remembered his voice from his role as the narrator of *The Civil War,* the public television series watched by nearly 40 million viewers in 1990. Shelby Foote's colorful commentary for the program made him an overnight celebrity to millions who had never read his brilliant trilogy on the Civil War. The PBS series stimulated an unprecedented level of interest in Civil War history, battlefield tourism, and preservation of Civil War sites. Foote became one of the proposal's most ornery foes. Ken Burns, the soft-spoken filmmaker who had overseen production of *The Civil War,* was working on a new project with Disney when his former collaborators announced their opposition to Disney's America. At the risk of jeopardizing his relationship with Disney, Burns, too, joined the cause. Because of a four-year release agreement with the Public Broadcasting System, millions saw *The Civil War* again in the summer of 1994, just as the historians launched their toughest attacks on Disney's plans.

In spite of the prizewinning authors and prominent historians in Protect Historic America and the growing national attention they commanded, members of the group felt like underdogs. After all, they had taken on the

Walt Disney Company and all the resources at its command. The historians were not optimistic. "Out there is a treasure that belongs to all of us," McCullough said about the Piedmont. "If it looks like Orlando five years from now, we'll at least know that we put up the warning flags and tried to stop it."

If Disney's site selection team had gone scouting for red flags in the early stages of planning they would have found plenty. Twenty years before, in 1973, the Marriott hotel chain had announced an agreement with Prince William County officials to construct a "Great American Theme Park" at the southwestern corner of the Manassas battlefield, site of significant activity during the Second Battle of Manassas in 1862. A National Park Service archaeologist later discovered more evidence of slave life on that site than at any other place in the region, including Mount Vernon and Monticello, the plantation homes of George Washington and Thomas Jefferson.[44] For years, federal officials had tried to include that tract of land in the battlefield park, but county officials, desiring development, objected. Though Marriott's proposal drew loud opposition swiftly, Prince William County officials gave their quick approval, only to see it overturned on a legal technicality at the end of a lengthy lawsuit four years later. Once again, federal officials tried to acquire the tract, whose value was then assessed in the range of $2 million, and add it to the park. But, again, they were dissuaded by officials from Prince William County.

As recently as 1988, a national outcry stopped bulldozers from leveling historic Stuart's Hill for a shopping mall called William Center. Stuart's Hill was the site of Robert E. Lee's headquarters during the Second Battle of Manassas and was also a burial place for Confederate dead. The threat to the battlefield attracted the attention of Arkansas senator Dale Bumpers, who, with the help of other members of Congress, persuaded his colleagues to save it while they could. One of them, New Hampshire senator Gordon Humphrey, argued that the mall would "turn the Manassas Battlefield into little more than a pastoral backdrop for another metropolitan concrete complex."[45] That controversy, dubbed the "Third Battle of Manassas" in the press, put local preservationists like Annie Snyder of the Save the Battlefield Coalition in the national spotlight. (Controversies over preservation of the battlefield date back even before the siting of an interstate highway in the 1950s.) A former marine who farmed land near the Manassas battlefield, Snyder could have made a small fortune by going along with the mall and then selling her farm to a developer. Instead, she became the star witness for preservation. At a hearing on the battlefield at the U.S. Capitol, Snyder told senators that "an outraged nation rises in righteous ire to protest this huge shopping mall that will violate the integrity of the Manassas battlefield park." She presented the petitions of seventy-five thousand people who asked that the site be saved.

"This is a thing whose time has come," Snyder said, because "they have a Manassas. They have something that is imperiled in their own state. They love our national treasures, our national parks, our national battlefields, and they want them protected." Within months, President Ronald Reagan signed a measure to purchase the land from the developer, add it to the battlefield park, and preserve it in perpetuity. The cost was $118 million, considerably more than the $2 million appraisal just a few years before the controversy had erupted.

The Walt Disney Company disregarded these precedents. Though the company spent millions of dollars to conceive its project and negotiate with real estate brokers, landowners, and public officials, it spent virtually no time with the public before its surprise announcement and seemed unprepared for the negative public reaction when it came. "I expected to be taken around on people's shoulders," Eisner said. Snyder, the veteran of previous preservation skirmishes, bluntly called Disney's America "an insult to Virginia." She and her allies were determined to fight it, and they made committed and formidable foes. Stonewall Jackson had preached their tactics to a fellow officer after the Battle of Cross Keys, in the nearby Shenandoah Valley. Always surprise the enemy, Jackson advised, strike, and never let up so long as you have strength to follow. "Such tactics will win every time, and a small army may thus destroy a large one in detail, and repeated victory will make it invincible."[46] Disney's army neglected philosopher George Santayana's admonition that those who fail to study history are doomed to repeat it.

The 1988 fight over the shopping mall made Americans aware of the vulnerability of America's Civil War battlefields, some of the most significant of which were being plowed under, paved over, and swept away for legitimate but poorly sited projects. Others were being gobbled up or unwittingly strangled by the slow expansion of multilane highways over ancient two-lane roads. A federal Civil War Sites Advisory Commission report, issued only months before Disney announced its plans, warned that "the nation's Civil War heritage is in grave danger. It is being demolished and bulldozed at an alarming pace." Of all the battlefields within a half-hour drive of the future Disney development, three—Manassas, Brandy Station, and Bristoe Station—were among the most important sites at the highest risk of being damaged irreversibly. Of the additional battlefields within an hour's drive of Disney's site, five more were in critical need of protection: Chancellorsville, Wilderness, Cedar Creek, First Kernstown, and Mine Run. Historian James McPherson, a member of the battlefield commission, warned that if Disney's development went ahead as proposed, the pressures on all of the sites would accelerate faster than the nation's ability to preserve them. "Some of them would be doomed to extinction," he said.

Disney executives never provided any clues that the company would be willing to reconsider its proposal, but Disney's corporate history showed that the company had been sensitive to appeals on behalf of preservation before. In the late 1980s, Disney's Buena Vista Pictures purchased the El Capitan, a landmark theater on Hollywood Boulevard in Los Angeles. Originally erected as a show stage in 1926, the theater was remodeled as a movie house in 1942, when its name changed to the Paramount. Buena Vista Pictures planned to cut the old theater up into a modern multiscreen cinema. But preservationists, speaking on behalf of the landmark and its importance to the history of Hollywood Boulevard, persuaded the new owners to restore the structure using historic rehabilitation tax credits. The company re-assessed its original plans, decided to restore the El Capitan to its original luster, and turned the landmark into a successful showcase for Disney pro-ductions. The restored theater became a catalyst for new efforts to revive the area's theater district, winning awards from the Los Angeles Conservancy (the citywide preservation group) and the National Trust for Historic Preser-vation a year before Disney's America was announced.

Disney's experiment with preservation in Los Angeles led the company to pursue a similar effort in the East. In the middle of the debate in Virginia, Disney announced intentions to restore the New Amsterdam Theater, a ninety-one-year-old historic landmark on New York's Forty-second Street near Times Square. From 1913 to 1927, the New Amsterdam had showcased the Ziegfeld Follies and performances by Irving Berlin, W. C. Fields, Will Rogers, and other popular entertainers. The restoration plan was the idea of architect Robert A. M. Stern, who taught historic preservation at Columbia University and also served on Disney's board of directors. In early 1993, Eis-ner became interested in Stern's idea and went to see the theater for himself. Outside, the building was surrounded by the seediness of Times Square's adult entertainment. Inside, it was strewn with debris from a renovation ef-fort abandoned years before. Pools of water stood on the floor and mush-rooms sprouted on wooden risers. Eisner told *New York Times* writer David Dunlap that he was "astonished that this once grand theater could have be-come so run-down." Still, Disney's CEO saw potential in the place and thought, "Wouldn't it be marvelous if this theater and this whole district could be brought back to their former glorious stature?" With its gutsy com-mitment to restore the abandoned New Amsterdam Theater, the Disney Company became a private partner of the local groups New 42d Street Inc. and the 42d Street Development Project and catalyzed one of the most excit-ing preservation efforts anywhere.

Disney's vice president for corporate real estate, David L. Malmuth, said the company's decision to rehabilitate the run-down theater in such a freewheeling urban environment had not been an easy one. For forty years, the company's routine development formula had been to build attractions in pristine environments over which the company had complete control. This was Times Square, and the project was a gamble. "The judgment we were trying to make was whether this was the right time to make a bold move," Malmuth said. "Those are the tough calls to make, because you could be very wrong."[47]

In Virginia, critics of Disney's America wondered how the company could have been so wrong in choosing the site it did. A month before Disney went public with its plans, a council of local governments in Virginia, Maryland, and the District of Columbia had adopted a set of goals for the region's future. The goals were the consensus of a two-hundred-member committee, the Partnership for Regional Excellence, comprising regional business, civic, and environmental-group leaders. Together, they looked at development trends across metropolitan Washington and concluded that low-density sprawl at the region's fringe threatened regional ability to sustain a prosperous economy, a stable society, a healthy environment, and a high quality of life for its residents. Over the next twenty-five years, the population of the District of Columbia would hardly change, but the population of northern Virginia would rise by 57 percent and employment in northern Virginia would rise by 72 percent.[48]

"The real question is what kind of growth is right for this region?" asked Dana Nottingham, director of development for Disney's America, at one of the many public hearings on the project. "Will it be clean, economically secure growth that provides a foundation for responsible land use? Or the fragmented, reactive development, born of economic desperation, that wise communities today seek to avoid?" To its critics, Disney's America represented leapfrog sprawl at its worst. Planning consultant Ed Risse said it had the potential to alter the northern Virginia landscape more than any project since the Pentagon was built south of the Potomac. In rebuttal, boosters of Disney's America said their opponents were fooling themselves if they thought rural Haymarket would never be developed on the scale that Disney proposed. "The reality is that you are going to see a new edge city in Haymarket," said Michael Vanderpool. "The Disney project will accelerate it to some extent."[49] But Joel Garreau, who chronicled the explosion of northern Virginia's suburban development in his book *Edge City*, offered a more realistic view of the future. "I don't expect many new edge cities to be built in the rest of the country for the next 20 years, simply because the market can't absorb them," Garreau wrote. "Instead, I see enormous demand for public funds to retrofit the edge cities we have already built to make them more efficient, more civilized, and more environmentally friendly."[50] Oliver Carr, a

major real estate developer in downtown Washington and a former president
of the Greater Washington Board of Trade, said, "We do need economic development, but it's got to be thoughtfully placed. The quality of life in the region is what I think creates the greatest magnet for the region, and if we
demean it then we demean our prospects economically."[51]

To protect the region's economic potential, environment, and quality of
life, the panel of civic leaders assembled by the regional Council of Governments had urged local authorities to redraft their old zoning laws that encouraged sprawl. They recommended the concentration of new development
along existing transportation infrastructure to get maximum return from investments made already. They recommended the preservation of older communities threatened by disinvestment as well as the development of new
communities in more appealing, compact ways. They said the "model for
these new suburban centers would be Georgetown, Leesburg, Old Town
Alexandria, and Reston," the most compact and some of the most desirable
places to live in the metropolitan region.

Disney's own marketing research showed that more compact new communities built around traditional town centers could indeed appeal to potential home buyers. Accused of accelerating sprawl in northern Virginia, the
Disney Company, ironically, was already planning alternatives to sprawl on
five thousand acres of its property in Florida, at a place called Celebration.
In a break from conventional formulas for placeless subdivisions or gated
housing complexes around a golf course, Disney hired a hall of fame of
American architects and community planners to design a new city for twenty
thousand. The new community was to be modeled after traditional towns
where families lived on tree-lined streets in houses built in traditional styles,
within walking distance of a town center filled with offices, apartments,
stores, and schools. Architect Robert Stern, whose firm designed Celebration's master plan along with the New York firm headed by Jaquelin Robertson, said the team sought ideas for the new community in historic Beaufort
and Charleston, South Carolina, and Florida's Coral Gables and Winter Park,
as well as in Seaside, the most widely reviewed New Urbanist development
in America, on the Gulf Coast near Pensacola.

Located across Interstate 4 from the Walt Disney World resort, Celebration is promoted in company literature as "a real place," with "everything a
town should have. Homes with front porches. A vibrant downtown where
you run into friends. A business district whose buildings have distinctive
looks. . . . And overall, the look and feel of a warm and friendly neighborhood." Because the Disney Company controlled the locale, it did not have to
haggle with public zoning authorities or private lenders stuck in the mind-set
that imagines only sprawl. But Stern said one of the greatest difficulties in

creating Celebration was converting building contractors to the idea that they could construct new houses in more appealing ways for a variety of household incomes. Many of them, Stern said, build one project well early in their lives and replicate the same formula for the rest of their careers. In marketing Celebration, the company made explicit appeals to a nostalgia for historic communities that predate sprawl, a tacit admission from one of the largest development companies in America that sprawl has left many Americans unsatisfied. "I've been around enough places to know that unless a community has some kind of heart to it, there's not much to it," Disney's Peter Rummell told Russ Rymer, author of a book on Florida towns.[52] The company's intent at Celebration, Rummell said, was to create a location "that feels like a place that has a tradition, even though it doesn't."

As an alternative to sprawl, Celebration was laudable. But Disney's attempt to manufacture a semblance of history where it did not exist in Florida only exposed the ridiculousness of what the company attempted to do in Virginia's Piedmont. As awareness of Disney's America spread, the idea was subjected to ridicule in cartoons and editorials nationwide. Though the approval process in Prince William County moved steadily in Disney's favor, a growing chorus of voices from across the country urged Disney to withdraw. The more the public fight dragged on, the more Disney's legendary luster dimmed.

By late summer, Disney's senior executives realized that the company didn't need the growing headache of Disney's America. Early statewide polls had shown Disney's America winning the support of a majority of Virginians, who favored economic activity and potential jobs, but public opinion had turned against the proposal as the full impact became apparent. "At first I thought Disney might be a good idea for the area," said Karen Walton, the co-owner of the new Kris and Karen's sandwich shop in Haymarket. "Then I got to thinking about all the factors, the environment, taxes, police, fire, schools. . . . It's not Disney I oppose so much, it's the fact that people have so little control over the junk that'll go up around it."[53] Across Virginia, almost no one without a financial stake in the proposal was adamantly for it. As the controversy wore on, opposition groups such as the Piedmont Environmental Council dug in their heels. Environmental organizations, such as the Chesapeake Bay Foundation and the Environmental Defense Fund, had joined the cause, virtually guaranteeing lengthy and costly litigation over environmental impacts on watersheds, water quality, and clean air. The outcome was far from certain, and Disney had already spent huge sums on lobbyists and lawyers. The tab for Disney's America, before any ground had been broken, was growing larger by the day.

John Cooke, a senior Disney executive uninvolved in Disney's America but sensitive to public opposition, helped persuade his colleagues that the company should cut its losses. In the final week of September 1994, less than a year after announcing Disney's America to the public, Eisner informed his board of the decision. Within a matter of days, the company announced the news on Disney stationery. At the top of the release was a smiling Mickey Mouse, with arms and white-gloved paws outstretched, as if opening an animated show. "Disney to Seek New Site," read the headline. The company acknowledged the widespread concern "about the possible impact of our park on historic sites in this unique area," saying "we have always tried to be sensitive to the issue." But uncertainty about the eventual outcome of the project had led the company to seek "a new location so we can move the process forward," the statement announced. "We certainly cannot let a particular site undermine that goal by becoming a source of divisiveness."

In truth, Disney's America was not a "source of divisiveness" as much as a symptom of a division between advocates of development and preservation over the assumption that if economies are to grow, places must be sacrificed. In this case, it was a civil war of sorts between residents of Prince William County over their county's future; a contest between suburban and rural counties over the future of northern Virginia; and a debate among multiple jurisdictions over the future of the greater Washington metropolitan region. In the words of Rudy Abramson, a former *Los Angeles Times* reporter who served as a spokesman for Protect Historic America and later wrote a book about the Piedmont, *Hallowed Ground:* "The theme park controversy was a crucial moment for a region already under relentless pressure and not yet organized to chart its future."[54]

In the aftermath of Disney's America, preservationists shared a sense of having won the battle while losing the war. Just days before the Disney Company pulled out of Virginia, for instance, the Prince William County Planning Commission approved the plan for Disney's America by a vote of seven to one. The solitary vote against the proposal was cast by Richard Hefter, the only commissioner who represented Disney's immediate neighbors in the western end of the county. Until Prince William County's fiscal situation can be remedied by other means such as revenue sharing among counties in the region, regional opposition to the county's "anything goes" posture toward commercial development will continue. Only a few months following the demise of Disney's America, furthermore, Virginia's legislature rejected a Growth Strategies Act that was six years in the making. After heavy lobbying by the governor's office and the Virginia Association of Realtors, lawmakers failed to come to terms with Virginia's need for a statewide growth-management strategy to resolve development conflicts between competing counties in a region.

On the very day the Prince William County Planning Commission approved Disney's America, officials representing autonomous jurisdictions in metropolitan Washington showed themselves to be as mindless as gridlock on the region's roads, the most visible product of regional dysfunction. The thirty-four-member Transportation Planning Board of the regional Council of Governments had to determine how best to spend $2.2 billion on future transportation projects, including road improvements for Disney's America, as part of a twenty-five-year transportation plan. Some board members candidly admitted that the plan failed to meet regional transportation needs. By 2020, the total number of miles driven by people in the region would increase by 70 percent, but highway capacity would expand by only 20 percent. Rush-hour traffic in the evening would triple. Three-quarters of the transportation budget would have to fund maintenance of existing infrastructure, leaving little money to expand existing roads. Tailpipe emissions would have to be reduced by some 25 percent over the next five years to meet clean air standards. Yet, sprawling development patterns would force drivers to travel more miles, offsetting reductions in pollution. The spread of far-flung work sites and shopping centers would do little to help the unemployed who were isolated in urban centers. The Metro subway system, which took $10 billion in taxpayers' money to construct and another $300 million a year to operate, was losing ridership. Road improvement for Disney's America was a trip in the wrong direction, but the board gave the highway expansion for Disney's America a green light and approved the twenty-five-year plan.

Without serious regional planning for the growth of metropolitan Washington, the future of communities in northern Virginia, Maryland, and the District of Columbia will be determined without the thoughtful coordination of local jurisdictions working toward common goals. Without regional cooperation or some regional authority to impose it, regionwide warnings about the costs of sprawl and new guidelines for alternative forms of development are unenforceable. "In the absence of a truly regional strategy, the region as a whole and its parts are becoming increasingly dysfunctional," warned the report of the Partnership for Regional Excellence. Local governments across northern Virginia alone had already planned and zoned fifteen times the amount of land needed to accommodate job growth and other nonresidential development projected for the next twenty years, noted the *Washington Post's* Benjamin Forgey. Such unrealistic planning will inevitably lead to more new places built in sloppy ways. As Forgey wrote, "This is regional planning—if it can be so called—at its excessive, uncoordinated worst."[55]

The controversy over Disney's America was more than a classic battle between developers and NIMBYs (Not in My Back Yard) and BANANAs (Build Absolutely Nothing Anywhere Near Anything), although specimens of each were evident in the fight. For a group of nationally known historians and writers, the issue was about stewardship of the "Cradle of Democracy," a unique region where momentous events in American history occurred. For average Americans, some from as far away as central Florida and Southern California, it was about the landscape where history is being written. For them, it was a referendum on sprawl, a rare opportunity to voice their objections to patterns of urbanization that have robbed so many special places of their identity and left their inhabitants agitated.

The controversy resonated because similar stories are played out on smaller scales with growing frequency in countless communities across the country. Major developments are proposed (and opposed) that have potential to alter the shape and character of their surroundings in profound and fundamental ways. Most of these local controversies don't involve national treasures like Virginia's northern Piedmont or entertainment giants like Disney or famous figures like David McCullough. But many proposals are driven by the same factors: developers who use stealth strategies to buy prime land; the desire of some public officials to add to their tax base at almost any cost; the premise that all new development projects must serve only automobile travel and deny people the choice of walking from one place to another; and, all too frequently, the failure, or absence, of sensible land-use planning. Many of these projects stem from tenets deeply rooted in American culture: a craving for boundless growth, a perception of unlimited land and economic resources, a preference for fresh starts over maintaining what we have, a belief that property owners should be allowed to do whatever they want with their holdings regardless of their neighbors, and an inability to recognize the interdependence of land-use decisions, how such things as zoning laws and transportation plans ultimately shape our surrounding built environment. In most instances, saying no to bad proposals is the only option some Americans have, because state and local officials have yet to create a process that lets them say yes to better alternatives.

The need for alternatives and alternative methods for reaching decisions is overdue. Following Disney's withdrawal, Mike Hoover, president of the Prince William County/Greater Manassas Chamber of Commerce, said that a major corporation could never again come into the surrounding territory, assemble land secretly, and spring a huge project on an unsuspecting public. The grounds for a legal challenge were too great, because people would demand a greater say over the future of their communities. "You have to build regional support," Hoover said. "When you back people into a corner, they come out fighting."[56] To avoid reactionary backlash against unexpected proposals, communities need to establish what is worth preserving and how best to preserve it. Such a consensus would save everyone time, money, and trouble, especially developers. In the absence of that kind of understanding, Disney's America was vulnerable to competing visions of the future: one set by

Prince William County officials, another laid out by the regional Council of Governments, and still another outlined by the national Civil War Sites Advisory Commission, to name but a few. Those competing visions have yet to be reconciled. Worse, no process exists to reconcile them.

Where democracy cannot solve such dilemmas, heavy hands will dictate the terms, as Disney has done at Celebration. To its credit, Disney has consciously developed at Celebration a model for improving suburban development patterns nationwide. As critic Russ Rymer observed, how ironic that Walt Disney's futuristic Experimental Prototype Community of Tomorrow would wind up becoming the Experimental Prototype Community of Yesterday.[57] But can others build places like it elsewhere, without Disney's level of corporate control to overcome the resistance of zoning officials and real estate lobbies invested in the status quo? In the relatively recent history of community planning, utopias have never really materialized as their visionaries planned them. And prototypes of well-designed communities have often failed to inspire spin-offs or little more than a cheap knockoff or two. Lowering expectations of what Celebration can accomplish, architect Robert Stern said, "It's not utopia. It's a real proposition. It's a textbook of ideas that have validity and are being tested here. But, if it doesn't work, well, we'll have to try something else."[58] Stern's healthy skepticism is justified. The publicity lavished on new or proposed traditional town developments is encouraging, but whether it offers more hype than hope remains to be seen.

In 1968, before most of today's New Urbanists were in architecture school, urbanist William H. Whyte wrote, "Urbanity is not something that can be lacquered on; it is the quality produced by the great concentration of diverse functions and a huge market to support the diversity. The center needs a hinterland to draw upon, but it cannot be in the hinterland; it must be in the center. This is the fundamental contradiction in the new town concept of self-containment."[59] Perhaps a lasting contribution of New Urbanism will be to rekindle interest in the urbanism that exists already. To date, the American preservation movement has enjoyed far more success in reclaiming historic environments—traditional neighborhoods, small-town Main Streets, and large downtown districts—than others have had in building facsimiles of them.

Americans deserve and demand good places. We deserve to share the evidence of our history. We deserve living environments better than the ones sprawl has offered us. But stopping bad development from happening does not guarantee that good development will occur. That guarantee can only be earned one neighborhood, one town, one city at a time. To fully understand that challenge, we need to be aware of the forces, attitudes, values, and personalities that have driven us to the places we are today.

2

THE MISPLACING OF AMERICA

Things fall apart; the center cannot hold;
Mere anarchy is loosed upon the world.

—William Butler Yeats, "The Second Coming"

When the nineteenth century drew to a close, Americans used the occasion to pause and reflect on the conditions of the environments they inhabited. In the years since the Civil War, the expansion of industry and waves of immigration had changed a rural nation of small communities into an industrial nation of large ones. In the "Gilded Age," as Mark Twain named it, Americans proudly produced great wealth and built some of the largest cities of the world. Looking back upon their progress, however, some realized that in the rush to get ahead, something had gone wrong.

In the boom years, once familiar communities had grown to giant size, exploded by new technologies beyond recognition, beyond an ability to function well, beyond the ability of citizens to control the forces that shaped everyday life. Political and business leaders, invested in the paths of progress, had grown indifferent to the consequences, to the horrid living conditions of the city. The last decades of the late nineteenth century were indeed hard times for urban Americans. Immigrant families piled on top of one another in high-rise tenements or ground-hugging shanties, enduring inhumane conditions. Poor sanitation and poor hygiene led to high rates of disease and infant mortality. The concentration of the poor in such badly built environments bred social pathologies and drove crime rates abnormally high. The public environment—the urban streets and streetscapes—symbolized the urban chaos: carriages and wagons clashed with one another in congested streets and intersections while industry and commerce jostled for the choicest parcels of land in a competitive race for profits. The social functions of the built environment remained neglected until documentations of the squalor opened Americans' eyes and helped to bring on a national soul-searching about the direction of American life.

According to Mel Scott, a historian of American urban development, "the chaotic, congested city spawned by the nineteenth century was soon to become the object of intense concern and the subject of innumerable muckraking articles, social surveys, civic improvement schemes, reform campaigns, and innovative laws, all aimed at making the urban environment worthy of a great and powerful country."[1] Throughout the nation, from large cities to small towns, Americans organized themselves in coalitions united by civic pride. They carved out public parks for poor and rich alike. They enforced building codes to promote better living conditions, improve sanitation, limit fire hazards, and prevent untimely deaths. They cleaned up dirty streets and eliminated unsightly billboards in crowded areas. Without a more humane built environment, they believed, America would be hard-pressed to build a more humane society. Civic reform became a national grassroots movement.

In Harrisburg, the capital city of Pennsylvania, citizens launched a cleanup campaign called the "City Beautiful," a name that became better identified with a style of monumental civic design promoted at the World's Columbian Exposition in Chicago's Jackson Park in 1893. There, an obscure historian named Frederick Jackson Turner announced in a lecture the closure of the American frontier, the "meeting point between savagery and civilization," while world-famous architects and landscape planners opened the door to a higher form of urban civilization for America. Together, they designed and erected an outdoor museum of classically proportioned monumental buildings arranged around grand boulevards, fountains, pools, and public parks, giving millions of Americans their first glimpse of an environment built more carefully than their own. "Millions of visitors, accustomed to urban ugliness, saw for the first time a splendid example of civic design and beauty in the classic pattern and on a grand scale and they liked it," wrote one historian of the event. "Throughout the nation people began to wonder why cities couldn't be as orderly and beautiful as the Columbian Exposition."[2]

The event spawned countless efforts in America's cities to build monumental civic architecture—sober and symmetrical neoclassical courthouses, customhouses, post offices, libraries, and railroad stations—as well as grand boulevards and park spaces intended as visible marks of civic order. While designing his plan for Chicago in 1907, Daniel Burnham, master architect of the 1893 Exposition, offered this advice: "Make no little plans; they have no magic to stir men's blood and probably will not be realized. Make big plans; aim high in hope and work, remembering that a nobler, logical diagram once recorded will never die, but long after we are gone will be a living thing, asserting itself with ever growing insistency. Remember that our sons and grandsons are going to do things that would stagger us. Let your watchword be order and your beacon beauty."[3] Burnham's effect was to bring to American cities the urban-planning tradition that had transformed the compact medieval cities of Europe into the spacious and ordered baroque environments in St. Petersburg and Paris. In Europe, the transformation had depended on the absolute power of monarchs and their administrators. In America, it required only civil authorities eager to leave their marks during their short terms in office, leaders who possessed the "edifice complex" of urban redevelopment. In places such as Chicago, Cleveland, Denver, Indianapolis, San Francisco, St. Louis, and the nation's capital, the improvement of the public urban realm did not solve all urban problems. But in the words of Mel Scott, the movement "touched the deep longing of a nation suffering from a loss of continuity with history for visual assurance of maturity and success."[4]

If that response to the industrial city of the late nineteenth century was meant to repair it, another was to run from it. Though country estates and residential suburbs had already begun to attract the wealthy, an English social reformer, Ebenezer Howard, envisioned a mass movement to flee the city limits and create utopias on open land. Born in 1850, Howard lived briefly in America in an unsuccessful attempt to make a life for himself on the American frontier. In 1876, he returned to England, where he was troubled by the divisions between the urban rich and poor. Fearing those divisions ultimately would lead to political turmoil in Britain, Howard decided, in the words of author Robert Fishman, that "large cities had no place in the society of the future."[5] In their place, Howard proposed to resettle residents of London in the countryside, in what he called "Garden Cities of Tomorrow." Howard's garden cities were not to be the exclusive, expensive residential suburbs he had seen in Chicago. They were to be independent towns, of thirty thousand residents at most, living in compact, self-contained communities that included factories, marketplaces, and farms, surrounded by a belt of undeveloped land to contain the size of each settlement and provide residents with accessible places for recreation and fresh air. As Howard saw it, the garden city would blend the best of town and country, allowing residents to experience the neighborliness of urban districts in the tranquillity of a rural setting, without the disadvantages of either industrial pollution or rural isolation. Howard saw the combined natural and built environments as a tool for achieving highly idealistic social aims, to cure urban alienation and foster fellowship and civic pride in new communities stabilized by cooperative ownership open to cross sections of society. "Above all, the allure of the garden city resided in its promise to redefine and strengthen community in a modern world that challenged and reduced community significance."[6] Howard's garden cities were never fully realized, but the underlying premise of his utopian dream, that urban centers could be abandoned in favor of forming new communities in the countryside, would become national policy in the United States.

A decade after Howard's plans became well known, the public-spirited Russell Sage Foundation launched the construction of Forest Hills Gardens, a planned suburb of Manhattan in Queens. Designed by Frederick Law Olmsted Jr. and Grosvenor Atterbury, Forest Hills was an urban village comprising houses and apartments of varying sizes intended for a population mixed in age and income, as well as shops and civic buildings placed at important focal points, within walking distance of the homes, all unified by a common architectural style and arranged around carefully planned streets and green spaces.[7] Though the tremendous appeal of Forest Hills made the community too expensive for a diverse class of occupants, Olmsted and Atterbury succeeded in constructing a popular new community with a distinctive local identity. They had achieved in America what British designers Raymond Unwin and Barry Parker had accomplished in England in diluting Howard's utopian garden city into the more practical garden suburb. Rediscovering the appeal of the preindustrial English village, Unwin and Parker promoted the village concept as a traditional model for new communities. According to British urban historian Peter Hall, they "raised the art of civic design to a level of pure genius."[8] In their work, they strove to show "that the architect and planner were the guardians of social and aesthetic life, maintaining and enhancing the traditional values of the community for future generations."[9] Their work in England and Unwin's 1909 book, *Town Planning in Practice*, became so influential in America that suburban home builders, unimpressed with America's vernacular architectural traditions, began building new houses, apartments, and neighborhood stores in the English Tudor style.

Across America, cities led by reform-minded civic leaders sought out talented planners to help them map their future. In high demand was John Nolen, who in his career oversaw the development of some four hundred separate town plans, half of which were realized. In his 1911 scheme for Madison, the capital of Wisconsin, Nolen struck out against the failures of laissez-faire urbanization that had scarred America's built environment since the end of the Civil War. He said that if Americans wanted to build great places in which to live and work, they would have to do more to make them happen; they would have to build more than the isolated monumental structures of the City Beautiful; they would require a broader understanding of and desire to shape the patterns that define the character of a place, its streets and streetscapes. "The most important features of city planning," Nolen said, "are not the public buildings, not the railroad approaches, not even the parks and playgrounds. They are the location of streets, the establishment of block lines, the subdivisions of property into lots, the regulations of building, and the housing of people," the kind of regulations that would eventually become codified in public zoning and building codes. Nolen noted at the time that "the fixing and extension of these features is too often left practically without effective regulation to the decision of private individuals. That these individuals are often lacking in knowledge, in taste, in high or even fair civic motives; that they are often controlled by ignorance, caprice, and selfishness, the present character of American city suburbs bears abundant testimony."[10]

Even the private sector had to acknowledge that the results of laissez-faire urbanization had been neither efficient nor attractive. Haphazard growth had created chaotic places. The urban realm had been shaped not by utopians such as Howard, or talented professional designers such as Nolen, but more likely by speculators interested in squeezing every dollar of profit from urban property, regardless of the outcome. Disreputable realtors, called "curbstoners," subdivided lots, sold what they could, then dumped the remainder and moved on. Those who built homes on a new street early could find themselves a few years later living next to a foundry, a tannery, a brewery, or some other noisy or smelly nuisance. Complaints about neighbors were often charged with racial, ethnic, and class tensions, over the spread of laundries operated by Chinese immigrants in Los Angeles neighborhoods, for instance, or the spread of immigrant sweatshops up New York's Fifth Avenue, into established areas of fashionable trade. In Berkeley, California, manufacturers complained that dwellings were encroaching on their industrial areas. In New York City, a new skyscraper blocked sunlight from neighboring structures, forcing workers inside them to conduct their business in shadows. Such conflicts led to the passage of zoning laws, which created zones restricted for specific purposes and set standards for the placement of buildings and the density of human settlement. Zoning provided for the orderly and efficient growth of the city, supplanting the City Beautiful with the City Efficient or City Functional.

The predictability that zoning brought to the expansion of cities also shrank the constituency for an orderly built environment. The responsibility fell out of the hands of civic and business coalitions and into the offices of zoning officials, road engineers, and other bureaucratic technicians who answered to their political clients, who in turn answered to their clients in the private sector. In an early critique still echoed to this day, Frederick L. Ackerman, an architect and planner whose values were shaped in the Progressive era, attacked his profession for straying from its civic mission, for neglecting "the causes which give rise to existing maladjustments," and for becoming too concerned with "the right of the individual to use the community as a machine for procuring individual profits and benefits, without regard to what happens to the community."[11]

Exhausted by Progressive reform and the First World War, Americans in the 1920s yearned for a "return to normalcy" and retreated from public concerns into domesticity, encouraged by a proliferation of advertisements for consumer goods and appliances, everything from radios and toasters to telephones and laundry machines, even new houses that had the electrical outlets to accommodate the new appliances.[12] The motorcar, mass-produced and made affordable by the genius of Henry Ford, was the ultimate emblem of machine-age mass consumption. Before the United States had entered the war, Americans possessed a little more than 2 million automobiles. By 1927, there was one for every five people.[13] In the days before streets became dominated by automobiles, they had served as byways for strolling, shopping, congregating, even as playing fields for childhood games. Though trolleys, delivery wagons, and pedestrians competed for space, streets were shared by different modes of travel moving at different speeds. Streetcar ridership reached its peak in 1923, after which it fell off as trolley lines fell victim to lobbies for auto, oil, rubber tire, and road-building industries. Unlike today's public transit systems, the early trolley lines were privately owned, the routes were poorly coordinated, and the systems suffered from a lack of public investment. Most lines actually operated at a loss, sponsored by speculators who used them to inflate the property values of undeveloped land. Because of their bad reputations, public regulators refused to improve the lines and limited the fares their operators could charge, dooming most of them to financial failure.[14] "Americans taxed and harassed public transportation," wrote historian Kenneth T. Jackson, "even while subsidizing the automobile like a pampered child."[15] Before the automobile became dominant, streets and sidewalks brought citizens together; afterward, streets drove citizens apart. The need for sidewalks in many places simply disappeared.

According to Clarence Perry, who contributed to the first regional plan for New York City in 1929, the "automobile menace" required Americans to construct new environments to shield people from the dangers of the motorcar while at the same time allowing a community to thrive in an economy that increasingly reduced personal contact.[16] Like Progressive reformers before him, Perry was concerned with the creation of places where immigrants could become assimilated to American culture. Having lived at Forest Hills Gardens, with its compact scale that encouraged neighborliness, Perry promoted construction of the "neighborhood unit" as a new model for community development. Each neighborhood would contain about five thousand to seven thousand people, in homes built no farther than a half mile from an elementary school at the center. The neighborhood would be bordered by clusters of shops on streets at the perimeter, within a quarter mile of every home. Perry determined the distances as the natural limits for short, comfortable walks.[17] His ideas shaped the development of early twentieth-century subdivisions, the most influential of which was Radburn, in Fairlawn, New Jersey.

Begun in 1927, when the United States owned 85 percent of the world's automobiles, Radburn gained national fame as a "town for the motor age."[18] Its most defining characteristic was the protection of its occupants from the nuisance of the automobile. Houses were placed on quiet culs-de-sac, and the entrances to homes were turned away from the street toward private gardens. Traffic not generated by residents was kept out of the neighborhood by the absence or limitation of through streets. A pathway allowed local children to walk to the nearby public school without having to walk along the road. But Radburn was not a community for social assimilation, as Perry had encouraged. Instead, it was a refuge whose occupancy was limited to white households of larger than average incomes. Whites of modest means were priced out and Jews and blacks were kept out with restrictive covenants. Radburn appealed to America's growing desire for privacy and protection. Historian Mel Scott claimed that "plans for the project excited more interest than those for any other new community of the decade."[19] Radburn reinforced not only social separation, but spatial separation, too, particularly through new suburban traffic patterns. According to Peter Rowe of Harvard's Graduate School of Design, "The concept of roads and streets as multipurpose and well-integrated realms of the city gave way."[20] At Radburn, the size and routes of roads were determined by the volume of traffic they were to carry. The guiding concept was to move cars through the area like blood through the human body. Large arterial roads outside the development would carry the heaviest traffic; roads through the neighborhood would get progressively smaller until reaching the culs-de-sac, the tiny capillaries at the end of circulation. The drawback of the scheme, of course, was that pushing so much traffic onto the arterial roads eventually clogged them, while neighborhood streets stood empty and unused. Clarence Perry's idealistic vision for a new community form in the age of the automobile could not hold. The centrifugal forces dispersing America's population were already dissolving the glue that held communities together. America was well on its way toward a newly built environment of separate zones for separate purposes, populated by separate classes and separate races who traveled on separate roads built for separate speeds.

"Cross-roads are an enemy to traffic," declared a modern designer who attacked frequent intersections in historic cities as obstacles to the steady flow of fast-moving traffic. "A city made for speed is made for success," he said.[21] His name was Charles-Edouard Jeanneret, a Swiss-born architect who practiced in France under the pseudonym "Le Corbusier." Reinventing the historic city, Le Corbusier assumed, would be as simple as reinventing his name. The old city was chaotic, slow, congested, encumbered by layers of historic complexity, the product of organic evolution, adapted slowly over time to meet the economic and social needs of each successive generation. Corbusier preferred revolution to evolution. He was eager to wipe the surface of the city clean, obliterating its history, variety, and human scale to realize the promise of new technology that made possible an environment of high-speed travel and high-rise towers open to sunlight and fresh air. In his "Contemporary City for Three Million People," Corbusier proposed "the city for our times," a collection of symmetrical, mass-produced, high-rise towers built for hyperdensity living, surrounded at ground level by empty open spaces, intersected by efficient high-speed roadways. "The city of to-day is a dying thing because it is not geometrical," he said. We must "replace our haphazard arrangements . . . by a uniform layout. The result of a true geometrical layout is repetition . . . standard . . . uniformity."[22] In 1925, Corbusier presented his plan for the renewal of Paris, which proposed "demolition of the historic city 'north of the Seine' "[23] and in its place, the construction of eighteen identical towers built to a height of seven hundred feet each, spaced out like massive tombstones in a giant cemetery. The scheme shocked Parisians as cold, empty, and lifeless, nothing more than monotony on a monumental scale. In the Paris city council, Corbusier was attacked as a "barbarian."[24] In response, the architect said that city planning was "too important to be left to the citizens."[25]

To leave one's mark on a place by erasing the contributions of those who came before demands the arrogance of an ego of heroic proportions, but Corbusier supplied that, too. "I could . . . be master of the environment in which all this takes place," he declared with no trace of modesty, placing himself in the tradition of autocratic urban administrators such as Baron Georges-Eugene Haussmann, who rebuilt the center of Paris for Napoleon III some seventy-five years earlier.[26] Praising Louis XIV, the Sun King who built Versailles, Corbusier wrote, "Homage to a great town planner. The despot conceived immense projects and realized them."[27] Corbusier's method was offensive, but more offensive was his model of what a city should be: a place that serves the functional demands of technology to build taller and travel faster at the expense of the needs of humanity for human contact. Oblivious of the way his high-rise towers would isolate occupants in anonymity, he said, "A house is a machine to live in." Rejected by Parisians, who clung protectively to their historic city, Corbusier was brought to the United States by a private foundation for a speaking tour of twenty cities. In the New World, he was welcomed as a genius.

Traditionally, architects were bound by respect for the locales in which they worked. It imposed a healthy degree of humility on both the designer and the design. Even the early skyscrapers that rose arrogantly above the old city still conformed to traditional building patterns at street level. Liberating themselves from traditional constraints, the modernist school of architects gave up the cohesive city for the pursuit of individuality, for gratification of the ego, for a desire to stand out for the sake of standing out. "Its pioneers, Gropius, Mies van der Rohe, Le Corbusier, as well as their followers right up to the present time, were united in despising the structure of the traditional city as it had been painstakingly built up over the centuries. They were determined to outrage it as much as possible," said architectural historian Vincent Scully.[28] They revolted against the understanding that buildings have to "get along with each other lawfully the way people have to do in a community."[29] And in place of traditional urbanism, modernists like Ludwig Hilberseimer proposed "his endless miles of high-rise slabs, his landscapes of hell, out of which the mass housing of the 1950s took shape, much of it to be dynamited as wholly unlivable hardly more than 20 years later."[30] In cities throughout America, Scully added, "Le Corbusier's cataclysmic vision of freeways and superblocks proved the most persuasive image of all. And through the agency of Redevelopment, and in alliance with departments of Transportation and their traffic engineers, it eventually came to lay the centers of most American cities in ruins."[31]

■　■　■

Only months after the stock market crash of 1929 brought the ebullient optimism of the Roaring Twenties to an end, Frank Lloyd Wright, America's most distinguished architect, addressed an audience at Princeton University and announced, "I believe the city, as we know it today, is to die." It was a bold prediction. Only a decade before, the United States had become an urbanized nation. The census of 1920 was the first to report that a majority of America's citizens resided in its cities. Yet, Wright suspected that the centripetal pull of the centralized city would someday come to an end. In his book *The Disappearing City*, first published in 1932, he predicted that just as the motorcar was replacing the horse and buggy, the telephone and radio would eventually replace the need for face-to-face communication. The spread of electricity to rural America, inexpensive building materials, and mass-production construction methods would also encourage a decentralized settlement form. The machine, an agent of oppression in the industrial city, Wright said, would become an agent of liberation.

For Frank Lloyd Wright, a son of the American prairie, the city could not disappear fast enough. He felt that it stifled the individual, that it made him a prisoner to big business and big government, that it made him a slave to the "Landlord, Machinelord, and Moneylord that own and Rent the old City."[32] Salvation of genuine American democracy, he believed, could only come about through decentralizing urban America and scattering its population out "upon the whole surface of the Nation."[33] "A free America," he said, "democratic in the sense that our forefathers intended it to be, means just this: *individual* freedom for all." The transformation of technology would lead to a transformation of human values, he said. The search by Americans to express their individuality, what he called the reawakened ideal of freedom in the individual, "is destined to become the greatest single spiritual force moving mankind against the Timebound City making Decentralization a great necessary movement not only possible but an imminent necessity. Inevitable! . . .

"Soon there will be little not reaching him at his own fireside by broadcasting, television, and publication," Wright predicted, long before television was to become a part of everyday life. "The 'movies' through television, will soon be seen and heard better at home than in any hall. . . . Symphony concerts, operas, and lectures will eventually be taken more easily into the home than people there can be taken to the great halls in old style, and be heard more satisfactorily in congenial company." The individual would re-create in the home, his own private space, what public places once provided: entertainment and the exchange of information. "No longer any need exists for futile racing to and from a common center, tired out but racing back and forth again."[34] Commerce would follow the individual into the countryside. "The great highways are in the process of becoming the decentralized metropolis," he said. He called roadside service stations the "future distribution stations in embryo." Stations with good locations would evolve into "a neighborhood distribution center, meeting place, restaurant, restroom, or whatever is needed. A thousand centers as city equivalents to every town or city we now have, will be the result of this advance agent of decentralization." Chain stores would become more efficient at distributing goods than any competitors in the centralized city. In the face of these trends, the main task for the architect, as Wright saw it, was "How easiest and soonest to assist the social unit in escaping the gradual paralysis of individual independence that is characteristic of the machine-made moron?"[35]

Wright's answer was a new pattern of settlement, which he called "Broadacre City." If Le Corbusier wanted to reinvent the traditional city by stretching it to the sky, Frank Lloyd Wright wanted to stretch it to the horizon. But, unlike Ebenezer Howard, who sought to blend the best of town and country, Wright sought to eliminate both. "The dividing lines between town and country are even now gradually disappearing," he said. "It will soon become unnecessary to concentrate in masses for any purpose whatsoever. . . . Even the small town is too large." Both town and country he saw merging into a universal form of "general non-urban development." In Wright's Broadacre City, Americans would settle across the landscape in concentrations no greater than one person per acre. America had the land to make it possible; "in these United States there are about fifty-seven green acres each, for every man, woman and child within our borders."[36] Broadacre City would be intentionally placeless, as Wright said in his autobiography, "nowhere, yet everywhere."[37] Roads would stretch to the horizon for unobstructed high-speed travel, dotted with modern architecture liberated from adherence to traditional styles, which limited the individuality of the artist and separated man from harmonizing the natural landscape. As Wright dreamed it, Broadacre City would have none of the ugliness, the power lines, telephone poles, and road-clogging traffic of the city. "Most important to us as a People is the fact that a more livable Life now demands a more livable City."[38]

Where the greatest living architect in America saw utopia, others saw disaster. Wright, the cantankerous artist who lived in near self-imposed exile from society after a bitter divorce, had ignored the social and cultural factors that drew people to the centers of population, the basic human need for social contact, for community, for civilization. Catherine Bauer, a contemporary critic, called Broadacre City an "endless roadtown," an "anti-city" of distances so vast it would foster absolute dependence on the machines Wright loathed to replace human interaction, destroying the physical setting for community in the process.[39] At best, Frank Lloyd Wright's Broadacre City offered more freedom for the individual in an egalitarian setting. At its worst, it was a road map for individualism to run amok across the countryside, every man for himself at the expense of communities shared by all, the selfish vision of a solipsistic mind. Wright's plans for Broadacre City were never taken seriously by those in authority, but as much as anyone, the man understood the decentralization of human settlement already under way. He clairvoyantly anticipated the self-liberation and extreme individualism that would shape America's built environment over the remainder of the century.

■   ■   ■

Lewis Mumford, a founder of the Regional Planning Association of America, said the nation was witnessing the fourth great migration of its history. As he put it, the first migration was the pioneer settlement of the continent. The second was the development of towns and cities. The third was the recent migration of Americans from farms to urban areas. And the fourth migration was the decentralization made possible by the development of new transportation and communication technologies. Drawing lessons from earlier

American experience, Mumford and others formed the RPAA to shape the direction of urbanization in constructive ways and to head off re-creations of the slums and environmental chaos of the nineteenth-century industrial city. "Fortunately for us, the fourth migration is only beginning," Mumford wrote, and "we may either permit it to crystallize in a formation quite as bad as that of our earlier migrations, or we may turn it to better account into new channels."[40]

Mumford and his colleagues were influenced heavily by the work of Patrick Geddes, a Scot interested in the careful rehabilitation of historic urban districts and urban planning on a regional scale to guide the growth of cities. As early as 1915, Geddes foresaw the possibility that America's northeastern cities would eventually spill into one another, draining urban cores as the reservoirs of civilization and leading to a waste of natural resources at their peripheries. Without action to check these trends, he warned, "the expectation is not absurd that the not too distant future will see practically one vast City-line along the Atlantic Coast for five hundred miles. . . . Towns must now cease to spread like expanding ink-stains and grease spots."[41] By 1937, a U.S. federal agency established to examine trends in urbanization warned the nation that a lack of adequate housing and transportation in urban centers as well as the lack of regional political authorities to guide development beyond the urban border threatened America's cities and its natural resources with inevitable sprawl. In the midst of an economic depression, however, sprawling urban growth was a problem America's leaders felt the nation could afford.

The most radical attempt to shape the settlement of the urban frontier was undertaken by a New Deal agency, the Resettlement Administration, headed by Rexford Guy Tugwell, an agricultural economist from Columbia University. Tugwell understood how the increasing mechanization of agriculture would displace farm laborers, depopulate rural America, and send migrants to urban areas in search of jobs and housing. To accommodate the migration, Tugwell developed a plan to construct high-density housing beyond the borders of cities, on open farmland. "My idea is to just go outside centers of population, pick up cheap land, build a whole community, and entice people into it. Then go back into the cities and tear down slums and make parks of them," wrote Tugwell in his diary.[42] During the short life of the four-year program, only three of Tugwell's towns were built: Greenbelt, Maryland, outside of Washington, D.C.; Greenhills, Ohio, outside of Cincinnati; and Greendale, Wisconsin, outside of Milwaukee. The so-called Tugwelltowns made foes quickly. To the idealists, they failed to materialize into independent "whole communities" as Tugwell had conceived. To others, they were viewed as inferior to the suburbs erected by the private sector.

The architecture struck many as crude, and the development process, entirely controlled by federal agencies, angered private building contractors and local political leaders, all of whom saw the federal government stepping on their turf.[43] Though "new towns" were attempted again a generation later, the socialistic program did not fit American culture. What did fit, however, was Tugwell's stated belief that the United States government could sanction and finance the abandonment and destruction of urban areas. That task initially fell to another depression-era federal agency called the FHA.

The Federal Housing Administration was established in 1934 in response to depression-era needs to encourage the construction of new homes and create work for unemployed building tradesmen. Because of so many foreclosures and bank failures, lending institutions had become reluctant to loan money for the purchase of homes, and prevailing mortgage terms priced potential home buyers out of the market anyway. Before the FHA, buyers typically made down payments of about 50 percent of the price of their new homes, then paid off the mortgage within five to seven years at an interest rate between 6 and 8 percent. At the end of the repayment period, buyers paid all the interest charges in full in a single balloon payment. To cover the interest charge, some buyers had to take out a second mortgage with an interest rate of 18 percent, which was due in three years.[44] The new FHA-insured mortgages allowed Americans to purchase homes with a down payment of as little as 10 percent, extending the repayment period up to thirty years, with an interest rate of 5.5 percent. The passage of the GI Bill in 1944 made housing even more affordable to some 16 million veterans. The Veterans Administration provided mortgage insurance with no down payment required. Because of the housing shortage that had grown worse over the depression and World War II, some found that buying a new home cost less than renting a substandard apartment.[45]

The FHA set strict criteria for determining which places were suitable for mortgage insurance, favoring new locations at the expense of older ones. To measure the suitability of a location for mortgage insurance, the FHA looked first and foremost for serious threats to future property values: evidence of blight and decay and any signs of African Americans or other racial or ethnic groups who might not suit a potential buyer's preference for all-white neighborhoods. A single house occupied by a black family in an urban neighborhood, even one tucked away on an inconspicuous side street, was enough for the FHA to label a predominantly white neighborhood as unfit for mortgage insurance. Areas that failed to meet the test were deemed too risky and "redlined" on confidential maps shared with bankers, whose lack of investment in those neighborhoods doomed many of them to eventual decline. Using the FHA's ranking system, the fate of areas was determined by grades in eight specific categories. The top category, "relative economic stability," accounted for 40 percent. The next most important category, "protection from adverse influences," a euphemism for saying an area was free of racial minorities, counted for 20 percent. Less important categories included "freedom from special hazards," "utilities," "transportation," "taxes," and "general appeal." All of these criteria gave almost exclusive attention to market values or the stability of property values and placed virtually no value on the social stability of a community. The last of the eight categories, the "adequacy of civic, social, and commercial centers," was worth only 5 percent.[46] To the bean counters in the FHA, the ability of a neighborhood setting to sustain community relationships was among the lowest of its priorities.

Promotion of home ownership was a national policy with both social as well as economic goals. Since the Russian Revolution in 1917, America's leaders had promoted home ownership as a way to stave off unrest among the masses. During the depression, moreover, a time of rampant foreclosures and business failures, the FHA's mission was to get Americans back to work building houses, to get families housed in homes of their own, and to protect mortgages against foreclosures in the future. All were worthy goals and the FHA was extremely successful in its mission, but at a great price to the nation's established neighborhoods and the strength of its communities. The FHA was not in the business of guaranteeing sound communities, just profitable ones. In fact, one FHA bulletin in 1938 offered guidance to home builders under the title "Planning Profitable Neighborhoods." The pamphlet showed developers how to follow FHA specifications to create a homogeneous residential subdivision of houses that stood apart from one another at standard distances on streets of standard widths. By standardizing subdivision design, the FHA could more easily predict a stable market for the houses whose mortgages it insured. But it did so by turning away from designs for sociable, walkable neighborhoods. The bulletin labeled traditional neighborhoods scaled to the pedestrian as "Bad." Those neighborhoods comprised short blocks and narrow streets. The houses were closer together, sometimes interrupted by an occasional corner store. The intensity of foot traffic made the sidewalks more lively and safe and the narrowness of streets kept traffic slow. Turning away from the wisdom contained in the best traditional places, the FHA bulletin labeled new subdivisions with longer blocks and wider streets and homes set back from the street on larger lots as "Good."[47] The design offered suburbanites more space, more privacy, and more use of the automobile, but it also turned them into prisoners of the home and the car. Just as Ebenezer Howard's garden city was reduced to the garden suburb, Clarence Perry's neighborhood unit was now reduced to the auto-oriented subdivision. As Lewis Mumford wrote, the "pedestrian scale of the suburb disappeared, and with it, most of its individuality and charm. The suburb ceased to be a neighborhood unit: it became a low density mass."[48]

The FHA-financed subdivision was homogeneous, not only by design, but also by occupancy. In a break with suburbs designed for the wealthy in the nineteenth century, which allowed for apartments over garages for the chauffeur, or small apartments attached to the main house for domestic help or aging in-laws, the FHA discouraged apartments from residential subdivisions altogether. Properties with apartments were a threat to standardized accounting, their values and marketability to middle-class families were more difficult to predict, and tenants of any kind were seen as undesirable neighbors. The FHA excluded nonwhite residents by promoting the use of covenants to protect a subdivision's racial purity. As Charles Abrams put it, the FHA "adopted a racial policy that could well have been culled from the Nuremberg laws" of Nazi Germany.[49] Whereas stability in traditional villages, towns, and neighborhoods depended on shared values that could take generations to evolve, the perceived stability of the instant subdivision depended on limiting those areas to one segment of the housing market, one class, one age group, one race.

Those who preferred to stay in the old neighborhood, where ties among extended relatives and neighbors were often strong, found it difficult to do so. Anyone who wanted to upgrade the family's old home, move down the block from relatives, or stay in town close to work found that home-repair loans, as they were offered then, provided limited help. Most homeowners had trouble getting financing for anything other than relatively minor or inexpensive repairs. By redlining entire urban neighborhoods, furthermore, the FHA encouraged longtime urban residents to sell and move, depriving the urban housing market of its middle-class buyers. In St. Louis, for example, all but 9 percent of FHA-insured mortgages from 1935 to 1939 were located in the suburbs.[50] When the FHA didn't draw residents out of familiar neighborhoods, blockbusters who exploited the mass migration of southern blacks to northern cities found ways to push them out. Warning white residents that black home buyers were about to move in, the con artists bought houses cheap from panicked buyers and sold them at exorbitant prices to black families eager to find any home in the racially restricted marketplace. Even in places untouched by blockbusting, federal home mortgage insurance policies helped to guarantee the conversion of once sound urban areas to urban slums. In existing neighborhoods, the effect was further declining property values, which meant fewer taxes to the city treasury, which stretched the city's budget and led to a decline in services, which encouraged more residents to move out only to be replaced by residents of lower means.

■ ■ ■

As blight spread through cities like tumors, the nation passed another housing measure that called for "the elimination of unsafe and insanitary housing conditions, for the eradication of slums." The Housing Act of 1937 identified a slum as "any area where dwellings predominate which by reason of dilapidation, over crowding, faulty arrangement and design, lack of ventilation, light or sanitary facilities, or any combination of these factors, are detrimental to safety, health or morals."[51] Under the law, federal tax dollars would help fund the construction of one new unit of public housing for each unit of dilapidated housing that localities tore down.[52] It was a well-intentioned measure to improve declining urban areas, house Americans of modest means, and provide the building trades with work. But the measure did as much as the FHA to concentrate poverty in the urban core. It also institutionalized as national policy the wholesale clearance of the built environment rather than its repair.

When smart business leaders of the era began to realize that to raze block after block of existing housing was both wasteful and costly, they sought alternative remedies for the problems of slums—not for idealistic reasons, but out of financial self-interest. By the end of the 1930s, the Federal Home Loan Bank Board, with an estimated $7 billion at stake in older urban real estate, saw urban deterioration as a threat to its investments. The board had collected surveys of 230 cities in America, with locations graded according to lending criteria and data compiled into confidential "security maps." The maps showed locations eligible for new investment and locations written off. Recognizing staggering losses in the making, the board launched a study to examine the threats to existing neighborhoods and what, if anything, could be done to save them.

No doubt, America was growing in impressive ways. Longtime property owners in traditional neighborhoods were fleeing substandard housing for new houses in the suburbs. Industry was escaping high urban land costs, high taxes, and traffic congestion for less expensive open spaces more suitable for new plants, trucking, and parking for employees. But the board noted that "while America was growing, it was also wasting away." Cities faced the loss of taxpaying residents and the rise of crime, health, and fire hazards in declining areas. The board's study noted that Cleveland spent seven times more on fire protection per person in slums than it did in the city as a whole, three times more per person on tuberculosis control, and three times more on police. In Cleveland's slums, the infant mortality rate was two and a half times greater than in the city as a whole. The story was similar in cities throughout the nation. A national survey identified as much as one-sixth of all urban dwellings "unfit for decent habitation." The marketplace, left to its own devices, could not maintain or revitalize most of these areas. Some form of public intervention was required. Slum clearance and new construction, the approach favored by the Housing Act of 1937, "will be slow and costly" and will produce undesirable side effects, the board's study announced. Little effort was being made to rehouse the displaced, who threatened to overwhelm the demographic stability of neighborhoods they moved into. The government's housing program was incomplete, the board declared. It was too heavily weighted toward the stimulation of new construction at the expense of repairing what existed. As the board reported, "It has left the *preservation of existing standard housing* virtually untouched." (Emphasis in original.) The board called this "wastage" that represented "tremendous losses" for the public and private sectors alike, and sought a "preventive program so vigilant groups of homeowners can reverse community disintegration before it attains a definitively destructive momentum." The board urged America "to consolidate our material and social gains and to conserve our economic and human resources," saying, "stronger accent must be placed on the development of maximum benefits from what we already possess." No wiser statement at the time was more widely ignored.

The board argued that the costly surgery needed in so many urban communities could be avoided by a less costly preventive method, namely, "neighborhood conservation." In cooperation with the Home Owners Loan Corporation, it launched a community conservation test project, which, if successful, could become a national model.[53] The pilot project was undertaken in 1940 in Waverly, a neighborhood of seven thousand residents of Baltimore. Waverly was found to be representative of stable neighborhoods vulnerable to nearby blight though the neighborhood itself was not blighted. Waverly's brick row houses, typical of Baltimore, were in strong demand, and its social composition was judged safe according to the racial biases of lending institutions. Its housing stock was relatively sound. Of the 1,610 houses in the neighborhood, half were in need of repairs, but only one warranted demolition. The study found that overall, Waverly "is essentially sound structurally, economically and socially. It is worth preserving and it can be preserved." But the study also found reasons for intervening. Houses in the worst shape were typically occupied by owners who needed more help with maintenance than was provided by limited home-repair loans. The neighborhood was plagued with "infection foci"—large billboards, obtrusive signs over corner stores, and filling stations—and the pattern of traffic on some neighborhood streets needed to be rerouted.

The test project initiated a five-month, districtwide effort that began by educating neighbors on the project's goals in order to overcome the skepticism of outsiders and resistance to government programs. A local civic organization, the Waverly Conservation League, was formed, and a master plan for the neighborhood was prepared. The sponsors provided experienced professionals who gave residents technical guidance and detailed recommendations on how to repair, upgrade, and maintain their houses. The neighborhood organized a fix up Waverly campaign and gave out awards to homeowners who improved their properties. Some streets were altered to reconfigure traffic patterns. Borrowing exclusionary tactics from the FHA, the project encouraged social barriers, such as deed restrictions, to limit the neighborhood from "undesirable residents and encroachment and infection by contiguous substandard districts." When the demonstration project was over, the neighborhood was improved. Lenders happily reported that sales of foreclosed properties, once stagnant, had shot up sharply. "The formula for the successful treatment of the area's developing malady is not costly nor is it dramatic," the report said. "It is a single, preventive remedy which has aptly been called 'organized neighborhood housekeeping' " that relied on "conservation and continued community effort." The board expressed its hope that its experience in Waverly "may one day inspire the establishment, in every large city, of a 'Department of Conservation' whose sole function" will be "to promote community stabilization projects in potentially and partially depreciated sections throughout the city." If consistently followed, the board predicted, this approach would "halt the process of physical, social, and economic disintegration which is so insidiously and restlessly attacking great urban districts throughout the United States."

More than a half century later, Waverly is a stable neighborhood composed of working families of Baltimore. But the approach undertaken in Waverly did not alter national policy at the time. The demonstration project failed to excite the imagination of policymakers because it required patience. It did not produce visible results quickly or dramatically enough for politicians eager to demonstrate change. It required energetic leadership, either an organized group of residents or some agency to coordinate the effort. Few, if any, local institutions at the time were in place to take up such a responsibility. It also required atypical home-improvement loans, and lenders who had assumed foreclosed property were usually unwilling to chase those losses with additional investments. American culture in the age of advertising and mass consumption was too conditioned to discard things and replace them, rather than repair them. Some opinion leaders preached the virtues of decentralization, arguing that the loss of population in the cities would ease urban congestion, free up space for urban parks, and bring high land values down to more reasonable levels. Frank Lloyd Wright even told the people of Pittsburgh in 1940 that their city would in all probability "have to be abandoned, eventually to be a rusty ruin and tumble into the river, staining the waters with oxide of iron for another half-century."[54] A generation later, in 1972, the National Survey of Housing Abandonment would declare that "entire neighborhoods housing hundreds of thousands of central-city dwellers are in advanced stages of being abandoned by their owners."[55] Two decades after that, in 1991, the United States could claim "over nine million vacant year-round housing units" or "in other words, about one in every 12 homes."[56]

■ ■ ■

While the FHA followed Wright's advice to resettle urbanites on open land beyond the urban core, it viewed the famed architect's house designs with skepticism. Such houses, the FHA felt, were too radical, too new. They were fine for wealthy clients of daring architects, but in a market dominated by the tastes of middle-class Americans, they were untested and risky. They could very well turn out to be a fad with little long-term staying power.[57] Though the FHA would later approve specifications for standardized "ranch" houses based on the "Usonian" houses Wright planned for Broadacre City, the FHA promoted new houses built in traditional styles. "Colonial" architecture had been gaining popularity after the nation's centennial of 1876 and more so after the White Pine Lumber Company began to publish monographs of colonial buildings in 1915 as a way to increase consumer demand for white pine in new construction. John D. Rockefeller's reconstruction of Colonial Williamsburg, begun in 1926, added to the desire for new buildings that mimicked eighteenth-century styles. With the FHA's blessing, the colonial revival was ensured long-term staying power. While modern architects designed houses with flat roofs and blank facades that avoided references to the past or the character of their surrounding built environment, the FHA stimulated consumer demand for traditional styles—without the traditional settings. As one critic put it, the FHA copied buildings that surrounded the New England village green but failed to copy the congenial community scale in which these structures had evolved.[58] The FHA's influence also smothered regional vernacular styles that reflected the climate, culture, and natural materials of a region. In place of regional architecture, the FHA helped to ensure the construction of identical houses in identical subdivisions from coast to coast. As Kenneth T. Jackson noted, "by the 1960s the casual suburban visitor would have a hard time deciphering whether she was in the environs of Boston or Dallas."[59]

All of this happened much more quickly after 1948, when Levitt and Sons undertook the construction of Levittown, on Long Island, twenty-three miles from downtown Manhattan. Containing seventeen thousand homes housing some eighty-two thousand people, it became the largest single housing development in American history. Compared to the pace and scale of previous subdivisions, Levittown was enormous and went up almost overnight. Previous subdivisions had been put up by builders who worked down a street one house at a time. They depended on highly skilled labor capable of doing a wide range of tasks. The skill and time involved for custom work kept costs high. At Levittown, the Levitts did for the suburban house what Henry Ford did for the automobile. They streamlined production—"the site became the factory"—and put out houses easier, quicker, and cheaper than anyone had before.[60] By 1955, subdivisions accounted for more than three-quarters of all new housing in metropolitan areas.[61]

The new economies of scale in land development and construction industries created massive sprawlscapes, the by-products of large-scale developers of generic product types: houses by Levitt and Sons, regional shopping centers by Edward J. DeBartolo. Such environments appeared to be the outcome of a random collision of market forces, but they were actually the intended result of rigid rules, from FHA specifications at the federal level to local zoning laws and subdivision codes that dictated the layout of the suburban landscape, replicated by mimeograph and passed among suburban officials from one county to the next. In fact, identical or similar rules applied in localities nationwide dictated the homogenization of what Kenneth T. Jackson called the "Crabgrass Frontier." "While being sold under fictions associated with individualism and patriotism, suburban living during mid-century became one of the most bureaucratically controlled and uniform types of development in American history," wrote Keller Easterling in his compilation of community designs, *American Town Plans*.[62] In spite of this fact, Vice President Richard M. Nixon told Soviet premier Nikita Khrushchev in the famous kitchen debate of 1959, "We do not want to have decisions made at the top by one government official that all houses should be built the same way."[63]

One effect of zoning and the rigidity with which it was applied on newly developed land was to disconnect the elements that had traditionally held a community and its citizens together. Though the construction of Forest Hills Gardens had shown America that it was possible to combine houses, apartments, and shops in appealing new "mixed-use" environments, the enactment of exclusive "single use" zones widened the distances between home and work and school and stores in order to minimize zoning conflicts. Levittown and its clones, for example, with only half the density of a typical turn-of-the-century streetcar suburb,[64] struck some critics, such as Mumford, as half-empty, void of the density and variety necessary to sustain social bonds between neighbors of different ages and incomes. "Levitt loathed critics like Mumford," wrote David Halberstam, who interviewed William Levitt for his book *The Fifties*. "When people spoke to him of the texture of a community,

he turned cold: He was in the business of putting up good low-cost housing;
he was not in charge of human relations after the building was finished."[65]
Sociologist Herbert Gans, who lived among the "Levittowners," found the
place a good environment for war veterans and their wives and babies. But
he also discovered that the environment isolated Levittown's youth. Deprived of the social stimulation offered in walkable small towns or urban
neighborhoods, Levittown's teenagers grew alienated, restless, angry, and
rebellious.[66] With builders like Levitt in the legitimate business of constructing houses and agencies such as the FHA in the legitimate business of insur-
ing mortgages, no one was minding the business of preserving America's
public realm.

■   ■   ■

Even before World War II, the effects of the depression and the initial decentralization of urban populations and some manufacturing industries led
public officials and business leaders to realize that allowing trends to continue as they were would leave cities severely disadvantaged. The 1940 census revealed that "the ten largest cities in the nation had either lost
population or grown at a slower rate than the country as a whole."[67] In
Boston, Cleveland, Philadelphia, and St. Louis, all cities that lost population
in the 1930s, neighborhoods saw longtime resident families leave, never to
return. Falling property values lowered urban tax bases. Many cities responded by raising taxes and cutting back the quality of services. Landlords
invested less in the maintenance of their structures.[68] According to historian
Thomas O'Connor, "Blighted districts covered almost one-third of the built
up parts of Brooklyn; nearly one-fourth of Birmingham's dwelling units were
located in declining areas; more than a quarter of Cleveland's population
lived in run-down neighborhoods; and Chicago's Loop was surrounded by a
three-mile-wide band of obsolete, wretched buildings."[69] In 1942, St. Louis
planners had reported that their city of 800,000 residents was "fast becoming
a decadent city . . . well on the way toward decline of its total population to
500,000 by 1980 or 1990."[70] Clearly, something drastic needed to be done to
check the declining conditions in America's cities, to provide employment after wartime, and to prevent the nation from sliding back into depression.
When the war ended, Americans saw Europeans digging out of bombed-out
rubble, rebuilding their cities from the ground up. Some Americans wished
they could be so lucky. "Having no benefit from the devastating bomb ourselves," observed Frank Lloyd Wright, America's "V for Victory may look
more like V for Vanquished."[71]

The urgent problem of housing topped the postwar agenda. Veterans de-
served better housing than the substandard dwellings or crowded apart-

ments that awaited their return. The National Association of Housing Officials estimated a need for half a million dwellings for new families after the war. Housing advocates pressed for more public housing for low-income occupants, whose needs the marketplace had never satisfactorily met. Urban business leaders argued for the clearance of slums to recapture the wasting potential of land values downtown.[72] And slum clearances, a federal policy under the New Deal, gained even greater currency in the postwar era. A congressional committee, chaired by Republican senator Robert Taft, called for "a new form of assistance to cities in ridding themselves of unhealthful housing conditions and of restoring blighted areas to productive use by private enterprise."[73] By clearing slums from the urban landscape, such reasoning went, the conditions that produced the slums in the first place could be eliminated. That view became the foundation for the Housing Act of 1949, legislation that later came to be known as "urban renewal."

According to the Housing Act of 1949, city authorities with power of eminent domain could seize property in areas identified as slums, purchase it with the help of federal funds, then sell the assembled area to a private developer for redevelopment. Among the law's laudable goals were the erection of "housing of sound standards of design, construction, livability, and size for adequate family life"; the construction of "well-planned, integrated residential neighborhoods";[74] and "the realization as soon as feasible of the goal of a decent home and a suitable living environment for every American family."[75] All too frequently, the results were something else: monstrous housing projects of faulty design, poorly planned neighborhoods that were seldom integrated with surrounding areas, and, in most cases, the displacement of residents without the provision of alternative housing.

Within a matter of years, policymakers realized the 1949 law would fall short of its goals and eliminate only 200,000 dwellings out of 5 million slated for removal nationwide. The low estimate of the cost to clear every blighted district in the nation was $3,000 per unit, or $15 billion in all, roughly equal to federal appropriations for the Marshall Plan to rebuild Europe.[76] Another 15 million dwellings did not require clearance but needed some form of conservation to prevent blight. To bring those dwellings to habitable conditions would cost the public only $600 each, because most of the costs would be carried by property owners. This approach was recommended for neighborhoods farther away from the central business districts, in places where potential land values were too small to justify huge public investments in large-scale clearance and redevelopment. Lacking funds to clear every blighted district in the nation, policymakers amended urban renewal programs in 1954 to encourage conservation methods as a practical alternative.[77] The new program called for stricter enforcement of building codes and authorized the FHA to insure mortgages on preexisting, new, and low-income housing in blighted districts, although it would be years before lawmakers would change the FHA's racial policies and address their lingering economic impact.[78] By 1964, 229 urban renewal projects throughout the country were involved in rehabilitation efforts, including a much publicized effort in Providence, Rhode Island, where preservationists had rescued the College Hill district, a historic residential area near Brown University. But efforts such as these were limited. William L. Slayton, commissioner of the Federal Urban Renewal Administration under President Kennedy, testified that "rehabilitation is even more difficult and complex than clearance and redevelopment, primarily because accomplishment depends so much upon the decisions and voluntary actions of many individual owners of a great variety of separate properties. . . . The process requires a great degree of participation by the local citizenry [and] skilled guidance for small property owners," as well as lending assistance. Slayton said that lack of experience in this area both at the federal level and among "the construction industry in general resulted in a slow start."[79]

While Europeans carefully restored their patrimony damaged by war (the citizens of Warsaw went so far as to reconstruct their demolished centuries-old downtown), prosperous Americans were less concerned with the city of yesterday and more eager to build Corbusier's City of Tomorrow with its high-rise towers and high-speed lanes. "Although the American scarcely thought of his car as an instrument for reshaping the city, it was to prove the most potent means of crippling central business districts and upbuilding outlying shopping areas that had ever been invented," wrote Mel Scott. "It was the most effective device for spreading the city over a vast territory that history had ever seen. Its potential for destruction and for construction was, in short, awesome."[80]

■ ■ ■

The Great Depression and World War II had put a hold on car purchases until car ownership picked up in the 1950s for the first time since 1929. With more cars and trucks traveling at greater speeds on congested narrow streets and clogged country lanes came growing demands for better roads that would carry more traffic at a smoother pace and a faster rate. In 1939, Paul Hoffman, the president of the Studebaker Corporation, said, "Many of our cities are almost as antiquated, trafficwise, as if they had medieval walls, moats, drawbridges."[81] Downtown interests agreed. America's historic cities were not built for the automobile, and it showed. Delivery trucks were held up in traffic. Commuters were stalled on the way to and from their jobs. Merchants said congestion in the streets and a lack of parking spaces kept customers from coming through their doors. But rather than design a transportation system to get the most out of America's cities, America redesigned its cities to get the most out of the automobile. "If we are to have the full use of automobiles, cities must be remade," Hoffman said.[82] Paving the way, General Motors erected a model city remade for highways called "the World of 1960" and displayed it in the "Futurama" exhibit at the New York World's Fair.

Traffic problems had been a national issue since the First World War, when the lack of efficient truck routes had slowed the transport of wartime supplies. The federal government began to send money to states that upgraded their rural roads, and after the war it created the Bureau of Public Roads to map a national system of routes that would link America's cities. But by 1939, when interest in the interstate system revived, the bureau was still but a small office in the U.S. Department of Agriculture and there was "surprisingly little cross-country traffic" to warrant the expense of new rural highways.[83] What limited highway construction had taken place had occurred in metropolitan areas. One of the early routes, for example, the Bronx River Parkway, begun in 1906 and completed in 1924, carried motorists along a ten-mile stretch through suburban New York in Westchester County's scenic Bronx River valley. Conceived partly as a device to relieve pollution of the Bronx River, the parkway was a triumph of careful road building and thoughtful land-use planning.[84] The result was an intentionally scenic drive, carefully routed to take advantage of the beauty of the natural terrain, complemented by the skilled work of talented landscape architects. Its design influenced other parkways in the region—the Long Island State Parkway, begun in 1926, the Hutchinson River Parkway, completed in 1928, the Saw Mill Parkway, completed in 1929, and the Merritt Parkway, completed in 1938—and others elsewhere in the country, including the Mount Vernon National Parkway, completed across the Potomac River from the nation's capital in 1932.[85]

During the New Deal era, the Bureau of Public Roads modified the original concept of an "interstate highway system" into an "interregional highway system," inspired by the German "autobahn," which linked Frankfurt and Darmstadt and provided significant employment for German workers under the Nazi regime.[86] Like the autobahn, interregional highways in the United States would provide employment and improve travel. But as author Stephen Goddard observed, "The autobahns may have inspired the interregional highways, but on one element they differed fundamentally: the German roads sought to serve the cities, while the American roads aimed to change them. The variance would become startlingly apparent a generation later."[87]

The "interregional system of highways has potentials for beneficial effects upon urban areas beyond any tools that have as yet been devised if the use is designed and directed by superior intelligence," Thomas H. McDonald, head of the Bureau of Public Roads, told an assembly of the American Society of Civil Engineers in 1943. "But," he warned, "the same tool may be used to produce disappointing, if not bad, effects."

Urban sprawl was already draining cities of industry, population, and retail trade, McDonald said. Beyond city boundaries, "sporadic urban expansion is left largely to the operation of subdividers" and "the zoning of land is designated greatly in excess of actual need or reasonable future demand." This, McDonald said, created illusory property values on the urban fringe and wasted property in the urban core, in the form of unused building lots, high vacancies, low rents, and deteriorating values. Few serious minds could argue any "economic or social reasons that justify robbing the historic center. To the Greeks, a city was not merely an agglomeration of buildings, but an association of men with common habits, needs and interests. By united effort, they endeavored to create for themselves acceptable and convenient surroundings for life. . . . Our cities are worth preserving," he said. "To survive, the city center must [remain] economically, socially, and functionally, the heart of the city."

As McDonald saw it, a new system of interregional highways could ensure that historic centers of population would remain the centers of their metropolitan regions. In theory, the new highways would bring in people more conveniently, and new circumferential highways, also called ring roads or beltways, built around the perimeters of urban settlement, would allow trucks to bypass the urban core, relieving downtowns of unnecessary congestion. In reality, the system turned America's cities inside out and did it so thoroughly that one wonders what America's highway planners were thinking at the time.

In fairness to McDonald, he was aware of potential pitfalls. For the system to be effective, he said, the construction of highways should wait until a metropolitan area has agreed on a plan for how it should develop. But he knew such an ideal scenario was "an impossible administrative problem" as long as a "plethora of independent government units"—counties, townships, water and sewer districts—continued to bid against each other "for municipal revenues, legal powers and administrative prestige within a metropolitan area that is essentially a social and economic entity." Looking ahead to the consequences for the postwar era, McDonald said, "Whether or not there is acceptance of a rational course and control of development, the provision of interregional routes will exert a powerful influence in shaping the future development of the city."

"The postwar highway era is here!" declared Robert Moses, the most influential road builder in American history.[88] From 1924 to 1968—through the terms of seven U.S. presidents, six governors of New York, and five different mayors of New York City—Moses controlled the largest local and statewide empire of public works projects in America. As head of New York's slum clearance committee, he oversaw the demolition of urban districts, the construction of private housing projects, and the provision of public housing for half a million people. As the kingpin of urban redevelopment, Moses was the dominant force in the construction of Lincoln Center, the New York Coliseum, Shea Stadium, and the United Nations headquarters. He built beaches, parks, and playgrounds across the metropolitan region. But his specialty was expressways. As the head of quasi-autonomous transit authorities, Moses oversaw the construction of hundreds of miles of parkways and highways and became the nation's most consulted expert on how to tear historic sections of cities apart to accommodate the automobile. A disciple of Corbusier, he was the Baron Haussmann for the modern era. In his biography of Moses, *The Power Broker*, author Robert Caro estimates that Moses evicted or displaced up to a quarter of a million people over the course of his long career. "He tore out the hearts of a score of neighborhoods," wrote Caro, "communities the size of small cities themselves, communities that had been lively, friendly places to live, the vital parts of the city that made New York Home to its people."[89] Disdainful of mass transit, Moses bled the city's transit system and ignored pleas to plan highways with future transit routes in mind, all in favor of building more and more highways that invited more traffic, increased congestion, lengthened commutes, guaranteed the sprawl of a region far beyond the needs of its growing population, and, by Caro's account, turned the world's best mass transit system into its worst. "Neighborhood feelings, urban planning considerations, cost, aesthetics, common humanity, common sense—none of these mattered in laying out the routes of New York's great roads," wrote Caro. "The only consideration that mattered was Robert Moses' will."[90] Moses was a man of such arrogance and contempt for those who stood in his path that the head of the Community Development Office of the Federal Urban Renewal Administration could fairly say that "nothing outside of Russia is more dictatorial than the highway official."[91] But Robert Moses never had to endure the stress he inflicted on others. Born in the age of the horse and buggy, Moses left the driving to his chauffeurs throughout his long career.[92]

As head of the Bureau of Public Roads, Thomas McDonald didn't care much for the methods Moses promoted. Instead, McDonald urged highway officials to think twice about razing neighborhoods and evicting people from their homes. He urged them to plan routes with economic and social values in mind. He even questioned the assumption that running highways through America's cities would alone solve urban traffic problems. The war, he said, had demonstrated the need for partial reliance on other modes of travel, railroads as well as shipping. As for the circulation of metropolitan residents, McDonald warned that a total reliance on the private automobile to handle commuter traffic would be asking the car and urban highways to do more than they possibly could, leading to inevitable disaster. Unless cities made better attempts to move people by other means, "The traffic problems of the larger cities may become well nigh insoluble."

Upon taking office, President Dwight Eisenhower edged McDonald aside in favor of a replacement more acceptable to the producers of oil, autos, and rubber tires, the all-powerful road-building lobbies. Robert Moses called on Washington to spend $50 billion—almost two-thirds of the annual federal budget at the time—on the construction of new highways.[93] Though Congress had already authorized a forty-thousand-mile "National System of Interstate and Defense Highways" in 1944, it had left half of the funding up to the states. With states either unwilling or unable to meet the costs, less than 1 percent of the planned mileage had been built by 1952.[94] To revive the effort, Eisenhower proposed his own "grand plan" and emphasized its importance to national defense. While some accused Eisenhower of exploiting cold war fears to promote his plan, others saw a genuine cold war rationale. In 1948, the National Security Resources Board had warned the nation that the concentration of industry in urban centers left the American economy too vulnerable to a Soviet nuclear attack. Identifying ninety-two cities as potential targets, it set out "to persuade American industry to disperse its plants throughout the country," ideally in cities of fifty thousand or less.[95] Out of fear that enemies would decimate America's cities, some Americans decided to dismantle them first, unwittingly following the example of the Muscovites who burned their city in anticipation of Napoleon's arrival.

When Congress passed the Federal Aid Highway Act in 1956, 90 percent of the funding for the interstate system came from a highway trust fund fueled by a federal tax on gasoline. Unwilling to build new highways before, state and city officials clamored for the easy money, regardless of their traffic needs. Daniel Patrick Moynihan, then an assistant professor of political science at Syracuse University, criticized the measure in *The Reporter* magazine, arguing that most of America's traffic existed in fourteen states in the northeastern quadrant of the country, but "a Democratic Congress dominated by Southern and Western representatives" had seen to it that 72 percent of the mileage would occur in entirely undeveloped regions.[96] As for the nation's cities, Moynihan claimed many would have improved their transit systems had money been as readily available. Across metropolitan regions,

Thomas McDonald's calls for linking highway construction with careful land-use planning were answered much too late. Instead of studying a metropolitan area to decide where development should go, highway engineers studied traffic trends and then built highways where traffic was projected to grow the worst—without questioning whether the long-term consequences were best for the urban region as a whole. Not until the mid-1960s did the nation plan highways with the protection of social and environmental values in mind. Not until 1970 did the nation make a long-term commitment to funding urban transit.[97] Even now, few metropolitan areas manage regional expansion seriously. Bertram D. Tallamy, who oversaw the development of federal highways in the 1950s and 1960s, said the system was built on principles taught by Robert Moses.[98] According to Moses, the most basic principle was this: "You can draw any kind of picture you want on a clean slate, but when you're operating in an overbuilt metropolis, you have to hack your way with a meat axe."[99]

In city after city, the suddenly available sums of money led to mindlessness. Urban historian Mel Scott put it this way: "Though transportation had been the most powerful force throughout American history in shaping the development of cities and concentrating greater proportions of the population in urban areas, vast sums of money were now going to be spent on a highway program related neither to a national urban policy nor a comprehensive transportation program."[100] Lewis Mumford said that "the most charitable thing to assume about this action is that they hadn't the faintest notion of what they were doing. Within the next fifteen years they will doubtless find out; but by that time it will be too late to correct all the damage to our cities and our countryside."[101] Just three short years later, the destruction of the urban built environment for highway projects was so severe that Mumford added, "The time is approaching in many cities when there will be every facility for moving about the city and no possible reason for going there."[102]

■   ■   ■

By coincidence, 1956, the year that gave America its interstate highway system, also gave America the first fully enclosed, climate-controlled, regional shopping mall, Southdale, in suburban Minneapolis. The early auto-oriented roadside marketplaces, like the small rows of shops that sprouted at streetcar stops before, had a local focus and served small local markets. They were little more than shopping villages for their surrounding communities. One of the first was developer Jesse Clyde Nichols's Country Club Plaza, built outside Kansas City in 1923 for his Country Club District, begun in 1907 as the first suburb to be reached by automobile. The plaza was a compact cluster of stores, sidewalks, and parking spaces built to resemble the center of a traditional small town, and its design reflected the visual character of the surrounding area. That arrangement was common in the first wave of auto-oriented shopping centers. As Peter Rowe has said, "almost all early examples referred back to a traditional model of development, one that stressed small-town, villagelike values of cheerful familiarity, personal service, convenience, and quality. Individuality in the architecture and appearance of specific stores took precedence over mass consumption."[103] In 1931, Highland Park Village, a community shopping center tucked into an area of single-family homes in suburban Dallas, broke from the pattern and became, to Rowe's eye, "the first major shopping center to turn away from the street."[104] It became the first shopping center to turn inward on itself and turn its back on the neighboring residential area. That development set off another trend in the evolution of the roadside marketplace. If shopping could occur in places completely independent from the places where people lived, new centers for shopping could go almost anyplace where roads brought people over inexpensive real estate. That happened in 1945, when a chain of farmers' markets spread across the West, modeled on a depression-era farmers' market in Beverly Hills that had been built on an inexpensive site, accessible to farmer and urban customer alike.[105]

As more Americans took to the road, more retailers took advantage of the steady volume of potential customers. Beginning in Kansas City in 1921, a White Castle hamburger stand grew into a chain of one hundred stores within a decade, years before Ray Kroc took the McDonald brothers' operation in San Bernardino and replicated it into an international fast-food franchise. From fast food to gasoline to motel rooms, regardless of the product, the marketing was the same. Familiar roadside architecture—cheap to build, easy to replicate, and easy to recognize from behind the wheel of a moving vehicle—catered to the mobile American, who demanded predictability in unfamiliar places. Soon, roads in all kinds of places began to look and feel just like roads in any other place along the ubiquitous car-bound strip that author Philip Langdon has called "the fume-laden corridor of commerce."[106]

Frank Lloyd Wright, whose Broadacre City was ridiculed by critics, could at least feel vindicated by the sight of cities disappearing into low-density sprawls across the wide horizon. In his biography of Wright, Herbert Muschamp recounted how Wright took Finnish architect Alvar Aalto on a tour of the sprawling suburbs of Boston in the 1950s. According to Muschamp, "Wright smiled beatifically, extended a magisterial hand out over the passing landscape, and proudly exclaimed, 'All this I have made possible.'" Muschamp asked, "How could an intelligent person say such a thing and keep a straight face? It is as though Einstein had beamed over Hiroshima. Didn't the Adventurer in Wright want to roar with laughter at the thought that the greatest architect of all time had made possible the conversion of America's natural paradise to an asphalt continent of Holiday Inns, Tastee-Freeze stands, automobile graveyards, billboards, smog, tract housing, mortgaged and franchised coast to coast?"[107]

As downtown department stores followed the expanding market base in suburbia, smaller retailers followed the department stores into regional clusters of roadside retail outlets. In suburban Boston, Wright could have taken Aalto to see one of the early ones, a place called Shoppers World, which opened on the outskirts of Framingham in 1951. The designers of Shoppers World called it a "double-decked mainstreet." With more awe than affection, others called it "one stop shopping machinery." Shoppers World held the equivalent of almost ten city blocks of retail development surrounded by acres of parking spaces. With an aluminum dome for a roof, it looked like "a spacecraft that had landed in a clearing within the woods."[108]

When the Dayton company went ahead with plans for its shopping center outside of Minneapolis in 1953, the job went to architect Victor Gruen. Gruen, who had come to the United States after fleeing Austria in 1938, was disturbed by the erosion of America's compact communities and the littering of its landscape with sprawling development. "Landscape and nature have become mere incidents within suburban spreads," Gruen said. "Instead of the city with its rooted citizens, we have urban sprawl with its drifting, nomadic inhabitants." Gruen saw a way to recentralize in the countryside all that had been dispersed from the old urban centers. He saw a compact and efficient pedestrian-oriented marketplace, less consumptive of the natural landscape than the commercial roadside strip. He saw a place for personal interaction in an impersonal built environment.

At Southdale, Gruen's dumbbell-shaped design called for a department store at either end of a two-story row of smaller stores, all joined under the same roof, surrounded by vast parking lots and buffered from neighboring real estate by acres of undeveloped land. Gruen's clients were skeptical, but there were precedents. Cleveland, for instance, had its five-story indoor urban arcade of 1890; London had seen Joseph Paxton's Crystal Palace in the Great Exhibition of 1851; and Milan still had its impressive four-story Galleria. All were massive structures that held rows of shops and boutiques or exhibits under a single roof, like city streets inside a greenhouse. The earlier enclosures were built for pedestrians in urban areas, but Gruen's clients needed to capture customers who could drive up to the very doors of suburban stores.[109] Was it unreasonable to expect suburban customers to park and walk for hundreds of yards? The developers took a gamble, and the project went ahead. Southdale became a success. Not only did people shop there, they spent time there, and Southdale turned the roadside shopping pit stop into a destination all its own.[110] Soon, malls were landing in clearances in the woods wherever potential markets could support them, usually at the junction of major highways, in anticipation of future residential development.[111]

The new suburban shopping center, Gruen felt, could become a new center of community. "We can restore the lost sense of commitment and belonging," he said; "we can counteract the phenomenon of alienation, isolation and loneliness and achieve a sense of identification and participation."[112] But Gruen, a native of Vienna, the historic Austrian city with a lively downtown pedestrian precinct, eventually became disenchanted with the ability of suburban malls to serve the social functions of the traditional downtown districts they replaced. Author William Kowinski recalled speaking to one of Gruen's former colleagues about this. "When I was talking to architect Cesar Pelli at Yale, he referred to the vast economic and social consequence of the malls' magnetism, and the power of large malls when they appear outside existing communities. 'Towns disappear,' he said. It was an awesome phrase. Towns disappear!"[113]

■ ■ ■

Across America, true community centers were disintegrating. In her 1961 book, *The Death and Life of Great American Cities,* Jane Jacobs praised the human scale of traditional urban environments, the variety of its street life, and the sidewalk traffic that made for safe, vibrant, and appealing places. Yet all of these great qualities, she warned, were under siege from modernist planning orthodoxy. "Downtowns and other neighborhoods that are marvels of close-grained intricacy and compact mutual support are casually disemboweled. Landmarks are crumbled or are so sundered from their contexts in city life as to become irrelevant trivialities. City character is blurred until every place becomes more like every other place, all adding up to Noplace."[114]

Five years later, a report of the U.S. Conference of Mayors' Special Committee on Historic Preservation alerted policymakers that America was perpetuating a terrible mistake by destroying the best of its built environment in order to improve it. Of all the historic landmarks of local identity recorded in detail over the previous three decades by the National Park Service's Historic American Buildings Survey, nearly half had been demolished or mutilated beyond recognition. The records had become a collection of "death masks" of America's most historically and architecturally significant structures.[115] Of the 145 landmarks the survey saw fit to record in San Francisco, only 23 were still intact. In Chicago, where nearly 300 buildings had been surveyed, nearly one-sixth were gone. In New Jersey, 20 percent of the 735 structures recorded were destroyed or too badly damaged to be of any public significance. Likewise, in New York City, one-fifth of the 250 landmarks surveyed were razed or ruined, including Pennsylvania Station, a structure so monumental that its demolition in 1965 shocked the city and the nation, too. Beyond the loss of great landmarks, entire districts were also leveled. "Minor buildings, in the aggregate, create the urban scene. They are the body of any city," wrote Carl Feiss. The "body is being rapidly carved up bit by bit and sometimes in whole chunks. The process has been so drastic in some cities that absolutely nothing is left. History is dead in such a city as though it had never existed, although there is still perhaps a bone or two lying around bleaching."[116]

"Radical Reconstruction" was the name given to the botched effort to reorganize the South after the Civil War. It failed in its mission, left antagonists even more hostile to the federal government, and unwittingly encouraged the extreme social divisions of Jim Crow segregation. The term also describes how America attempted to reorganize its urban form in the postwar years, cataclysmic clearances and reconstructions at the expense of a sustainable, organic process of repair and regeneration. As architectural historian James Marston Fitch describes it, "An organic process of growth and repair must create a gradual sequence of changes, and these changes must be distributed evenly across every level of scale. There must be as much attention to the repair of details . . . as to the creation of brand-new buildings. Only then can an environment stay balanced both as a whole and in its parts, at every moment of its history." According to University of California professor and author Christopher Alexander, "All the good environments that we know have this in common." Fitch explains:

> They are whole and alive because they have grown slowly over long periods of time, piece by piece. The pieces are small—and there are always a balanced number of projects going forward at every scale. If one building is being built, there are, simultaneously, many repairs and changes going forward at smaller scales all around the building. . . . This attitude to the repair of the environment has been commonplace for thousands of years in traditional cultures.
>
> But in modern urban developments, the environment grows in massive chunks. . . . Once a building is built, says Alexander, it is considered finished; it is not part of a long sequence of repair projects. These "finished" buildings are assumed to have a certain finite lifetime. . . . The fundamental assumption is that it is better to be in a new building than in an old building: and the money spent on

the environment is concentrated in the huge new projects, while the money spent maintaining old buildings is reduced to a bare minimum.[117]

In their rush to replace the historic city, the product of generations, with the City of Tomorrow, Americans took environments full of intricate and interweaving parts and trashed them, often creating little in their place but a no-man's-land of gaping, empty holes. "The street goes, human scale goes, pedestrian scale goes, variety goes—everything goes," said Vincent Scully. "Our cities lie destroyed all around us, and, of course, as the cities were destroyed, the terrible thing in American society and politics is that the communities of the center of the city were destroyed with them."[118]

Though urban renewal gave some fading locations new leases on economic life, many others were left in ruins, typically those with the poorest and least politically connected constituencies. In Boston, the demolition of the humble West End neighborhood for high-rise, high-rent apartment towers became a nationally notorious example of "urban removal," the destruction of living, breathing communities by abusive, authoritarian planners. According to Boston historian Thomas O'Connor, "One elderly Jewish woman from Russia described the process as though the Cossacks themselves had come riding into her neighborhood."[119] In Los Angeles, the riots that erupted in Watts in 1964 shocked the entire nation. Among the factors that investigators believed to be responsible for the rage was the disruption of familiar environments by the construction of urban highways and new high-rise public housing.

Soon, urban renewal was attacked from both the left and the right. Martin Anderson, a professor at Columbia University who would later become a domestic policy adviser to President Ronald Reagan, called urban renewal a fiasco, first in an article in the *Harvard Business Review* and later in a book, *The Federal Bulldozer.* Anderson said the program had failed to live up to its original goals of eliminating slums, producing a sufficient supply of housing, and "a decent home and a suitable living environment for every American family."[120] He argued that the marketplace, if left alone, would have been more efficient than federal spending. Others, including real estate specialists as well as government administrators, responded that the failure of the marketplace to maintain and improve existing housing as well as meet the demand for affordable housing is what brought on urban renewal to begin with. Corbusier, whose urban plans had inspired Americans to sack their own cities and the people who inhabited them, died in 1965, just as others began to reassess how destructive his dogma really was. Though the man has been dead for three decades, monuments to his utopian visions survive him: the dead streets and deadly public housing projects throughout urban America. As British planner Peter Hall has written, "The evil that Corbusier did lives after him."[121]

The most tragic outcome of all, perhaps, is that the City of Tomorrow was justified by conditions prevalent in the 1920s, the congestion that prevented further concentration of the urban core. By the time America's experiment with urban Radical Reconstruction had reverted back to a more traditional process of organic, piecemeal urban redevelopment, the city had already decentralized. Billions had been spent to build an urban form that upon completion made many places obsolete. Even the alarming prediction of St. Louis planners in 1942—that their city of 800,000 residents could shrink to 500,000 by 1980 or 1990—proved to be too optimistic. By 1990, the population of St. Louis had fallen to 397,000. As Kenneth T. Jackson reported, "Many of its old neighborhoods have become dispiriting collections of eviscerated homes and vacant lots. Aging warehouses and grimy loft factories are now open to the sky; weeds cover once busy railroad sidings."[122]

■   ■   ■

From 1973 to 1985, the United States lost 5 million blue-collar jobs. Over the same time, the nation gained from 82 million to 110 million new jobs in service fields.[123] As fewer people commuted to work in an urban center, more and more commuted from suburban homes to suburban job sites, especially former housewives newly added to the workforce. In the 1970s, suburbs contained just a quarter of the office space in metropolitan areas, but by 1984 they held the majority.[124] By the mid-1980s, the development of suburban workplaces had grown so vast that hundreds of suburbs had become independent of urban centers. Urban historian Robert Fishman said that these suburbs, with their own housing subdivisions, retail shopping centers, and employment centers, had all the makings of independent cities and could no longer be called suburbs; they represented a new urban form altogether. Author Joel Garreau called them "edge cities." Financed partly by generous local subsidies for suburban development as well as generous federal tax benefits for real estate construction, most of them had developed during the 1970s and 1980s on what had been farmland only a generation before.[125] Employment opportunities at the edge of urban America in turn stretched the reach of the metropolitan region. From 1970 to 1990, the population of metropolitan Los Angeles grew by 45 percent, but the land area of the metropolis sprawled by a whopping 300 percent beyond its former size.[126] Over the same period, the size of greater Philadelphia grew by 32 percent in size while its population actually shrank by 3 percent.[127] Metropolitan Cleveland also declined in population while its area expanded by a third.[128]

Clevelanders call their town "the Comeback City," taking pride in their dynamic mayor, Michael White, and popular recent additions to the city's traditional core: the new baseball park, Jacobs Field; the Rock and Roll Hall of Fame; and the revitalized historic warehouse district called the Flats. But the nickname "Comeback City" hides reality. Few of the city's former residents are coming back. Many more are leaving. Thomas Bier, director of the Housing Policy Research Program at Cleveland State University, studied residential migration in the Cleveland metropolitan market from 1987 to 1991 and discovered that migration "outward was five times greater than movement inward."[129] Residents of the inner city are moving to the inner suburbs; residents of the inner suburbs are moving to the outer suburbs; and residents of the outer suburbs are moving beyond them into formerly rural exurbia. As Bier notes, the general pattern of outward migration has existed since at least the 1930s and is "largely the result of supportive government policies," a willingness on the part of local, county, state, and federal governments to fund new infrastructure such as new roads and new schools in outlying areas while spending relatively little money to maintain the quality of residential areas closer to Cleveland's core. What is new, Bier found, is that the pattern of desertion and dispersal is no longer confined to inner Cleveland. Residents abandon the inner suburbs almost as fast as they do the city. "Cleveland and its inner suburbs have been unwittingly undermined by federal and state government," Bier says. "Vulnerable suburbs," he warns, "are those with the lowest priced housing located next to or near the city of Cleveland, places such as Parma, Maple Heights and Euclid"—middle-class areas whose longtime residents have begun to leave. "The present risk is that over the next 20–30 years, Cuyahoga County will follow the city of Cleveland into distressed fiscal condition, which would in turn further jeopardize the economic condition of the multi-county Cleveland region."

What is happening in greater Cleveland is happening nationwide as aging suburbs lose the appeal they had when they were new. "We're seeing two things: continued exurban expansion and increasing decline of older suburbs," write William Lucy and David Phillips, professors of urban and environmental planning at the University of Virginia, who have tracked these trends for municipalities and business interests in Virginia. According to their research, from 1960 to 1990, the nation's twenty-five largest cities all experienced a decline in median family income, but so did some of the suburbs in all but four of those cities, and some of those suburbs "are growing poorer at an even faster rate than the cities they surround."[130] By their measure, family income dropped faster in almost half of the suburbs around Atlanta and the District of Columbia than it did in those two central cities themselves. Areas unable to sustain themselves continue to be left behind, along with wasting public investments in roads, water and sewer systems, schools, hospitals, and other local institutions. In spite of flight, however, taxpayers, property owners, and businesses cannot disassociate themselves from problems in neighboring locales. According to the Federal Reserve Bank of Philadelphia, the health of suburbs is linked to the health of the urban centers they surround. When cities do well, suburbs benefit, too. Conversely, when a city declines, its suburbs go down with it. Conditions of the core set the tone for investment in the metropolitan region as a whole.[131]

When a metropolitan region sprawls, moreover, everyone eventually picks up a portion of the tab for the extra costs of extending public infrastructure, such as roads and school districts and fire and police protection, to outlying areas. Sprawl means higher taxes to duplicate what already exists. Every older community contains an enormous investment of public funds in downtown streets, sidewalks, and the like. When this investment—public assets that are already paid for—is abandoned or used at a fraction of its capacity, taxpayer dollars are wasted. Sprawl is not only outrageously expensive, it's fiscally irresponsible. And it's insatiable, too. While the size of the average American household has shrunk, the size of the average new house has grown. In 1970, married couples with children represented the largest share of the housing market. By 1990, nuclear family households were outnumbered by married couples living by themselves. Yet, the American housing industry constructs bigger houses for smaller families built farther apart than at any time since rural homesteading. On the edges of urban regions it is not uncommon to see developments going up on former farmland that has been cut up into large five-acre lots to accommodate "McMansions" or "trophy houses" for affluent couples with nary a child at home. Philip Langdon has pointed out that the three-car garage (about seven thousand square feet in size) is almost as large as an entire first-generation suburban house at Levittown. Factor in the excessive widths of roads in these new subdivisions, roads barely used at all, and one can easily understand how residential sprawl stretches the metropolitan limits.

A complete dependence on the automobile to move around poorly planned sprawlscapes is said to give us more freedom and mobility, but it may actually give us less. Americans spend more time driving vaster distances in the car than ever, commuting to work, running errands, and chauffeuring children, much of the time stuck in slow-moving traffic. America's love affair with the automobile has become an addiction in the environment of sprawl, where most have no choice but to drive for every need. Children and the elderly who are unable to drive have no alternative but to stay shut

Auto
probs. ✓

in, with few or no places to go within walking distance of the home. Working people without cars, most likely the working poor left behind in urban neighborhoods and aging inner suburbs, are trapped, too, finding it difficult, if not impossible, to commute via buses to new jobs created in sprawling locations.

The shape of a fragmented, disintegrated metropolis has, in turn, shaped a similar society. Hartford, Connecticut, "once embodied middle-class urbanity sustained by smokeless, genteel businesses like insurance companies," wrote columnist George Will, who visited the city in 1996.[132] Now, "Hartford is the nation's eighth poorest city and has the nation's highest illegitimacy rate." Its school system's test scores rank lowest in Connecticut, and the unemployment rate among adult public housing residents is 94 percent. In 1950, Hartford's population was 358,081, and more than 340,000 residents, or 96 percent, were white. By 1990, the city's population had dropped by 61 percent, to 139,739, and only some 55,000 residents, or 40 percent, were white. Demographically, the metropolitan area had become one of thirty in the nation where Hispanic Americans are most segregated.[133] Economically, Hartford itself had become "the emaciated core of a metropolitan area of 1.1 million"—in a state with the highest per capita income in America.[134]

As divisions and distances between Americans have widened, so have gaps in social trust. According to surveys conducted annually by the National Opinion Research Center, trust among Americans is in decline, especially among persons born after World War II.[135] Some theorists believe the shape of the built environment to be a major culprit. As early as the 1950s, British sociologists Michael Young and Peter Willmott tracked the migration of residents from a closely knit working-class neighborhood in East London to a new housing subdivision. In the neighborhood, they discovered that social solidarity was the product of common ties to a shared place, a common sense of turf and familiarity among neighbors formed by frequent contact on sidewalks, in local stores and pubs, and outside schools. This kind of casual contact was critical, they felt, because it occurred between neighbors who otherwise would not invite each other into their homes. But when the same residents moved to the new, lower-density housing estate, a place with one-fifth as many people per acre, "the culture of friendliness and familiarity was replaced by distrust, social privacy, and materialism."[136] Why? "Their lives outside the family are no longer centered on people; their lives are centered on the house. This change from a people-centered to a house-centered existence is one of the fundamental changes resulting from the migration."[137] In the United States, a home-centered existence was the norm, the American Dream. In fact, as political scientist Robert Putnam has noted, the home is so central to the American lifestyle that "television absorbs 40 percent of the average American's free time."[138]

Sociologist Ray Oldenburg, author of *The Great Good Place: Cafes, Coffee Shops, Community Centers, Beauty Parlors, General Stores, Bars, Hangouts, and How They Get You Through The Day*, argues that Americans have little choice but to retreat into the sanctuary of their family rooms because of the disappearance of local gathering places that used to be within walking distance of their homes and workplaces. He blames rigid single-use zoning districts for eliminating traditional neighborhood gathering places, the local tavern or corner store, where people could stop off and linger, blow off steam, form acquaintances, and cement the kind of attachment to neighbors necessary for civic trust. Americans, Oldenburg writes, are spending too much time at home and work, expecting too much from either environment, putting strains on family or business relationships, leading to stress that shows up in anger on the job, depression, dependence on drugs and alcohol, and high rates of divorce. "The average individual has not yet caught on to the problems of place and still tends to blame other factors for the hardships imposed by bad urban design," he writes.[139]

When Oldenburg came across a 1968 copy of *The Community Builders Handbook,* published by the Urban Land Institute, a national trade association of developers, the sociologist was surprised to find that the only type of public gathering place mentioned in the manual was bowling alleys, and they were described as "poor money makers." *The Community Builders Handbook* was not about building communities but about building shopping centers.[140] Oldenburg writes, "The course of urban growth and development in the United States has been hostile to an informal public life; we are failing to provide either suitable or sufficient gathering places necessary for it."[141] The French, he notes, have their neighborhood bistros and sidewalk cafés; the Italians, their public piazzas; the Irish and British, their local pubs; the Viennese, their coffeehouses; the Germans, their beer gardens; and the Japanese, their teahouses. What do the majority of Americans who live in places zoned for single uses have? Nothing within walking distance. What little exists within a short driving distance is most likely to be a franchise intended for quick transactions more than social interaction. "A habitat that discourages association, one in which people withdraw to privacy as turtles into their shells, denies community and leaves people lonely in the midst of many," says the sociologist.[142] When Oldenburg urges Americans to consider the emptiness of sprawling single-use environments, some accuse him of trying to turn back the clock in order to bring back the past. "We don't want the past," Oldenburg protests. "We can't have the past. We don't need the past. *We need the places!*"[143]

As habitats for community have eroded, so too has the true meaning of the word. Today, "community" more commonly describes any rootless collection of interests rather than people rooted in a place—people tied by fellowship or even kinship to one another, to a shared past, and to a common interest in the future.

The pseudocommunity of the interest group can never replace what the genuine community provides: a place (not a marketplace) for cooperation more than competition, a home where people of disparate views can speak face-to-face, stand accountable to one another, reconcile their differences, and reach agreements on action to be taken up by all. "Self-governing communities, not individuals, are the basic units of democratic society," argued the late historian Christopher Lasch. "It is the decline of those communities, more than anything else, that calls the future of democracy into question."[144]

When Democracy Builds is the title of a book by Frank Lloyd Wright, who elevated the private home above the public realm and urged his countrymen to desert their neighbors for the open frontier. A more fitting title would have been "When Democracy Decays."

Wright once said, "Clients have asked me: How far should we go out, Mr. Wright? I say: 'Just ten times as far as you think you ought to go!—and go soon and go fast.' " Wright himself went far off into the horizon and purchased eight hundred acres of the Arizona desert, some twenty-six miles from Phoenix. Before long, however, the exodus that Wright had advocated caught up to him. As architect Robert A. M. Stern recounts in his book *Pride of Place: Building the American Dream,* Frank Lloyd Wright became "the victim of his own prophecies. Americans, whether or not they had ever heard of him, followed Wright's counsel to drive onto the freeway and move into the country, and the miniature haciendas of suburban Phoenix had reached his Paradise Valley doorstep."[145] Instead of welcoming the new arrivals with open arms, Wright went to court to stop the erection of their power lines that were to mar his views. He lost his case. The machine had triumphed over man and nature after all.

As well as anyone, Wright foresaw the forces of decentralization: new technology and a new desire for self-liberation. But he failed to anticipate the consequences. To go ten times farther than we think we can go is to liberate ourselves from reasonable "constraints of time and place," from our responsibility to those with whom we share them, and to deny that any of this carries a price."[146] And so, as the twentieth century nears its close, Americans continue to flee not the polluted, congested industrial city of the late nineteenth century, but a mess of modern making, trading emptied environments for new environments of emptiness, unwilling or unable to preserve the places we leave behind, caught in an ever widening gyre of abandonment and sprawl.

3

BLUFF CITY

It was tougher than war, tougher than the Yankee Brigadier
Chalmers and his artillery and all his sappers with dynamite and
crowbars and cans of kerosene. But it wasn't tougher than the
ringing of a cash register bell. It had to go—obliterated, effaced,
no trace left—so that a sprawling octopus covering the country
from Portland, Maine to Oregon can dispense in cut-rate bargain
lots, bananas and toilet paper.

They call this progress. But they don't say where it's going; also
there are some of us who would like the chance to say whether or
not we want the ride.

—William Faulkner, from a letter to *The Oxford Eagle* recalling
the demolition of an Oxford, Mississippi, landmark while protest-
ing the proposed demolition of the Lafayette County Courthouse

When the founders of Memphis, Tennessee, chose their city's
name in 1819, they translated "Memphis" to mean "beautiful and established," taking the name of a place in Egypt whose ruins had vanished along
the Nile thousands of years before. Because of choices made by the
founders' successors, the ruins of modern Memphis now line the banks of
the Mississippi River less than two centuries after the city's birth.

Parts of Memphis make the place like no other city in America: the barbecue pits, rhythm and blues, and Graceland, home of the King of Rock and
Roll. But too much of Memphis is like too many other cities in America: a
nine-to-five downtown, neighborhoods in decline, and homogenized, sprawling strip development as far as the eye can see. In fact, travelers who arrive
in Memphis through the airport or the interstate highways will see little of
what makes Memphis . . . Memphis. To see authentic Memphis is to go
where few Memphians ever go themselves.

Fronting the Mississippi River in the original heart of Memphis is Cotton
Row, a four-block-long wall of historic brick buildings. Here, from antebel-

lum offices and turn-of-the-century warehouses, cotton factors and cotton brokers ran the largest inland cotton market in the world. On the eve of the Civil War, some four hundred thousand bales of cotton came through this part of town. Roustabouts, stevedores, and draymen hauled them by the cartload, up a cobblestone landing and into warehouses, where they waited to travel to textile mills in New England. A few bales still pass through this part of town each October or November, but the bustling activity is gone. So are the draymen and the "squidges," the apprentice brokers trained to grade the quality of raw cotton by sight and touch. Gone from the sidewalks on Cotton Row are crowds of any kind. The historic blocks of Front Street facing the majestic river are almost ruins lining the banks of the American Nile.

Just behind Cotton Row runs historic Main Street, a ten-block stretch of commercial buildings, most of which date from the late nineteenth and early twentieth centuries. Some are short brick buildings built just after the Civil War. Some are magnificent turn-of-the-century "skyscrapers." But on Main Street today, storefronts at street level are mostly empty. Windows above are empty, too, except for an occasional poster advertising cut-rate deals on "Leasable Space." Though downtown still employs a daytime workforce of fifty thousand people, few, if any, are seen here.

Main Street was *the* main street when a mule-drawn streetcar line first traversed it in 1866. Electric trolleys took their place, and then disappeared for decades, until the city brought them back in 1993. The restored trolley line was intended to bring traffic to Main Street, and in a way it has, but the trolleys no longer function as they once did. A photograph taken on an August afternoon in 1912 shows fourteen streetcars on two blocks of Main Street, while pedestrians fill the sidewalks with activity. More than eighty years later, a trolley runs about every ten minutes on average. On some runs, it carries more tourists than Memphians, who can easily walk down Main Street in the time it takes to wait for a ride. In restoring the trolley line, the city has bluffed the visitor into believing Main Street is alive. But how can a city ask visitors to appreciate a place that too many locals obviously do not appreciate themselves? Memphis may be the only city in America where fifty cents buys a ride on a restored streetcar line through a veritable theme park of urban disinvestment.

Ask any knowledgeable Memphian when civilization departed downtown, and chances are he or she will respond with an exact date in history: April 4, 1968, the day Martin Luther King Jr. fell victim to a sniper's bullet, a block off South Main on the balcony of the Lorraine Motel. That tragic event wounded the psyche of the city in ways from which it has yet to fully recover, but the answer is too convenient, offered as if the trigger finger of a single gunman exonerates citizens of any role in the abandonment of their downtown. In truth, flight from the city's historic core more accurately coincides with the death of something else: the reign of Edward Hull Crump's political machine, which ruled Memphis and surrounding Shelby County over the span of forty-five years.

When Crump was first elected mayor in 1909, Memphis was ninety years old. Unlike southern frontier settlements that sprouted loosely around a courthouse at a crossroads, the founding of Memphis was an urban undertaking from the start. The original proprietors, James Winchester, John Overton, and Andrew Jackson, laid out a town of 362 lots, bisected by streets that ran parallel and perpendicular to the Mississippi. From the beginning the location's greatest advantage was the river. Travel down the Mississippi from its junction with the Ohio River, as novelty steamboats still do today, and you pass strategic points along the way, the bluffs that provided safe havens above the floodplain, sites for Spanish and American forts, and this permanent settlement on the "Fourth Chickasaw Bluff," named for the tribe that lost the territory to American Manifest Destiny.

Chickasaw natives knew this spot to be the most convenient river crossing in the region, a fact that did not escape the city's American settlers. In 1820, proprietor John Overton pitched an advertisement to potential investors: "The plan and local situation of Memphis are such . . . that it is destined to become a large and populous city."[1] In anticipation of his city's expected growth, Overton boasted of the founders' foresight to improve property values by setting aside four blocks of real estate as public squares and along the river "an ample vacant space, reserved as a promenade."[2]

As a young river city in the glory days of steamboats, Memphis blossomed along with St. Louis and Cincinnati, attracting a large number of immigrants from Germany and Ireland. Though Memphis shared commerce and cultural influences with the industrial cities upriver, its economy and social system were rooted in the slave-owning South. For a century, cotton magnates resisted the kind of large-scale industrialization that swept the North. All of this confused the city's regional identity. Memphis was clearly in the South, but it had much in common with the early Midwest. At some point, people decided to split the difference and call their region the "Mid South"—not the Deep South, not the upper South, not the coastal South, but an inland market area that spans western Tennessee, eastern Arkansas, northern Mississippi, western Kentucky, and southeastern Missouri.

Roughly equidistant from St. Louis and New Orleans, Memphis grew slowly in antebellum times and survived the Civil War physically unscathed, although an infamous race riot unsettled the city in 1866 during Reconstruction. During the 1870s, the river city was all but abandoned when a series of yellow fever epidemics decimated the population and bankrupted the city treasury, and Memphis, unable to govern itself, lost its city charter. Citizens with the wealth and influence to restore the place to health skipped town and moved east, to Nashville or farther beyond, leaving their hometown to the care of a few diligent businessmen who intervened to remedy the ills of poor sanitation and bring the city back from bankruptcy. By this time, the spread of railroads, the drainage of Delta wetlands, and the harvest of ancient forests turned Memphis into one of the world's leading markets for hardwood timber. With cotton prices in decline, timber provided new fortunes that rebuilt the decrepit town. The first electric streetcars arrived in 1881, replacing the mule-drawn vehicles that had run down Main Street since the end of the Civil War. Then the Great Bridge over the Mississippi opened in 1892, the first railroad bridge south of St. Louis to link the East and West. The railroad junctions kept commerce concentrated along Front and Main Streets downtown, where the wonders of new steel construction methods, elevators, and electric lights gave rise to the city's first skyscraper in 1895. At eleven stories, the building was the tallest in the South. There, Memphians commanded a rooftop view of the Delta for the price of a dime. Many of the surviving buildings in the city's historic downtown took form during this prosperous era, when locals changed their understanding of the ancient name "Memphis" to mean "place of good abode."

The economic boom that fueled the growth of Memphis, also attracted tens of thousands of rural migrants unprepared for urban life. Young and single laborers poured their wages into raucous saloons, gambling halls, and houses of ill repute, giving Memphis a reputation as a rowdy, uncivilized town. The city became America's "Murder Capital," in honor of its homicide rate, which in one year neared 90 murders per 100,000 people, more than ten times the national average and well above New Orleans's own record of 75 per 100,000 set in 1995.[3] "The economic elite of Memphis, the cotton brokers and Factors on Front Street, gave little attention to local government," writes Memphis historian David M. Tucker. "In more than a hundred years of existence, Memphis had produced no statesman whom her citizens cared to dignify with a bronze statue."[4] Ed Crump, who had migrated to Memphis as a poor, skinny kid from the north Mississippi town of Holly Springs, stepped in to fill the void.

From his election as mayor in 1909 until his death in 1954, Crump was the boss man and Memphis was his plantation. He came to Memphis seeking order and imposed it from his office on Main Street across from City Hall, where he built an insurance business and long-lived political machine. "Ed Crump was essentially a highly moral man, and Memphis was an exceedingly sinful city," wrote Turner Catledge, who covered the city as a young reporter for the *Memphis Commercial Appeal*. "The city challenged Crump's zeal and piety. He wanted to remake it in his own image—honest, moral, efficient. The problem was that Crump believed so passionately in his own purity that he thought his noble ends justified whatever ignoble means he chose to employ. So, he became a pious, but very ruthless dictator."[5] As the self-elected chairman of the city and county's unofficial board of directors (his puppets and protégés in political offices), Crump tamed Memphis. He even commissioned local bandleader W. C. Handy to compose a tune now known as the "Memphis Blues," with the refrain "Mr. Crump don't 'low no easy riders here." The song said more about political dissenters than it did about unruly rowdies, for Crump winked at gambling and bootlegging for a quarter century until the vice industries no longer served his political interests. As a civic leader, Crump was a man of contradictions. A racist and staunch segregationist, he enfranchised blacks and fought off the Ku Klux Klan, the only organization that could rival his own. As a congressman in Washington for two terms, he voted consistently with Franklin Roosevelt's New Deal, yet back in Memphis he was suspicious of federal intervention in local affairs and opposed industrial labor unions.

As Memphis grew, Crump molded the city in his own image, from a place marked by its past rural poverty into a maturing city of sober, traditional buildings deserving of national respect. The prominent buildings Memphis erected in the Crump years reflected variety within the bounds of conformity to classical architectural traditions. Perhaps none was as graceful as the 1909 Shelby County Courthouse, a monumental limestone landmark flanked by marble statues carved to honor Wisdom, Authority, Justice, Liberty, Peace, and Prosperity. As Eugene J. Johnson and Robert D. Russell Jr. write in their history of Memphis architecture, "This building says 'Good Government' and says it well."[6] At the southern end of downtown, Union Station was erected in 1912. "This monumental building made arrivals and departures the exciting events they were supposed to be in the great days of the railroads," write Johnson and Russell, who call the elaborate structure "the finest Beaux-Arts building the city ever had."[7] Memphis historian Robert A. Sigafoos calls it a "symbol of local progress" built upon the assumption that "the more grandiose or elegant the structure, the greater the community pride. It was the city's calling card extended to business and tourist visitors."[8] In a similar spirit, the Federal Customs House on the riverfront at the center of town was rebuilt in granite in 1929. The most prominent side was graced with a row of paired columns after Senator Kenneth D. McKellar instructed the architect to make the building complement the neoclassical county courthouse and a prominent bank building nearby.[9]

Privately built structures took pride in the face they presented to the public, too. On Main Street, the Columbia Mutual Tower (now the vacant

Lincoln America Tower), a twenty-one-story building clad in white tiles, gave the Memphis skyline a stunning small-scale replica of Cass Gilbert's Woolworth Building in New York. Between 1923 and 1929, Memphis added 1 million square feet of office space downtown, culminating with the twenty-nine-story Sterick Building, the tallest building in Memphis for the next thirty-five years. At the northern end of Main Street, the Italian Renaissance Ellis Auditorium was completed in 1924, while at the southern end, the Orpheum Theater, an ornate show palace, was completed in 1928.

It did not take long for these developments to translate into local pride. By the end of World War I, on the occasion of the city's centennial, Memphis was calling itself the "Wonder City of the South." Though the depression took a toll, Crump paid the unemployed to keep the city clean. "By the end of World War II, Memphis was one of the cleanest, quietest, healthiest, most law-abiding, and most beautiful cities in the nation," writes Memphis historian John E. Harkins. "Indeed, in many ways the muddy, pestilential little hamlet atop the Fourth Chickasaw Bluff had become like its namesake—stable and beautiful and a 'place of good abode.' "[10]

Crump dominated Memphis affairs during a time of unprecedented prosperity and physical change, from the days of mule-drawn drays to the advent of the interstate highways. Four decades after his death in 1954, he is still spoken of with deference as "Mr. Crump" by anyone old enough to remember him, everyone from former busboys to present-day bankers, even reform-minded opponents who once compared him to Benito Mussolini, the Italian dictator who made the trains run on time. But where Crump delivered order, he also stifled disagreement and imagination. In striving to make Memphis a city worthy of national respect, Crump wanted the city to grow almost at any cost, so he ignored warnings of chaotic development sprouting on the urban rim. A nearsighted man who wore thick, round, black-rimmed glasses two decades after they went out of fashion, Crump could not foresee what awaited Memphis down the road.

In most large cities in the United States, America's victory in World War II was enough to unleash energy pent up by the war effort and years of the Great Depression. Memphis had to await the departure of old men who preserved the prewar order for another decade. By the time the next generation of leaders took charge after Crump's death in 1954, they went out of their way to prove to the rest of America that Memphis was not a dowdy southern backwater run by a tyrannical clique of country bumpkins. Nothing symbolized the birth of a new era as much as the rising pop culture phenomenon Elvis Presley, whose first regional hit, "That's All Right," emerged from the Memphis Sun Records studio in 1954. That same year, the U.S. Supreme Court ruled in *Brown v. Board of Education of Topeka,* signaling that a half century of Jim Crow segregation was heading toward an inevitable and disruptive close.

Liberated from the heavy hand of the past, Memphis chose to free itself from the confines of its traditional downtown. As new suburban homeowners and merchants ran away from aging buildings, downtown property owners, in fear of being left behind by the new competition, modernized the city's appearance. It was no longer enough for Memphis to be merely a "place of good abode." Progress demanded change. In 1957, Goldsmith's department store on Main Street, the longtime retail hub of the Mid South region, covered its 1901 exterior with pink porcelain panels in order to appeal to shoppers attracted to new suburban roadside stores.[11] Up the street, an entire block of elaborate three- and four-story nineteenth-century commercial buildings fell to the wrecker's ball. The site was taken over by a dull, blank box of a department store, the image of a roadside retail outlet that would have been more at home in the middle of a suburban parking lot.

Throughout the city, historic Victorian structures were reconstructed to appear less Victorian. In 1958, the Cossitt Library—a Romanesque red sandstone landmark built in 1893 and framed at ground level by a graceful terrace overlooking the Mississippi River—was chopped apart and deconstructed. Its remains were hidden behind a blank modernist extension. The library was "one of the few great monumental structures in the city . . . an imposing structure of great power and dignity," write Johnson and Russell. According to the authors, "The loss of no old building in Memphis is more regrettable."[12]

The new public buildings downtown were unlike anything the city had ever seen. In 1959, Memphis broke ground for a new civic center that would eventually include a new city hall; county, state, and federal office buildings; as well as a structure for the Federal Reserve Bank. They were clustered around a plaza that swallowed four entire blocks and gobbled the traditional street patterns and sidewalks. Civic Center became less a plaza for pedestrians than a pedestal for modern buildings that stood apart from their surroundings, a fitting symbol for any government that grows out of touch with the public it aims to serve. The new county building, with ugly aluminum screens adorning its exterior, was a brutalistic form of art accessible only to artistes. Memphians called it the "Bedspring Hotel."[13]

The pace of progress downtown was measured also by movement up, into massive projects that dwarfed the scale of the traditional city. In 1964, the First National Bank opened its new twenty-five-story office tower. The amount of office space in the structure was equivalent to two-thirds of the office space built in the 1920s boom alone. It was followed by the construction of two more towers, one of them thirty-eight stories tall, the tallest building erected in the city since 1929. Offering modern amenities, dramatic views, and proximity to the courts and the Civic Center, the top-class office space attracted the highest-paying tenants in the city. But the competitive race to the top of the skyline had unintended side effects on the downtown as a whole. Memphis was not Manhattan, where land is scarce and therefore expensive, where the tallest of buildings can be justified. As far back as 1922, the famed urban planner Harland Bartholomew of St. Louis urged Memphis to declare a height limit of twelve stories for all new downtown buildings. In spite of their rising popularity nationwide, tall buildings, Bartholomew knew, congested downtowns and deprived them of light and freely flowing air.[14] Memphis ignored him, and by the late 1960s, the height of structures was more than an issue about congestion and sunlight. By vacuuming tenants from older structures up into upper-story space, the new towers compressed the downtown into a few blocks ringed by parking lots, leaving Memphis to witness the slow rot of formerly occupied structures ringed by empty sidewalks.[15]

Having given little thought to managing its vertical growth, Memphis gave even less consideration to containing its horizontal expansion, pursuing a policy of more is always better. Following World War II, real estate analysts predicted Memphis would grow to 1 million people by 1995. Clearly, the increase in population would have to be accommodated by the development of open land; but even then, with the forecast in hand, Memphis did little to shape the consequences. As a city prevented from growing westward by a river that flooded lower ground on the opposite bank, Memphis had three directions in which to expand. Land to the north held the least desirable sites. Land to the south was limited by the Mississippi state line. Much of the migrating money moved east, away from the river.

As early as the 1920s, Bartholomew had warned the city to contain the eastward movement. To prevent uneven metropolitan growth and the migration of too many residents in one direction, the planner urged Memphis to build better roads traversing the city from north to south, but local leaders resisted, allowing speculators and land developers operating east of downtown to set the terms. In 1940, Bartholomew wrote to new mayor Walter Chandler warning that blighted residential districts around the downtown would drive residents even farther from the city's core. He urged the city to rehabilitate aging, dilapidated housing in order to improve property values in central Memphis, and he urged the city to limit development at the city's perimeter. But Memphis did little to meet the goals.

The city's longtime planning official died in 1948 and was not replaced during seven critical years when federally insured home mortgages and Veterans Administration loans reconfigured the settlement of Shelby County. Beyond the city limits, farms were subdivided for homes before annexation, leaving the private sector to shape the new suburbs in chaotic and often sloppy ways. Unimproved roads running from north to south made the eastern growth of Memphis more imbalanced. Little control was imposed over the proliferation of unsightly commercial strips. One chronicler of the era claimed the chaotic new landscape revealed Shelby County's unwritten policy of anything goes—unless someone objects.[16]

Because of reform candidate Edmund Orgill, who wanted to check the political influence of real estate developers, the lack of metropolitan planning became a major campaign issue in the 1955 mayor's race. But when it came to taming incoherent urbanization, the new Orgill administration was ineffectual. Though Orgill succeeded in creating a combined Memphis and Shelby County Planning Commission, it was disbanded after twenty-one years during which it presided helplessly over the sprawl of greater Memphis, its decisions overturned by elected officials or judges when they went against the wishes of powerful private interests. Throughout the 1960s, moreover, when city-planning staff argued for containing new commercial strip development in cohesive clusters, more influential private interests again had their way.[17]

Architect Louis Sullivan said that when it comes to the shape of buildings, or anything in nature, "form ever follows function, and this is the law." When it comes to the shape of cities, the corollary to Sullivan's law is that form follows transportation.[18] Throughout history, cities have risen at the busiest intersections of travel and commerce, regardless of the transportation used. Born in an age when steamboats gave birth to inland river cities, downtown Memphis was still the unrivaled center of a city of twenty-four square miles as late as the 1920s. Then, goods were moved by rail or river and the circulation of citizens was borne by multiple modes of travel, over paved streets, dirt roads, downtown sidewalks, and 127 miles of tracks for streetcars that carried 161,000 riders daily, the equivalent of two-thirds of the city's population. Eighty percent of streetcar routes ran down Main Street, making the location the busiest spot in town.[19] By 1956, three of every four downtown workers commuted to work by bus, but 131,000 cars still arrived each day in a downtown with only 20,000 parking spaces.[20] Downtown had become cramped, congested, and clogged. The modern era valued movement, and downtown Memphis was moving at a crawl.

New highways were begun in 1958, and the completion of the southern loop of I-240, the expressway that rings the city, was completed by 1963, literally paving the way for many white Memphians to abandon the core of the city after the passage of civil rights laws and the desegregation of public housing. By comparison with other cities, Memphis was integrated relatively peacefully, beginning with buses and the library even before passage of the Civil Rights Act of 1964.[21] A few public schools were integrated in 1961 and all of them by 1966. But when the legal barriers between the races were removed, the physical distance between the races expanded greatly; whites moved out of their old neighborhoods and blacks moved up, into better housing that whites had left behind. Integration gave way to separatism, both white and black, as whites abandoned the city's core and blacks, unhappy with the slow pace of change, resorted to militant demands for political power.

The stubborn refusal of Memphis mayor Henry Loeb to settle a strike by sanitation workers in 1968 led to a black boycott of downtown businesses, whose retail sales sank by 35 percent. Martin Luther King Jr. was in town trying to resolve the strike peacefully when he was killed. When some followers of King blamed Memphis for his death, the city as a whole felt unfairly stigmatized. "Memphis has been wrongfully and irrationally blamed for the murder of Martin Luther King Jr.," declared Tennessee judge Preston Battle when he sentenced James Earl Ray. "Neither the defendant nor the victim lived in Memphis. Their orbits merely intersected here."[22] The assassination also shattered King's dream of nonviolent change as a small riot convulsed the historically black portion of downtown Memphis. It was just one of 172 riots that flared in American cities, leading to twenty-seven thousand arrests, eclipsing the violence in Birmingham in 1963, Watts in 1964, Chicago in 1966, and Newark and Detroit in 1967.[23]

The tragedy in Memphis in 1968 did not kill downtown Memphis; it merely accelerated trends already under way. In 1949, when Memphis saw its first suburban-style shopping center go up on a major artery leading out of town, downtown merchants captured 28 percent of the region's retail sales; by 1967, downtown retail sales had dropped to 7 percent.[24] By 1966, moreover, sites three miles east of the downtown had sprouted new office towers closer to the homes of executives, offering quality space with a shorter commute and unlimited free parking. After the events of 1968, more downtown tenants deserted their buildings for the new ones east of town.

The absence of people on the sidewalks downtown fed fears about declining public safety, as did the growing share of vacant or blighted blocks. To eradicate the problem, Memphis razed whole blocks together. During this period Memphis lost its most significant historic area, the district surrounding Beale Street. In 1934, black business leader George W. Lee called Beale Street "the Main Street of Negro America."[25] In its most vibrant years, from the 1880s until Tennessee's prohibition of alcohol in 1916, Beale Street was a nationally recognized center of urban African American culture. In the 1880s, when whites began to depart the district after the arrival of the electric streetcar, entrepreneur Robert R. Church began to buy up properties

and became the reputed first black millionaire in the South. Only a generation after the abolition of slavery, Beale Street gave rise to "black capitalism,"
to banks, insurance companies, newspapers, mansions, and churches built by
and for black Memphians. Here, Ida B. Wells waged her public campaigns
against lynchings. And here, clothing stores and pawnshops attracted thousands of rural blacks from throughout the Delta to shop on Saturday morn-
ings while food stands and lunchrooms drew customers with fried fish and
barbecued pork. Saturday night swelled the saloons, honky-tonks, and jazz
joints with the sounds of harmonicas, banjos, and jug bands playing the blues
brought to Memphis from Mississippi cotton plantations. For a generation,
Beale Street was to black America what Harlem and Chicago's Bronzeville
became in the age of jazz.[26]

After World War I, when blacks began to migrate north in large numbers
in search of jobs, Beale Street's vibrancy began to fade. By the 1960s, the
district was depressed, but still standing. In 1964, a master plan of the Memphis Housing Authority approved the demolition of the Beale Street area for
a shopping mall, arguing that the historic area "has been permitted to deteriorate to a point where little remains, from a practical standpoint, of its
lively past." A few years before, Mayor Orgill had announced plans to use
urban renewal funds to clean up Beale Street and transform it into a local
version of Bourbon Street in New Orleans. Those ideas were put on hold in
1966 when the National Park Service designated two blocks of Beale Street
a National Historic Landmark, the only one in Memphis, and the first district in the city to be listed in the National Register of Historic Places, the
nation's official inventory of places worth preserving. Though the distinc-
tions prevented federal funds from being used to tear down designated
landmarks, all but two short blocks on Beale Street later became "the devastated victim of an urban renewal program about which one cannot say
enough bad things . . . one of the saddest examples of what Urban Renewal
did to American cities," according to Memphis architectural historians Johnson and Russell.[27] In response to the tragedy of 1968, the fear of unrest so
close to downtown offices led federal officials to approve the city's urban renewal plan in 1969. In the words of Johnson and Russell, the assassination of
Dr. King "led to the assassination of Beale Street." Fourteen million federal
dollars were spent to remove 1,500 residents and all but 65 of 625 buildings
from a 113-acre area cleared for "renewal."[28] But when anticipated redevelopment of the empty blocks failed to materialize, locals began calling the
bulldozed acreage the "DMZ," an acronym author Grady Clay redefined for
urban America as the "dangerous movement zone."[29] The *Memphis Press-
Scimitar,* the city's evening newspaper, editorialized that city actions had
"destroyed Beale Street, and with it, a part of Memphis."[30]

Between 1957 and 1977, urban renewal in Memphis undertook eleven projects over 560 acres, demolishing a total of three thousand structures.[31] "Under questionable leadership, the Memphis Housing Authority began what was essentially an all-out effort to destroy the nineteenth century urban areas immediately to the east and south of the downtown," writes Robert D. Russell Jr. "Entire blocks, entire neighborhoods were dynamited and bull-dozed—simply, so it seems, to get rid of what was there: both the houses and their inhabitants. It was at this time that the area stretching east from down-town . . . assumed its present devastated appearance. Most of the part of the city that had been built up during the boom years of the 1880s and 1890s was wiped out in the 1960s."[32] Among the most imposing landmarks lost was Union Station, one of two passenger stations in the city. The underutilized station came down after fifty-eight years, replaced by an industrial postal fa-cility imprisoned behind a chain-link fence.

By the time the dust from the demolitions settled, the unfamiliar empti-ness further demoralized the town. In 1973, the chamber of commerce, en-couraged by home builder and Holiday Inn cofounder Wallace Johnson, launched a "Believe in Memphis" campaign to improve civic morale. Nor-man Vincent Peale came to preach the power of positive thinking. "Mem-phis's greatest assets are its problems," Peale said. He called the problems "a sign of life . . . a device by which communities grow strong. Believe in Mem-phis; believe in yourself; believe in God; believe in your country; believe in people; believe in your future. If you believe in Memphis and talk it up and work it up, a greater Memphis will flow back to you."[33] The sloganeering, however, was no substitute for the people who were gone. Memphis had be-come the city that turned its back on the river and ran away from its historic downtown.

When a new Hyatt hotel went up at the perimeter of the city in 1974, at the intersection of I-240 and Poplar Avenue, the main east-west route out of town, the *Memphis Commercial Appeal* blithely predicted that the structure "is the maypole around which Memphis will revolve."[34] Since the age of the steamboats, the maypole of Memphis had been the riverfront Customs House and the Gayoso Hotel, eclipsed in the twentieth century by the Peabody Hotel. Following its reconstruction after a fire in 1924, the Peabody became the residence of some of the city's most prominent citizens. It hosted plenty of others in its Plantation Rooftop ballroom, which offered cool breezes before the introduction of air-conditioning. "The Mississippi Delta begins in the lobby of the Peabody Hotel and ends on Catfish Row in Vicks-burg," wrote David Cohn in his 1935 book, *God Shakes Creation*. Stand in the lobby of the Peabody, he said, and "ultimately you will see everybody who is anybody in the Delta." By 1975, however, the city that gave birth to the roadside motel chain Holiday Inn watched as the Peabody went bankrupt and closed. It was sold at an auction on the steps of the Shelby County Courthouse for one-tenth of the cost of its construction fifty years before.

Main Street shut down, too. At the cost of $7 million, Memphis closed off ten blocks of the street to vehicular traffic in 1976, creating a pedestrian zone renamed the Mid America Mall. Main Street tried to compete with suburbia by trying to become suburban, but all the mall did was clean Main Street out, emphasizing its emptiness. Said one local observer, "There was no convincing evidence that the Mall helped to brighten the downtown retail economy."[35] No gimmick could remedy the fact that downtown was no longer the central business district of Memphis. It had become more accurately a "peripheral" business district, the tattered edge of a sprawling metropolis, isolated along the river behind a new north-south boulevard named for the actor Danny Thomas.

From the end of World War II until 1977, the population of Memphis grew by only one-half, but the area of the city grew to five and a half times its former size, from 51 square miles in 1945 to roughly 280 square miles thirty years later. The rapid expansion of the city over so great an area spread investments in Memphis thin, draining the historic core to feed the extension of the rim. Bluff City became "Donut City," with all the sugarcoated development at the outer edges and a hole left in the core. "Progress" had left the city demoralized. The death of Elvis Presley in 1977 only dampened spirits further, while that same year the last downtown movie house, Loew's Palace Theatre, where Elvis himself had worked as a teenage usher, turned off its lights for good. "By mid 1977 the Chamber of Commerce was on the verge of economic collapse, and some business leaders had withdrawn from trying to solve the city's problems. . . . Crime accelerated and streets became less and less safe," writes Memphis historian John E. Harkins. "The local economy remained sluggish, characterized by low wages and underemployment. Worst of all, some Memphians seemed to have lost their sense of identity, purpose and local pride."[36]

Determined to save one last piece of their historic city, preservationists belonging to the group Memphis Heritage waged a futile public campaign to rescue a historic mansion on Union Avenue, the city's "gaudiest and finest example of robber-baron Victorian."[37] In his definitive history of the suburbanization of the United States, *Crabgrass Frontier*, Columbia University historian Kenneth T. Jackson, a native of Memphis, recalls how the "elegant stone mansion," one of Union Avenue's last surviving landmarks, "was leveled to make room for another fast food outlet. Within three years, the plastic-and-glass hamburger emporium was bankrupt, but the scar on Union Avenue remained."[38]

Not far from the site, another historic residential district at Vance and Pontotoc Streets fell apart so thoroughly that it was taken off the National Register of Historic Places. Though the Memphis chapter of the Association for the Preservation of Tennessee Antiquities had saved two blocks of ante-bellum and Gilded Age mansions on Adams Avenue as "Victorian Village," the city disappeared around them, collapsing into parking lots for the grow-ing mid-Memphis medical center. The house museums became forlorn or-phans of the past. With residue like Victorian Village in mind, Walter Muir Whitehill, a prominent American preservationist, urged others of a similar bent to broaden their mission from the rescue of a few lonely relics to the re-vitalization of entire districts for everyday needs. "We urgently need to im-prove the quality of our lives and of our surroundings," he said, "rather than to create little paradises of nostalgia in an ocean of superhighways and loud-speakers, billboards, neon signs, parking lots, used-car dumps, and hot dog stands."[39]

Throughout Memphis, avenues with high volumes of traffic sported wave after wave of what Whitehill feared most. Today, the metropolitan area claims nearly fifty-five square feet of retail space for every person, about triple the national average and quadruple the amount that retail analysts say is necessary, subjecting Memphians to the spreading visual pollution of road-side signs and asphalt lots and the blighting influence of declining commer-cial strips. Because of an unmitigated building binge, the east Memphis office market surpassed downtown in total size by the mid-1980s, adding more commercial space in little over a decade than downtown had erected over more than 125 years, creating rival urban centers within the city limits, each competing against the other for private investment and public tax dol-lars. By the mid-1990s, the "edge city" in east Memphis had nearly twice as much office space as downtown, leaving downtown with a glut of vacant, un-marketable buildings.

For all of the quantifiable growth, east Memphis is empty in its own way. As architect and community planner Peter Calthorpe has written, edge cities lack "the fundamental qualities of real towns: pedestrian scale, an identifi-able center and edge, integrated use and population, and defined public space," in short, the factors that humanize and civilize the built environ-ment.[40] In east Memphis, there is no need to define public space or provide for pedestrians because virtually all outdoor movement takes place within the confines of a car, at a pace that makes intricate definitions of space un-necessary.

East Memphis is a drive-through city. Were it not for license plates that say "Tennessee," you would be hard-pressed to tell where you are. Nothing there exists to inspire affection or attachment, either to the place or to those who inhabit it. Defenders of such places claim they represent the efficient dispersal of activities from the congested urban core, yet they are hardly as efficient as a walkable downtown, and they beg vital questions that cannot be answered by a banker's spreadsheet. As Joel Garreau has asked, "Will we ever be proud of this place? Will we ever drag our visiting relatives out to show off our Edge City? Will we ever feel—for this generation and the ones that follow—that it's a good place to be young? To have a Fourth of July parade? Will it ever be the place we want to call home?"[41]

Christopher B. Leinberger, managing partner of the largest independent real estate consulting firm in the country, claims these loosely clustered cores of development cannot evolve in constructive ways as long as 70 percent of their land remains sacrificed to surface parking and traffic lanes. When they become saturated with automobiles and reach the limits of their highway capacity, they repel additional businesses from locating there, driving them to locate ten miles farther into the countryside, creating a market for new housing built another fifteen miles beyond that. In Memphis, congestion in the metro core around the Poplar Avenue/I-240 intersection, ten miles east of downtown, has pushed new development further east, into Germantown, beyond the city limits. This, in turn, has encouraged workers to relocate in Collierville or Cordova, some fifteen to twenty-five miles east of downtown, in places with little emotional connection to other sections of the metropolis. Until now, the popular response to the congestion created by sprawl has been to sprawl even more and create more traffic congestion down the road, more environmental degradation, more abandonment of existing places and the people left behind. "As a nation, we continue to ignore the negative consequences of how we are building where 75 percent of all Americans live," Leinberger says.[42]

Traditional downtowns and new edge cities that avoid a declining fate, Leinberger predicts, will be those that benefit from a nearby supply of high-end housing, vibrant shopping or entertainment attractions, and an urbanizing core—places that grow not by mere horizontal expansion, but by "densifying," by filling in the gaps between structures to achieve a density that allows people to reach multiple destinations on foot once they have parked their cars, creating what Leinberger calls a "heart" and an appealing local identity of their own.

Developer Jack Belz, the distinguished-looking second-generation leader of a Memphis development firm that owned fifteen Holiday Inn franchises, discovered potential value in the unique identity of historic Memphis when he bought the bankrupt Peabody Hotel in 1975. Taking advantage of federal tax credits awarded for the rehabilitation of commercial properties listed in the National Register of Historic Places as well as a federal Community

Development Block Grant and a range of local financial incentives, Belz restored the Peabody to its former glory, even returning live ducks to the lobby fountain, a tradition begun as a prank by hotel manager Frank Schutt back in 1932. When the hotel reopened in 1981, it became a magnet that drew Memphians and their out-of-town guests back to the river. If a single building had the power to lift a city's spirits, others in Memphis began to imagine what a cluster of rehabilitated buildings could do.

The restoration of the Peabody Hotel was indeed a turning point for how Memphians perceived their historic downtown. If it was no longer the unrivaled business and retail center of the Mid South region, neither was it just a scrap heap of vacated structures. It was still the harbor of local history, a symbolic anchor for a population that had drifted away from its roots, an irreplaceable environment that would be appreciated more as time wore on.

Belz was not the first to discover value in downtown's empty landmarks. The adaptive reuse of historic Memphis structures had begun in 1974, when architect Jack Tucker renovated into condos a three-story brick commercial building that dated from the 1850s. "When I moved down here, people told me I was crazy," Tucker said, "but it's worked out well." After Tucker's pioneering effort, others followed, stimulated in part by federal tax credits for the rehabilitation of income-producing properties listed on the National Register of Historic Places. In 1977, when Memphis created its Center City Commission to redevelop downtown as the economic, cultural, and governmental heart of Memphis and surrounding Shelby County, downtown was home to only five hundred residents. That number grew to five thousand by 1994, and is expected to double by the year 2000.

In 1995, real estate attorney Mimi Phillips, president of the local preservation group Memphis Heritage, moved her law firm into the restored eleven-story 1912 Falls Building on Cotton Row, only blocks away from the county courthouse and other law firms in town. "I had an office out in east Memphis and I just couldn't stand it," Phillips said. "You can't go to lunch there without getting in your car. You can't do anything in east Memphis without using your car, and because everybody is in their car, Poplar Avenue is a nightmare. The only people who walk in east Memphis are Orthodox Jews." In spite of those drawbacks, Phillips acknowledged that east Memphis continues to expand. "The money and energy being invested in urban sprawl is just sad. It's sick. The core of Memphis is just being eaten alive."

Though downtown vacancies mean that rents downtown are one-third cheaper than in east Memphis and parking is relatively easy and inexpensive, the sidewalks still do not carry enough pedestrian traffic to diminish the fear of crime. Ironically, when Memphis was "Murder Capital of America," the city did not suffer the same fear that drove residents away during the yellow fever epidemics of the 1870s. With people on the streets, Memphians felt safer then than they do today. "In Memphis the homicide rate in 1984, although deplorably high, was only about half what it was in 1915, when the Bluff City was regionally famous as a 'murder capital,' " notes Kenneth T. Jackson. "Yet Memphis's central business district was bustling and vibrant in 1915, in 1985, it is quiet and forlorn."[43] A decade later, the district is less forlorn, but the fear of crime persists. "I have legal clients who are afraid to come downtown," Phillips said. "I have clients who have lived in Memphis all their lives, but they live in east Memphis now, and I have to tell them how to get to Front Street."

On Front Street, at the top of the 1924 Cotton Exchange Building on Cotton Row, works Henry Turley, a Memphis developer whose office overlooks the downtown and the naturally pristine flood basin on the Arkansas side of the river. Turley is a tall man with graying hair and a folksy forcefulness reminiscent of the intimidating charm of Lyndon Johnson. He has developed numerous significant projects downtown, but he understands the pull of new homes and office space built on greener pastures. "Why live in a place that makes you pay more to get less?" he asked. "Why pay twice as much in taxes to get crime and shitty schools?" Why, then, has Turley stayed downtown? "I think sprawl is destructive," he said. "Downtown is the one place where the real estate guy can provide a sense of interaction and common ground, a point of commonality, a shared place and shared history. And I never could quite get used to the idea of throwing away a perfectly good city."

Turley walked to his balcony and looked north out over the rooftops of buildings on Cotton Row and Main Street. "We are a city that is not terribly long on capital assets. A huge amount of our assets are tied up in these old buildings you see here, and sewers and electric systems and what not. For us to throw that away and create a new one is not nearly so good as to deploy that capital in a productive way. To destroy our social fabric and waste our economic assets just makes no sense to me."

Turley has sought success in projects such as the restored Cotton Exchange Building or his conversion of the 1923 Shrine Building into downtown housing in 1976, the first large-scale adaptive reuse of a historic building in Memphis. Yet, he called his achievements "nothing but an uphill battle, like swimming upstream. It's easy to sprawl. It's hard to redevelop. Urban redevelopment requires a coordinated effort, a consensus behind a vision of what you want and what you're doing. We've never had an activist government or shared a vision of what should be done. Our private sector, not unlike that in the early days of L.A., has always invested in the eastern movement, so the private sector is driving things east; the government sector is inactive and lacking in focus; and there is very little interaction between the two. There's not much common vision. And all of this is overarched by racial distrust."

In the 1990s, Memphis elected for the first time a black mayor, Willie Herenton, the former superintendent of schools, who has enjoyed praise from all corners of the city. But Turley contended that the persistent racial divide prevents the population from reaching a consensus about how it ought to grow, blocking the formation of a government effective enough to take it there. In Turley's mind, it is a legacy of the Delta culture. "We are very much agrarian, and we never fully believed in the urban undertaking and became urban. We just built a town."

But Memphis is more than just a town. It is a sprawling metropolis that has spread for 280 square miles across three states. Within the city limits alone, Memphis by 1980 had a lower population density than Phoenix or Houston, two Sun Belt cities often singled out for their loose and chaotic patterns of development. In some parts of Memphis, the clutter of sprawl is so shocking it appears the city has grown by accident rather than according to any plan. "Oh my God, we don't believe in planning!" Turley said with roaring laughter. "If the developers are going to be in charge, and if you're going to have weak government, where do you want it weakest? If you're in the real estate business, you don't mind a strong police force, but you don't want anybody fooling with your private property rights. So we have institutionalized this weakness."

A major consequence of that weakness is a half-empty historic core, and a Main Street lined with vacancies on either side. On one highly visible corner just a block from city hall, a massive brick commercial building from the turn of the century sat rotting behind a chain-link fence for years because its owners, a real estate syndicate from out of state, gained more tax advantages by letting the landmark fall apart than by staving off its decay. Not far away stand the empty office of E. H. Crump and the vacated headquarters of Union Planters Bank, one of the oldest and largest banks in Memphis, which abandoned its 1924 building for a new East Memphis home.

"I've gone before the establishment in Memphis, people whose great-grandfathers were the founders of the city, and I've told them, 'You can create the market downtown. I can't. I'm just an architect,'" Jack Tucker said. "I've had clients doing small projects that are good for Memphis and the banks won't talk to them." The architect mentioned former clients who had plans to convert a historic three-story bank building into office space downtown. "These guys were cotton brokers who trade millions every day, and they couldn't get a bank to loan them the money for their project." Tucker claimed they went to thirty mortgage companies and were turned down by every one until they finally secured a loan from a bank located far beyond downtown, past the I-240 limits. "When I came to town," Tucker said, "you could go to the banks and say, 'You have investments in property downtown. We have a downtown project that will help protect your investments.' And you had a little leverage with them." Now, he said, "You can't get lenders to participate in anything that's not a multimillion-dollar project. They don't want to mess with a small loan. If I asked them for ten million dollars, they might talk to me. But if the paperwork costs them the same, they'd rather go with the big loan than the small one."

Henry Turley, who has secured financing for his large projects in the past, dreams of ways to draw Memphians back to the river to the city's birthplace. He called the intersection of Beale Street and the Mississippi River historically "the most important place in the city and one of the most significant places in the country." But of the six blocks on either side of Beale Street closest to the river, four are given over to parking lots where supply is so plentiful that motorists can park their cars for as little as a dollar a day. Though the *Delta Queen,* a riverboat for vacationers, stops nearby twenty-seven times a year, Memphis doesn't capitalize on the river as it could. Instead, Turley said, "We capitalize on the freedom of anarchy. It's cheap and there are no rules. We sell sprawl. That's what we offer. But the flip side of the lack of order and anarchy is freedom, entrepreneurship, and creativity. Come to Shelby County. You're on your own. Be a pioneer."

Turley has attracted national attention as a pioneer in the movement called New Urbanism, led by architects, planners, and builders who advocate better-designed communities as remedies for placeless urban sprawl. Turley is a partner in two communities in Memphis, a $100 million development on the river south of downtown called South Bluffs and a larger, $150 million development called Harbortown on Mud Island in the river across from downtown. Both resemble the scale and density of the walkable streetcar suburbs built in mid-Memphis from the 1890s through the 1920s, before formulas for subdivisions and auto-dependent commercial strips took hold. What makes Turley's projects unique among the hundreds of so-called neo-traditional developments going up across the country is the fact that they are located in an urban setting rather than at the metropolitan edge. But in spite of hype about how such places de-emphasize the private domain in favor of "the architecture of community," these two projects are essentially residential enclaves that appeal to exclusivity. South Bluffs is guarded by a gate at its entrance, and Harbortown on Mud Island is as isolated as any medieval fortress behind a moat.

One mile east of downtown, a more remarkable thing is happening in a neighborhood called Evergreen, a classic suburb of the streetcar era filled with well-kept bungalows on tree-lined streets. In 1958, highway officials planned an expressway through the neighborhood and nearby Overton Park, the city's premier public space since 1905 and the inspiration for Peter Taylor's short story "The Old Forest." Though the highway route was chosen as the path of least resistance (over an old streetcar line through the park), a local group called Citizens to Preserve Overton Park fought it from the start.

"When I first got involved, I thought it unlikely that we would be able to win the case," said Charlie Newman, the Memphis lawyer who argued their case before the United States Supreme Court. "In those days, the environmental movement didn't exist. A lot of people who didn't want the highway built didn't have the stomach to fight it." But it turned out to be a nationally significant precedent. In March of 1971, Supreme Court justices decided that highway builders in Memphis had failed to search for a "feasible and prudent alternative" as called for in 1966 and 1968 laws passed to prevent the unnecessary paving of parkland and historic sites for highways. A *New York Times* editorial called the decision "A Defeat for the Bulldozer" and "good news for cities across the country that are still contending with the mania of those who would sacrifice the serene values of a green parkland to frenetic movement through a concrete wasteland."[44]

While the case was argued, however, homes in Evergreen were seized and demolished to make way for the highway construction. Though houses were torn down and lots stood empty, mature oak trees were left standing pending a decision, sparing Evergreen's empty house lots the appearance of a clear-cut forest. After the case was finally decided against the highway, Mayor Richard C. Hackett's administration began to sell the empty lots to people who would build new single-family homes; new houses costing as much as three hundred thousand dollars went up in a neighborhood of homes then selling on average for under one hundred thousand dollars. Because the neighborhood was a locally protected historic district, the city was able to ensure that the size and design of the new homes fit comfortably with existing neighboring houses, preserving the identity of the district as a whole.

Throughout mid-Memphis, preservationists have maintained several historic residential districts, but they have been unable to prevent others from disappearing. Having already lost much of Beale Street and other historic residential districts in the 1970s, Memphis in the 1990s lost a district called "the Pinch" at the north end of downtown. In antebellum years, the Pinch attracted poor Irish immigrants whose "pinchgut" appearance gave the area its name. After the yellow fever epidemics of the 1870s, the early houses were torn down and the neighborhood was rebuilt in the 1890s for Jews and Italians.

After decades of decline, preservationists tried to have the Pinch protected by city hall, but private interests overruled them, and most of the district's humble brick houses came down after Memphis opened the Pyramid in 1991. Built along the riverfront, the Pyramid is a $63 million, thirty-two-story-high basketball arena modeled on the Pyramids of Egypt. First proposed in 1975, the feature was inspired by the desire of civic leaders to keep pace with St. Louis to the north, which tore out pieces of its historic fabric to construct the Gateway Arch. Though the Pyramid created a demand for sports bars and other entertainment venues in a few Pinch buildings, the new arena also created a demand for parking. Most of the Pinch wound up demolished for parking lots.

"America is a destructive place, driven by the destructive nature of capitalism," said Turley, who opposed the attempt to have the Pinch protected, allegedly because he didn't want the Pyramid built near his South Bluffs development site. "If you're going to grow and compete, you have to destroy. Sometimes, someone has to say, 'Calm down. You're being too destructive. Hold on a minute.' But that doesn't happen here."

Throughout downtown, Memphis shows evidence of a place in such desperate straits that it is willing to accept any development proposal, even if it means sacrificing the city's traditional scale and appeal. The riverfront, envisioned by the city's founders as "an ample vacant space reserved as a promenade," has been sold off over the years piece by piece, to a point where only two park blocks remain. Monumental civic landmarks like the Federal Customs House are flanked by parking garages. A fire station built in 1967 is little more than a blank, beige brick parking garage for fire engines. Several blocks downriver, a squat low-rise apartment complex interrupts the public's view of the river from Vance Street. The complex, called Riverbluff Place, is the creation and home of developer Henry Turley. "I blocked it off," Turley admitted about the river view. "When I built it, I knew I was perpetrating a small sin, but I thought that repopulating the city was important and that it was good on balance. It was one of my design sins, but no other town in America would let me get away with that."

On Main Street at Court Square, one of the remaining original park blocks not sold off for construction, a hotel chain has built a motel-style building criticized as "a Hampton Inn on the interstate." The latest addition to the riverfront, meanwhile, is a glass box of an office building, the new home for a locally based auto parts company called Auto Zone. The company's well-intentioned chairman, Pitt Hyde, saw it as a way to invest in downtown and move nine hundred employees into the city's historic core. A noble gesture to be sure, but the building fails in this location. Its reflective glass gives employees inside an impressive view of the river, but it mars the riverfront and Cotton Row. Looking at the building from the outside is a bit unnerving, like trying to have a conversation with someone wearing chrome-

tinted reflective sunglasses. At the other end of Cotton Row, where the dilapidated King Cotton Hotel was demolished for construction of the Morgan
Keegan Tower in 1986, critics called the new office building—the first in the
city in thirteen years—an "alien" and "a minor eastward sally from the
glitzkrieg being waged in Houston and Dallas."[45] Memphis still awaits an innovative contemporary architect to design a new structure that complements
its traditional built environment. Until now, new projects have seemed content to borrow suburban formulas, ignoring a warning offered by native son
Kenneth T. Jackson a decade ago: "Too late, municipal leaders will realize
that a slavish duplication of suburbia destroys the urban fabric that makes
cities interesting."[46]

The wisdom of that warning may have finally come home to Memphis. If
it has, the timing is not too late. Having ripped out the failed Mid America
Mall, Memphis restored the name of Main Street and built the trolley line
for $33 million, using transportation funds formerly earmarked for the can-
celed interstate highway through Overton Park. Though the infrequency of
trolley cars limits ridership, the system's greatest contribution is the way it
has reduced the psychological distance between one end of downtown and
the other, linking sites, streets, and a streetscape that suffered divisions in
the past. At the southern end of the line, businessman Pitt Hyde and others
deserve praise for their efforts to help create the National Civil Rights Museum in the former Lorraine Motel. In the 1980s, the motel's imminent closure raised a public dilemma over what to do with the building. Because the
motel had long attracted visitors seeking to mourn the slain civil rights
leader, the museum was proposed as a way to recognize the work of his life,
to show that his dream did not die with him. Some called the project a waste
of money; others said a visitor-oriented museum would only erase the pain
of the past; while others still said it would prevent events of the past from
being forgotten, forcing people in the present to look history in the eye and
come to terms with it. As poet Maya Angelou, a veteran of King's Southern
Christian Leadership Conference, put it, "The very idea of having a civil
rights museum in this city ennobles the city. It doesn't erase the past. It en-
riches it."[47] Dedicated in 1993, the landmark is one of the most moving sites
in Memphis.

As Memphis looks ahead to its bicentennial in the year 2019, coming to
terms with its history is the best option the city has. In the 1980s, Memphis
advertised itself as "America's Distribution Center," a nod to its history as the
cotton and hardwood capital of the Mid South as well as its status as the
headquarters of Federal Express. "Since its founding, Memphis has always
been a place to pass through," said local preservation consultant John Hopkins. The problem with that identity, however, is that it speaks of Memphis as

a pit stop for overnight packages instead of a destination for people, a place to settle down and proudly call home.

With a more welcoming nod to the city's cultural traditions, Memphis now calls itself the "Home of the Blues and the Birthplace of Rock 'n' Roll." Two decades after his death, Elvis is a major local industry. Since opening to the public in 1982, Graceland has grown into what could be the third most visited house museum in America, after the White House and George Washington's Mount Vernon. After a $28 million investment, the two surviving blocks of the Beale Street historic district have come alive, attracting visitors to exhibits on the musical legacy of Memphis, to the home of bandleader W. C. Handy, and to blues clubs and other popular nightspots.

As the South as a region becomes ever more homogenized by the spread of suburban subdivisions, chain restaurants, and retail outlet malls, the magnetism of this traditional downtown grows stronger. The historic cores of Nashville, Birmingham, Little Rock, and Jackson, Mississippi, never reached the maturity of the one in Memphis, and what is left of those cities is even less well preserved. A traveler from the region would have to go as far as New Orleans or Cincinnati to find an environment filled with more variety and historic complexity than downtown Memphis. Clearly, tourism presents Memphis with promising opportunities.

More promising is how downtown is discovered more each year by Memphians themselves, drawn to the river for weekend recreation and for annual festivals and carnivals celebrating the city's music and famous barbecue. If downtown is to avoid becoming merely a theme park for visitors, however, locals will need to return in greater numbers, for periods longer than the time it takes to attend a special event. If Memphis civic and business leaders make more of a determined effort, it is not inconceivable that a generation from now many of downtown's vacancies could be filled.

The market for apartments in converted historic structures is healthy and expanding. In 1995, 97 percent of downtown's new housing units were occupied. Smart developers have caught on to the fact that single people living alone now represent a quarter of all households, as large a share of the national housing market as nuclear families, which have dropped from more than 40 percent of the market in 1970. The most recent addition to downtown living opportunities stems from the conversion of the long-vacant 1910 Exchange Building on Court Square into affordable apartments.

The most exciting project in Memphis—one of the largest federally certified historic rehabilitation projects under way in the United States—is being undertaken only a few blocks up Main Street by a firm that bills itself as a national trendsetter in the development of suburban factory outlet malls: Belz Enterprises, restorers of the Peabody Hotel. Using a diverse pool of public financial incentives, including one last remaining federal Urban Development Action Grant awarded Memphis more than fifteen years ago, Belz is developing a $100 million project called Peabody Place, which includes the $45 million rehabilitation of two historic blocks and new construction on blocks across the street. The centerpiece of the project, the long-vacant Gayoso Hotel, has been converted into 156 units of mixed-rate housing, all of them leased in three months. Behind it, the former Goldsmith's department store, the 1891 Riley Building, and the 1915 Majestic Theater are evolving into a complex of offices, apartments, and shops at street level. Across Main Street a new retail complex and a new office building are being built into which the Belz firm is moving its offices from its former quarters located behind an industrial park in outer Memphis. Critics will find fault with some particulars, but, as a whole, the project is an impressive and encouraging patchwork of old and new.

Among other landmarks already slated for redevelopment is Central Station, a railroad terminal on South Main Street at the southern terminus of the trolley line. Built in 1914, the eight-story redbrick station was a staging point for the great migration of southern blacks to northern cities, when passengers stood on the platform with all their belongings in bags or cardboard boxes waiting to board the *City of New Orleans* to Chicago. Lately, train stops have dwindled to two a day at odd hours, which has left the station empty and its dusty windows prime targets for vandals. With funding from the city and federal sources, the site will become a transit junction for city buses and the trolley line while the station itself will eventually house affordable apartments. Renovation of the empty eyesore should remove an obstacle to the rehabilitation of the rows of historic two-story brick commercial buildings that have stood vacant on South Main Street for years.

Throughout downtown Memphis, the functions of old structures may change over time, but one function of the historic built environment will endure: to serve as the place of assimilation, where people, cultures, and time are layered into one.

"The kind of culture that can maintain reasonable human commitments takes centuries to create but only a few generations to destroy," writes James Q. Wilson in *The Moral Sense*. Fortunately for Memphians, their fragile historic physical links are not all destroyed. Indeed, if one of the nation's leading sprawl developers can invest so much in the preservation of the city's built environment, there must be hope that the historic core of Memphis may again become "beautiful and established" and "a place of good abode."

Almost every city in America has gone through some variation of the Memphis experience, but, as Memphis shows, it is not too late to reinvigorate what has been left behind. The place has done so before. A century ago,

Memphis avoided the fate of its Egyptian namesake by rebounding from the yellow fever and an infamous race riot during Reconstruction to enjoy its most vibrant and creative days. By inhabiting emptied streets, strangers became neighbors; through face-to-face contact, they calmed their fears, made choices about their future, and took responsibility as citizens of the rehabilitated town.

Memphis today, like most places in America, grows more by chance than by choice. Like Memphians today, we can continue to settle for the kind of places we get, leaving the fate of our communities to chance, or we can demand, preserve, and build the kinds of places we want. Either way, that choice is up to us.

4

NEW TOOLS FOR OLDER NEIGHBORHOODS

Different places on the face of the earth have different vital efflu-
ence, different vibration, different chemical exhalation, different
polarity with different stars: call it what you like. But the spirit of
place is a great reality.

—D. H. Lawrence, "The Spirit of Place"

Some people measure the worth of a city by the number of major-
league sports teams it can claim. Philadelphia has four; St. Louis has three;
Buffalo has two; Green Bay is content with one. Countless places with none
long to become "a major-league city." Sports teams, like historic landmarks,
are sources of civic pride, objects of public affection and admiration. Like
historic landmarks, however, franchises can easily disappear, leaving their ad-
mirers with terrible feelings of loss and even betrayal. Brooklyn still grieves
for its Dodgers, who left town for Los Angeles in 1958. Baltimore felt less
than whole without its Colts, who moved to Indianapolis. Cleveland mourns
the departure of its beloved Browns. But if Baltimore and Cleveland suffer at
all today, it is not from the loss of professional football but from the loss of
professional residents who once called the city home.

Baltimore and Cleveland are among nineteen major American cities in serious economic decline, according to David Rusk, the former mayor of Albu-
querque, who has studied the conditions of cities in comparison to their
suburbs. From a distance, Baltimore, with its revitalized inner harbor and
the new Oriole Park at Camden Yards, would appear to be a city on the rebound. But up close, as Rusk points out in his book, *Baltimore Unbound,*
"Baltimore City is programmed for inexorable decline," racked by insur-
mountable poverty and crime. Affluent residents of the Baltimore region are
moving farthest from the center, abandoning the core to poor residents who
can't afford to move. Cleveland in 1950 was home to 62 percent of all the
people in its metropolitan region. Over the next forty years, Cleveland lost
almost half of its population as its middle class fled to the suburbs, leaving

the city with only 18 percent of the metropolitan population. By 1989, the average income of Cleveland's residents had fallen to 54 percent of the average income of suburbanites. According to Rusk, when a city loses more than 20 percent of its population, when its minority population rises above 30 percent, and when the average income of city residents falls below 70 percent of the average income of suburbanites, a city can no longer reverse those trends, passing what he calls "the point of no return." As Rusk notes, "no city that has passed that point of no return has ever come back." And no such city will ever reverse those trends without the cooperation of its neighboring suburban jurisdictions.[1] By these criteria, reconsider Philadelphia, St. Louis, Buffalo, and Green Bay as "major-league cities." Only Green Bay has not passed Rusk's "point of no return."

"The image of the successful central business district assiduously cultivated by city planners and municipal administrators in the 1970s and 80s, with glamorous skyscrapers and exciting cultural showplaces, has turned out to be a false measure of urban health," writes urban historian Witold Rybczynski. "Neighborhoods are the lifeblood of any city."[2] But healthy neighborhoods remain healthy only when they regenerate themselves, when they attract new residents and reinvestment. Declining neighborhoods are places that have lost their appeal to both longtime and prospective residents, who choose to move elsewhere. Attracting no replacements comparable to the residents who leave, the neighborhood suffers, driving more residents away. If the vicious cycle continues, the neighborhood declines until a point where almost every resident who remains wants out, too, and it becomes "a perpetual slum."[3]

As pieces of the larger urban community, neighborhoods, especially older, inner-city neighborhoods, are affected less by the deliberate choices of their residents than by other forces. "The process by which venerable neighborhoods, many of which were prosperous only twenty to forty years ago, have turned into slums involves myriad forces ranging from poverty to drugs to racism to disintegrating families," writes Winifred Gallagher, author of *The Power of Place.* But she adds that the physical signs of neighborhood disintegration such as abandoned buildings and vacant lots "are not just symbols of the disastrous change in the urban ecology but also active agents in its downward spiral."[4]

In their "Broken Windows" thesis, James Q. Wilson and George Kelling explain the dynamics at work in the decline of once sound neighborhoods. First, physical evidence of decay appears: broken windows, crumbling building exteriors, and litter on sidewalks. When not removed quickly—whether because of poverty, ignorance about the importance of routine maintenance, the lax enforcement of building-code violations, or absentee property ownership—signs of decay linger until they become constant fixtures in an area.

Intimidated by the negative signals, neighbors begin to feel defeated and withdraw into their homes, less willing to speak up about signs of neglect. Vandals take their withdrawal as a signal to misbehave, and public order gradually decays along with the physical deterioration. The typical response of neighbors is to withdraw even further, which then invites worse criminal behavior to these places, where the fear of getting caught has been reduced.

"The physical characteristics and appearance of a neighborhood *do* matter when those who would break the law select the location for their crimes," argues Henry C. Cisneros, the former mayor of San Antonio who became secretary of housing and urban development during the first Clinton administration.[5] As evidence, Cisneros points to research gathered in a fifty-block area of Baltimore that showed how higher rates of crime were linked to places marked by a physical deterioration of streetfronts. "The way we feel about the place where we live governs our motivation to take care of it or to neglect it," Cisneros says, and "neighborhood characteristics signal how strongly residents are likely to respond when they identify criminal activity in their midst."

Fostering a shared sense of turf or "territoriality" among residents of a community is a strong deterrent to crime and decay. But many public community redevelopment programs of the past never did enough to reach this goal. They often failed to leverage investment of private property owners, and they failed to change perceptions that a community was going in any direction other than a slide into decline. Had such efforts attracted private reinvestment to stave off the early phases of deterioration, the need for massive public intervention in some places might have been avoided. "Many neighborhoods that were clinging to the edge of stability a decade ago have since slid into chaos," writes Cisneros. The most devastated places, he noted, are those areas "where a sense of community has all but vanished, the least promising areas for reclamation."[6]

Migrations, whether across oceans or municipal boundaries, are the outcome of factors that push people away from one place and pull them to another. Cleveland's suburbanites did not abandon the city because the Cavaliers, the city's basketball team, moved some forty-five minutes away. Neither will those former residents follow the Cavaliers back to the city as the team returns after years of absence. Pushed out by dropping property values, declining schools, meaner streets, and rising taxes, residents of declining neighborhoods are pulled elsewhere by the opposite. It is this migratory pattern, played out in neighborhood after neighborhood, that pushes a city past Rusk's "point of no return." But these trends are not inevitable, or unalterable in every urban locale. As Jane Jacobs recognized nearly forty years ago, "The key link in a perpetual slum is that too many people move out of it too fast—and in the meantime dream of getting out. This is the link that has to be broken if any other efforts at overcoming slums or slum life are to be of the least avail."[7] In some places, as in the stories from Pittsburgh and New Orleans that follow, that cycle is being broken.

The "Field of Dreams" strategy of urban revitalization, "If you build it, they will come," can attract suburbanites to a city for a few hours. When pursued at the expense of other priorities, however, it neglects the fact that the first thing suburbs acquired—before shopping centers, schools, and corporate office campuses—was residents. Residents came first, and the rest followed: commerce, new jobs, and a growing tax base. Neighborhood preservationists understand this instinctively. For them, the operative phrase has always been, "If you maintain it, they will stay." Strong neighborhoods maintain themselves. Weaker ones demand intervention. Either way, the preservation of a neighborhood preserves more than buildings. It preserves people in a place, a community. When people stay, they make a statement that a place is worth inhabiting. Others join them. A neighborhood regenerates itself, and a city is healthier for it.

■ ■ ■

Thomas Jefferson's decision to buy the Louisiana Purchase from Napoleon in 1803 for the sum of $15 million extended American rule over one-third of today's continental United States. The Louisiana Purchase stretched from New Orleans at the Gulf of Mexico into what is now Canada and from the Mississippi River over the Great Plains to the Rocky Mountains. As a land speculator, Jefferson was the sharpest in American history. As a town planner, he was less accomplished. An experienced surveyor and architect, the president advocated the development of towns on the new frontier along grid patterns of rectangular blocks, bordered by straight streets that intersected at right angles. The grid pattern provided a quick, inexpensive, and orderly way to map new towns, but as those early settlements expanded into cities, "what may have at first seemed like a vision of a new world of urban rationality all too quickly blurred into an impression of sterile dullness," writes John Reps, the historian of early town planning in America.[8] Young cities in America's heartland grew in monotonous blocks, over unimaginative street patterns that often failed to complement the qualities of the local topography and natural landscape. For private developers who dictated the shape of urban growth, Reps notes, "mediocre planning, or worse, yielded generous financial returns," so "new areas mechanically repeated almost endlessly the grid street system without any relieving features." New Orleans, however, expanded differently.

Like other settlements of the colonial era, from the Spanish pueblos of the Southwest to the early villages of New England to the coastal cities of

Philadelphia, Annapolis, and Savannah, New Orleans was more carefully conceived. In the 1720s, the city began to develop along the plans of French American settlers, who envisioned a city of small square blocks built around an open public square of a parade ground, placed at a prominent spot along the Mississippi River. There, French and later Spanish colonists developed their architectural traditions into a distinctive regional style, just as they had throughout the Caribbean and along the Gulf of Mexico. They built structures on the very edge of streets and covered them with long, low-pitched roofs that protected homes from the tropical sun and rain.[9] They distinguished their homes with long windows, second-story balconies, private courtyards, and walled gardens, sacrificing neither privacy nor neighborliness in their designs.

After 1803, Americans who came to the city of the "Creoles" (people of mixed French, Spanish, and African descent) built houses in Anglo-American styles, Federal and later Greek Revival town houses, set back from the street, bordered by more spacious yards. As the city expanded, however, the original plan for streets and squares expanded with it. New Orleans grew from a single district behind a garrison into a city of distinctive "faubourgs," a French term that described a "town outside the wall." According to Witold Rybczynski, "When new districts, or faubourgs, were laid out, they included similarly proportioned blocks and central squares, but instead of simply extending the French grid, the American planners adjusted the angle of the new gridded areas to follow the curve of the Mississippi, which created interesting relationships between the different districts where the grids intersected. As the entire geometry shifted, the early inhabitants of New Orleans knew when they were passing from one faubourg to another; arriving at the square they knew they were in the heart of the district."[10]

First-time visitors to New Orleans who spend little time outside the French Quarter, the oldest district (also known as the Vieux Carré), will miss the variety found in the Crescent City's other historic neighborhoods. The St. Charles Avenue streetcar gives visitors a glimpse of the Garden District, the premier address for early Anglo-American settlers, still home to their grand mansions, Frederick Law Olmsted's Audubon Park, and Tulane University. Other interesting historic neighborhoods are easier to miss, such as the Lower Garden District, built after 1805 around a magnificent park called Coliseum Square, where streets are named for the Muses, the daughters of Zeus in Greek mythology. Esplanade Ridge, another district, spans both sides of Esplanade Avenue, the Creole community's grand boulevard equivalent to the Anglo-Americans' St. Charles Avenue. One of the most remote historic districts in the city, Algiers Point, is located on the opposite bank of the Mississippi River from the French Quarter, where its physical separation from the rest of the city's early faubourgs makes the place feel like a self-contained town. Because of its diverse cultural legacies and remarkable state of preservation, New Orleans is a city of historic neighborhoods unlike any other in the United States. But while some of the city's neighborhoods are in sound shape, others seem to hang on by the slenderest of threads. Incredibly, even the future of the French Quarter was in doubt at various moments throughout the twentieth century.

The Vieux Carré was a slum in the 1920s when writers Sherwood Anderson and William Faulkner moved there to enjoy its timeless but well-worn charms. An organized effort to preserve the district formed the Vieux Carré Commission in 1925, although the district was not regulated formally until 1937, six years after the Battery in Charleston, South Carolina, became the first locally protected historic district in the United States. Later, the 1960s became a critical decade for preservation of the French Quarter when New Orleans pursued a plan for an urban expressway that Robert Moses, the New York road builder, had mapped out for the city in 1946. The plan included the construction of a forty-foot-high elevated expressway through the French Quarter, along the Mississippi River. Initial opposition to the plan was mainly limited to irate residents of the historic district until a group of New Orleanians calling themselves HELP (Help Establish Logical Planning) published a full-page advertisement against the highway in the *New Orleans Times-Picayune*. Attorney Bill Borah, a leader of the group, said the ad "rocked this town. It was like a flare going up for an invasion. The fight that followed was hostile and vicious, but we ended up changing the basic power structure in this town, how things got built and where the money went."

Funded by a private foundation with ties to New Orleans, the Stern family fund in New York, opponents went to other cities to research local fights against urban highways and formed a national coalition to change federal transportation laws. "We were a long shot," Borah recalled. The city's establishment was lined up against them. Local business leaders, the mayor, the city council, the city's newspaper, even the governor and Louisiana's two U.S. senators were united behind the highway. Borah recalled how one local officeholder even claimed that the best thing that could happen to the French Quarter would be for a fire to burn it to the ground. "New Orleans had no respect for its history," he said.

The highway opponents realized that their only chance to rescue the French Quarter was to go over the heads of local leaders and appeal to public opinion nationwide. "The only way this thing was going be stopped was to make this a national issue," Borah said. The most clever publicity stunt was pulled by local activist Martha Robinson, who printed up postcards that showed an elevated highway obscuring Jackson Square and St. Louis Cathedral. A headline above the scene announced, "Greetings from the Vieux Carré!" As the postcards arrived in the mailboxes of news editors throughout the country, the conflict grew into a national news story, attracting the attention of policymakers in Washington. In 1966, Congress amended transportation laws to protect historic and natural environments from reckless highway construction. Soon thereafter, the New Orleans–led coalition was the first antihighway group to appear before the new federal highway administrator. The Nixon administration's secretary of transportation, John Volpe, effectively halted the French Quarter expressway in 1969, when he refused to grant the project federal funds. "That's when the city began to realize that it was different," Borah said. "It was not Atlanta. It was not Dallas. It was unique, and the historic buildings were the reason people came here. People began to see that preservation was good for the city."

Three decades later, 10 million people visit New Orleans each year, contributing an estimated $3.5 billion to the local economy, making tourism the only industry in the city to rival petrochemicals. In November of 1995, *Condé Nast Traveler* magazine identified New Orleans as the nation's third most popular destination city after San Francisco and Santa Fe, two other places distinguished by their longtime attention to preservation. In New Orleans, some 60,000 people are employed in the tourist trades, but tourism has put strains on the city, too. The French Quarter, still a residential neighborhood, is constantly under siege from commercialization that threatens to destroy the very character people come to see. As New York City preservationist Roberta Brandes Gratz writes in her book *The Living City*, "in the 1980s hotel/convention centers and other outsider-directed formulas, rather than the more appropriate projects and programs geared to the local populace, have become favorite downtown 'revitalizers.' The danger is that these projects either fail miserably or work so well that the outsiders overwhelm the local ambience, new hotels dwarf the scale of the historic locale, outside vehicular traffic impedes local movement, and residents and locally owned businesses are replaced by tourists and tourist-oriented activity. Any place left primarily to tourists ceases to be a real place and eventually loses its appeal even to tourists."[11]

Some charge that the concentration of tourist interests around the French Quarter distracts the city and its business leadership from doing more to promote the revitalization of other areas of New Orleans. The state historic preservation office estimates that half of the city's territory and up to as many as forty thousand separate buildings are listed in the National Register of

Historic Places. Twelve separate areas in New Orleans are designated as local historic districts, a distinction that carries more protection of historic landmarks than a listing in the National Register.

The popularity of preservation in New Orleans has grown visibly in recent decades. A world's fair in the 1980s raised awareness of the city's warehouse district and stimulated the revitalization of historic office buildings and the conversion of old warehouses to downtown apartments. Interest in the historic character of New Orleans was also stimulated by a series of popular books on the city's architecture produced by a local organization, Friends of the Cabildo. And bad planning decisions that erased historic streets and ruined neighborhoods for elevated expressways still catalyze the preservation movement here. Claiborne Avenue, for instance, the traditional path of black Mardi Gras parades, was all but wiped out by an overhead expressway. Still, New Orleans has escaped much of the physical damage seen in other cities. Though some areas were cleared for new public housing developments during the depression, New Orleans shows few scars from postwar urban renewal. According to Borah, the Louisiana legislature "called it a Communist plot and wouldn't allow it to happen in the state of Louisiana. That's one of the reasons that New Orleans didn't get destroyed the way other cities did." Much of historic New Orleans has actually survived intact because of the poverty of past generations, who lacked the money to modernize structures or tear them down and rebuild. The city also escaped the urban race riots of the 1960s. Because of its Creole legacy, New Orleans has always been a racially diverse place, more integrated and less racially hostile than the average American city. But social tensions have risen in recent decades, accelerating with the disappearance of jobs after the oil bust in the early 1980s and the appearance of crack cocaine a few years later.

Like most large cities, New Orleans has lost large portions of its middle class, both white and black, fleeing crime. Property theft is so pervasive that some residents simply shrug it off as an unavoidable fact of local life. The city's murder rate in 1995—75 homicides per 100,000 people—was tops in the nation and far above the national average for a city of its size. In 1960, New Orleans was home to 627,525 people; by 1990, the population had fallen to 496,938, a loss of more than 20 percent over thirty years. Many residents live on some form of public assistance, but the city's wealthier residents, who never really abandoned their fashionable districts, keep the per capita income in Orleans Parish even with, or greater than, per capita income in suburban parishes. In the city's least stable neighborhoods, however, the migration has turned into outright evacuation, as the loss of neighborhood businesses and social ties has created vacuums filled by drugs, gangs, and violence. In many neighborhoods, affordable historic houses stand abandoned. In 1995, New Orleans had some thirty-seven thousand units of vacant housing scattered across the city.

New Orleans lawyer and preservationist Camille Strachan grew up on a ranch in central Florida and moved with her husband Duncan into a large Greek Revival house on Coliseum Square in the Lower Garden District in 1971. They were urban pioneers in the back-to-the-city movement, when a generation's search for affordable housing led many baby boomers into long-neglected historic urban neighborhoods. The Lower Garden District was one of them, and the Strachans helped establish the Coliseum Square Commission, which after the Vieux Carré Commission became the second historic district commission in the city. "When I came to New Orleans, my neighborhood was considered a backwater, but the city was a landlord's dream, because the occupancy was so high," Strachan said. Twenty years later, 80 percent of housing in the city was owned by landlords, but many of their former tenants were gone. Federal mortgage subsidies had financed the early flight to the suburbs, to places like Metairie, much of it covered by low-density ranch house developments, where the main commercial street is a garish strip of plastic signs and asphalt parking lots named in honor of the victors of World War II, Veterans Boulevard. A local property assessor once told Strachan that "twenty thousand men went to war from the Irish Channel [a blue-collar district along the river], but when the war ended, they couldn't get the financing to move back in." Because of mortgage rules, even those who preferred to stay in the old districts had to give up the places they called home. "When we arrived in New Orleans, the parents of those veterans were still living in these neighborhoods," Strachan said as she drove through one nearly deserted section of the city. As the old residents died, however, few new residents took their places. Many who remained could not afford to maintain their houses. Whole blocks of formerly inhabited homes crumbled in a matter of years.

Central City, a neighborhood within a couple of miles of the downtown, is an apocalyptic setting of urban devastation: block after block of abandoned houses interrupted by empty lots strewn with debris and overgrown weeds. The neighborhood's central artery, Dryades Street, was a busy commercial district until racial divisions led to a boycott of white-owned businesses in the 1960s that drove most merchants away. The neighborhood declined quickly and never recovered. Dryades Street, renamed Oretha Castle Haley Boulevard, after a local civil rights activist, is now a depressing row of empty storefronts, boarded-up windows, and burned-out buildings whose front facades have fallen down while interior walls collapse slowly into piles of brick and plaster. Along the street sit the remnants of recent public street improvement programs, wooden park benches stuck into the sidewalks, facing nothing but urban emptiness. "When you don't have jobs and you don't have people, you have deterioration. Look around," Strachan said as she drove down a street lined with abandoned houses and empty lots. "There's nobody here. There's not even a market for crack."

Several minutes later, Strachan arrived in the heart of Central City, where an entire block of traditional shotgun houses have been rehabilitated for low-income occupants. The project was financed, in part, by federal tax credits offered for the creation of low-income housing and rehabilitation of income-producing buildings listed in the National Register. The houses appear to be well kept. The exteriors are freshly painted. There is no graffiti in sight. Across the street is the Sixth District Police Station, as strong a deterrent to crime as any New Orleans neighborhood will ever see. The houses are inhabited. The block demonstrates that it is indeed possible to preserve a place when conditions are right, even in the midst of despair. New Orleans may not be able to preserve every neighborhood, but the conditions of this particular neighborhood serve as a warning for others where the city does not try.

Strachan's own neighborhood, the Lower Garden District, is "teetering between hope and hopelessness," announced a headline in the *Times-Picayune*, which ran a series of articles in 1992 on conditions in the city's historic neighborhoods.[12] Unlike Central City, the Lower Garden District was created for the city's well-to-do. When prosperous early residents were replaced after the Civil War by Reconstruction carpetbaggers and scalawags, the district began a long decline. But the elaborate homes survived long enough to attract, by the early 1970s, a new generation of buyers eager to put their investment and energy into the improvement of the neighborhood. One of the first fights they waged was to stop a proposed bridge over the Mississippi River that would have split the district down the middle while isolating between two ramps one of the city's finest public parks, Coliseum Square. When the new residents couldn't get a hearing with public officials, Duncan Strachan, a collector of armored military vehicles, loaded a few neighbors into his half-track personnel carrier (wheels on the front axle, tank tracks on the back) and drove up to the front door of the old Roosevelt Hotel downtown, where the new governor, Edwin Edwards, was meeting inside. The group refused to leave without an audience with the governor. Edwards, a rogue of a character, came out of the hotel, took one look, smiled, and said, "Come on in." The bridge was never built as planned.

"After one rousing decade of rehabilitation and a subsequent decade on hold, the Lower Garden District is once again at a crossroads," wrote *Times-Picayune* reporter Elizabeth Mullener. "It has been hit hard by urban flight, vacancy and abandonment. It has been plagued by crime and afflicted by poverty. And now, for every house that has been lovingly restored, two more have been abandoned and left to die a humiliating death."

In the late 1980s, when the Lower Garden District showed alarming new evidence of decline, preservationists stepped in to stop the decay. An entire block of Magazine Street, the neighborhood's main commercial thorough-fare, had become almost entirely vacated. After one lender foreclosed on most of the buildings, a few residents decided they had to do something if they were to save their neighborhood. They approached the Preservation Resource Center, the citywide advocate for historic preservation founded in 1974 and managed since 1981 by a dynamic and feisty preservationist named Patty Gay.

In the late 1970s, the Preservation Resource Center had preserved a two-story Federal brick town house at 604 Julia Street, part of a row of historic houses converted to professional offices in downtown's Lafayette Square dis-trict. Aware of the PRC's work, the Lower Garden District residents asked the PRC to become the organizational catalyst for the preservation of Maga-zine Street's historic commercial buildings. The PRC agreed to market the foreclosed properties to potential buyers if the lender would finance the pur-chases and rehabilitations. Seeking advice from preservation revolving funds in other cities, the PRC enlisted the expertise of Lee Adler, the preservation-ist in Savannah who had run one of the first of such funds in the country. Adler came to New Orleans, looked at Magazine Street, and urged the group to expand its effort from an attempt to save a few isolated properties to a community-wide preservation program. According to Patty Gay, Adler told them, "Don't just do one block. Target a much bigger area. Get options on other properties and expand." With Adler's advice, the PRC widened its fo-cus to twenty-four blocks. "We soon found we could market the area," Gay said, "but buyers had no way of getting loans to pay for the renovation of abandoned structures." Vacant buildings are commonly so deteriorated that banks or other lending institutions will not risk loaning buyers money to ac-quire and renovate them. "If we were going to attract buyers, we had to offer them some kind of rehab financing," Gay said.

To accomplish what the private housing market in New Orleans would not or could not do, the Preservation Resource Center in 1988 launched Opera-tion Comeback, a program to help people overcome obstacles to buying and rehabilitating vacant houses in the city's historic neighborhoods. (The name of the program says as much about attracting residents to the city as it does about revitalizing the city's older neighborhoods.) Interested buyers first at-tend workshops that introduce them to the steps involved in buying and re-habilitating a vacant building. Those who qualify for a mortgage then shop for a vacant house in one of seven neighborhoods targeted by the program.

Once the buyers settle on a property, they work out rehabilitation plans with a contractor. With plans in hand, they submit their proposal and renovation bids to Operation Comeback staff. If the plans and the bids are reasonable, Operation Comeback will then purchase the vacant property on behalf of the buyer. The buyer in turn gives Operation Comeback a down payment equal to 5 percent of acquisition and rehabilitation costs. As the house is renovated, Operation Comeback staff oversee the work of contractors with help from professionals who volunteer their services to the program through the local chapter of the American Institute of Architects. Past volunteers have included architects from Koch & Wilson, a leading local firm, as well as Eean McNaughton, a prominent New Orleans architect who oversaw the 1994 renovation of the old state capitol in Baton Rouge. During the renovation, Operation Comeback pays contractors in stages, drawing on a line of credit at a local bank, while buyers pay the monthly interest on Operation Comeback's loan. Buyers also contribute their own labor to the project. When the renovation is completed, Operation Comeback sells the rehabilitated house to the buyer for an amount equal to the purchase price plus the cost of repairs and any taxes and fees. As a nonprofit program whose administrative costs are funded by private donations to the Preservation Resource Center as well by a grant from the city of New Orleans, Operation Comeback does not charge for the technical assistance it provides, nor does it charge higher than market rates on interim financing.

When Operation Comeback began in 1988, Patty Gay explained, "Whitney Bank gave us a line of credit for one hundred fifty thousand dollars. We started out slow. We were only doing about one or two houses at a time." After the initial successes proved to be profitable, the bank extended the credit line to a million dollars, enabling the program to renovate as many as twelve properties at a time. In 1992, the *Times-Picayune* compared the results of Operation Comeback to the results of the state's Community Improvement Agency, which operates in New Orleans on public funds. Both organizations aim to attract buyers to vacant houses in the city's neighborhoods. Both had similar budgets in 1992, roughly $220,000 each. According to the report, Operation Comeback had rescued, or stimulated others to rescue, one hundred houses, while the Community Improvement Agency had rescued none. The agency had never even invoked its power to seize abandoned properties from neglectful owners and sell them to buyers who would rehabilitate them. Even more astonishing was the fact that Operation Comeback had a staff of two, while the Community Improvement Agency had a staff of fourteen.[13]

Alexander Garvin, a New York City planning commissioner, teacher at Yale University, and author of *The American City: What Works, What Doesn't*, defines successful city planning as "public action that generates a desirable, widespread, and sustained private market reaction."[14] By that measure, Operation Comeback has become a success, using its limited resources to attract buyers who have invested several million dollars into aging neighborhoods, restored abandoned properties to the city's tax rolls, and increased the property values of other houses within sight of formerly blighted eyesores. More than a dozen lenders in New Orleans now offer loans to finance the acquisition and renovation of blighted buildings. By introducing potential buyers to these lenders, Operation Comeback's small staff is able to spend less time on financing preservation and more time on rehabilitation and marketing efforts.

Still a young program, Operation Comeback is refining its technique. In the early stages, Operation Comeback also had a difficult time attracting prospective buyers. "We tried to involve realtors," Gay said. "We want realtors to be involved, because we don't want to be real estate agents, but realtors don't get too excited about selling a house for ten thousand dollars where somebody puts one hundred thousand dollars into repairs because their commission is still on ten thousand dollars."

To attract potential buyers, Operation Comeback launched a marketing program called Live in a Landmark. Working with seven different neighborhood associations, the Live in a Landmark program sponsors two tours in each participating neighborhood every year. One tour introduces buyers to vacant houses for sale while the other tour showcases homes already renovated and occupied. One unique advantage of the tours is that they give potential property owners a chance to learn directly from residents, rather than just a realtor, about a neighborhood and its amenities. According to the marketing program's director, Annie Avery, Live in a Landmark has enjoyed the most success in places where neighborhood associations are strongest: in Algiers Point, the historic district across the river from the French Quarter; in Esplanade Ridge, a neighborhood where shotgun cottages have been purchased and renovated for as little as sixty thousand dollars and more ornate Victorian houses have been done for over three times that amount; in Faubourg St. John, another neighborhood of diverse housing sizes and styles adjacent to the green lawns of City Park; in Bywater, a neighborhood of affordable shotgun houses wedged between the Mississippi River and the city's Industrial Canal; and in the Lower Garden District, where small houses have been redone for as little as fifty-three thousand dollars and larger ones, including a five-thousand-square-foot Greek Revival house off Coliseum Square, have been bought and fixed for over a quarter of a million dollars. The social impact of the effort, however, cannot be quantified in dollars. Home buyers who go through the experience typically develop a strong attachment to their neighborhoods and readily contribute to neighborhood association activities like crime watches and cleanup campaigns. No one can put a price tag on civic pride and the restoration of hope on blocks where it had disappeared.

Thanks to a $126,000 grant from the city in 1994, the Live in a Landmark program developed an imaging system that lets prospective buyers examine a range of properties quickly and easily from a computer screen in Operation Comeback headquarters. The grant enabled students at the University of New Orleans to videotape hundreds of vacant properties in Operation Comeback neighborhoods and transfer those images to the computer system. Live in a Landmark has even gone on-line, with a site on the World Wide Web that offers browsers a virtual tour of properties in sixteen historic districts in New Orleans.

Patty Gay, the PRC's executive director, knows that city life is not for everybody, especially in New Orleans, where the incidence of crime is high. Camille Strachan conceded that "with our culture and the climate, we have an unusually high tolerance of public eccentricity." Still, while a majority of Americans opt for privacy and security in suburbia, Gay insists that a steady stream of people is still drawn to the city's historic neighborhoods, especially for the housing bargains. For first-time or financially strapped home buyers, a small but restorable vacant shotgun cottage is generally an affordable deal. For others, including increasing numbers of "empty nesters" in the aging baby boom generation, the city's historic neighborhoods offer a unique quality of life. With no children in school or in the home, they feel more free to live closer to downtown, where commutes to work are short and trips home from the office take them down a boulevard lined by mature live oak trees instead of congested highway strips flooded with glaring lights. They prefer to live in mixed-use neighborhoods, where they can walk to corner stores, a restaurant, or a dry cleaner, without hopping in their cars. Most of them are simply drawn to historic houses, with their high ceilings, hardwood floors, hidden patios or porches, and other details unavailable in new housing. All of this New Orleans has in abundance.

"We have so many places that other cities would just kill for," said Camille Strachan. Therein lies part of the city's problem. In a city with a wealth of historic houses, many of the neighborhoods still suffer from disinvestment, facing great competition for limited amounts of reinvestment. By comparison, Roberta Brandes Gratz notes how in Columbus, Ohio, a city with fewer historic districts, the energy of preservationists concentrated years ago on a single location, German Village, a compact neighborhood of Victorian brick houses on narrow streets lined with brick sidewalks. German Village is now one of the most appealing neighborhoods in Columbus, while New Orleans's historic neighborhoods struggle against decline.

The properties rehabilitated by Operation Comeback across seven different districts do not alone make a dramatic visible impact in a city with thousands of vacant houses. This fact may lead the program to eventually narrow its geographic focus. But Patty Gay points out that every rehabilitated property makes a contribution to the city that ripples throughout its neighborhood. "When a house that has been sitting there for years with peeling paint starts getting fixed up, people nearby start working on their own houses," she said. "You don't feel like putting money into repairs on your house when you see all the houses around you just getting worse and worse, but when somebody comes in and fixes a house, you are inspired. There is a ripple effect." Based on visual inspections and an exhaustive study of building permits at city hall, Operation Comeback estimates that for every property it has helped to renovate, two more have been renovated by neighboring property owners acting on their own.

In the Lower Garden District, where foreclosed properties first spawned the Operation Comeback program, Magazine Street's numerous vacancies have been filled by clusters of antique merchants and artists who took advantage of the low rents in the old two-story brick commercial buildings. "Every shop is occupied," Strachan said on one block, pointing out that some shop owners even live in the apartments upstairs. The street is also home to several restaurants, a popular coffeehouse, and various local stores, small businesses, and offices, all of which attract pedestrians throughout the day—not enough traffic to overwhelm the residential character of the surrounding area but enough to make the place feel safer than empty streets elsewhere in New Orleans. With porches lined up in rows over the sidewalks, the relatively quiet street seems more like a sleepy setting in Texas than a vibrant commercial strip in a large metropolis. Strachan said she keeps her law office in one of the buildings because "it's just like the main street of a small town, where rednecks like me can feel at home."

Judged by "the ripple effect," Operation Comeback has clearly improved small sections of the city. But an even greater effect ripples from another PRC-sponsored program, Christmas in October. On two weekends in every October since 1988, thousands of volunteers have performed basic repair work on blighted community buildings or run-down houses whose low-income, elderly, or disabled occupants need assistance with property maintenance. The average household income of the program's beneficiaries in New Orleans is $9,500 a year. In 1995, some 3,500 volunteers worked on sixty-five separate properties across New Orleans. They painted a century-old courthouse in Algiers Point and performed structural and cosmetic repairs to a Creole cottage that houses a low-income family in Treme, a small neighborhood behind the French Quarter. All of the work is done in districts eligible for listing in the National Register of Historic Places, but historic preservation is not the leading mission. Christmas in October assists longtime New Orleans residents whose presence stabilizes their neighborhoods against decline or gentrification. The effort grew out of a program that began in Midlands, Texas, two decades ago and has spread to 380 places nationwide under an umbrella organization based in Washington, D.C., called Christmas in April. (In most places, April is an ideal month for performing outdoor building renovations, but October is a better month in New Orleans.) A grant from the city of New Orleans funds the program's administrative costs, including a year-round, full-time staff of two. The program also leverages thousands of dollars in contributions from volunteers, neighborhood and professional associations, corporations, and local businesses.

Launching the program was not easy. "Initially, we encountered a lot of skepticism," said Gay, who noted that the legacies of failed neighborhood improvement programs made people reluctant to become involved. "But as the years go by, it is easier to convince people. Every year we get better." In 1995, volunteers and businesses donated over $630,000 in labor and services. From 1988 to 1995, Christmas in October helped repair 341 separate houses and community landmarks. By improving the worst eyesores on any given block, Christmas in October has given thousands of homeowners and their neighbors a financial and emotional lift that often inspires neighbors to rehabilitate their properties on their own. Elderly homeowners who benefit from the program are typically shut-ins, frightened and withdrawn from their neighborhoods. Improving their homes improves their morale, as well as the morale of volunteers, who often sign up with coworkers as a team representing a single office or employer. Participating businesses report that their volunteers actually get along better at work after the experience, said Tracey Hogan, who works on the program year-round. And neighborhood associations, Hogan said, are happier to collaborate on constructive efforts to improve their neighborhoods, a relief from more fatiguing reactive battles to defend their neighborhoods from external threats.

Preservationists in New Orleans have effectively constructed a community-wide approach to neighborhood preservation similar to the way that community policing maintains neighborhood safety: organize residents to prevent further deterioration before existing deterioration invites more. "I remember being a little girl when Dryades Street in Central City was a vibrant place," said Annie Avery, the fifty-eight-year-old director of Live in a Landmark. "Now you go there and you're afraid. But many of our neighborhoods are coming back, and if we continue doing what we're doing, ten years from now some neighborhoods are going to have a totally new look." Patty Gay wishes her organization's approach would influence other social service efforts, which often focus solely on providing help to individuals or individual families. "By working with neighborhood associations," she said, "you don't just address quality of life inside the home, you're also addressing the quality-of-life issue inside the neighborhood. And you're helping the neighborhood association build up its effectiveness."

What sets Gay's organization apart from non-preservation-oriented community development corporations is that the Preservation Resource Center does not view attracting higher-income individuals to a neighborhood as a threat to the neighborhood's longtime residents. No neighborhood can be stabilized without halting population decline, she argued. Still, "grassroots preservationists face opposition when they propose attracting home buyers—any home buyers—to blighted historic neighborhoods, even though this would be the single most beneficial means to reverse decline."[15] When new residents reclaim abandoned properties, the poor in those neighborhoods stand to benefit most, she said. Yet urban policies "almost never take action to increase the urban middle class, because of the risk of displacement," even though "displacement occurs when neighborhoods are not stable and when buildings deteriorate to an uninhabited state. Displacement occurs when residents of any income level are forced to move out because of crime." While public subsidies have fueled the spread of urban sprawl, she said, other subsidies "have institutionalized our cities as enclaves for the poor. . . . We have confined our urban revitalization efforts and considerable resources to poverty programs. We have ignored the need for diversity and jobs generated by an urban middle class."[16]

Nothing in New Orleans illustrates Gay's argument better than the St. Thomas public housing complex in the Lower Garden District. When built in 1939, the first generation of low-rise brick buildings, now shaded by mature oak trees, was a popular place to live. Over time, however, its low-income working residents were displaced to make room for residents with no income. It was a well-intentioned attempt to direct limited public dollars to the people most in need, but by lumping the chronically unemployed together in one location, it turned stable housing developments into concentration camps of misery. By 1995, most of the windows at St. Thomas were boarded up; two-thirds of the 1,500 units appeared vacant. Its chain-link fences topped with razor-sharp wire resembled the perimeters of public detention centers, places designed to keep criminals in, not the other way around.

To remedy the failure at St. Thomas, private sources in New Orleans will contribute up to $30 million, matched by an equal or greater federal grant, to make the housing units habitable and safe—for the tenants as well as the residents of surrounding neighborhoods. The project is part of a nationwide program begun under U.S. Department of Housing and Urban Development secretary Henry Cisneros to rid the nation of its 100,000 worst public housing units by the year 2000. At St. Thomas, the housing units in the worst condition, the ones built after World War II, will come down. Some of the depression-era units will come down, too, reducing the size of the development from 1,500 units to 750. Some units will be reserved for working tenants, to prevent another concentration of unemployed in one location. New housing units will be more compatible with traditional houses in the historic district, removing the visual stigma forced on public housing occupants. On neighboring blocks, vacant public houses built in suburban styles on empty lots during the 1960s and 1970s will also come down, removing more blighting influences from the district. The plan will also restore the neighborhood's traditional street pattern, gobbled up by the housing complex years ago. Across the street from the St. Thomas project, a nonprofit group has already rehabilitated existing single-family homes for relatives of St. Thomas residents. Camille Strachan, who lives less than a mile away, calls the renovated houses "tiny candles in a big stadium, but candles nonetheless."

"I'm probably more cynical than most," Strachan admitted. "We face enormous problems, but individual organizations and individuals can make a difference."

One such individual is Joseph Canizaro, a real estate developer who owns seventy-two acres of property near St. Thomas. Canizaro is not just any developer. Over twenty-five years, his company has overseen $1 billion of real estate development in New Orleans. In 1995, he became president of the Urban Land Institute, the national umbrella organization for developers. In short, Canizaro is the kind of guy who can get the attention of officials at city hall and public housing bureaucrats in Washington. "One day about three or four years ago, I opened the *Times-Picayune,* our local newspaper, and saw a full two-page spread on the Lower Garden District," Canizaro said in a profile in the ULI's magazine, *Urban Land.* "The area had a lot of problems, but some organizations and associations were attempting to restore and bring the neighborhood back. It intrigued me. Since we had an interest in the area, I thought we could work with the neighbors to further improve the area." Working with residents of St. Thomas and civic leaders in the Lower Garden District, Canizaro formed a nonprofit group to plan and carry out the revitalization of St. Thomas and its immediate area. "You might say I had an ulterior motive," the developer said candidly. "I told them that my 72 acres would become more valuable if the entire Lower Garden District area becomes an asset instead of a liability. I told them that's the reason I'm here."[17]

The multimillion-dollar project to fix St. Thomas is a headline grabber—it is costly and dramatic. By contrast, the Preservation Resource Center's efforts to prevent other neighborhoods from one day becoming more like St. Thomas get less attention than they deserve. Still, the administration of the city's latest mayor, Marc Morial, has done some things to help. For example, the city has streamlined the process for seizing abandoned property and selling it to would-be renovators. In a break with past policies, the city has also lifted income restrictions that prevented middle-class home buyers from qualifying for loans under the city's Home Mortgage Authority Program. The city has also provided partial funding for the Preservation Resource Center's Live in a Landmark and Christmas in October programs. But support from the city for such activities is limited, Patty Gay said. The city's indifference could stem from Louisiana's "homestead exemption," which prevents New Orleans (but not municipalities in its suburbs) from collecting property taxes on the first seventy-five thousand dollars of a home's appraised value. But Gay said the issue goes deeper than that: "Incremental development has no appeal to the politicians and the general public. They say, 'We love the Imax theater. We love the aquarium. We love the zoo. We love road races.'" But talk to them about attracting new residents to the city's historic neighborhoods, and "they say it won't happen." A decade ago, nobody lived in the warehouse district downtown, she pointed out. The first apartments there didn't become available until the mid-1980s. "Now, we have over two thousand people living there, yet people will still tell me, 'It won't happen.'" Though preservationists in New Orleans have rescued abandoned buildings, reinvigorated run-down areas with reinvestment, created construction jobs, raised property values and tax assessments, built community pride, and lifted the image of the city in the minds of its citizens and visitors, Gay feels the city does not support preservation as a serious economic development tool.

By contrast, the city's time-consuming efforts to foster a gambling industry have failed to produce a profitable return. In 1992, under the administration of Mayor Sidney Bartholemew, New Orleans paved the way for a casino that was to have generated up to $1 billion in business each year and twenty-five thousand jobs. The casino opened three years late in 1995, fell two-thirds short of projected gross revenue, produced only two thousand jobs, and went bankrupt within five months. Though gambling has dealt New Orleans nothing but a losing hand, today the city, under Mayor Marc Morial, continues to encourage the construction of a casino on the site of a demolished convention center, the Rivergate, a 1960s modernist version of a Greek temple. The seven-acre site is surrounded by five historic districts listed in the National Register of Historic Places. The casino/hotel/entertainment complex will ultimately siphon investment that might otherwise go into the revitalization of existing districts, predicts Thomas Tucker, a New Orleans lawyer who helped write the city's landmark preservation ordinance and chaired the Central Business District's Historic District Landmark Commission when the casino was proposed. Tucker, who accurately foresaw the failure of the first casino, does not claim any gift of clairvoyance. "Cannibalization is easy to predict," he said.

In New Orleans, as in other places, it is only after preservationists have taken the financial risk out of locations that political and business interests seek to capitalize on the newly created value. "Where preservation has been successful, that's where developers want to be," said Patty Gay. "There is a willingness here to sacrifice the character of the city of New Orleans for the fast buck," said Camille Strachan. "It's inconceivable to me that any administration wouldn't take steps to give the goose that lays the golden eggs some corn, instead of killing it." To cash in the hard-won preservation of this historic city is "wrongheaded, narrow-minded," said Bill Borah, the attorney who fought off the elevated expressway through the French Quarter and now teaches preservation planning to a young generation of New Orleanians. "You don't have to be a rocket scientist to see that the biggest growth industry of this place is dependent on the evidence of our history. This whole place is a living museum. Our greatest asset is the physical stuff. You don't have to change New Orleans to bring it to life. All you have to do is rehabilitate what's here."

■　■　■

Pittsburgh is one of America's most interesting postindustrial cities. Discard outdated impressions of a city of steel mills and smokestacks; Pittsburgh is said to be home to more Fortune 500 companies than any city except New York and Chicago. Yet, in an era of look-alike postindustrial cities, Pittsburgh remains a distinctive place.

For all of the changes of recent decades, Pittsburgh is still a city of hills, where houses sit on hilltops, where houses are perched on slopes, and where thousands more lie nestled in neat rows in the bottoms below. San Francisco has its cable cars, but the hills of Pittsburgh have the oldest funiculars in use, including a railcar from 1877 that carries passengers up an incline of thirty-five degrees to the top of Mount Washington's 450 feet. Pittsburgh is still a river city, too. At the base of the hills run three wide rivers. The Allegheny flows from the northeast and the Monongahela flows from the southeast until they join at the center of Pittsburgh to become the Ohio River, flowing west. On maps, the three rivers form a sideways letter Y.

Legend has it that George Washington, as a colonel in the French and Indian War, was so struck by the advantages of the terrain that he convinced the British army to seize the French Fort Duquesne here in 1754 and erect at the junction of the rivers a stronger fortification. The new fort, the largest and most expensive ever constructed in the thirteen British colonies, was named for William Pitt, then a leader in the British Parliament in London.[18] Today, that very site is the tip of downtown known as the Golden Triangle, and its roads along the riverbanks or streets along the hilltops provide a panoramic view of the city's skyline. "To see Manhattan, you need to go to New Jersey. To see Chicago, you have to be out on Lake Michigan. But here, you can see Pittsburgh from any angle," said Pittsburgh archivist Albert Tannler.

The rivers brought initial wealth to Pittsburgh, but the great fortunes came from the hills. The hills supplied the coal for the furnaces that made Pittsburgh the "Forge of the Universe," an early producer of glass, then "Iron City" and, later, a producer of steel after the Civil War, when a judge named Thomas Mellon quit the bench to become a banker. Mellon claimed that any man who couldn't make a fortune in Pittsburgh was too dumb to make a dollar.[19] In ways more literal than not, the city's economy caught fire. In 1868, a writer for the *Atlantic Monthly* called Pittsburgh "Hell with the Lid Taken Off."[20]

To Lewis Mumford, the Pittsburgh of that era, like Newark, New Jersey, Youngstown, Ohio, and Gary, Indiana, was a quintessential Coketown. "Examine it with eye, ear, nose, skin," Mumford wrote, "its prevailing color was black. Black clouds of smoke rolled out of the factory chimneys, and railroad yards, which often cut clean into the town, mangling the very organism, spreading soot and cinders everywhere." Dark industrial pollution hung over the city so low to the ground that streetlamps were kept lit twenty-four hours a day. "In this new environment," said Mumford, "black clothes were only a protective coloration, not a form of mourning; the black stovepipe hat was almost a functional design." Soot and smudges from coal grease were everywhere: on clothes, on hands, in washbasins, and in the air. The smoke fouled the rivers and blunted tastes, aesthetic as well as culinary. "Even well-to-do people began to eat canned goods and stale foods, even when fresh ones were available, because they could no longer tell the difference," Mumford explained.[21] And so it was by no coincidence that a local entrepreneur named H. J. Heinz capitalized on the opportunity and made a fortune marketing more than "57 varieties" of processed foods.

Pittsburghers shrugged off the daily dreariness, but outsiders found it depressing. "The ugliness of the majority of American cities is the first thing which strikes a foreigner," wrote Charles Mulford Robinson, the nation's leading public advocate of the City Beautiful movement. "The ugliness is not only offensive to the eye, but it is repellent to the soul. Men need beauty precisely as they need fresh air and clear skies. To condemn them to live among the ugly surroundings, under skies blackened with smoke, is to deaden their sensibility [and] rob their lives of one great element of interest and dignity."

As Pittsburgh historian Roy Lubove recounted, when a 1907 city survey aroused alarm with its "wholesale condemnation of Pittsburgh's social institutions," local philanthropy was already transforming a new section of the city, Oakland, into a monumental "Civic Center."[22] Pittsburgh's leading capitalists filled the location with grand structures inspired by classical, Gothic, and Renaissance designs, starting with the Carnegie Institute, begun in 1892; it was followed by the Phipps Conservatory (1893); St. Paul's Cathedral (1903); St. Nicholas Cathedral (1904); the Soldiers and Sailors Memorial (1907); Thaw Hall of the University of Pittsburgh (1908); the Pittsburgh Athletic Association (1909); the Twentieth Century Club (1910); the Historic Society of Western Pennsylvania (1912); Masonic Temple (1914); the first Mellon Institute (1915); the University Club (1923); the Young Men's Hebrew Association (1924); the Cathedral of Learning (1926); the second Mellon Institute, at Carnegie-Mellon University (1931); Heinz Chapel (1934); and the Stephen Foster Memorial (1935).[23] Few American cities built as many monumental landmarks in one place.

Lubove called the Oakland civic center "an archetype of responsible capitalism and entrepreneurship, expressed in the neoclassical architecture which had dominated the Chicago Exposition." The aim was for Pittsburghers to "translate into their own lives the values and ideals expressed in their civic environment: aesthetic and cultural achievement, discipline, rationality, harmony, order, pride and self-respect." And to a certain extent they did. As architectural historian Franklin Toker notes, "Pittsburghers enjoyed their buildings so much that their favorite deck of cards in 1912 carried the images of fifty-two of them, plus jokers."[24]

But there was also a humbler side of Pittsburgh, underappreciated at the time. For every public library, concert hall, and institute financed by Andrew Carnegie, for every public conservatory built by his partner Henry Phipps, for every public park created by a Schenley, for every Presbyterian church paid for by a Mellon, for every university hall funded by a Thaw, Pittsburgh had hundreds of streets, scores of parishes, and dozens of neighborhoods built by laboring classes, by immigrants from Germany, Ireland, Ukraine, Poland, Lithuania, Slovakia, Greece, Croatia, Serbia, Russia, indeed from all over Europe, as well as the neighborhoods built by the city's African Americans. And while the City Beautiful brought order and dignity to Pittsburgh's civic realm, it did little to improve the quality of life of the average citizen. In 1927, H. L. Mencken, columnist for the *Baltimore Sun*, was so appalled by the living conditions he saw in Pittsburgh that he declared, "Never before has a great community applied what it had so meagerly to the rational purposes of human life."[25]

All of this began to change in 1946, when Pittsburgh created America's first postwar urban redevelopment authority, overseen by Mayor (and later Governor) David Lawrence, who was overseen by financier Richard King Mellon, founder of the Allegheny Conference on Community Development. It was R. K. Mellon, more than any other individual, who recruited the city's corporate elite to "rebuild rather than abandon Pittsburgh."[26] Over the next quarter century, Pittsburgh spent half a billion dollars to tidy up its natural and built environments, to cleanse its polluted air and dirty water, and to encourage new productive uses of its obsolete industrial sites and rotting slums. It was nothing short of cataclysmic, done according to a design philosophy that Lubove describes as "international style architecture combined with Corbusier's nightmarish Radiant City, executed through the Urban Redevelopment Authority's large-scale clearance projects."

The largest chunk of the old city to go was the Lower Hill, a neighborhood adjacent to the Golden Triangle and populated by the city's poorest and least politically connected African American citizens. In 1955, the city demolished some 1,300 Lower Hill buildings, home to roughly eight thousand people and over four hundred businesses, to clear the site for redevelopment. In their place went up the eighteen-thousand-seat stainless-steel-domed Civic Arena, a flying saucer landed on an asphalt field of parking lots. As refugees from the Lower Hill evictions migrated across the Allegheny River into Pittsburgh's North Side neighborhoods, city hall prepared to demolish those neighborhoods also. According to Pittsburgh historian Walter Kidney, "a North Side survey in 1951 found no romance in housing that was 41 percent slum and six-tenths of a percent fully satisfactory."[27] The core of the North Side, a neighborhood called Allegheny, was bulldozed for Allegheny Center, a windowless fortress of a shopping mall, an office tower, and a private housing complex. New highways mowed down other aging neighborhoods nearby, and downriver rose an even larger isolated fortress, Three Rivers Stadium. In Allegheny, whole blocks of historic Pittsburgh were carted to the landfill—brick houses, churches, parish halls, and corner stores, over five hundred buildings in all, including the 1863 North Side Market House. "This great square hall, with its slim pillars and its large uncluttered space, ornamented above with the delicate tracery of the roof trusses, was like a grand church dedicated to commerce," wrote Pittsburgh architectural historian James Van Trump, who claimed it was a shame to see irreplaceable landmarks go when they might be put to good use instead. In the rush to redevelop, Pittsburgh was shedding its special character. "When

Pittsburgh un-smoked itself, half of its visual mystery and drama departed," Van Trump remarked wistfully.[28]

"Pittsburgh's redemption was conceived in terms of liberation from the past, including an unsavory environment: liberation from smoke, from floods, from blighted residential and commercial structures, from a top heavy, aging industrial economy," wrote Lubove. "In essence, Pittsburgh's very survival was dependent upon disassociation from its history, including an architecture which no longer symbolized progress but instead, clutter, which had to be eliminated."[29] Another writer described the prevailing public attitude in 1964: "Pittsburgh's great effort has been to remake itself, to change as fast as it can from the environment of the old nineteenth-century technology into the sleek new forms of the future. . . . The city welcomes tomorrow, because yesterday was hard and unlovely. . . . The town has no worship of landmarks. Instead, it takes its pleasure in the swing of the headache ball and the crash of falling brick."[30]

The era was called the "Pittsburgh Renaissance." But Lubove, recalling Robinson's critique of the City Beautiful's shortcomings, reminded Pittsburgh that the "civic renaissance would be incomplete" until the urban reform movement "descended into the slums."[31]

Judged on that standard, the true renaissance in Pittsburgh began in the winter of 1964, when Arthur Ziegler, a professor of English at Carnegie-Mellon University, and architectural historian James Van Trump found themselves in one of Pittsburgh's slums, Manchester, on the North Side. There, on the 1300 block of Liverpool Street, the two men looked up at a row of Victorian houses scheduled to come down and "resolved to find an alternative to redevelopment by demolition," Ziegler recalled. Until that point, historic preservation was monopolized by antiquarians, genealogical societies, and gentrifiers. The Pittsburghers made preservation the tool of altruistic civic reformers.[32] "We had a deep commitment to finding means to revitalize neighborhoods without removing either the historic buildings or the inhabitants," Ziegler said. Together, he and Van Trump and willing allies founded the Pittsburgh History & Landmarks Foundation, which grew into one of the most innovative and accomplished local private preservation organizations in the United States.

With a one-hundred-thousand-dollar grant from the Sarah Mellon Scaife Foundation in 1966, the organization began to rehabilitate blighted houses in a North Side neighborhood called the Mexican War Streets. Laid out in 1848, the neighborhood's streets were named for battles in the war. Its Italianate and late Victorian houses had declined so much that the city's 1954 master plan called for the area's wholesale demolition and replacement with symmetrical modern complexes similar to prevailing public housing schemes. "It was decaying, but not decayed," Ziegler said. The neighborhood "needed more time to become a ghetto. Longtime residents were reluctantly leaving and only the poor were replacing them." Banks would not lend mortgages there. "For investment it attracted only the slumlord," he said. To stem the decay, Ziegler's Landmarks Foundation began to offer technical architectural and construction advice to residents willing to restore their homes. But Ziegler quickly recognized that advice was not enough. Just as Pittsburgh would have to diversify its economy to replace jobs in its shrinking steel industry, the Mexican War Streets would have to attract new residents and new investment or risk being pulled under by the weight of concentrated poverty. At the same time, Ziegler's group didn't want to displace existing residents if they could avoid it. As Ziegler said, his foundation was "committed to saving not only the buildings in a neighborhood but also the neighborhood's people, or at least as many as possible."

The plan targeted the most blighted houses on a block, buying out slumlords, eliminating overcrowding in rooming houses, improving the run-down properties and attracting working residents to the area. The foundation struck a deal with the city's Urban Redevelopment Authority to lease rehabilitated homes back to the city for rental to low-income residents, one of the first such arrangements in the nation. The progress inspired other property owners to undertake preservation efforts of their own. By Ziegler's estimate, for every dollar his group invested in the preservation of the Mexican War Streets neighborhood, its residents invested six more. In the first five years, the foundation restored and rehabilitated fourteen houses while longtime residents rehabilitated fifty-one more, and new owners attracted to the neighborhood restored an additional thirty-eight, all in a small twelve-block neighborhood of roughly three hundred houses. Property values rose 10 percent on average over the same period. The slumming of the Mexican War Streets had been halted.

Ziegler was also very much aware of the effort's social dimension. In a 1972 article, "The Quest for Community Self-Determination," Ziegler said the Mexican War Streets effort was "developing in all these people a new sense of neighborhood." He acknowledged that "most of these people actually have little in common; however, the renewal of this historic district and the goals of this urban experiment have given them common cause." This was intentional all along, he said. "We felt the burden of responsibility for solving local problems would be placed squarely on the shoulders of the local people. They would have to work on their own behalf and not look to us as omnipresent problem solver and benefactor," he said, echoing views of conservative sociologist Robert Nisbet, whose 1969 book, *The Quest for Community: A Study in the Ethics of Order and Freedom*, warned of how bureaucratic efforts of large, centralized governments stifled the development of healthy community ties. "Before our arrival, this neighborhood had lost its ability to determine its future. It was on the ineluctable course of going bad, like any organism. It had lost the means of regeneration," Ziegler said. "We provided a new injection of energy, of life.... We have really freed—or at least started the process of freeing—this area to determine what it wants for itself."[33]

Ziegler's foundation then moved across Pittsburgh's rivers to its South Side, to a white working-class neighborhood formerly known as Birmingham, an area of mills and humble homes not more than five minutes from downtown. The threat to the South Side was not the wholesale clearance schemes of city hall, but wholesale depopulation. Though still a relatively stable neighborhood of longtime residents with strong loyalty to their local parishes and impressive, historic churches—such as St. John the Baptist (Ukrainian), with its eight onion-shaped domes, St. Casimir's (Lithuanian), and St. Adalbert's (Polish)—the South Side was aging, and few new residents were moving in. (From 1950 to 1990, its population dropped by 68 percent.) But in physical respects, the neighborhood was remarkably intact, with most of its modest row houses standing as they did when constructed in the nineteenth century, though original facades and stone doorsteps were often hidden behind vinyl siding and aluminum awnings. Decay on the mile-long business district, East Carson Street, could not be hidden so easily. One-fifth of all shopfronts on the eighteen-block commercial street were empty. Suburban shopping centers siphoned customers by offering more plentiful choices. Rigorous maintenance of the historic two- and three-story masonry buildings was not the highest priority of landlords deprived of rental income lost to vacancies. Looking at East Carson Street, one could reasonably foresee a faded urban environment pockmarked by empty storefronts shuttered for good behind graffiti-covered grates.

With assistance from the local chapter of the American Institute of Architects, the Pittsburgh History & Landmarks Foundation launched in 1968 a program to restore East Carson Street's commercial buildings, in cooperation with the South Side Chamber of Commerce and neighborhood community council. With another grant from the Sarah Mellon Scaife Foundation in 1970, the Landmarks Foundation offered free professional guidance on facade restorations and street improvements. As a demonstration project, the PH&LF purchased and restored a three-story brick commercial building to show that the preservation of East Carson Street's properties was both affordable and beneficial for the landlords. Working through the South Side Local Development Company, preservationists helped to make Pittsburghers appreciate what was there: not just its buildings, but the community that inhabited them. The Landmarks Foundation even published a biography and book of recipes of a Serbian immigrant and South Side restaurant owner, Vukevich Evosevich.

In 1985, East Carson Street became one of the first seven urban commercial districts to join the National Trust for Historic Preservation's Main Street program, which helps primarily small cities and towns devise strategies to preserve and revive historic local business districts.[34] Since joining the Main Street network, East Carson Street has gained 150 restored building facades, 120 new businesses, 750 new jobs, and over $20 million in private investment. Rents have risen from $7 per square foot in 1985 to $12 a decade later.[35] Because improvements have occurred gradually, businesses that cater to longtime local residents coexist alongside galleries and boutiques, bars and restaurants aimed at younger crowds.

"Back in 1968, there were vacant storefronts all over the place. Now, this is *the* booming street in Pittsburgh, and it is teeming with nightlife," Ziegler said. "We didn't come in and force people to do it," he said, noting that no regulations or rules were forced on property owners. Instead, preservationists simply set examples and offered help and financial incentives through the South Side Local Development Company to people who wanted to do the same. Only some twenty-five years after the effort to preserve East Carson Street began did the Pittsburgh City Council designate the area a local historic district, making it worthy of official protection. The vitality of the commercial corridor has also created a market for new housing along the adjacent South Side riverfront, as well as interest in the redevelopment of a 110-acre riverfront site once occupied by a steel mill at the eastern end of the community. Standing on East Carson Street on a frosty February afternoon, Ziegler said, "Historic preservation can be the underlying basis of community renewal, human renewal, and economic renewal. Preservation is not some isolated cultural benefit. I don't think of preservation as an end in itself. I see it as a means to create an operating community of concerned and reasonably happy people."

Manchester, a North Side neighborhood and Pittsburgh's largest historic district, was far from a community of happy people when the Pittsburgh History and Landmarks Foundation began working there in 1967. First settled in 1832, Manchester had declined from a respectable nineteenth-century neighborhood of Victorian mansions and two-story town houses into a nearly abandoned slum. Though Manchester had been a racially mixed neighborhood for years, white residents began to flee after the city's demolition of the Lower Hill caused black families to migrate to Pittsburgh's North Side in greater numbers. The neighborhood went into serious decline when a new highway was built along its edge. Manchester's nadir followed the urban riots that erupted in 1968 after the assassination of Martin Luther King Jr., when the population, as high as 18,000 after World War II, fell to its low of 1,200. In little more than a generation, a stable neighborhood had become a ghetto of burned-out buildings, vacant houses with missing windows, and empty lots littered with trash, all compounded by absentee property owners, indifferent slumlords, and residents deprived of hope.

Working with community residents, the Landmarks Foundation helped organize a community development corporation, the Manchester Citizens Corporation. In a departure from slum clearance policies, Pittsburgh's Urban Redevelopment Authority hired the organization in 1970 to study conditions in Manchester and make recommendations on how to preserve existing buildings, using tax dollars that would have funded demolitions and construction of new public housing. Some black residents of Manchester, however, were skeptical of the city's offer. A few remembered the URA's evictions when the Lower Hill was cleared for downtown real estate developers. Some resented offers of help from whites after white flight had taken its local toll. One of the skeptics was a dynamic young community activist named Stanley Lowe.

Born in 1950, when Manchester was a predominantly white neighborhood, Lowe grew up in an era of relative stability only to see it disintegrate as he matured. "After King died, inner-city neighborhoods went through a very traumatic period," he said. "The massive white flight said something about the neighborhood. People were running from the neighborhood to suburbia, and many in the neighborhoods could not leave." To make the neighborhood more appealing, Lowe said, "we decided to build suburbia in the inner city." In the early 1970s, Lowe helped coordinate the demolition of Manchester's blighted brick row houses, replacing them with new "tract houses" that Arthur Ziegler described as "the white man's dream of suburbia." In terms of size, the new houses weren't much larger, but their horizontal orientation demanded larger lots. In order to build a little over a hundred new homes, Lowe said, "I killed about four or five hundred houses."

At the time, Lowe thought he was doing good by Manchester. "We were building what white folks were running to. We were building what other folks thought were the things to have." After a few years, however, he realized that the people who had left were not coming back. "It really had nothing to do with the [new] buildings, and it took me a long time to realize that," he said. In an era of riots and decay, "there was no reason to be proud" of the special qualities that made Manchester a unique place, Lowe recalled. The urge at the time was to be more like everyplace else. Lowe said Ziegler "tried to talk me into saving old buildings," but he wouldn't think of it. With persistent persuasion, however, Ziegler finally convinced Lowe and others to travel in the mid-1970s to Cincinnati, where a community activist named Carl Westmoreland had led efforts since 1967 to preserve Mount Auburn, an African American neighborhood with a history and appearance similar to Pittsburgh's Manchester. Ziegler knew of historic districts becoming gentrified across the country, but Westmoreland's effort in Cincinnati was different. There, preservation was not the work of outsiders, but of longtime residents. "The only thing unique about us is that most of the renovation is being done by the people who live here," Westmoreland told author Roberta Brandes Gratz. But few knew about the effort, because, as Westmoreland explained, too many people "mistakenly view preservation as an elitist activity, not as a tool to revitalize inner-city, low-to-moderate income neighborhoods."[36]

With their eyes opened by what they saw in Cincinnati, Lowe and other Manchester activists then traveled to Georgetown, the venerable historic district in Washington, D.C. "We were shocked beyond our wildest imagination to learn that Georgetown at one time was an African American neighborhood," Lowe said. "Everywhere we went, we saw houses and streetscapes similar to our own." (A decade before, author Jane Jacobs had called a Pittsburgh neighborhood "the workingman's Georgetown.") Once in Georgetown, Lowe and his fellow visitors from Pittsburgh looked at each other and said, "These buildings look just like our buildings back home, only we throw this kind of stuff away." At that point, Lowe said he realized that "in order for me to continue building suburban tract housing, it required me to destroy my heritage, my neighborhood—and that was too big a price to pay." That's when Stanley Lowe became a preservationist.

After joining Ziegler at the Landmarks Foundation and becoming manager of its revolving loan fund in 1984, Lowe helped his fellow Manchester residents rehabilitate some eight hundred houses in the neighborhood, more than half of its housing stock. Though many of its residents live in poverty and more than 10 percent of its housing remained vacant in 1995, Manchester was one of only three neighborhoods in the city to grow during the 1980s. By 1995, the population had reached 3,600, almost three times what it had been before the neighborhood preservation effort began. "I've seen property values here rise two, three, four thousand percent," Lowe said. "There was a time when you could buy a vacant house here for six hundred dollars. You'd be lucky to get a vacant house in Manchester now for thirty or forty thousand." According to the 1990 census, the majority of Manchester's houses were valued between $45,000 and $125,000. In 1993, the Manchester Citizens Corporation purchased a historic stone mansion and its carriage house at a public auction, renovated the property, and converted it into its neighborhood headquarters. "We bought this house for twenty thousand dollars,"

Lowe said, noting that two years later it was appraised at $211,000. In 1994, the group built seven new brick town houses on empty lots. The new homes, modeled after historic houses in the neighborhood, are hard to distinguish from originals on the same street. They were sold to new owners whose monthly mortgage and interest payments average $450 per month. The MCC's newsletter called the success "a tremendous strategic shift in ideology" away from slum clearance schemes that "saw over 900 historic homes demolished to make way for the suburban dream." In 1995, the MCC won a grant from the U.S. Department of Housing and Urban Development to remove blighted public housing projects and replace them with more traditional single-family homes. In 1996, the neighborhood held a "demolition party," kicked off by Mayor Tom Murphy on a bulldozer, who proudly said, "Manchester will become the first community in Pittsburgh to demolish public housing as we know it."

"We're trying to correct past mistakes," said Lowe, who left the Landmarks Foundation to become executive director of the Pittsburgh Housing Authority under Mayor Murphy. "The old concept of public housing didn't work," he said. "The poorest of the poor stay in public housing. The crime rates are the highest. It is the most segregated." And the shoddy design only stigmatizes occupants, he said. "Every existing house in the neighborhood reinforces the fact that their house is different. It sends a signal to the people in public housing that you don't belong." The new brick row houses going up will help solve that problem. Rhonda Brandon, the Manchester Community Corporation's executive director, predicted, "From the outside, you're not going to be able to distinguish public housing from private houses."

The MCC also plans to convert a large vacant Victorian mansion into ten affordable apartments and assume control of ninety-four publicly subsidized apartments in historic buildings that show neglect from absentee ownership. More new row houses will be built on vacant lots. All of this is part of a multi-year, $40 million neighborhood revitalization strategy that calls for residents to secure local ownership of all the properties in Manchester, increase the neighborhood's rate of home ownership, and rid the district of blighting influences, vacancies, and drug activity. "When we build these houses, we have an opportunity to start fresh," said Lowe, who noted that bricks and mortgages alone will not heal the neighborhood completely. "You can't be in preservation in Manchester without dealing with the gangs and employment. You have to be involved with lots of quality-of-life issues"—helping people get off and stay off drugs, teaching job skills to the unemployed, encouraging steady work habits, and attracting potential employers to the light industrial sites nearby. When the MCC held a ninety-day neighborhood cleanup campaign, for instance, the organization hired rival local gangs to do the work as a way to structure a truce on the streets and foster among gang members a sense of ownership in the community's comeback. Lowe recalled how no one taught him to appreciate Manchester when he was young. Now he speaks in moving terms about a neighborhood landmark, the Anderson Manor, whose original owner once shared a love of reading with youngsters, one of whom was immigrant Andrew Carnegie, who grew up to finance the construction of libraries in communities across the United States.

Lowe is now considering how to structure a pilot program that will encourage homeowners to maintain their houses and stave off the blight that lowers the value of surrounding properties. "You have to stay on top of maintenance problems like graffiti—as soon as you see it, get rid of it," Lowe said. To remove the blighting influence of some 150 vacant houses in the neighborhood that have been seized by the city for back taxes, the MCC is searching for ways to stabilize their facades until the day when new owners might come and rehabilitate their interiors. The idea is not too far-fetched. Manchester, Pittsburgh's largest historic district, is a special place. It is blessed by strong community stewardship in a location with unique appeal, a neighborhood on flat land in a city of hills, on a spot just across the Allegheny River from the downtown.

The problems facing Manchester and neighborhoods like it are "solvable," Lowe said. "Fifty percent of the job is just getting people as excited about this as you are, getting people to believe in themselves, and in the buildings." Many efforts fail, he said, because "sometimes, we want to do too much for other people. But once we show people that preservation is economically viable, that it works, it's like old-time religion to them: give me more."

Preservation in Pittsburgh is not just about low-income residents discovering preservation, but preservationists discovering low-income residents, people like Harriet Henson, who led public housing tenants in a fight to reclaim another African American neighborhood, Brighton Place, not far from Manchester on the North Side. Having won a class-action lawsuit against HUD for failing to maintain their properties, Henson's two-hundred-member group wanted to do more, but none of them could get loans to buy and rehabilitate the inexpensive three-story brick row houses or other run-down properties in the neighborhood. Stanley Lowe remembers Henson coming to him and saying, "We want to turn our place around, but I have crack-infested bars all around me, and until we deal with these bars, we're never going to be able to revitalize our neighborhood."

"We had given up on Brighton Place," said Arthur Ziegler. "We never thought we could do it." But Henson's commitment convinced his foundation to loan her tenants group a quarter of a million dollars to buy out and shut down two nuisance bars that harbored, in Henson's words, "every illegal activity you can imagine." Henson's group then created a headquarters in one of the former bars and used the remainder of the loan to buy half a dozen houses, renovate them, and lease them back to public housing tenants. "Until Arthur loaned us the money, we couldn't get anyone to take us seriously," Henson said. Gradually, her group paid back the loan, plus interest. Then, with grants from the city and private foundations, the North Side tenants rehabilitated a total of thirty-four housing units on two blocks that were added to the National Register of Historic Places. And they protected their hard-won gains with stepped-up security patrols. "Before, I had a different view of preservation," Henson said. "To me, it was just about saving a bunch of raggedy old buildings." After restoring the exteriors of buildings, securing patrols on the streets, and working with community police, "a lot of the fear of crime has been removed," she said. "The housing looks better. People seem to be proud. Now, I can see the potential that was here all along." Henson scoffs at experts who say poor neighborhoods can't be improved, that the only strategy should be to help their residents move out. "Stanley Lowe and his group proved it wrong in Manchester in the 1970s, and we're proving it wrong today. If you make up your mind that you want to change it, you can change it." Self-motivation accounts for some of the success on Brighton Place, but money accounts for more. As Henson said at her desk in her neighborhood office, "If it had not been for Arthur, we wouldn't be sitting here today."

None of the preservation activity at Brighton Place or Manchester could happen without access to capital that was denied those places during decades of redlining and disinvestment. "We need capital in our neighborhoods. We need investment," Lowe said. "If you want to find out whether or not a neighborhood will survive or die, you need to count the dollars. Follow the money."

In 1988, the *Atlanta Constitution* won a Pulitzer Prize for its review of mortgage lending by savings and loan institutions in America's large cities. Research discovered that Pittsburgh's Allegheny County had the highest concentration of bank deposits per capita of any place in America after Manhattan, but lenders there had a record of making few or no loans to people in low-income inner-city neighborhoods. In fact, the paper reported that Pittsburgh savings and loans had the second most discriminatory record in the nation. The Community Reinvestment Act of 1977 had required lenders to do business with creditworthy applicants in underserved urban and rural areas. But not until 1989, when the law was strengthened after the collapse of the savings and loan industry, did lenders have to disclose information about mortgage applicants. This new requirement provided the critical information for watchdog groups to track lenders' compliance with the objectives of community reinvestment laws.

When the parent company of Union National Bank of Pittsburgh requested that federal banking regulators approve a merger with Pennbancorp, the Manchester Citizens Corporation examined Union's mortgage disclosure data and discovered that Manchester had been effectively redlined by the bank. Before seeking to resolve the problem with Union's officers, MCC joined with seventeen other neighborhood organizations to form the Pittsburgh Community Reinvestment Group. It was funded by Ziegler's Landmarks Foundation and inspired by a Chicago effort led by community activist Gale Cincotta, whose group had helped to write federal community reinvestment legislation. For months, Union National Bank resisted appeals from Pittsburgh activists to improve its community lending record, until the bank's desire to get approval for its merger led to an agreement with community leaders in 1989. The product of the bank merger, Integra Bank, pledged $109 million in loans to Pittsburgh's underserved areas over the next five years, including a loan of half a million dollars to the Pittsburgh History & Landmark Foundation's Preservation Loan Fund.

With money from the PH&LF's loan fund, the community reinvestment group then undertook an extensive evaluation of the neighborhood lending practices of Pittsburgh's four major commercial banks over the most recent four-year period. The study showed that Equibank, the mortgage lender with the worst record in Pittsburgh's low- and moderate-income African American neighborhoods, had avoided low-risk applicants in those communities while chasing speculative investments in Florida and western states. Another major lender, Dollar Bank, showed a less than stellar record. After negotiations to correct Dollar Bank's lending practices failed, Lowe said his group "went to the mayor and said, 'Why do you have your money in this bank?' " The mayor, Sophie Masloff, read the group's report and called the bank's president, expecting to settle the issue. Masloff was an elderly former city councillor whose short height and gentle demeanor made her seem more like a kind Russian grandmother than an urban political boss. According to Lowe, the bank's president brushed off the mayor, telling her, "Leave us alone. You run the city. We run the bank." The following day, the city informed the bank that it intended to withdraw $25 million in deposits. "When you start moving that kind of cash around, it gets people's attention," Lowe said.

In a similar episode, when National City Bank in Cleveland, with assets totaling $35 billion, announced plans to acquire Pittsburgh's $14.6 billion Integra Bank, the community reinvestment coalition approached bank officials in Cleveland about improving community lending in Pittsburgh. "They dissed us pretty bad," Lowe said. But with the support of city hall, the school board, local hospitals, and sympathetic foundations, Lowe said, institutions in Pittsburgh "were prepared within seven days to withdraw a hundred million dollars from Integra Bank." As a last resort, the coalition of community groups was prepared to file a formal protest with federal regulators reviewing the merger. "We know that before we file any protest, we have a responsibility, just as the lender does, to be diligent," Lowe said. "When you file a protest, it's necessary to have your facts together. You must make sure that you have your coalition together, that your correspondence file is complete, that your home mortgage lending record is accurate, and on and on and on." After National City Bank in Cleveland failed to respond to the PCRG's requests, the coalition's member organizations resolved to file their complaints. "The next day, the Cleveland Fed had fifty protests," Lowe said. Unanimity is part of the coalition's strength; member organizations act together or not at all. When federal regulators called Lowe with an offer from the bank in Cleveland to settle the protests, Lowe said, "Fine, I'll withdraw them all. And the Fed said, 'You can withdraw them all?' And I said, 'Certainly; it's not a problem.' And the man at the Fed said, 'Wait, let me get this straight; you can send one letter with your signature and just wipe them all out?' I said, 'Absolutely.' They were in shock."

Thanks to meticulous research and a disciplined approach, the coalition has earned the respect of Pittsburgh's political and civic elites, a valuable asset when negotiating with banking officials. "Generally, not-for-profit neighborhood groups in many people's minds are synonymous for 'dumb, stupid, and ignorant,' " Lowe said. "You have to position yourself to be the complete opposite." The coalition always tries negotiation and cooperation before confrontation, looking for situations where the needs of a community overlap with the needs of banks that want to improve their community lending practices. In Manchester, Lowe said, when residents drew up their long-term $40 million neighborhood revitalization strategy, they identified all the credit risks in the neighborhood on a map, including blighted public housing units, poorly maintained apartments, and drug trade locations. "We knew that if we didn't take care of them, the banks wouldn't touch us," Lowe said. "So we went to the banks and said, 'We have put a plan together to change our neighborhood. We know, Mr. Banker, that you can't invest here until we deal with these problems. We tell you what, Mr. Banker. We'll take care of this. This is not your job. It's our job. And we'll deal with it. But when we do, it'll be time for you to invest.' "

Five years after the community reinvestment coalition was founded, Pittsburgh lenders have committed more than $2.5 billion for loans in formerly underserved communities. In 1995, Integra Bank alone pledged another $1.67 billion in loans by the year 2000, the largest community reinvestment agreement in the United States. Mayor Tom Murphy hailed the agreement, saying "the public dollar cannot be the only investment in many neighborhoods." Eleven savings and loan institutions formed a program that offers loans of up to $75,000 to start small businesses in low-to-moderate-income neighborhoods and historic districts. And Mellon Bank has launched a $10 million Comprehensive Neighborhood Development Initiative that allows community groups to approach the bank with a long-term comprehensive revitalization strategy, which bank officials then help to refine and finance. "A lot of community groups do a house here, or a house there," said Scott Brown, Mellon's community reinvestment officer. "But if an organization has a neighborhood plan, we're able to work them through the process," from planning, to design, to mortgage lending, to construction. To cultivate goodwill and trust, the community reinvestment coalition honors the city's most cooperative bankers with annual awards. As part of their compliance with the Community Reinvestment Act, Pittsburgh banks have assumed the administrative costs of the community reinvestment coalition, about $250,000 a year, although the Pittsburgh History & Landmarks Foundation still funds the coalition's annual analysis of community lending data, entitled "Follow the Money."

In Pittsburgh, preservationists have tapped capital in the city to advance neighborhood restoration, which, as Lowe noted, has advanced "economic development and a sense of pride, a sense of belonging. We have helped people in our neighborhoods understand that the pie is bigger than they ever imagined," he said. "All we ask people to do is try the system."

Howard Slaughter Jr., a former vice president and community reinvestment officer at Dollar Bank, left his job to manage the Landmarks Foundation's revolving loan fund when Lowe moved to city hall. "When I had a chance to go to work for a lowly nonprofit, my colleagues thought I was crazy." Why give up the salary and the tickets to the skyboxes? his colleagues asked him. "But it wasn't about money," Slaughter said. "Banks do what they have to do to get by, and I wanted to see more done." For Slaughter, promoting preservation full-time was his way to do more. "Most people don't stop to realize that restoring a building and adapting it for a new use creates jobs, provides business opportunities, adds to the stability of a neighborhood, and encourages further restoration activity."

When Slaughter took charge of the loan fund, one of the first things he did was to persuade the Landmarks Foundation to raise the interest rate on its loans, from 2 or 3 percent to prime rate. "I wanted the fund to sustain itself over the long term," he said, believing that if the fund was going to make the riskiest loans, the ones that conventional sources would not make, the nonprofit organization was justified in asking for a little more from borrowers. Besides, he said, "every dime we make goes back into the fund to do more, and the more successful we are, the easier it is to raise more money. And in the time that I have been here, we have not had any defaults."

Thanks to a capital campaign in the early 1980s, the loan fund has grown from the original $100,000 gift from the Sarah Mellon Scaife Foundation to over $2 million. Instead of using the fund's deposits to purchase properties, as the Landmarks Foundation did in its early years, the fund makes loans to other neighborhood-based nonprofit groups that purchase and restore historic landmarks in their communities. Major projects to date include the conversion of the 1888 St. Mary's Priory, a former convent once threatened with demolition for Interstate 279, into an inn; the preservation of the home of environmentalist Rachel Carson, author of *Silent Spring;* and the creation of a brewery pub and restaurant in the 1883 Eberhardt & Ober Brewery.

With assistance from Partners for Sacred Places, a national organization based in Philadelphia, the Landmarks Foundation has offered dwindling congregations at historic churches and synagogues technical assistance with the maintenance and restoration of their structures. Following the success of the Steeples Project, started in Boston by the nonprofit Historic Boston Incorporated, the Pittsburgh organization has helped raise public awareness of the serious maintenance crises facing churches with limited financial resources but virtually unlimited social and civic missions. Twice in two decades, for instance, the Pittsburgh foundation has persuaded the Immaculate Heart of Mary Church to keep its copper-covered dome, the most identifiable landmark in Pittsburgh's Polish Hill neighborhood. Concern for Pittsburgh's landmark churches and the community services they provide even inspired a documentary aired on local station WQED-TV, entitled *Holy Pittsburgh.*

The loan fund has also helped stimulate interest in the redevelopment of industrial brick warehouses along the Allegheny River, in a section of the city called the Strip for its strip of produce vendors. In 1996, the fund loaned ninety-nine thousand dollars to the Hill District Community Development Corporation to acquire and renovate the 1927 New Grenada Theater, an old jazz palace that years ago sank into disrepair.

For all of its projects, the Pittsburgh History & Landmarks Foundation won national acclaim for its redevelopment of an underutilized railyard complex along the Monongahela River into Station Square, a marketplace of shops and restaurants, offices, and a new hotel. In the early 1970s, after a city plan to demolish historic buildings on the site was shelved, Ziegler saw an opportunity to remake the setting into a location for the upscale shops and dining that Pittsburgh didn't have. San Francisco had already redeveloped Ghirardelli Square; Boston was about to open a new festival marketplace at Quincy Market, behind Faneuil Hall. "The city needed an attraction," Ziegler said. "We were the tenth largest corporate city in America, and we had a blue-collar bias." But when Ziegler and his colleagues proposed the idea, Pittsburgh's preservationists couldn't get any institutional support. "Everybody said it wouldn't work," Ziegler said. "The city planning agency even tried to stop us," he said.

It took Pittsburgh a long time to realize the potential of its waterfront. As far back as 1910, planner Frederick Law Olmsted Jr. and others had criticized Pittsburgh for not using its riverfronts as public attractions, in the way European cities had done for centuries. According to historian Roy Lubove, the critics claimed Pittsburgh had neglected its unique riverbanks as places for "recreation . . . civic respect . . . happiness . . . loyalty and local pride," and blamed the city's negligence on "the wasteful commercialism of the later nineteenth century, [which drove the notion] that economical and useful things were normally ugly" and that appealing places were only "to be sought in things otherwise useless." By the 1970s, however, the deindustrialization of the city's riverfronts and the return of clean rivers allowed visionaries like Ziegler to see the long-ignored potential, even if public officials remained closed-minded. "Bureaucrats are not known to have a lot of imagination," Ziegler said. "We're free to go out and do what comes to mind." So, with a $5 million grant from Richard Mellon Scaife's Allegheny Foundation, the Station Square project went ahead. Ziegler remembers Scaife telling him, "Just do what you did in the neighborhoods and all the rest will work."

The redevelopment of Station Square proceeded in gradual, deliberate phases. The plan concentrated on creating amenities for locals first, then attractions for tourists later. "Like a city, we would let it grow by itself," Ziegler said. One building was renovated for shops. The former waiting hall of the 1901 Pittsburgh & Lake Erie Railroad station was converted into the Grand Concourse Restaurant after a $2 million investment from Detroit restaurateur Charles A. Muer. The restaurant became the "the forty-first largest grossing restaurant in America," Ziegler said, "and we couldn't get a dime of financing" from conventional sources. Other parts of the historic industrial complex gradually took on new uses, including shops and more restaurants, even offices in the former station whose windows offered prime views of the Golden Triangle and Pittsburgh's rivers and hills. (Ziegler claimed a corner office on the building's fourth floor.) The Scaife Family Foundation then awarded $4.1 million for a park along the river to showcase steelmaking machinery salvaged from the region's mills. Before long, Station Square was the most visited attraction in Pittsburgh, drawing an estimated 85 percent of tourists to the city and 3 million total visitors a year. A hotel at the site claimed the highest occupancy rate of any hotel in the city. By Ziegler's account, Station Square has stimulated the creation of over 140 businesses, with three thousand employees, office space that is 98 percent leased, and annual property and parking taxes of $4 million. In 1994, the Landmarks Foundation sold its interest in Station Square and adjacent developable sites to private developers for $25.5 million, with the proceeds endowing the foundation's work. Sitting inside his Station Square office, Ziegler's voice is filled with pride in discussing the financial success, but there is a trace of bitterness over others' early lack of faith in the project's potential. Sounding like Harriet Henson, who credited Ziegler's foundation with financing the preservation of Brighton Place, Ziegler has not forgotten the philanthropist who allowed the Station Square proposal to proceed. "Without Dick Scaife, none of this would be here."

One of the lessons in Pittsburgh, whether at Station Square, East Carson Street, or Manchester, is that all historic buildings—except the most treasured cultural monuments under subsidized stewardship—have to remain economically viable if they are to provide any lasting public benefits. "Architecture is an art wholly based upon continuing utility, and utility is in turn grounded in the market place," Ziegler once wrote. "When you accept that circumstance and apply the techniques of finance, real estate, and construction to the problems at hand, you compete on equal terms with the forces that destroy buildings."[37]

Having challenged those forces within Pittsburgh, Ziegler now fears they lurk beyond the city's hills, in the sprawling metropolitan area that has grown to more than 2 million people, even as Pittsburgh has lost 45 percent of its population (over 300,000 citizens) since 1950, when the "Pittsburgh Renaissance" began. "We look at our city and we see that we have a great skyline. The city looks robust," Ziegler said. But Pittsburgh has lost jobs and taxpaying residents and is losing more as its population ages. "We've already seen some of our stronger neighborhoods begin to weaken," he said. "Once, we were the leading city on how to revitalize, but we've fallen behind, and now we want to catch up." To do so, Pittsburgh has gambled on an expensive new international airport, over the hills and fifteen miles from the Golden Triangle. Until now, transportation and topography had kept the city contained. Metropolitan Pittsburgh never built a suburban circumferential expressway or an edge city that would have displaced the economic power of its historic core. But now, growth is accelerating at the periphery, near the highways, on open land, stimulating interest in a suburban beltway after so many years without one. Ziegler fears the implications for Pittsburgh's residents with no access to new suburban jobs and for their neighborhoods, the places he has worked to preserve from the bottom up for a generation.

"This city still believes that from the top all improvements will flow," he said. "Pittsburgh still worships the Mellon-Lawrence leadership of the 1950s.

They did some wonderful things. They cleaned the air. They cleaned the water. But they also unleashed huge forces of demolition, none of which has worked and all of which have cost huge amounts of money." First, taxpayers paid to buy blighted real estate and tear old structures down. They paid again to build new public housing in its place. They paid again to maintain the public housing, and paid again to tear it down. They paid yet again to build something better in its place. While over all those years the historic structures that survived stood the test of time. Ziegler once estimated that by stopping the URA's North Side demolition plan in the 1970s, preservationists saved taxpayers $100 million. More tax dollars remain invested in older sections of the city. What happens to that investment now is in Pittsburgh's hands.

Architectural historian Franklin Toker warned that Pittsburgh's future success may come "at the price of its own remarkable heritage. The old Pittsburgh had terrible economic disparities, but it forged itself by its great labor into one of the most distinctive of world cities. It was a production center, and production (unlike services or the information industry) is tied to a place. The old Pittsburgh *was* a place, and it showed its confidence of place in a hundred ways, including its food, its speech, and its architecture. Whether the new Pittsburgh will be so distinctive is not yet clear."[38]

"We made some horrible mistakes," said Stanley Lowe, who once demolished his own neighborhood in order to preserve it. "The tragedy about it is that we made so many monumental mistakes, people don't even know we made them, because they don't have any memories of what was here to evaluate the mistakes we made.

"We have so little left to protect. I'm doing this because I have a sense of duty to protect the community. Others may not feel the same way when I'm gone, but I hope we will have protected enough of the fabric that people will be just as offended as I am when others stand up and say, 'Tear it down.'

"There was a time when I didn't understand that, but now I understand why. What we have is irreplaceable. When you tear a building down, you must be absolutely sure. There must be no doubt. You must be unequivocal that you are doing the correct thing. Because when you tear down the buildings, you're tearing down the neighborhood, and they don't come back as fast as they disappear."

■　■　■

Neighborhood preservation has always been a grassroots activity, whether in Charleston's Battery and the French Quarter in the 1930s, Philadelphia's Society Hill and College Hill in Providence in the 1950s, or Pittsburgh's Manchester and South Side in the 1990s. If the neighborhood preservation movement has changed significantly over those decades, it has certainly become more democratic, evolving from a former focus on districts inhabited solely by elites to places home to a broader spectrum of society.

Some of the most encouraging instances of neighborhood preservation today are occurring in historically African American neighborhoods, the kind of places written off for decades by mortgage lenders and urban renewal policies. Huguenin Heights, a racially mixed six-block area of 80 homes in Macon, Georgia, is being restored by the Macon Heritage Foundation, with assistance from the Community Partners initiative of the National Trust for Historic Preservation. Similar projects are taking place in the Farish Street district in Jackson, Mississippi, and Atlanta's Sweet Auburn neighborhood, the home of Martin Luther King Jr., where a community-based nonprofit group, the Historic District Development Corporation, is rehabilitating existing homes and constructing new ones on vacant lots. Ransom Place, the oldest black neighborhood in Indianapolis, a small district of some four dozen houses on six blocks, was rehabilitated by committed residents and inspired the formation of the National Association for African American Heritage Preservation to promote the recognition of historically black communities in other cities. Betts-Longworth in the west end of Cincinnati, a neighborhood ripped apart by decades of urban renewal schemes, was "on the verge of demolition" as recently as 1987, until the last remaining residents prodded the city to help patch up the historic district.[39] In 1993, Peak's Suburban and Tenth Street, two historic neighborhoods in Dallas, along with six others in the city, were threatened with demolition plans. Resistance from community groups and preservationists led the city to create a package of incentives to encourage rehabilitation of homes there, promoted by the advocacy group Preservation Dallas. Similar work is carried out by the Cleveland Restoration Society, the Providence Preservation Society, and local preservation groups in every region of the country.

Thousands of neighborhoods are in dire need of such visionary, energetic leadership. According to the Committee for Economic Development, a business-funded research organization in New York, "one-third of the neighborhoods in the nation's 100 largest cities are either distressed or on the brink of falling into distress. About 17 million people live in those neighborhoods."[40] Clearly, preservation-related revitalization strategies cannot save all of them. Yet, community after community is proving that reinvestment in the historic built environment offers some of the best hope for improving a community's self-image, increasing civic activism, luring new residents to replace the ones who have left, and bolstering long-term neighborhood stability. As author Winifred Gallagher has stated, "Part of the tragedy of the cities isn't that no one knows what to do about them, but that we know some things that could help yet haven't done them."[41] Environmental psychologist

Ralph Taylor, a professor of criminal justice at Temple University in Philadelphia and author of *Human Territorial Functioning,* has said, "If I could do one thing to improve urban life, I'd rehab all the vacant housing."[42]

To be successful, neighborhood preservation efforts require self-motivated residents, money, and institutionalized leadership with the expertise to do the job. Declining neighborhoods are ones that have lacked those ingredients for success. As Ronald Grzywinski, founder of Chicago's Shorebank Corporation, told writer Rochelle L. Stanfield, "If this country is ever going to get serious about rebuilding neighborhoods for the benefit of the people who are there, we've got to create self-sustaining institutions that can play long-term."[43]

To help fulfill this need, the Ford Foundation created the nonprofit Local Initiatives Support Corporation in 1979. Over the last two decades, LISC has dispensed technical advice to foster community development corporations in neighborhoods throughout the country, along with $2 billion in grants, loans, and equity raised from 1,500 corporations and other foundations, most of which has funded the rehabilitation or construction of sixty-four thousand homes nationwide. "People who don't experience cities firsthand only know about the mayhem on the local late-night TV news, but there are positive things going on. There is an increasing roster of neighborhood turnaround stories," said Paul Grogan, LISC's CEO since 1986.

Success begins, Grogan said, when "residents take responsibility" for their surroundings, instead of simply waiting for government to do it all. "Many groups start out fixing one house, or just a few," he said, "yet, generating victories one at a time is the way to begin to turn the tide." Every small success builds confidence, and confidence is what gives people the courage to climb one step higher.

Such efforts have a better chance of succeeding today than in the past, Grogan said, because of webs of support formed relatively recently by foundations, banks, and city halls. "Years ago, most mayors hated the idea of community development corporations," said Grogan, who managed neighborhood redevelopment for the city of Boston in the 1980s after the traumatic era of urban renewal. "They felt that strong neighborhood groups were trouble. But that's changed." In a time when federal money for cities has slowed to a trickle, strong neighborhood groups are viewed less as obstructionists blocking federally funded urban renewal projects and more as necessary partners in urban revitalization strategies that begin from the grass roots up.

Limited public funding, moreover, has forced local organizations to hunt for private sources of investment, bringing a market sensibility and private sector discipline to public and nonprofit efforts. "When something involves nothing but public money, it's very hard to discipline the process," Grogan said. At the same time, however, where there is no public investment, there is often no leverage to discipline the marketplace or attract private capital to places that need it desperately. The core of LISC's mission, as Grogan described it, is to put private capital to work to "break down the isolation of places where the mainstream private sector has all but disappeared." The mission is being fulfilled, Grogan insists. Investors have realized profits from neighborhood housing efforts. Retailers have begun to discover the purchasing power of consumers in underserved urban markets. And "banks are dying to get good loans," he said. Thanks to tools such as the Community Reinvestment Act, he said, "there has been a credit revolution in the inner city—responsible for meteoric rises in black and Hispanic home ownership rates." He acknowledged that the community investment records of banks and insurance companies still leave room for improvement. But the important fact to realize, he said, is that "we have come a long way from the days of massive redlining."

"This process has grown up organically, house by house, block by block, beneath the radar screen," he said. "It's very hard for us to track these things that are very important to society. But, on the other hand, that's an advantage."

Grogan claimed that the many efforts of the Great Society failed not just because of too much public money, but also because expectations of success were set unreasonably high, leading to a "pessimism that government can't do anything right." Success stories, however, are what change perceptions of what can be achieved. And Americans have yet to hear enough of the success stories. As Grogan explained, "Our greatest problem today stems from a lack of confidence as much as a lack of money."

In Pittsburgh, New Orleans, and places like them, preservation has become less an end in itself and more a tool of neighborhood regeneration, a way of attracting investment, energy, and affection to places whose futures would be in doubt without it. It is not the work of preservationists acting alone but of preservationists working in tandem with community development corporations, public offices, private lenders, real estate agencies, and others toward a variety of goals: community stabilization, the creation of affordable housing, and local economic development.

In all of these cities, preservationists have learned that the preservation of a neighborhood is about more than the preservation of its buildings. It is about the preservation of people in a place, the preservation of community, the preservation of places that people are proud to call their homes. When preservationists say that a particular place matters, they are also saying something just as important—that its people matter, too.

5

THE REVIVAL OF MAIN STREET

This old town was built by hand
In the dustbowl of the Mother Land
There must be rock beneath this sand
Oh, I'll be damned
This town still stands.

—Janis Ian and Jon Vezner, "This Old Town"

There is a scene in Frank Capra's 1946 film, *It's a Wonderful Life,* in which the fictional town of Bedford Falls goes to hell in a hurry. George Bailey, president of the local building and loan played by Jimmy Stewart, desperately wants to escape "this measly crummy old town" in order to "build things, plan modern cities" and "travel the world." When depression drives him to the brink of suicide on Christmas Eve, Bailey, like Scrooge in *A Christmas Carol,* is shocked into his senses by a nightmare vision of his community's future without him: Main Street has become mean street; family gathering spots have given way to gin mills; all the buildings have become the property of a greedy, tyrannical landlord who calls townspeople "suckers"; sidewalks have become empty, dark, and scary at night, filled only with the occasional bum begging for a drink. Viewing the film inside their downtown theaters in 1946, few moviegoers could have anticipated how this fictional scenario would play itself out in their own hometowns for real.

At the end of World War II, Main Street was the unrivaled center of retail trade and the cultural heart of small-town communities. Main Street held the heritage of previous generations in all its historic buildings and accumulated public investments in such things as sidewalks and streetlamps. It was the seat of local government as well as the public meeting ground for casual conversations or formal gatherings, the place to hold a holiday parade or an annual local festival. Main Street was the place to shop, to conduct business, to entertain, and to trade local news, if not in the town's theater or restaurants, then simply on a park bench, at the lunch counter or soda fountain, in the barbershop or beauty parlor. People were plentiful on Main Street, in part because many of them lived nearby, if not around the corner on a leafy residential street, then above a store or an office in an affordable apartment upstairs, within walking distance of everything in town. Main Street was inhabited at all hours of the day. In only a few decades, however, the means of mutual support broke down and dissolved.

The American landscape is littered with ghost towns in places where local economies have vanished: an old mining town in Montana, a farming town in North Dakota, or a coal town in Kentucky. Unable to diversify their economies and find ways for residents to stay employed, places withered away, leaving only skeletons of buildings behind. But even places that managed to sustain the health of their economies had trouble sustaining the health of Main Street in the face of evolutionary changes in transportation. In 1945, the average trade area of an American small town was about fifteen miles, because residents of a town were unwilling to travel much farther than fifteen miles for routine shopping. After Americans gave up the saddle for the car seat and traded in the horse-drawn wagon for the pickup truck, the average trade area stretched beyond fifty miles, a huge difference with significant implications for Main Street business districts.

Throughout history, businesses have clustered at the intersections, regardless of the transportation used. The stagecoach made the crossroads tavern a necessity. Tall ships gave rise to port towns. Steamboats gave birth to river cities. Large cities sprang up at the busiest railroad junctions. Urban business districts grew up along the trolley lines. Small towns evolved from rows of buildings around a depot. In small-town America, Main Streets were *the main street* because they were the most efficient places for distributing goods and services. But the interstate highways changed all that. Main Streets lost their monopoly on traffic to new roads on the edge of town, built so truckers and other long-distance travelers could avoid the inconvenience of downtown congestion, its parked cars and pedestrians in the crosswalks.

Development that followed the traffic bypassed the downtown economy, too. Grocers were among the first downtown merchants to desert Main Street business districts for large tracts of cheap land along the highways. More spacious sites allowed grocery stores to stock greater inventories for growing families who carted goods home in the car. Other businesses, dependent on the traffic generated by grocery shopping, soon followed. Downtown's business mix was dissected and scattered across the strips, closer to the new, government-financed subdivisions where consumers lived.

Adopting new building and zoning codes after the war, some towns actually pushed residents out of downtown when they outlawed apartments in the upper stories of downtown commercial buildings. The stated rationale was to protect tenants from fires or other imagined dangers, but the real reason was the narrow mind-set of single-use zoning applied retroactively to traditional mixed-use districts. Deprived of income from residential tenants, downtown landlords found it harder to maintain their structures. As buildings began to look more shabby, the exodus of high-paying tenants accelerated. Doctors, dentists, and other professionals who kept offices on Main Street moved to new buildings closer to new residential areas. Factories left their old brick mills by the river for suburban industrial parks. Post offices abandoned town for more efficient space. Even county governments, with a great stake in the health of their county seats, left local Main Streets, shifting offices and employees to new suburban facilities modeled after stand-alone corporate campuses. Back downtown, building codes and lending criteria written for new suburban structures discouraged the conversion of familiar landmarks to other uses. Within a few decades, downtown became a stomping ground for herds of white elephant buildings like vacant department stores and abandoned railroad hotels. Main Street theaters lost moviegoers to the drive-ins and television, which, along with air-conditioning, kept more people inside their homes.

The new intersections of travel, meanwhile, gave rise to the roadside retail center. At the end of World War II, America had only 8 suburban shopping centers. In 1950, there were 100. By 1960, the number had climbed to 3,000. By 1985, there were 22,000 more, responsible for half of all retail sales in America. In 1992, when the Mall of America, America's largest, opened in Bloomington, Minnesota, there were nearly 40,000 shopping centers throughout the country, 1,835 of them regional shopping malls.[1] Mobile consumers expected familiarity wherever they went, and national chains responded to the challenge. Careful research and savvy marketing by the retail giants allowed them to capture the bulk of retail sales, aided by downtown merchants who were slow to respond to changing trends.

Still, many merchants on Main Street clung to their old hours—Monday through Friday, nine to five—indifferent to the inconvenience to the growing number of women in the workplace. Many Main Street retailers, who had never faced competition within their trade area before, never mastered the basics of good marketing and merchandising. Instead of attracting shoppers with enticing window displays, their storefronts showcased mannequins adorned with clothes long out of fashion bleaching in the midday sun, failing to lure potential customers. New shopping centers commanded high rents and the fastest-growing businesses. Low rents on Main Street attracted marginal enterprises, thrift stores and fly-by-night vendors. Main Street's bargain-basement atmosphere only repelled customers even more.

In spite of the low prices in low-end stores, Main Street could not compete with the real bargains offered by the discount retailers and wholesale warehouse clubs that offered a wider variety of goods at the lowest possible price. In 1962, a merchant who spotted the weakness of retailers on small-town Main Streets as well as the strength of discount department store chains opened his first store in Rogers, Arkansas. The entrepreneur, Sam Walton, named it Wal-Mart Discount City. Walton's concept was so successful that by 1990, he had become America's largest retailer. A few years after his death in 1992, the Wal-Mart chain had captured nearly 15 percent of the nation's sales of "department store type merchandise," outselling every corporation in America but General Motors, Ford, and Exxon. The mission of Wal-Mart stores and others like them (Kmart and Target also opened in 1962) is to compete on prices, keep costs low, sell goods quickly, and make high profits for stockholders who live elsewhere. For shoppers, they're a bargain. But some communities get more than they bargained for when the efficient distribution of inexpensive goods carries a price tag unnoticed at the checkout counter.

Iowa State University economist Kenneth Stone discovered that five years after a Wal-Mart store opened in Iowa, neighboring communities of under five thousand people within a twenty-mile radius of the store typically saw a "cumulative net sales reduction of 25.4 percent."[2] Ten years after Wal-Mart entered the state, Stone found, half of Iowa's men's and boy's apparel stores had folded, along with 37 percent of Iowa's hardware stores.[3] The weak stores couldn't compete. Some people who shed tears for the lost businesses probably would not have shopped at them anyway, but the loss of so many local businesses over so short a time also amounts to the loss of local economies and local culture, conditions that affect everyone in a community. When retail chains expand faster than a community's ability to absorb new sales, the local retail market's center of gravity shifts away from Main Street to a commercial strip on the edge of town. As business downtown drops off, stores and offices close or relocate. Facing a loss of rental income, property owners cut back on maintenance. Facing a loss of tax revenues, local governments cut back on services. Facing diminished services, people stay away. When the business leadership leaves downtown, civic leadership follows, and a community crumbles.

One businessman in Iowa said that the millions of dollars deposited in a local bank by a national retail outlet "aren't there long enough to smoke the floors" before they are whisked away to a corporate headquarters in another state. That is money that never circulates through the local economy, money that is never loaned to local residents and business owners to improve their properties, money that never filters down to local charities and civic causes, money that never buys advertising in local newspapers, often the only forum for debating and solving local problems. According to analysts, a locally owned store in a locally owned building typically reinvests 85 percent of its profits in the local economy, but a typical fast-food franchise reinvests only 20 percent of its profits in the local economy.[4] In 1992, presidential candidate Ross Perot warned that the North American Free Trade Agreement would cause a "giant sucking sound"—the loss of American jobs pulled across the border into Mexico. In many of America's smaller towns, the sound you hear is that of local profits siphoned off to faraway corporate headquarters in the United States, like the one in Bentonville, Arkansas, where, according to a 1995 estimate by *Forbes* magazine, Wal-Mart's founding family has amassed a fortune in excess of $21 billion.

The marketplace allows each of us to shop where we choose, but the market is distorted when choices are denied or overruled. During more humble days for his chain, Sam Walton reportedly said, "If some community, for whatever reason, doesn't want us in there, we aren't interested in going in and creating a fuss." Having abandoned that philosophy, Walton's successors have used their company's size to elbow their way into small communities that refuse to welcome them. When Independence, Iowa, objected to the retailer's plans to build in their hometown, the chain threatened to build in a neighboring community and siphon local sales away. The opposition caved. In time, the two-block local Main Street became pocked with empty buildings, and Independence, Iowa, in effect, lost its independence. The same fate befell Rockport, Texas, Hamilton, Alabama, and countless other towns like them. Donaldsonville, Louisiana, a town of seven thousand between New Orleans and Baton Rouge, has effectively closed, having lost scores of locally owned businesses after a national discount chain came to town. As businesses closed, as shopkeepers lost their wages and the purchasing power of Donaldsonville's consumers fell, the retail chain eventually sold its building to local buyers and then abandoned it, leaving shoppers in Donaldsonville little choice but to drive thirty minutes away to shop at the next outlet in the same discount chain that deserted their town. With its Main Street gone and the discount department store departed, Donaldsonville has the dubious distinction of having died twice. Hearne, a Texas town of five thousand roughly fifty miles southeast of Waco, suffered a similar fate.

"We remain mystified that community after community considers it a more significant victory to entice a new discount superstore or shopping mall inside its boundaries than to rebuild the vibrance of its historic center," said Kennedy Smith, who has traveled to 1,500 communities in all fifty states as head of the National Trust for Historic Preservation's Main Street Center.

"Very few municipal planning offices have any idea how much commercial space is supportable in their communities," she said. As a result, they "have failed to balance new commercial development with their capacity to support new commercial development."

The retail building binge has left too many stores with too few shoppers coming through their doors, driving profit margins down while encouraging strong chains to expand in an attempt to beat the competition. From 1974 to 1985, the amount of retail space in America grew by 80 percent, far outpacing the growth in personal income adjusted for inflation.[5] In the 1980s, when retail sales inched up only 7.4 percent, retail space grew by a whopping 40 percent.[6] Though metropolitan Dallas in 1996 had 39 percent more retail space per person than the national average, the Nordstrom department store chain that year became the eleventh one in town. Explaining the mission of the retailer, Daniel Nordstrom, one of six copresidents of the Seattle-based company, said, "All you are doing is going after market share from other stores."[7]

In 1996, King of Prussia, Pennsylvania, in suburban Philadelphia, became home to the largest "super regional" mall on the East Coast. With 9 anchor department stores, 450 smaller stores, and parking for thirteen thousand vehicles at a time, one prognosticator said the 2.8-million-square-foot plaza "will make the standard three-anchor regional mall look like a mom-and-pop trading post."[8] Sales at the mall are expected to double and approach $1 billion a year by the turn of the century. Unless disposable income in the region rises just as quickly, sales elsewhere in the region will drop. Though the retail marketplace is saturated in location after location, the construction of new shopping centers continues unabated. "It's Darwin's theory," said Mark Schoifet, spokesman for the International Council of Shopping Centers. "The strong will get stronger and the weak will have to find a way to survive."[9]

While shoppers are exposed to more plentiful choices, communities are littered with the by-products of retail competition. Communities confront not only empty downtown Main Streets, but also boarded-up first-generation shopping centers, the new suburban slums. With nearly 5 billion square feet of retail space, the United States has more than 19 square feet for every American, up from 4 square feet in 1960. Half a billion of that sits empty, the equivalent of more than four thousand abandoned shopping centers or "dead malls." If retail construction were to come to a halt, analysts predict that it would still take Americans decades to fill all the space that exists already.

Still, towns are willing to add more space at almost any cost. In Darien, Georgia, an outlet mall developer received an abatement on all property taxes for thirteen years, costing a community of fewer than two thousand people approximately $250,000 in annual tax revenues. In Terrell, Texas, a developer told the town, "I don't care how you get the money, but this is what we need from you to make this a viable site." In response, the town gave him nearly $3 million worth of incentives: all utilities and water and sewer lines to and through the site, a mile-long, four-lane road through the project, a traffic signal, and $125,000 annually to market the site for seven years. Some developers show real innovation in getting government to pay for their projects. In Vicksburg, Mississippi, a developer of an outlying mall placed the main drive in the center of the project, then dedicated it back as a city street so the city will pay to maintain it. The developer then asked the state to construct a frontage road connection worth $1.5 million. These people know a good thing when they see it. The head of one development firm boasted, "Inducement packages are a significant part of the development of every one of our centers, averaging well into seven figures per project." This particular developer's portfolio includes seventeen retail outlet centers across the country. He estimated his company has received "a total of fifty million dollars of inducements" from local, county, and state governments. Historic downtowns don't automatically dissolve into sprawl—taxpayers actually *pay* developers to do the job.

"Of all the lessons we have learned in the Main Street Center's first fifteen years," said Smith, "none is more compelling than the urgent need to shift the American community-development paradigm from one of unquestioned growth to one of sustainability and conservation. Our local governments are crumbling under the crippling fiscal burden of supporting superfluous commercial development, while existing commercial buildings—our historic downtowns—sit vacant and deteriorating."

More than in the past, communities now realize that they don't have to be shaped by chance, by the whims of chain-store representatives or out-of-town developers. They are learning that communities can be shaped by choice, and they are choosing what they want their communities to be. The people of Westford, a town of 17,500 in northeastern Massachusetts, just said no to Wal-Mart. In the historic village of East Aurora, in upstate New York, citizens ousted local officials in an election and replaced them with new leaders who refused to cave in to superstore intimidation, who refused to fall for sprawl's illusory promises of job gains, tax revenues, and bargain prices without any detrimental costs to East Aurora's existing businesses, jobs, and tax base. In 1994, the Vermont Environmental Board denied a national discount retailer permission to build a one-hundred-thousand-square-foot outlet in St. Alban's, a town of 7,400 people. The board studied the proposal and found that it would create more retail space than the local trade area could absorb; it would cost taxpayers three dollars for every one dollar in public benefits; and it would cost the area's economy more jobs than the new store would produce. Similarly, in Illinois, DuPage County's planning department in 1991 tallied up the public costs of more commercial development and found that the costs outweighed the gains.

More and more communities have concluded that their future goes beyond numbers at the bottom line. Al Norman, who organized his neighbors to defeat a Wal-Mart store in Greenfield, Massachusetts, believes passionately that it does. Norman organizes citizens in other communities through a nationwide network of self-described Sprawl Busters. "There's one thing you can't buy at a Wal-mart," Norman says, "and that's small-town quality of life." Norman and his band of Sprawl Busters refuse to see themselves solely as consumers merely looking for the cheapest bargains. They see themselves as citizens responsible for the vitality of the places they call home. "Life is about more than cheap underwear," Norman says. John Bachman, managing principal of Edward Jones & Company, the financial services firm with more brokers and agents on local Main Streets than any other firm in the United States, has also challenged the notion that places should be shaped only by a marketplace mentality. Speaking to Main Street advocates in 1996, he said, "We have to decide if we want to be a nation of people based on transactions or relationships, a society of isolation or one based on community."

Because of people like Bachman and Norman, small cities and towns are becoming more careful when making choices that determine their own futures. Saying no to sprawl is one choice—an important choice—but not one that in itself is likely to revive a faded Main Street or bring a community together. Achieving those things requires other choices altogether.

■　■　■

In an era of abandoned shopping centers, it boggles the mind to recall that back in the 1960s and 1970s, traditional Main Streets tried to compete with strip malls by striving to look more like them. Merchants slapped highway-sized plastic signs on their two-story brick commercial buildings, as if those signs were necessary where street traffic flowed at fifteen miles an hour. To hide their historic storefronts from shoppers who preferred to spend their money in modern suburban stores, property owners covered grand old facades with slipcovers of aluminum siding and another short-lived improvement fad called Permastone. Taking cues from theme parks, some places dressed up their downtowns in silly costumes, the Wild West or Bavarian Village themes, ignoring their town's authentic history. Some communities closed off Main Street to auto traffic, forming pedestrian-only districts in a feeble attempt to mimic the malls, neglecting the traffic patterns that made Main Street viable. Countless places allowed convenience store chains, like 7-Eleven, to overwhelm pleasant sidewalks with asphalt parking lots and blank concrete block walls. In each of these instances, Main Streets strove to become suburban, to become anything but what they were, the traditional thoroughfares of America's towns. But changing how Main Street looked was no substitute for improving the business mix that was there. Too many downtowns still ignore this fact and seek salvation only through the quick and easy installation of park benches and colorful banners attached to lampposts, one of the latest beautification fads.

To help America's Main Streets compete against the forces eroding historic downtowns, Mary Means, then director of the Chicago office of the National Trust for Historic Preservation, launched a pilot program in 1977. The program was based on a belief that "big fix" renewal schemes typical of the 1970s, such as publicly sponsored pedestrian malls, did more harm than good. Such approaches often ignored the basic ways in which Main Streets have always worked, and they too often failed to rally business owners as full partners in the effort. Because every community is unique, the new program avoided a rigid, one-size-fits-all formula in favor of incremental improvements tailored to local needs. The testing grounds were three communities of different sizes; Galesburg, Illinois, Hot Springs, South Dakota, and Madison, Indiana. According to Kennedy Smith, the project's staff realized that in order to save historic downtown buildings, "the entire economy of the commercial district would have to be restructured. Buildings would have to be adapted for new economic uses. Merchants would need training and coaching. Promotional efforts would need to reposition the downtown in consumers' minds. Like the mall, the downtown needed a market strategy, an economic game plan."[10] Unlike the mall, the Main Street plan was based on "community self-determination and gradual transformation." The early promise of the program was helped by fortunate timing, coinciding with the creation of federal rehabilitation tax credits and Urban Development Action Grants, which demanded that public and private sectors work together on redevelopment projects. The eagerness of other communities to learn from the lessons of those three pilot programs—their successes as well as failures—led to the creation of the National Trust for Historic Preservation's Main Street Center in 1980.

Sixteen years later, the program has grown into a nationwide network of more than 1,200 participating Main Street communities in forty-three states. Working through statewide and citywide community development agencies or private organizations, the Main Street Center provides local teams of officials and business and civic leaders with the tools and technical assistance to revitalize their Main Street districts. The program is based on a four-part approach: the development of a strong organization to coordinate the effort and build local partnerships; the restructuring of the district's economy to fit consumer demand and develop new business niches in the market area; the rehabilitation of historic buildings and the district's physical environment; and promotional efforts to market local businesses and change public perceptions of the district as a whole. Over two decades, the Main Street program has helped communities of various sizes—from towns under five hundred people to cities over five hundred thousand—generate almost $6 billion in new investment in their downtowns. Across America, the program has helped attract 33,000 net new businesses, 115,000 net new jobs, and 34,000 historic building rehabilitation projects to downtown districts through the end of 1995. Main Street's success proves that lots of people prefer to spend money and time in traditional downtown environments when given desirable options. But the most remarkable aspect of the program may be its cost-effectiveness. For every dollar invested in a downtown by a local Main Street program, private and public sources on average invest another thirty. When counting only the dollars invested by local governments, the ratio is closer to sixty to one, making the Main Street program one of the most efficient local economic development tools in America today.

Communities join the Main Street Network because of a variety of threats to their downtowns. As we shall see in this chapter, places like tiny Bonaparte, Iowa, with fragile local economies desperately want to stave off imminent decline. Others, like Chippewa Falls, Wisconsin, face competition from large discount stores and suburban malls and seek to regain downtown's competitive edge. Some places that join the network, like Franklin, Tennessee, are once sleepy downtowns that suddenly find themselves in quickly growing locales. These places seek to steer new investment into downtown's historic buildings to preserve the local pride of place from being overwhelmed by sprawl. While the conditions and solutions in each locale may differ, the goal in every case is the same: to make downtown a better place.

■　■　■

Bonaparte, Iowa, population 465, has refused to die—not once, but several times throughout this century. Located in the southeastern corner of Iowa, on the banks of the Des Moines River, close to the Missouri border, Bonaparte grew up around a mill erected by William Meek in 1836. For years, Meek's Mill was the only grist mill for two hundred miles. When homesteaders in the region needed to grind large amounts of grain, they would pack up the wagon, make the long journey to Bonaparte, and remain in town for a week before heading home. Later in the century, railroads expanded Bonaparte's trade area and a new factory that manufactured men's pants brought additional income into the community from a thriving mail-order business. Growth in Bonaparte came to a halt in 1903, however, when a flood washed away the dam that powered the flour and woolen mills, putting the Meek brothers out of business. When a fire claimed fourteen buildings in the downtown that same year, it must have seemed as if Bonaparte would go out of business, too. Bonaparte hung on, however, even as more farm families disappeared each year and floods returned in 1947 and 1964. Manufacturing, a glove factory in particular, now employs more people than any other industry in town. Yet, by the time the farm crisis hit Iowa in the 1980s, Bonaparte's population had dwindled to barely a third of its turn-of-the-century peak.

Richard Critchfield, a journalist who traced the disappearance of rural communities in Iowa, reported, "Go around Iowa and you find old implement dealerships empty, hospitals just a third full. . . . Rural Iowa's one booming business is nursing homes; most have long waiting lists."[11] According to Iowa State University economist Kenneth Stone, towns under five thousand people in Iowa lost a third of their retail trade to larger neighboring towns in the years between 1979 and 1986. As a result, many local businesses went under, including nearly one-quarter of all grocery stores in the state and plenty of businesses in other categories such as hardware, clothing, and gas stations. "In Iowa, small towns don't die," wrote Critchfield. "Their Main Streets do."

Bonaparte's town clerk, Connie Meek, claimed that half of the incorporated towns in Iowa have populations under five hundred. "A lot of them are just dying," she said. The day of reckoning in Bonaparte came in 1986, when a "Going Out of Business" sign appeared in the window of White's Shopping Center, a longtime family-owned collection of small businesses in four adjacent downtown buildings: the town grocery, hardware, appliance, furniture, and clothing stores. The buildings dated from the late 1800s, and because they were contiguous, the owners had cut doors between them all, allowing shoppers to go from one store to another without having to go outside. The stores were quaint, but unable to compete with discount retailers in nearby Fairfield or shopping centers in Burlington, a city of twenty-seven thousand, thirty-five miles away.

Downtown Bonaparte at the time "was pretty ugly," Connie Meek recalled. "Very dismal," is how Gianna Barrow, the local postmaster, remembered it. "You didn't want to go to Bonaparte to shop in the stores," said resident Jacki Gunn. In White's Shopping Center, Gunn said, "you could see flames from the furnace in the basement through the holes in the floor." An old mannequin in a storefront window wore faded clothing of a style not popular since the 1950s. "The sidewalks were crumbling," Meek said. "And there must have been a sale on silver paint at some point in the past, because all of their buildings were painted silver," Barrow said.

Few fully fathomed the warning signals of decline until the day the "Going Out of Business" sign appeared. "Suddenly, people realized that Bonaparte's once bustling Main Street was starting to look like a ghost town," said Mike Gunn, vice president at a local plastics company, the town's largest employer.[12] The buildings were the focal point of Main Street, but they were in a poor state of repair. "It seemed inevitable that the buildings would be abandoned and torn down," he said. But it wasn't easy to let them go, because the buildings, "despite their shabbiness, still helped define the public face of Bonaparte." For many in town, he said, "the thought of losing these buildings altogether was unthinkable."

"What are we going to do with these buildings?" asked Steve Hainline, the operator of a service station across the street, when County Attorney Steve Reno pulled in for a fill-up. The two talked about forming a partnership to buy the buildings and recruited a friend, Bill Easter, who in turn brought in Mike Gunn. Each was willing to put up two thousand dollars as a down payment to buy the buildings. While negotiating the real estate transaction, they uncovered considerable support among their neighbors, so they called a town meeting one night to present their proposal, the creation of Township Stores, a community-owned corporation in which locals could invest up to two thousand dollars each. Over the next three weeks, fifty local investors came forward and Township Stores Inc. had raised one hundred thousand dollars in capital. Of those funds, forty thousand dollars went to buy the four buildings and sixty thousand was invested in building renovations. The first tenants were a small convenience-style grocery store, a hardware store, and a medical clinic, joined the following year by a law office and an insurance agency. But setbacks were encountered along the way. As cost overruns dried up the pool of money, Township Stores had to sell the second story above the grocery store as two condominiums. The grocery store tenant bailed out, but Township Stores, the landlord, took the struggling business over and turned it into a financial success. A historic theater acquired by Township Stores was converted into condominiums upstairs, with offices and a public meeting space on the ground floor. "All of the money invested in the buildings has come from local sources and all of the businesses serve local needs," Mike Gunn said. The greatest need, he said, was to give people "a quiet optimism about the future of this small Iowa town."

Like Bonaparte, small communities in rural areas far from metropolitan regions constantly face the challenge of how to sustain a local business through a change in ownership. Though a local business may be profitable and still serve critical local needs, such a business can disappear quickly if longtime owners don't cooperate with potential buyers or if potential buyers don't materialize. When a twenty-five-year-old café in downtown Atwood,

Illinois, population 1,200, closed in 1992, it was a serious blow to the community. Not only was the café one of few public places to eat, it was a downtown attraction, a traffic generator in this small central Illinois community about twenty miles east of Decatur. To save the café, a group of citizens banded together, twenty-two in all, and bought shares at $250 each, raising $60,000 to purchase the property. Some forty-seven volunteers gave 1,200 hours to the project. The café reopened and was sold to a single private owner two years later. By buying the business themselves, Atwood's citizens ensured a transition in ownership that might never have occurred if the restaurant had closed for good. Similarly, in Wooster, Ohio, when a large strip mall caused a 106-year-old family-owned downtown department store to hang a "For Sale" sign in its window, twenty local investors in this town of twenty-three thousand between Canton and Columbus bought the property, financed the renovation of the interior, and later leased it to a designer clothing store, the fortunate result of both concern for empty downtown real estate and confidence in the local retail marketplace.

In Bonaparte, the experience with Township Stores gave citizens more pride in their downtown and inspired them to have their historic five-block riverfront district, comprising thirty-nine structures in all, listed on the National Register of Historic Places in 1989. This made owners of commercial property in the district eligible for federal rehabilitation tax credits, an incentive to attract reinvestment in aging real estate. To further protect the downtown, Bonaparte created a historic district ordinance in 1990; and the town applied to join Iowa's statewide Main Street program, only to find that it was limited to towns of at least five thousand people. The size requirement drew communities large enough to hire full-time Main Street program staff. But Bonaparte's mayor, Rebecca Reynolds Knight, petitioned for a special small-town program, and Iowa created one. From 1986 through 1995, Bonaparte's property owners invested almost four hundred thousand dollars in the rehabilitation of thirty buildings and helped to create twenty new businesses, several business expansions, and thirty-one new jobs, a remarkable achievement given the town's small size.

Having won statewide recognition for its Main Street revitalization effort, Bonaparte's restoration achievements were severely damaged by the "hundred-year" flood of 1993. When the rains fell for days and the Des Moines River swelled, people waited and watched as water crept higher by the day. Volunteers sandbagged the Township Stores and stood ready to clean out the inventory on the shelves when the water got too high to hold back. Farmers, idled by water in their fields, donated their equipment to the effort. When the swollen river receded, water had damaged the structural integrity of downtown's historic buildings and had left all of them caked in mud. Noticing that old construction had fared the calamity better than new, Bonaparte's residents got a lesson in traditional building methods. Structures worst off were the ones with new oakwood floors and new basements lacking traditional ventilation. The older floors in town, built out of fir, remained intact. Recent generations had forgotten the old wisdom in their old buildings. "We found out after the flood why things were built the way they were," said Jacki Gunn. To fix the damage, this municipality with an average annual budget of $225,000 suddenly faced millions of dollars in repairs.

Bonaparte's participation in the Main Street Network and its listing in the National Register of Historic Places made the town eligible for unique forms of emergency assistance. The National Trust for Historic Preservation's disaster response office provided a grant that paid for architectural services to guide repairs to the historic district. The local district ordinance passed three years before came in handy when the owner of a flood-damaged corner building sought a demolition permit. The ordinance allowed the town to delay the demolition and give a potential buyer time to make an offer on the property, acquire it, and tap public flood-relief funds to help finance its stabilization.

Bonaparte faced yet another threat when a regional representative of the U.S. Postal Service decided to pull service out of the downtown post office, which had already survived at least three major floods since its construction in 1918. Bonaparte's postmaster, Gianna Barrow, appealed to her superiors to keep the mail service where it was. "When they built these buildings, they made them strong enough to withstand a flood," she said. But the postal service bureaucracy wanted a new building constructed on a concrete slab somewhere out of the flood zone. Barrow called supervisors in Des Moines and asked them to come see her building for themselves. After taking a look, the postal service kept operations where they had been all along and funded necessary repairs to the landmark structure, saving thousands of dollars that would have been spent on new construction and the waste of an existing building. "Even the post office is reinvesting in our downtown," Barrow said proudly.

After everything the town has been through, Bonaparte seems able to survive almost anything. "We just don't give up easily," said Connie Meek. Citizens, she said, "are coming to realize that historic preservation is important." Though downtown vacancies remain to be filled, Bonaparte has strengthened its confidence and pride. "We have our history, our historic buildings, and the river. That's what we got," Meek said. "So our buildings are important. We are proud to have a very pretty town."

About a hundred miles downriver from Bonaparte, Clarksville, Missouri, another historic community of fewer than five hundred people, has been rescued from the blight of downtown vacancies by local action. When citizens began their Main Street program in 1988, most commercial buildings in this town were boarded up. After local public investment triggered more investment from private sources, Clarksville has a viable commercial district, with sixteen new businesses and thirty-five new jobs. The vacancy rate for commercial structures has dropped from a high of 85 percent to the point where 75 percent of the buildings are now occupied. Since the program began, housing prices in Clarksville have tripled.

As in Bonaparte, Main Street communities throughout the country have also turned natural disasters into unnatural opportunities. When downtown Fort Bragg, California, was damaged by fire in 1987, the local Main Street program, with help from the community's lenders, businesses, and government, created incentives to encourage property owners to fix their buildings quickly. The community of 6,500 soon saw thirty-eight separate building rehabilitations and $1 million in local reinvestment. In Watsonville, California, after an earthquake shook downtown in 1989, merchants decided to carve out a niche in the regional marketplace by catering to 1.7 million Latino residents in and near the Santa Clara Valley. Consumer preferences of this large group were going unmet by conventional retailers. It took a natural disaster for Watsonville to realize the opportunity, but savvy ethnic niche marketing has brought new prosperity to this town of thirty-one thousand people.

"Any town has to figure out what its strengths are," said Bonaparte's Connie Meek. "You can't sit in City Hall and wait for things to happen. People in Des Moines aren't going to come to Bonaparte and say, 'We want to save your town.' You have to know what you want to do, seek out the help that's out there, and go to work."

■   ■   ■

"There's No Place Like This Place Anyplace" is the slogan of Chippewa Falls, a small city of thirteen thousand in northwestern Wisconsin. At first glance, Chippewa Falls appears to be a quintessential American Main Street town, with historic two- and three-story brick buildings lining both sides of Bridge Street, the main downtown commercial thoroughfare. Rather than coasting on its past, however, Chippewa Falls is a community that has organized itself to shape its future.

Originally settled by French Canadians in 1836, Chippewa Falls thrived as a frontier mill town, thanks to an abundance of white pine in Wisconsin's north woods and power from the Chippewa River. As the economy grew, the first settlers were joined by immigrants from Germany, Ireland, and Norway as well as pioneers from the eastern United States. After a fire cleared the town of its early wooden structures in 1869, downtown buildings were erected in brick and mortar. Of the 140 or so buildings downtown today, most along Bridge Street were built before 1911, when the last of the sawmills closed. "This was a booming town in the nineteenth century until they stripped the forest clear," explained Mayor Virginia Smith. With no more timber to cut into lumber, she said, "people started leaving and the city was losing businesses. They thought that was the end of Chippewa Falls, because after the mills closed, there was nothing here."

To avoid becoming a ghost town, business and civic leaders formed the Chippewa Falls Progressive League to promote a positive image, attract new industry, and make the transition from an economy based solely on logging to one based on manufacturing. "By golly, they got five shoe factories and a seven-million-dollar sugar beet industry, which was a lot in those days," Smith said. Today, all but one of the shoe factories are gone, and since the 1970s, manufacturing jobs have followed Cray Research, the locally based supercomputer producer, into industrial parks on the edge of town. Even the falls are gone, too, dammed years ago for electricity by the regional utility. Now, Chippewans are on another mission to revive their downtown economy.

The latest effort began in the late 1980s, when downtown retailers began to feel competition from new highway strip development, discount chain stores, and a regional shopping center in Eau Claire, a city of fifty-five thousand, fifteen minutes away. "We did not have an attractive downtown," said Kathy LaPlante, who worked at a department store on Bridge Street and later at the mall. "No one was taking good care of their buildings. Downtown interests were not organized to direct what was happening around us, and if we didn't address our downtown, there was no telling what would happen."

As a first step, the community spent twenty-five thousand dollars on a formal market analysis of area consumer spending and the health of downtown businesses. According to the research, "We were operating from a position of strength, but it was fragile," recalled city planner Jayson Smith (no relation to the mayor). Downtown Chippewa Falls was still intact. Only 8 percent of storefronts were vacant, and many of the businesses were locally owned establishments operated by families, such as Olson's, whose ice cream was known to lure travelers into town off the highway. Still, the district needed improvement and the market research showed significant unmet retail needs.

As Chippewa Falls formed a committee to come up with a downtown plan, the state of Wisconsin launched its statewide Main Street program and invited Chippewa Falls to join in 1988, the very first year. Though Jayson Smith was impressed by what he learned about Main Street, he urged the town to wait a year in order to build a strong local consensus for moving forward. "The Main Street lessons made sense to me," he said. "If you're going to preserve historic buildings, you just can't make museums out of them at the public's expense. You've got to make them economically viable." Chippewa Falls officials liked the fact that Main Street was a local self-help effort, coached and guided by statewide and nationwide expertise. But not every local official was as optimistic about Main Street as the city planner. Virginia Smith, a city councillor at the time, voted against it. "I have to admit, I was a skeptic. I said, 'Here's another government boondoggle that's going to require more city money.' I thought it'd never work.

"Downtown businesspeople are independent, and I didn't think you could get independent people to work together," she said. "Businesspeople called me and said they wanted no part of it. They said, 'We don't want a tax to re-build the downtown.' " But local Main Street advocates "were patient," she recalled. "They didn't force anything on people. They went to businesspeo-ple and said, 'This is what we'd like to do, and we'd like you to be a part of it.' " Jayson Smith described how he and his allies persuaded skeptics to come on board. "We began at the grass roots, started at the bottom, and worked our way up. We put together teams of people who would talk to mer-chants and property owners one-on-one. We had a very strong person-to-person campaign." The message? "You have to change with the marketplace if you're going to survive. You're not the only business in town anymore, so you've got to stop acting like the only business in town. That means you can't be mean to customers anymore. You might have to change your hours." To help persuade local business owners, the statewide Main Street staff came to Chippewa Falls to run an introductory training session and present slide shows of what had been done in other places.

Donovan Rypkema, a real estate and economic development consultant who works with the Main Street Center, asks community leaders to realize that "downtown is a business, and business needs management." Too few merchants on Main Street understand this basic fact and prefer instead to see their independence as their best competitive advantage. "There is no such thing as an independent business," Rypkema says. "The businesses downtown are *interdependent*." After hearing these kinds of arguments in the six-hour training session in Chippewa Falls, said Jayson Smith, "The skeptics walked out having gone from doubters to believers."

To fund the Main Street program, the city established a local Business Improvement District. The levy, $1.75 on every $1,000 of property value, is considerably lower than the statewide average of about $2.75, but it raises $36,000 a year, in addition to an annual city grant of $23,000, corporate con-tributions that total $40,000, and proceeds from fund-raising events. Kathy LaPlante, who had ten years of experience at a midwestern department store chain, was hired away from the mall in Eau Claire to become executive di-rector of the Main Street program. The local director is assisted by part-time staff, full-time volunteers, and countless others, including an active board of civic leaders. Over six years, Chippewa Falls Main Street has helped to attract eighty-nine new businesses and 621 new jobs downtown. Property owners have renovated 101 buildings and restored portions of 26 historic building exteriors. Private and public sources have invested more than $15 million in downtown properties and infrastructure, roughly $27 for every $1 spent by the Main Street program itself.

Downtown has also had its share of setbacks. A fire claimed half a block at the heart of Bridge Street in 1992. The following year, JCPenney abandoned its downtown store, and Spurgeon's, a regional department store chain, went bankrupt the year after that. The downtown also lost one of its three grocery stores, one of its two hardware stores, and two of five drugstores. "We actually had more variety of businesses before," confessed LaPlante. With the Main Street program in place, however, downtown was able to rebound from the closings quickly. The departure of some merchants created new openings for others. JCPenney's space was soon filled by a new outlet store opened by Mason Shoe, a local footwear manufacturer that relies mainly on catalog sales. The company is one of the oldest in Chippewa Falls, founded to supply boots to lumberjacks in the days of the sawmills. The volume of shoppers at Mason Shoe helped to entice a bookstore to move into space next door, away from its former location in a strip mall. By 1996, 95 percent of downtown storefronts were occupied. Some property owners collected rents up to three times the amount they received before the Main Street program began.

Chippewa Falls is gradually taking on the appearance of a healthy, vibrant downtown district. Many building improvement projects involve undoing alterations less than three decades old. "In the 1960s and 1970s, we saw a lot of aluminum siding go up on our historic buildings, and the stucco salesmen came through here, too, and convinced a lot of people that modernizing old buildings would help their businesses compete with the strip malls," said LaPlante. "Many of them also put up monster signage out front, which is fine for a commercial strip, but not here." As far back as 1964, the city ordered merchants to remove the garish signs that hung over Bridge Street's sidewalks. Thirty years later, Main Street encourages property owners to remove the false facades, offering financial incentives to those willing to restore their storefronts. Six community-based banks have committed a combined total of $400,000 dollars to a facade restoration loan fund, allowing Chippewa Falls Main Street to make loans of up to $50,000 for worthy projects. Bridge Street is regaining its prestige in small increments, allowing business tenants to keep pace with gradually rising rents.

LaPlante said that ten years ago, a visitor would have seen "a lot of uglier buildings, but we still have more of them than we'd like." In fact, at the gateway to the downtown district stands a structure labeled "ugliest building" at a past gathering of Main Street staff. The building was originally a stone-and-brick bank built in the classical form of a Grecian temple, until its ornamental details were chipped away and masked by protruding overhangs covered by a white stuccolike material. "As if that weren't bad enough, this building used to have fake evergreen trees stuck in its corners. They looked like giant toilet bowl brushes," LaPlante recalled. The remodeling job was the architectural equivalent of taking a classic three-button jacket from the 1920s and cutting it up for a 1970s leisure suit. Restoring the facade will not be as easy as changing a wardrobe.

"We haven't been good about keeping our historic places intact," said Mayor Virginia Smith. "My sister lives in Germany near a place with a city hall that's four hundred thirty years old. Here in the United States, we say, 'If it's old, let's tear it down.' But now, we've begun to say, 'Wait a minute, we have some interesting buildings downtown.' "

Because Chippewa Falls has no formal regulations to guide alterations to building exteriors in the historic district, compliance with design guidelines is strictly voluntary. That kind of flexibility means that results can be uneven. In an effort to do his part for Main Street, for example, one well-intentioned property owner "fixed" his aging sandstone storefront by painting it white—only to learn that sandstone doesn't hold paint for long. After the paint job, the storefront became more of a maintenance headache than before.

Alicia Goerhing, coordinator of Wisconsin's statewide Main Street office, called the restoration of historic buildings the most frustrating issue she faced when she served as a local Main Street program manager. Property owners need freedom to do things on their own, she said, "but if you don't guide them, two years later they'll realize what they did was wrong and get mad at you for not helping them get it right the first time." Because most small business owners lack expertise in property maintenance and restoration, "the process takes a tremendous amount of hand-holding from beginning to end," Goerhing said. The key is to make property owners feel comfortable enough to seek help when they need it. The Main Street program in Sheboygan Falls, in eastern Wisconsin, has helped property owners restore historic buildings to high standards in part because of the influence of a talented local architect affiliated with the program. Wisconsin's statewide program has a full-time staff architect who travels to participating towns, offers free technical advice on the spot, and even helps draw up rehabilitation plans. Like the building rehabilitation projects in Chippewa Falls, most of the work involves undoing past renovations. Goerhing noted how towns that never had altered their historic structures now find themselves further ahead. As an example, she pointed to Sharon, a town of 1,200 on Wisconsin's border with Illinois, roughly equidistant from Madison, Milwaukee, and Chicago. Sharon's downtown is full of

Modern office towers and urban flight transformed historic Main Street, Memphis, into a row of vacant buildings. Signs of vitality return in 1995. The sign at lower left says it all: SOMETHING GREAT IS GOING UP DOWNTOWN. (*Carter Wilkie*)

Over the last three decades, Pittsburgh's Manchester Citizens' Corporation has rebuilt pride and hope in a historic neighborhood that was down and out when the group began. (*Pittsburgh History and Landmarks Foundation*)

Tiny Bonaparte, Iowa, was in danger of becoming a ghost town when longtime business owners decided to close down. (*Photos of Bonaparte courtesy of The National Main Street Center of the National Trust for Historic Preservation*)

Taking responsibility for downtown's fate, citizens joined to purchase Bonaparte's threatened properties, including the Opera House, which was renovated into a community meeting hall and space for income-producing tenants.

This landmark at the gateway to Chippewa Falls, Wisconsin, was obscured by aluminum siding in an attempt to mimic the design of the modern strip mall. After the windows disappeared, the occupants did, too. (*Photos of Chippewa Falls courtesy of Metropolitan Building Project*)

ABOVE: Bricked-in windows were opened to their original proportions, which flooded the interior with light and improved the public's view of the building from the street.

ABOVE: Pride in downtown's history uncovered. A new owner begins removing alterations in 1995, revealing a century-old structure in need of restoration but still intact.

RIGHT: The owner plans to restore the original ground-level storefronts next, using rental income from tenants attracted to the renovated structure.

LEFT: Downtown Franklin, Tennessee, faded for years, prompting civic leaders to launch the local Main Street Program in 1984. (*Photos of Franklin courtesy of Downtown Franklin Association*)

RIGHT: Early twentieth-century structures along Franklin's Main Street held litttle magnetism in the age of interstate highways and regional shopping malls . . .

LEFT AND FACING PAGE, TOP: . . . until property owners, business leaders, and city hall reinvigorated Main Street as an appealing destination and a magnet for sidewalk traffic. Apartments above stores contribute to downtown's street life as well as its economy.

LEFT: Franklin's courthouse square, anchored by a monument to Confederate veterans, was enhanced by major public improvements to the streetscape beginning in 1991.

RIGHT: The square continues to serve as a focal point for public gatherings, including an annual summer festival that draws tens of thousands of visitors each year.

Neighbors in New Orleans help homeowners with repairs during an annual event dubbed "Christmas in October." (*Preservation Resource Center of New Orleans*)

Savvy investors, preservationists, and city officials turned warehouses in Lower Downtown into "LoDo," Denver's hottest historic district. Coors Field, a ballpark opened in 1995, graces the view down Wynkoop Street. (*Jim Lindberg*)

A visionary city government, a supportive foundation, and a community of artists revitalized Lowertown, a warehouse district in downtown St. Paul, Minnesota. (*John R. Murray*)

A farmer's market attracts weekend visitors to St. Paul's Lowertown historic district. (*John R. Murray*)

Pioneer Courthouse Square in Portland, Oregon, was once a parking lot. In 1984, it became the city's public "living room," with historic landmarks along the edges serving as its walls. (*Association for Portland Progress*)

Since the early 1970s, leaders in Portland have pursued policies that have helped to double the number of jobs downtown and protect the region's surrounding natural environment from unlimited urban sprawl. (*Association for Portland Progress*)

"turn-of-the-century buildings done in cream city brick," she said. "They never had enough money to remuddle their buildings, but now they don't need a lot of money to undo past mistakes."

The Chippewa Falls Main Street program has carefully avoided pushing historic district regulations until citizens become comfortable with the idea. "We're kind of conservative here," said City Planner Jayson Smith. "I personally believe that historic preservation is the approach to take to preserve the character and the heritage of your community, but we'd prefer to see it happen on a volunteer basis and build its own momentum until we reach the point when the downtown eventually comes to city hall and says, 'We think it's time to do this. We've got an investment in our downtown properties and now we want to protect it.' That's the only way it could get done in this community." LaPlante, the Main Street director, said property owners are motivated most by what their neighbors do. When one merchant restores a facade, others next door and across the street soon follow. "I don't think the loan pool is the only reason this is taking place," she said.

To encourage new business start-ups and expansions, a local commercial lender, Jerry Kuehl, came up with a novel idea to speed things along: an annual contest that awards five thousand dollars cash and a low-interest matching loan of twenty thousand dollars to the person who submits the best business plan. In 1995, the contest's first year, forty-seven people requested applications and four submitted plans. The winner was an Eau Claire telecommunications consultant who wanted to move his business to Chippewa Falls, rehabilitate a run-down nineteenth-century building on Bridge Street, and equip it with twenty-first-century technology: fiber-optic cables, videoconferencing equipment, wireless communications devices, and other telecommunications infrastructure.

Jayson Smith, the city planner, recalled that the building was owned by an elderly woman who couldn't keep it up. Tenants were fleeing; the building code inspector noticed serious violations. On the outside, the brick front was covered by a rectangular sheet of white aluminum, fifty feet tall by seventy-two feet wide, blocking second- and third-story windows. Original windows on the side of the building had been altered badly in a misguided attempt to save on heating bills. Inside, original walls dripped plaster chunks onto the floor. But the building was structurally sound and suffered no damage that couldn't be reversed. Ceilings on the second story were twelve feet high; ceilings on the third story were sixteen feet high. Behind the aluminum siding was light waiting to flood the interior. Underneath the linoleum floor was hardwood waiting to be buffed.

When Jeff Novak, the telecommunications consultant, saw the building for the first time, he could not believe the potential office space that was going wasted. He invested six hundred thousand dollars to purchase the property and restore it over the next five years. "You couldn't build a building like this today," Novak said while sitting in an office on the second floor. "I suppose I could have built something out in an industrial park for one-third what I'm spending on restoration here. But what would that building be worth in ten to fifteen years? This building is very well built. It's like an old Corvette. It's only going to get more valuable with age."

Novak said he was drawn to the traditional building because he didn't want his high-tech equipment to intimidate potential clients who come through the door. "The first time I stepped into this building, I felt like I was walking into a Dick Tracy movie," he said. He also didn't want his employees to experience the boredom he felt in suburban Milwaukee or Dallas. On Bridge Street, he said, they can walk out the front door to a coffee shop down the street without getting in their cars.

Ironically, one of Bridge Street's oldest buildings now houses the street's most cutting-edge industry. With technology lessening their isolation, more places like Chippewa Falls can participate in the information-age economy if their businesses equip themselves with the infrastructure, as Novak has done. "There are twenty-five different high-tech companies in Chippewa Falls, and they're not here because of Cray," Novak said. "They're here because Chippewa Falls is a nice place to live, a good place to raise kids, with a good sense of heritage." Novak said he was also drawn to the community by the eagerness of local officials to help a newcomer. "Most towns aren't like that," Novak claimed. "Too many of them are controlled by a good old boys club, and if you're not a member of the club, you don't get any help. Here, they just want to make this a better place." Goerhing described civic leaders in Chippewa Falls as "people who simply feel very strongly that downtown is the heart and soul of their community, and if downtown dies, the community dies."

The most impressive rehabilitation in Chippewa Falls so far is the conversion of an abandoned four-story brick shoe factory into apartments for low- and moderate-income tenants. For eighteen years, the building stood vacant, its windows smashed out and some of them filled in with concrete blocks. Though the owner was delinquent on county property taxes, the county would not assume ownership of the building because demolishing it would have cost more than two hundred thousand dollars. It was cheaper to let the structure stand there, and so it did, a terrible eyesore to anyone who drove through Chippewa Falls on State Highway 29. Efforts to put the vacant building to productive use had failed until 1992, when Warren Loveland, a Wisconsin entrepreneur with experience in rehabilitating historic structures, drove into town.

Loveland had come to Chippewa Falls wanting to see a former high school building, but the old school was already being converted into a performing arts center. When LaPlante took him by the old shoe factory instead, the developer was so impressed by its potential as housing that he bought an option on the building that day and soon structured a deal to convert the factory into apartments. Rehabilitation costs totaled nearly $2 million, covered by $942,000 in equity from investors, a $340,000 loan from a local bank, a $298,000 loan from a Community Development Block Grant, federal rehabilitation and low-income-housing tax credits, a $50,000 facade restoration loan from Chippewa Falls Main Street, and a thirty-year, no-interest loan of $198,000 from a tax increment financing district established by city hall, which froze local taxes on the property for thirty years. The financing was complicated, as was wading through state regulations that make it difficult to bring historic buildings into compliance with contemporary building codes. The city had to convince the state Department of Natural Resources to grant the project a waiver from restrictions on development in a floodplain, even redevelopment of buildings that existed before the rule. When the project was completed in 1994, every apartment was leased within five months of the opening. Two years later, a list of potential tenants waited to get in.

"Now, people say it was the right thing to do," said Mayor Smith, "but we were highly criticized for saving that building. It wasn't easy when people were questioning us, saying, 'Why are you spending that kind of money to fix that thing up?' But the building would have cost us more than two hundred thousand dollars just to demolish, and then where would we be? We'd have nothing there but another parking lot. As it stands now, that building is meeting some very important needs." In addition to providing thirty-two apartments in a town with a housing shortage, the building also pays thirty-eight thousand dollars a year in local taxes. "We're lucky to have residential areas right next to the downtown," she added. "That's what keeps the downtown alive."

In addition to hundreds of residents who live in neighborhoods within easy walking distance of the downtown district, 266 people live in downtown apartment buildings and another 100 live in apartments above stores or offices. The upstairs apartments provide constant pedestrian traffic on downtown sidewalks and lighted windows at night, giving downtown Chippewa Falls a feeling of being occupied and safe, instead of empty and dangerous. LaPlante said that seeing the new apartments in the old shoe factory makes her wonder how many potential apartments were lost forever when a historic woolen mill was torn down two years before the local Main Street program began.

In converting the vacant factory into housing, Chippewa Falls was lucky to solve the kind of vacancy that plagues downtowns for years. Many towns never do. Too many places fall into the trap of trying to solve their biggest vacancy first, becoming dispirited when they fail. They would get better returns from small, incremental improvements aimed at changing perceptions about a location. Results, not effort, are what catalyze more results over time. Alicia Goehring, Wisconsin's statewide Main Street director, explains why. Before coming to Wisconsin in 1988, Goehring was director of the local Main Street program in Burlington, Iowa, where the departure of a Woolworth department store emphasized the gaping holes in the downtown streetscape. Storefronts at the time were about 45 percent vacant. Goehring remembers some people saying, "If we can just get something in the Woolworth building, everything else will fall into place." But only after the little pieces fall into place is a downtown likely to fill its biggest vacancy. As Goehring said, "People don't take big risks in a downtown that hasn't seen investment in years."

To reinforce improvements and bring further activity to downtown Chippewa Falls, city officials had to wage a battle with county officers who wanted to invest millions in a new county building somewhere outside of town. County officials wanted a site that would reinforce their separation from the local jurisdiction. Chippewa Falls wanted downtown integration. Common sense prevailed. A 1994 expansion of the existing downtown county courthouse brought an extra 125 employees into the district on a daily basis. The town also saved an endangered historic mansion on the expansion site by giving new owners time to move it to a safe location.

After seven years of successful revitalization, Chippewa Falls in 1996 was hoping to attract, of all things, a retail department store. Though the last two department stores left Bridge Street in the previous decade, the city's regional market analysis showed strong unmet demand for women's and children's clothes. The city is hopeful a store will come forward, perhaps to occupy the site leveled by the 1991 fire that left a large hole in the heart of the downtown district. "We were criticized for buying that vacant lot, too," said Mayor Virginia Smith. "But we didn't want a gas station there. We didn't want fast food there." Whatever fills the highly visible spot will set the tone for all downtown development that follows, as critical an event to Bridge Street's character as the decision to build in brick after the fire in 1869.

Perhaps the greatest strength of the Chippewa Falls program is its promotional efforts, the ways in which it builds civic pride through public events and other forms of creative marketing. Six years ago, "there was nothing going on downtown," LaPlante said. "Now we have six events each year." Although LaPlante confessed that her town's slogan, "There's No Place Like This Place Anyplace," was "borrowed" from Seattle, what counts is that people are proud of what they have here. Walking down Bridge Street, LaPlante stopped in front of a four-story brick building and pointed to initials carved in decorative stone in its facade. "When schoolkids come downtown for a tour, we tell them to look up at the top of this building at the letters B.P.O.E. That stands for Benevolent Protective Order of Elks, but we tell them it stands for Best People on Earth."

Sometimes people need to be reminded. One local businessman who helps sponsor events downtown admitted that he never realized the unique appeal of his hometown until he went to a trade show in Chicago in 1991. "A lot of people came up to me and said, 'I just went through Chippewa Falls for the first time last year and you have a gorgeous city there,' " recalled Jake Leinenkugel, the fifth generation of his family to operate the brewery founded by his namesake, Jacob Leinenkugel, in 1867. "That really meant something to me, because I never really looked at Chippewa Falls that way, and I have been around for 40 years now."[13] The changes in the Leinenkugel family business have mirrored changes in small-town retailing. In the years following World War II, local breweries, like local retailers, suddenly faced giant competitors with greater distribution and lower costs. Small regional breweries that couldn't keep up were swallowed up. But Leinenkugel's held on long enough to enjoy a renaissance in consumer preference for quality over cost. Recent marketing research even found Chippewa Falls itself to be part of Leinenkugel's appeal. Customers identify the beer and its nineteenth-century brewery complex with a wholesome, friendly, small-town mystique, a refreshing alternative to the homogenized products from big-city breweries. Now the location itself is a headline attraction in company advertising: "Chippewa Falls, Home of Leinenkugel's Beer."

The question facing Leinenkugel's is the same one that faces Chippewa Falls: Is the fate of local business in the hands of local people or external forces beyond their control? Miller Brewing Company, owned by Philip Morris, bought the Leinenkugel Brewery in 1988, but retained the family management. Similarly, the largest local employer, Cray Research, has been sold by local owners to California-based Silicon Graphics and Johnson-Matthey, a British firm. And the state Department of Transportation, with local approval, has plans to build a highway bypass around downtown, which could very well invite a glut of retail space and undermine what people on Bridge Street are seeking to achieve.

"You can either direct the change in your downtown, or let change happen to you," warned Kathy LaPlante before leaving Chippewa Falls in 1996 to head the new statewide Main Street program in New Hampshire. If the past record of Chippewa Falls is any prelude of what's to come, Chippewans will weather the changes, regardless of what they may bring. They will adjust, adapt, and survive by keeping pace with the times, all without sacrificing their local heritage and pride of place.

■ ■ ■

Historic downtown Franklin, in the rolling hills of middle Tennessee, is so attractive it is hard to imagine the place has been anything but inviting ever since southerners built the imposing redbrick Greek Revival Williamson County Courthouse on Main Street here in 1858.

The courthouse is the public anchor of a classic southern courthouse square. A tall monument in the center honors Confederate soldiers who came to Franklin on November 30, 1864, intending to whip the Yankees before they got to Nashville, fifteen miles to the north. Instead the Confederates suffered seven thousand casualties, including the death of five generals and the wounding of seven more. Franklin paid for that defeat for a long time, for it took the local economy another 120 years to reach pre–Civil War strength. But the absence of a growing economy allowed the historic downtown to survive largely untouched and become Franklin's greatest community asset.

"Here in Franklin, we say we're fifteen miles and a hundred years down the road from Nashville," said Rudy Jordan, a founder and executive director of the Downtown Franklin Association. In truth, Franklin is not so much behind the times as it is ahead of them. The downtown has rebounded from decay to become one the most sought after day-trip destinations in the South, a model of success for places trying to keep their small-town character in high-growth locales.

In recent years wealth has returned to Williamson County, mostly due to Nashville's suburban expansion. "We are not a quickly growing community, we are an *explosively* growing community," said Mark Willoughby, a local stockbroker and president of the downtown association. As Rudy Jordan explained, "We are the fastest-growing county in the state and we have the highest income of any county in Tennessee, which means the development pressures are incredible." Since 1980, the population of Franklin has more than doubled, from 12,400 in 1980 to an estimated 27,700 in 1995. Over the same period, the county grew from 58,000 residents to over 100,000. As the Nashville metropolitan area has expanded, Franklin, a formerly rural county seat, has found itself the popular new home for affluent suburbanites, many of them newcomers from outside Tennessee. When General Motors built its Saturn plant in nearby Spring Hill in 1991, many of the company executives who came from Michigan moved to Franklin; recording-industry refugees from California and employees of Nashville's expanding health care industry have joined them. Country-and-western music stars have taken up residence on surrounding horse farms once owned by scions of Tennessee squires. "Our proximity to

Nashville has opened up a lot of opportunities for us," Jordan said. If there is anything remarkable about the influx of new money into Franklin, it is that a great deal of it has gone into reviving the historic downtown, instead of fueling the sprawl spreading across the suburban South like kudzu.

Anyone who saw Franklin two decades ago would be amazed to hear that downtown captured any new investment at all. When revitalization efforts began in the late 1970s, Jordan said, "downtown did not have much going for it. We had pool halls, thrift shops, and liquor stores. We even had a murder at a downtown café where a driver dragged the victim down the street under a car.

"We had broken sidewalks," Jordan said. "So many of the buildings flooded from time to time." Sidewalks were covered by a beat-up aluminum canopy that ran the length of the street. Historic storefronts were hidden behind aluminum siding. Some landlords were too lazy to take down signs that advertised businesses that had long since closed. "A building housing the Ben Franklin five-and-dime had burned. We had a lot of mysterious fires. We had so many discount shops and Going Out of Business signs. Main Street was really down and out."

Eager to pump new life into Main Street's deteriorating structures, Jordan and others began to look into local comeback strategies in 1978, a year after the National Trust for Historic Preservation launched its three pilot Main Street programs. "We piled people on buses and went to Charleston, to Savannah, to Madison, Indiana, and Louisville, wherever there was a preservation lesson to learn from," Jordan recalled. "We brought in experts to speak to us." Then they learned that experts were more willing to help if they paid them. "If you pay people to teach you, they will stick with you along the way," said Jordan, who now gets calls from other downtown groups seeking her advice and counsel.

As an outgrowth of that early effort, the Downtown Franklin Association was born in 1984 to bring together merchants, property owners, public officials, and local volunteers. It wasn't easy, Jordan said. "Some of the merchants thought we were nuts—some still do. City hall was against us. The chamber of commerce thought we were trying to form another chamber of commerce." One of the skeptics was Catherine Whitley, a women's clothing store owner. "At the time, I thought Rudy was a little out of her mind when she started this," Whitley said. "I told her, 'There is no way I would ever be on Main Street with the pool halls and the derelicts.'" Jordan said it took time to win the confidence of the merchants and even more time to get them to work together. "The good news is they're independent and want to do things differently than the malls," she said. "The bad news is they're independent and want to do things differently than the mall." But downtown advocates organized them, and, as Whitely said, "Main Street was renovated little by little."

In little over a decade, Main Street's thrift stores and pool halls have given way to boutiques and galleries stocked with works by local artisans—stained glass, sculpture, jewelry, and pottery—as well as antiques, upscale women's clothing, and gourmet coffee. There are few chain outlets on Main Street, mostly local flavor, and there is even a historic downtown movie theater still in operation. Thousands of visitors come here each year simply to stroll down an inviting, vibrant Main Street, something they can't do at home. Many stop here as part of a weekend trip to Nashville. Others stop here on their way to Civil War battlefields, antebellum plantations, and house museums. Franklin also benefits from being near the Natchez Trace Parkway that runs from Nashville to Natchez, Mississippi, as well as the Antebellum Trail, a regional heritage area in middle Tennessee. The heritage area uses preservation as a device to stimulate economic development in small communities throughout the region. Franklin's downtown association has capitalized on the visitor traffic by hosting two annual regional events, an arts festival in May and a jazz festival in August, on top of a local festival during the Christmas shopping season. The three events attract well over a hundred thousand visitors downtown each year, generating profits that fund Franklin's Main Street program.

Franklin's program is a mature one. It has passed the "catalyst" and "growth" phases, in which coalitions are organized, goals are set, and major reinvestment occurs. It has reached the "management" phase, in which downtown is kept in top condition and promoted actively. Franklin even markets itself on the World Wide Web at the downtown association's Internet address.

"Everything had to be done by years of persuasion," Jordan said. To encourage property owners to restore historic properties, volunteers donated time to work on facade improvements. They took down aluminum siding, scraped peeling paint, and applied mortar between old bricks. Property owners followed in kind by removing ugly signs, restoring their facades, and improving window displays. The downtown association recruited a merchant with credibility at city hall to persuade public officials to fund improvements of the streetscape: new sidewalks, new streetlamps, new water and sewer systems under a new street, and a refurbished courthouse square. The city kicked in more than $1 million, supplemented by $300,000 from the state highway department and $400,000 from downtown property owners. While the work went on, Main Street looked like a war zone. "It was like being pregnant—nine months of pure hell, but the reward is so wonderful," Whitley said. The result of years of work is one of the most appealing Main

Streets in the South. Jordan feels proud of the achievement, but she also feels a little lucky. "A friend of mine said the aldermen never would have done it if they really knew what it was going to cost," she said.

"In 1956, I was a page on the floor of the United States Senate when Congress was debating the interstate highway system," said Calvin Layhew, one of the developers who put his money on Main Street. "That was a time when the big move was out to the highways, and downtown started to feel the effect of the stores moving out." Franklin, like so many other towns, developed a negative attitude about the old downtown and tried to cover it up with things like aluminum siding. "I was the head of the chamber of commerce when this negativism was going on. I said, 'We need to seize on our qualities and not try to compete with the malls on their terms.' " Layhew should have known. By then, he had become the successful developer of a strip mall built across from a frequently visited plantation museum nearby. "I preached the benefits of improving downtown and the value of attracting tourism, but it was falling on deaf ears." Discouraged by Franklin's lack of civic pride, Layhew moved to California to make money in real estate. "Then one day, I got a call from my buddies back in Tennessee. They said, 'We have a chance to buy a bunch of historic buildings in Franklin. Downtown is dead, and they're cheap.' " Downtown vacancies were running over 50 percent at the time, Layhew said. "So I came back, and we bought seven buildings for three hundred fifty thousand dollars." Layhew decided Main Street needed a restaurant, so he planned to build one and sought a liquor license after some gentle diplomacy with the local Baptist church and Church of Christ. But Layhew had a tougher time winning the approval of local lenders. "Bankers are always on the back side of the curve," he said. "They are very conservative, but I had a feeling this was going to work, so I went to some others and said I needed seven hundred fifty thousand dollars to put into these old buildings." Layhew amassed more than a million dollars in debt before the restaurant even opened, when one local bank, of which Layhew had been a director, decided to foreclose on his property, calling in a liquidator. "The president of the bank told me, 'Franklin will never develop as you envision. Your dreams for Franklin will never materialize.' " But Layhew would not let go so easily. He auctioned off his farm and used the money to finance the restaurant. The restaurant became a success as well as a magnet for pedestrian traffic on Main Street's sidewalks. "We put the farm up for sale, put that money downtown, and now I like it when that banker comes into the restaurant and has to wait for a table," Layhew gloated. His biggest reward, Layhew said, was the return of local pride, something he feels "when I go into the restaurant on a Friday night to have a drink, listen to some jazz, take a look around, and see that the place is full."

Investors like Layhew who took early risks in the old downtown have laughed all the way to the bank. First-floor rents, less than $1 per square foot before the Main Street program began, have risen gradually over the years to $12 per square foot. Fourteen upper floors have been converted to apartments, some of which rent for as much as $1,200 a month. In 1994, the 220 businesses in downtown Franklin generated more than $18 million in gross annual sales, an increase of 42 percent in ten years. Tax assessments have tripled and in some cases even quadrupled from levels a decade before. By 1995, the total value of downtown commercial property exceeded $75 million.

"Franklin is very much a classy, classic town," boasted Rudy Jordan. And it shows. The buildings are beautiful. The sidewalks are spotless. If this were not the South, a cynical visitor might wonder if it was a bit too precious. About the only thing Jordan apologizes for is the appearance of the parking lots. Clearly, only a town with an economy in such sound shape can be so meticulous about every detail. "We will not compromise on design," Jordan said. "If you compromise on design, you become Anytown, U.S.A."

Anyone who spends time in metropolitan Nashville realizes why Franklin is so protective of its authentic Main Street environment. That environment, rare in this realm of sprawl, is the town's competitive edge. This is no phony country-western theme park erected overnight. "Go for quality," Jordan advises other places considering a Main Street program. "Don't go for a fad or some cutesy theme."

Like Franklin, the town of Eureka, California, home to twenty-seven thousand on Humboldt Bay on the northern coast of California, has developed itself carefully. Eureka used to thrive on forestry and fishing. Now, it's diversifying its economy to attract the benefits of tourism. A six-hour drive from either San Francisco or Portland, Oregon, Eureka is blessed by the coastal scenery, surrounding redwood forests, and the highest concentration of artists per capita of any locality in California. To tap this unique asset, the city council in 1994 designated forty-nine blocks around Eureka's Main Street a "Cultural Arts Resource District." The following year, the council passed an ordinance and changed local zoning and building codes in the district to allow the conversion of second and third floors into studio spaces where artists could live and work. Developers found the working studios cheaper to create than conventional apartments, and landlords used the extra income to restore their historic structures. The new tenants have created an active, permanent presence of people downtown. From April through September each year, businesses in the arts district stay open late on the first Saturday night of each month to accommodate weekend visitors. Eureka has become popular enough to support some fifty restaurants in its downtown district and smart enough to receive nine hundred thousand dollars in federal funds to clean up the appearance of Highway 101, the commercial corridor that runs through town.

In Franklin, preservation of the community's historic assets has become such a local religion that all candidates for the city council in 1995 spoke of the importance of maintaining Franklin's distinctive environment. "We have protected and preserved the positive aspects of the downtown in a time of rapid change," said City Administrator Jay Johnson. "It was difficult getting there. But today, we have an extremely viable downtown less than three miles from the largest mall in Tennessee." The Cool Springs Galleria, with five anchor department stores and parking for over seven thousand vehicles, is so large that it attracts shoppers from as far away as Alabama and northern Georgia. When it opened in 1991, the mall added nearly three times as much shopping space to the trade area as downtown Franklin had accumulated in all of its two-hundred-year history. "Downtown merchants said it was going to ruin us," said Dara Aldrige, who became the local Main Street program manager in 1996. But downtown Franklin was already improved before the mall was built. By the time the mall opened, Main Street merchants were ready to compete. "I'm sure the mall has hurt some of the merchants a little bit," Aldrige said, "but in other ways it has helped us, and we cooperate with the mall's management." Catherine Whitley, the downtown women's clothing store owner, says her shop benefits from spillover customers who might not shop in Franklin were it not for the huge mall three miles away. "We have a lot of traffic from Alabama and Georgia. People come up just for the day to shop and then to see historic downtown Franklin," she said. The mall's management allowed signs to be posted on its access roads pointing shoppers in the direction of "Historic Downtown Franklin." During the holiday shopping season, the downtown association borrows trolley-style tour buses from a summer resort to shuttle shoppers between the mall and Main Street.

Similar cooperation between downtowns and malls has occurred elsewhere. In San Marcos, Texas, home of thirty-seven thousand in the high-growth corridor between Austin and San Antonio, trolley-style buses link the historic downtown shopping district to nearby outlet malls. By marketing its Mexican-influenced architecture and Texas-made products in local stores, San Marcos has watched its vacancy rate drop from 35 percent to less than 5 percent, while rents have risen five times.

The greatest change in downtown Franklin over the years, according to Nancy Conway, the longtime director of the local chamber of commerce, is the increased "density" of businesses on each block. That density and variety could never occur in a strip mall, where single-use zoning reigns supreme and too much ground space is surrendered to surface parking. Such a variety can only evolve in a traditional downtown environment. Here, traffic from one activity generates traffic for another and small spaces serve as incubators for small businesses that neither require nor can afford prime real estate.

The importance of mutually reinforcing activity is seldom fully understood. In 1990, the U.S. Postal Service announced intentions to abandon its facility in downtown Franklin for a new one on a highway. "Small towns all over America are losing their downtown post offices to these monoliths on the interstate," Jordan said. "It is a sad day when people can't walk to their post office downtown." But Franklin's citizens had invested too much in their downtown to give up their post office without a fight. They called their congressman. Elderly residents organized to keep it in place. The National Trust for Historic Preservation put the post office on its 1991 list of America's Eleven Most Endangered Historic Places. Downtown advocates managed to keep the building on Main Street thanks to federal regulations that prevent federal tax dollars from funding projects that damage sites on the National Register of Historic Places.

Franklin's citizens have realized that Main Street is more than just a commercial district. It is more than the province of independent merchants or property owners. "The downtown is the hub, the heart of the community that sets the tone for Franklin," said Mark Willoughby, president of the downtown association. His predecessor, John Hackney, has said, "Other small towns have seen their historic Main Streets wither on the vine in the face of competition from malls and strip developments, but Franklin's Main Street is alive and well. We like to think the economic vitality of downtown helps give our community a sense of place. A town with no Main Street is a town with no heart."

■ ■ ■

National retail specialists see new hope for historic downtown retail districts. For one thing, historic Main Streets can age gracefully while aging shopping malls can only lose the appeal they had when they were new. The malls' share of the retail marketplace is already shrinking in the face of new competition from discount stores, mail-order catalog sales, home shopping networks on television, and even sales over the Internet. The amount of time Americans spent in malls dropped by 75 percent during the 1980s, from an average twelve hours per month per person in 1980 to four hours in 1990.

Consumers looking for more convenient ways to shop are making more trips to stand-alone "big box" stores that offer large varieties of a single category of products, like toys, office supplies, or electronics, under one roof. Their high volume allows the stores to offer deep discounts that kill the competition; hence their name, "category killers."

Research also shows that malls are losing their appeal among shoppers in their early twenties. Perhaps the malls are becoming victims of marketing strategies devised to target narrow but affluent groups of consumers by filling retail space with the same chain stores offering the same merchandise and the same piped-in music from coast to coast. Tom Moriarity, a retail development consultant in Washington who managed one of the first three local Main Street programs two decades ago in Madison, Indiana, claimed that aging baby boomers and the generation born after 1964 are seeking less "staged" and more "authentic" shopping environments that hold a wider variety of tenants and merchandise. A group of downtown merchants in a major American city has taken advantage of this trend already by posting advertisements that show a female college student next to the headline, "You have your whole life to shop in the suburbs. But why dwell on the negative?"

Small retailers depend on pedestrian traffic for drop-in customers. Activity that generates pedestrian traffic ultimately generates sales. That's why small retailers thrive along busy walkways and in pedestrian-friendly environments, whether on Main Street or inside a climate-controlled shopping mall. But many suburban shopping centers are designed for auto traffic only, and they are hurt most of all by their lack of mixed uses that draw people for reasons other than shopping. One important trend in the retail industry is "coupling"—when a bookstore adds a café, or a gas station adds a mini fast-food franchise. On this ground, Main Street districts have a built-in competitive edge. A traditional mixed-use environment can accommodate a wider variety of pedestrian attractions than a roadside retail center.

New distribution methods have also opened up new opportunities for Main Street merchants, who are no longer limited by the tiny trade area of their towns. Auto travel and weekend tourism have expanded trade areas dramatically, as have the rise in mail-order shopping and Internet sales. The Wal-Mart chain grew phenomenally in the 1980s thanks to a distribution system that allowed the retailer to skip regional wholesale distributors and serve as its own "middleman." Wal-Mart's distribution technology even created a retail monopoly in some locations. But now, new distribution tools have trickled down into the hands of small specialty retailers. Thanks to devices like the Internet, the fax machine, and overnight delivery services, mom-and-pop operations in remote locations can market narrow categories of goods—everything from Vermont maple syrup to Virginia country hams to southwestern salsa—to specialized audiences of consumers throughout the country. Stores that rely solely on local business can still employ E-mail to remind customers of upcoming sales and other promotional events. Even local category killers may face heavy competition from distant category killers that use toll-free telephone numbers to take orders. In 1996, almost half of the communities in the nationwide Main Street network reported having businesses that use the Internet to reach new customers. That same year, *Forbes* magazine reported that the growth in sales at category killers was slipping.

The only thing certain about retailing in America is that it is constantly changing. It is unrealistic to expect traditional downtown retailers in limited market areas to compete with discount chains on comparison items. On the other hand, downtowns that provide consumers with convenient and appealing places to shop for wider varieties of specialized goods and services will not only survive but thrive.

Retail chains understand this already. To expand their share of the retail marketplace, "chains must grow or die," Moriarity said. Chains that fail will leave behind more vacant buildings and empty asphalt lots on the strips. The chains that succeed, Moriarity predicted, will be those that treat downtowns as the next retail frontier. Citizens who choose to accept national retailers into their towns will have increasing power to set their own parameters. In Tulsa, Oklahoma, citizens persuaded Home Depot to locate its store downtown and incorporate the facade of an obsolete Art Deco building. After years of rejections, Wal-Mart finally got a foothold in Vermont only after conceding to local demands in Bennington, where the chain now occupies a fifty-thousand-square-foot site vacated by a Woolworth store. Though that store is one of Wal-Mart's smallest, its manager told a visitor in 1995 that the store's sales-to–floor space ratio was one of the highest in the Wal-Mart system. The second Wal-Mart in Vermont is slated to go into an empty Kmart building in downtown Rutland, even after Wal-Mart representatives claimed that the seventy-five-thousand-square-foot site didn't meet its economy of scale. It happened because Vermonters take recycling seriously.

"The economic and ecological gains our communities make by recycling bottles and cans pale in comparison to the gains we would make if we stopped littering the landscape with redundant commercial buildings and invested in recycling the ones we already have," said Kennedy Smith, director of the Main Street Center. The increasingly frugal fiscal environment in government at every level should only strengthen arguments about not squandering Main Street's tax base and accumulated public investments.

Small towns that maintain their historic character will more than likely maintain a comparative economic advantage over towns that do not. William A. Galston and Karen J. Baehler, authors of *Rural Development in the United States,* concluded that models of the past—"New Deal–style, large-scale federal public investment; industrial attraction campaigns; resource exploitation strategies—have all produced disappointing results."[14] They contend that small communities in rural America must tap their unique "locational assets" and "amenities of place"—their scenic natural and built environments—if they hope to attract investments and individuals in an era when both are highly mobile. Bruce Epsy's story illustrates the point. A representative of the financial services firm Edward Jones & Company, Epsy runs his business out of a converted 1940 gas station in Lake Wales, a town of 9,500 in central Florida. "The company hired me in 1986 and told me I could pick my own location," he said to Allen Freeman of *Preservation News.* "So my wife and I drove around the state on weekends while I was studying to take the New York Stock Exchange exam. When we arrived in Lake Wales one Sunday afternoon, we immediately noticed that it had a restored historic downtown that had been fixed up with beautiful landscaping. After driving around the lake, I looked at my wife and said, 'This is it.' "[15]

Considering the mobility of Americans, particularly retirees, Galston and Baehler predict that the rural locations worst off in the next century will be those with few "quality-of-life amenities." Why? "Rural places with substantial locational assets have commanded the lion's share of rural population and employments gains." Studies of Farm Belt counties for the Federal Reserve Bank of Kansas City and the National Governors Association confirm this conclusion. The most recent economic growth in America's Farm Belt towns has come from tourism, recreation, government facilities, and retirement-related activities rather than manufacturing or the extraction of natural resources.

Places that depend solely on income from mining, logging, fishing, and farming could see further job losses as productivity in these fields continues to rise, analysts predict. Farming, in fact, has become so productive over the last century that the U.S. Census Bureau, in 1993, stopped counting the few farmers left, calling them statistically insignificant. Communities once supported by local networks of farm families have suffered rapid depopulation. Facing limited opportunities at home, the young leave and do not return, causing a talent drain in communities unable to attract new residents— places that eventually fade as quietly as old cotton on the clothesline. Remote ghost towns only remind us just how much of our rural culture we have allowed to drift away.

Fortunately for America's rural communities, not all the trends are bleak. According to the U.S. Chamber of Commerce, tourism is on the way to becoming the top retail industry in America by the twenty-first century. That's good news for places worth visiting. Galston and Baehler suggest that strategies designed to attract outsiders to spend money in a locality "appear to be as effective as tangible exports for generating new local wealth." As competition for tourists increases, the best-kept places will fare the best, edging out localities that sacrifice their unique qualities of place to drastic overcommercialization.

Tourism does not go to places that have lost their souls, argues Arthur Frommer, a man with forty years of experience in the travel industry. Frommer notes that people travel for three reasons: for recreation, to see natural wonders, and to experience "the achievements of the past." Professionals call this last category "heritage tourism," one of the fastest-growing segments of the American travel industry. Of places "with no particular recreational appeal, those that have substantially preserved their past continue to enjoy tourism," Frommer said. "Those that haven't receive no tourism at all. It is as simple as that."[16] Carefully preserved and marketed well, a community's historic character is a valuable local economic asset.

Tourism has also helped introduce a generation of urbanities to a small-town quality of life they have never known. More of them appear to be opting for it, aided by advanced communication technologies that hold the potential to decentralize settlement patterns, allowing business operations to take place in some of the most remote locations imaginable. Yet, most high-technology-dependent businesses are still drawn to places with a talented workforce, universities, and international airports.[17] These factors do not suggest a reverse migration to rural America as much as an extension of the outer boundaries of metropolitan America, further into exurbia, a trend one analyst at the U.S. Department of Transportation calls "telesprawl."

Still, there are signs that the population loss in rural America has tapered off and that a reverse migration, albeit small, has begun. In the 1980s, 55 percent of nonmetropolitan areas in the United States lost population, but between 1990 and 1994, 74 percent of such areas grew. According to federal demographers, more than half of that growth represented migrants to small towns and rural areas. Many of them seek a safe and affordable refuge, away from the hectic pace of suburb-to-suburb commutes and the anomie of placeless urban sprawl. Some of them, like Jeff Novak, the telecommunications consultant in Chippewa Falls, are drawn to traditional Main Street environments by a craving for face-to-face contact, either because urban life has made such contact dangerous, or because sprawl, in an attempt to create a safe environment, has made random personal encounters all but impossible.

America's "nostalgia for the small town need not be construed as directed toward the town itself: it is rather a 'quest for community'—a nostalgia for a compassable and integral living unit," Max Lerner wrote in America as a Civilization forty years ago, when communities were far more integrated spatially than they are today. "The critical question is not whether the small town can be rehabilitated in the image of its earlier strength and growth—for clearly it cannot—but whether American life will be able to evolve any other integral community to replace it. This is what I call the problem of place in America, and unless it is somehow resolved, American life will become more jangled and fragmented than it is, and American personality will continue to be unquiet and unfulfilled."[18]

Starved for so long for places built on a human scale, where public life is manageable, where people go their own way while still sharing respect for local customs, Americans at the end of the twentieth century desperately want to feel at home. Public opinion surveys show that more Americans would prefer to live in a small town than in any other type of environment—city, suburb, or farm. Ironically, people are attracted to Main Streets by the ideal of small-town stability, but the most visited and prosperous Main Streets are actually ones that have undergone enormous change. They are not the Main Streets of yesterday, but the Main Streets of tomorrow.

"Nobody should try to revive a downtown with the rallying cry, 'Remember When?'" said Matt Wagner, a young former manager of Main Street Sheboygan Falls, Wisconsin. "Because, today, there is a whole group of people of a certain age who have only lived in malls and have never spent any real time in a downtown. They don't remember when, because for them, there never was a when."

Wagner is right. Main Street communities need not appeal to nostalgia for what is gone. They simply need to see their own potential and invest in what they have. If and when they do, their citizens, like George Bailey in Bedford Falls, will get a second chance at a wonderful life, a chance to see that, next time, things turn out for the best.

REINVENTING DOWNTOWN

There should be, in every life, a place . . . where you could come
and visit your past, and the past of your people, and know that
whatever happened outside, here timelessness lived.

— Anne Rivers Siddons, *Colony*

Many people who used to go downtown have few reasons to go
there anymore. Others avoid downtown simply out of fear: fear of strangers,
fear of a breakdown in civic order. For some, even the common suburban
subdivision is not safe enough. Seeking reassuring environments, an estimated 4 million Americans have retreated behind walls into housing complexes where access is restricted by a gate. Ironically, Americans are moving
into a form of settlement that gave rise to urban cores themselves.

Lewis Mumford argued that fear above all else spawned the birth of cities
in the Western world a millennium ago. Terrorized by bandits and barbarians
during the anarchy that followed the collapse of the Roman Empire, feudal
lords holed up in castles perched atop defensible hills while commoners in
valleys took refuge behind wooden stockades. Safety within the stockades
made possible sustained face-to-face contact. Strangers became neighbors.
They relaxed their fear, developed trust, formed mutual alliances, and became citizens of the medieval town.

To be a citizen of the town carried civic responsibilities, and to go outside
the town was to go beyond the "pale," or "fence post," the boundary of the
commonly protected jurisdiction. Over time, as the permanence of settlement was assured, wooden stockades gave way to walls of stone, and what
grew up behind the walls can be summarized in a word: civilization. According to Mumford, "The population flowed into these protected centers, built
and rebuilt them, and in a few centuries created perhaps the highest type of
urban civilization that had been known in Europe since the fifth century in
Greece."[1]

Size alone did not distinguish a great city. Such a place was marked by the maturity of its civilization. In addition to providing protection from external enemies and from internal conflict, through self-government and law, the city was home to the marketplace, the cathedral, the university, the public forum, and a variety of other places to sustain the culture and life and attention of the community as a whole.

In America today, the ingredients of a city are less likely to be concentrated in a downtown, within walking distance of one another as they have been for centuries elsewhere. We have busy metropolitan areas, but we have emptier downtowns. Many older metropolitan areas have lost their downtowns to urban sprawl; newer metropolitan regions never had them to begin with.

When the New Jersey Devils hockey team won the 1995 Stanley Cup championship, the franchise had no obvious location for a victory parade, so the team celebrated with fans outside the stadium in a parking lot. "It's too bad to have to rally in a parking lot, but there's no town to go to," one fan told a reporter from the *New York Times*. Syndicated columnist Calvin Trillin seized on the event as symbolic of the placelessness of contemporary American culture. "Like a lot of people in New Jersey and Long Island and Westchester County, N.Y., the Devils aren't exactly from anywhere," Trillin wrote. "They represent a market rather than a place—a certain number of people with a certain amount of disposable income living within a certain radius drawn on a map around the Meadowlands. If sports teams were named accurately, the new Stanley Cup champions would be called the Suburban Sprawl Devils."

In 1992, Governor Bill Clinton's presidential campaign sent the candidate on a trip through places where presidential candidates no longer journeyed. Clinton, his running mate, Senator Al Gore, and their wives hopped aboard a bus and traveled through the heartland, stopping at tiny towns and crossroads along the way. All summer long, their campaign aides, under the tutelage of Hollywood producer Mort Engelberg, had found historic settings as picturesque backdrops for the traveling entourage: the county courthouse in Wilmington, Ohio, the 1836 Greek Revival statehouse where Abraham Lincoln served as a state legislator in Vandalia, Illinois, as well as public squares in downtown St. Louis, Columbus, and Cleveland. But when their aides got to Youngstown, a declining city of steel mills in eastern Ohio, they found no public site in the downtown suitable as a setting for a large public event. Youngstown was still home to tens of thousands of people, downtown was still full of wonderful old buildings, but windows in the buildings were boarded up. Sidewalks were empty. The campaign wound up staging its rally in the parking lot of a suburban shopping mall. Its was an appropriate choice, for Youngstown, as it turned out, was the home of Edward J. DeBartolo, America's largest regional shopping mall developer, whose developments had displaced the centers of communities nationwide.

Not every American city has lost its downtown to the extent that Youngstown has. But people in most cities would agree that America's downtowns are not what they used to be. Does all this matter? Why should anyone care about the disinvestment that afflicts the downtown core? The health of a downtown is an important indicator of the economic health of the entire metropolitan community, affecting everything from property values in surrounding locations to a community's ability to attract investors to its economy. A number of studies have shown that the health of an entire region is tied to the economic health of its core. In other words, the image of downtown determines the image of the region as a whole. Ask someone to describe metropolitan Detroit, for example, and chances are they will never mention places like Oakland, a prosperous suburb.

The smallest of cities have major investments in their downtowns, in the structures themselves as well as in the infrastructure. In a time of fiscal austerity it is irresponsible to let them go to waste. Downtowns are important incubators for new small businesses, most of which are started in older buildings, where space is less expensive to lease. Downtowns tend to be home to independent, family-oriented businesses, which, unlike national chains, reinvest a large portion of their profits in the local economy, and support local civic institutions, schools, charities, and community projects.

The importance of downtowns, however, goes well beyond economics. With increasing density at the heart of a community, cities are made more livable and thus centrifugal pressures for sprawl are reduced. Downtown holds together the most varied mix of economic, civic, and social functions. It is the place where everyone can meet and interact, where monuments are located, where speeches are made, where parades are held and crowds are entertained. More than anyplace else, downtown gives a community its collective identity and thus its pride. It is the keystone that keeps the other pieces of the city in place. Downtown is the heart and soul of the metropolis.

Like other organisms, cities evolve and, with them, their downtowns. Old functions disappear, and new ones either replace them or move elsewhere. As we shall see, downtowns reinvented by creative thinking and entrepreneurial leadership are not leaving this evolution to chance.

■　■　■

Denver's history is a story of booms and busts, of prospectors, speculators, and liquidators, from the discovery of gold in 1858 to the collapse of savings and loans a century and a quarter later. Like the landscape, where the Front

Range of the Rocky Mountains meets the Great Plains, Denver's economy has risen to lofty peaks in one cycle only to fall flat in the next.

At first glance, there is no natural explanation for a metropolis of 2 million people to be here. Denver's South Platte River is neither wide nor widely used. Water is scarce, and the land is dry. Laying the first railroad tracks between the East and San Francisco, the Union Pacific Railroad bypassed tiny Denver in favor of Cheyenne, Wyoming. But Denver's business leaders bought their way onto the map. Digging into their pockets, they raised enough money, in only a matter of weeks, to build a railroad spur into town in 1870. Then commerce really flowed. By 1876, Denver was the capital of Colorado, a young state that grew rich quickly from the mining of silver.

During the great silver boom, Denver exploded, becoming the "Queen City of the Plains," the largest city in the West after San Francisco and Omaha, a busy railroad junction. But Denver's pace of growth was unsustainable. The federal repeal of the Sherman Silver Purchase Act in 1893, along with a national financial panic and economic depression that year, brought construction in Denver to a halt. Building permits sank by 95 percent within a year. Only then did the city finally pause to discover it was a mess. "Private dreams, schemes and greed [had] shaped the city's growth," wrote Denver historian Thomas J. Noel and preservationist Barbara S. Norgren. "The frontier of rugged individualism prevailed; there was little sense of community. Commercial buildings were thrown up recklessly."[2]

At the peak of the Progressive era's reactions to the ills of industrial urbanization, Mayor Robert Walter "Boss Bob" Speer, elected in 1904, asked the city's leadership to make Denver "the Paris of America."[3] Assisted by architect Edward Bennett, Daniel Burnham's assistant at the Chicago exposition in 1893, planner Charles M. Robinson, and landscape architect Frederick Law Olmsted Jr., Speer proposed the construction of a monumental civic center at the foot of the 1888 state capitol building steps, where a marker notes the exact altitude of 5,280 feet above sea level. With its monumental civic structures, formal public gardens, and gathering space for public events, the civic center's "ornamental value for the future cannot be measured by dollars," Speer said. The project would achieve the unmeasurable goal of making "our people proud of Denver."[4]

Investing huge sums in the city once again, Denver built its civic center, culminating with the completion of the City County Building in 1932, a new replacement for the old city hall. Launched in 1924, the "marble municipal palace" was plagued for years by highly publicized cost overruns, alterations, and construction delays. The fiasco cost Denver the public's confidence in large-scale physical improvements. It also cost Mayor Benjamin F. Stapleton his job after the *Denver Post* called him "the most incapable and utterly incompetent and extravagant mayor this city has ever had." For a generation at least, the age of the megaproject was over.[5]

In the bust that followed the early-twentieth-century boom in city building, Frank Lloyd Wright delivered a speech in Denver in 1948 and called his host city a "pig pile." According to Noel and Norgren, Wright "urged Denverites to decentralize and called for 'the obliteration of the great clusters of humanity we call cities.' " By the time of Wright's visit, Denver's oldest sections had not aged well. When the city's trolley system came to a complete stop in 1950, the oldest commercial thoroughfare in town, Larimer Street, had become skid row. Before the war, "concerned merchants formed the Larimer Street Improvement Association [and] persuaded the city to install bright new ornamental street lights that only illuminated the continuing decline."[6] By the mid-1950s, respectable businesses on Larimer Street had migrated elsewhere, leaving a low-rent district behind. The effort to clean up Larimer Street then shifted to more drastic measures. The city's power brokers decided that tearing down the street's old structures was not too great a sacrifice to rid the downtown of its "skid row bums," who were fed, clothed, and sheltered by religious missions. So Denver prepared to demolish thirty downtown blocks for urban renewal, the equivalent of cutting down old trees to rid your yard of squirrels.

Sifting through the ruins on Larimer Street like a prospector panning for gold was Dana Crawford, a pioneering preservationist in this land of pioneers. Born in Kansas and educated at Radcliffe in the early 1950s, Crawford focused on the 1400 block of Larimer Street, home to a few antique stores in a row of Victorian buildings. Dating to the silver boom, the ornate three- and four-story buildings had suffered damaging alterations, but Crawford had no trouble imagining them renovated for shops and restaurants. When Crawford had arrived in Denver, "there was no gathering place here," she recalled. Her goal, she said, was to give Denver the kind of attraction it did not have. Digging into the location's history, Crawford learned that the block was actually the birthplace of downtown Denver, the home of its earliest saloons, boardinghouses, banks, dry goods stores, blacksmith shops, and corrals. On one corner was the very site where Denver's founder, William Larimer, had built a log cabin using coffin lids as doors. As Larimer's wooden frontier town gave way to more-permanent masonry buildings after a fire in 1863, Larimer Street's Victorian grandeur earned Denver the nickname Queen City of the Plains. "I'm always attracted to good architecture," Crawford said, "and where you find good architecture, you find history." But others did not share her affection for the relics of Denver's past. "There was no preservation ethic," she said. To the officials in charge at city hall, Larimer Street's rundown structures didn't seem very historic at all. They were just shabby.

Crawford, however, was a contrarian, and like all smart contrarians with good timing, she found value selling at a discount. To gather inspiration for her Denver project, she traveled to St. Louis in 1963, to a place similar to Larimer Street called Gas Light Square. Like Crawford's spot in Denver, Gas Light Square was in "a ragged neighborhood," she said, but blessed with wide sidewalks and distinctive buildings that housed antique stores and restaurants. But Gas Light Square became "a victim of its own success and the ignorance of its management," she said. Rents rose so fast they drove out existing retail tenants and with them their daytime customers. Nighttime attractions developed a rowdy reputation, and safety was not managed well. As the location declined, establishments folded one by one until all of them were gone. "From Gas Light Square, I learned what not to do," Crawford said. To achieve better results, she decided to rule her Larimer Street buildings with more skill and discipline, learning from suburban shopping center managers how to organize independent specialty retailers and gain clout with public officials. After forming a partnership with investors and earning the support of Mayor Thomas Currigan, Crawford began work on the buildings in 1965, removing decrepit signs, uncovering historic storefronts, and undoing alterations to make the buildings more presentable. She got the city to narrow the traffic lanes for cars and widen the sidewalks for pedestrians. She enhanced the streetscape with period-style lampposts, gaslights, trees, and hanging baskets. To lease the buildings to specialty retail tenants quickly, she offered flexible rents (based on a percentage of sales as opposed to fixed amounts) until the block was half occupied. Lacking an anchor retail tenant, Crawford made the block's unique atmosphere the magnet, relying on the grouping of stores to draw customers, following what she called "the law of cumulative attraction." With expertise gained from a career in public relations, she organized special events and threw public parties to fill the place with crowds. "I promoted the hell out of that block," she said. Renamed Larimer Square, the district opened shortly after a new urban marketplace opened in San Francisco's rehabilitated Ghirardelli chocolate factory. Like Ghirardelli Square, Larimer Square reminded people how cities could be exciting, clean, safe, and fun, and that historic sites, if adaptively reused and managed well, could become unique assets too valuable for any city to throw away.

Crawford's success with Larimer Square, along with the city's pursuit of demolitions in the surrounding Skyline Renewal area, created momentum for the preservation of Denver's historic places. In 1967, the city created its landmark commission. In 1971, the local preservation group, Historic Denver, formed to rescue a Victorian house that once belonged to local philanthropist Molly Brown, who survived the sinking of the *Titanic* in 1912.

Larimer Square became the first district in the city added to the National Register of Historic Places, and at the same time, the city began to notice a much larger historic district just beyond Larimer Square called Lower Downtown.

A twenty-five block district of nineteenth- and early-twentieth-century warehouses and commercial buildings, the district was Denver's downtown in the age of rail, before horse-drawn streetcars and electric trolleys shifted the city's business district uptown. Around the rail yards sprang up foundries, factories, meatpacking plants, flour mills, breweries, cigar makers, saddle shops, western clothiers, and other wholesalers. After a fire in 1863 cleared the district of its original wooden structures, replacements were built in "warm orange-red brick, characterized by repetitive round, arched windows and bays, with simple brick cornices and arched brick facades," as Denver preservationist Barbara Gibson described them. After 1870, the railroad "brought new building materials such as pressed and cast metal, used for cornices, storefront columns, and window hoods, adding decoration to the plain facades of Denver's commercial buildings."[7] Steel reinforcements and new "vertical railways," as the elevator was first called, increased the size of structures and the storage space under one roof, leading the way for a new class of industrial warehouses. During the Gilded Age, the style of warehouses went from plain to prestigious after architect H. H. Richardson designed an elaborate warehouse for Marshall Field in Chicago in 1887. "Unlike industrial plants designed by engineers, most warehouses were the work of architects. Warehousers wanted prestigious buildings because they combined storage facilities with their corporate offices," wrote Noel and Norgren.[8] But the district's best days were numbered, as horse cars and then electric trolleys shifted the downtown several blocks away. When trolleys began to disappear from the city in the 1930s, Lower Downtown began to fade along with the painted advertisements on its brick warehouse walls. Trucking and new warehouse technology sent the district into decline, making some of the old industrial buildings obsolete. Streets grew emptier as the number of passenger trains arriving at Denver Union Terminal dwindled from scores each day to less than a handful.

Following Dana Crawford's preservation success at Larimer Square, the Lower Downtown was rezoned from an industrial area to a mixed-use district in 1974. This allowed the conversion of empty warehouses to office space and other uses. But the act stimulated little dramatic improvement in the area. Instead, Lower Downtown suffered a blitzkrieg of demolitions. When the energy crisis made oil extracted from Colorado shale a competitive alternative to oil from the Middle East, new money flowed into banks on Seventeenth Street, nicknamed the "Wall Street of the West." Speculators chasing sudden fortunes built high-rise office towers, doubling in a decade the space downtown Denver had built in the previous century. To accommodate all the automobiles driven into the city by occupants of the new high-rise towers, developers bought obsolete properties in the old Lower Downtown and demolished them for surface parking.

Worried that Denver's historic warehouse district was threatened with eventual destruction, preservationists began looking for strategies to save it from the building boom's demolition derby. A consultant for the National Trust for Historic Preservation went to Denver in 1981 and discovered a "limitless market for office development" that threatened to wipe out Lower Downtown's small historic structures. A visionless public sector gave little thought to the placement of new downtown office towers and parking lots. Private interests dictated the city agenda, and "unless substantial segments of the business community embrace preservation soon, there won't be much left," the consultant warned.

In 1982, the district was rezoned again with incentives for property owners who preserved the antique structures in the shadows of the high-rise buildings, but plans didn't work the way they were intended. The oil boom soon went bust. Caught with unmarketable old properties, some owners sought to demolish them rather than pay for upkeep and the taxes. The district would not be preserved without some stronger form of protection.

As early as 1981, preservationists had campaigned for the city to designate Lower Downtown a local historic district. Lisa Purdy, a former Historic Denver staffer, was one of the visionaries who imagined Lower Downtown revived as a vibrant mixed-use historic district, similar to Larimer Square, but on a larger scale. Purdy recalled that the constituency for new housing in Lower Downtown was particularly vocal—"people who believed that the key to making a vibrant city is that people have to live there to make it work." Skeptics saw little appeal in Lower Downtown's aging industrial buildings, with their dusty windows and crumbling facades. But, Purdy said, others "could see a gold mine if the buildings were protected from demolition. You could envision a great mixed-use district if the buildings could be used."

Denver's preservationists found support among the city's business leadership, which, according to Purdy, understood the concept "that Lower Downtown is what separates us from the suburbs. It is a great unique asset. If it gets wiped out, we've got nothing. We're like anywhere else." Business leaders told preservationists to make their case broad, that if they hoped to put together a wide coalition of allies the issue had to be about the future of Denver rather than the potential of one small area. Their chance came in 1984, when a new city administration, under Mayor Frederico Peña, began to compile a plan to guide changes to the downtown and the city's inner neighborhoods over the next fifty years. Coordinated by a twenty-eight-member committee of business and civic leaders, the plan called for, among other things, the construction of a new convention center and a new international airport, and the enhancement of the city's historic areas, especially the Lower Downtown and historic neighborhoods close by. The plan gave new energy to the movement to declare Lower Downtown a local historic district, to create protection for its landmarks, and to devise a review process to ensure that new development would be compatible.

Supported by city business leaders and a broad coalition of civic groups, the historic district designation was virulently opposed by a majority of Lower Downtown property owners. The most influential of them was Dana Crawford. After transforming the 1400 block of Larimer Street into Larimer Square, Crawford in 1980 had become a co-owner of the 1891 Oxford Hotel, in the heart of Lower Downtown, one block away from Denver's historic railroad station. Legendary in its early days, the hotel by the 1970s "was really just a flophouse," Crawford said. "But we thought it could be the cornerstone of development down here." After a three-year, $12 million restoration, the Oxford had reopened in 1983, drawing more attention to the district's other historic gems that awaited restoration.

Crawford plunged into Lower Downtown expecting the dormant area to blossom once again. "I had seen what Seattle had done in Pioneer Square, and other cities were willing to put money into historic areas to leverage private investment," she said. Pioneer Square was a run-down historic district of some forty blocks that grew more valuable after Seattle gave it local historic district protections in 1970. But Crawford opposed the creation of any district in Denver that would give others authority to review her projects, particularly the Ice House, a massive, prominent brick warehouse that Crawford intended to convert into a center for artistic designers. When preserving Denver's historic landmarks, she preferred to do things her own way, true to the regional culture of rugged individualism. She was more of a preservation-minded developer than a development-minded preservationist. She did not believe in preservation for preservation's sake, but as a means to other ends—in her case, her business, which was real estate. When speaking before audiences of preservationists, Crawford tells them that preservation is about real estate, and if they don't understand real estate, they don't belong in preservation.

Because of the absence of any national corporate headquarters in the city, decision making in Denver is influenced less by corporate power than by individuals with large egos and big dreams. "They think they're going to get lucky. They like the high-stakes game. And they believe if they are the ones who build it, they can fold it any time they please," said Kathleen Brooker, Historic Denver's president.

Once labeled the most powerful woman in town by a cover piece in the *Denver Post* magazine, Crawford was a powerful foe of the historic district's designation. She was admired, loved, and feared, all at the same time. "She has style. She has smarts. She has drive," the profile explained. "She is combative. She has a nasty streak. She is devious. She is self-serving. And she has made a difference in Denver."[9]

In opposing the designation, Crawford contributed her chutzpah, but other property owners provided the hysterics, predicting nothing but doom and gloom. A petition circulated by the Development Association of Lower Downtown, Incorporated, called the district a "depressed area in a depressed marketplace." With a districtwide vacancy rate of 40 percent in Lower Downtown, property owners had lost a bundle in the oil bust and feared new restrictions on development in the district would push them toward further losses. "These restrictions can only reduce the chances for new investors to inject new capital into the area," they said. "This can only result in some investors abandoning their property . . . decreasing the District tax base, having the buildings go into disrepair and potentially having them become derelict and condemned."

One Lower Downtown property owner who took a different view was Jerry Glick, a real estate developer and entrepreneur who had converted a 1903 seed warehouse to office space in 1985. Glick recalled that at one public hearing on the designation, "someone stood up and said every property owner is opposed to this, that if it goes through, it will be absolute disaster. It will hurt property values. Nothing good will ever come of it." Glick stood up and replied, "Wait a minute. I'm not sure that's true. In all likelihood, it could be good for the city and good for me economically. There's real character here that needs to be preserved."

A decade later, Glick professed, "I'm not really a preservationist," adding that he got his start in real estate "doing suburban stuff." But Glick said he was attracted to Lower Downtown because he admired the materials and the details in the old warehouses, especially when compared to new construction. "I liked the floors, the bricks, and the beams, and I thought if I liked it, then others would like it, too." Promoting the protection of the historic district, Glick appealed to Denver's entrepreneurial culture. He spoke of profits in Lower Downtown waiting to be mined. But the city council was still not sold.

Jennifer Moulton, an architect then working for the Downtown Denver Partnership, the downtown business lobby that supported the designation, collected stories of successful precedents in other cities to bolster the case in Denver. Studying several local historic districts across the country, Moulton and her allies gathered economic data, looking at property values over the five years before each designation and five years after. "In every single case, property values went up," Moulton said. She used the data to challenge property owners who predicted losses in Denver. "You show us one district in the country where the story is different," she said. "They didn't come up with a single one."

To further impress the city council, proponents of the designation produced visual displays, including three-dimensional models that showed undesirable changes to the district allowed by the city's zoning laws. City councillors could see for themselves the need for guidelines on the design of new buildings. But a process to review demolitions in the district, a sticking point for property owners, enjoyed less political support. Demolition review "was the hardest part to keep," said Lisa Purdy. "We absolutely would not give up on that. We said that if we don't have that in there, it's not worth getting. You can have design control all you want, but if the buildings go, you don't have the district, its history, its whole reason for being."

In a show of support for that position, Mayor Peña signaled that he would not sign legislation to create the historic district unless it included demolition review. At a crucial moment in city council deliberations, Peña's aide Tom Gougeon reportedly told councillors that the issue was more important to Denver's identity than even the convention center and the new airport: "I've never told you any of those is the single most important issue for the city, but I'm telling you that historic district designation for Lower Downtown is."[10]

Studying the components of Denver's long-term comprehensive plan, Mayor Peña knew the convention center and the airport could be achieved eventually. "But the most difficult challenge we had before us was how to revitalize downtown Denver," Peña said during an interview while serving as the Clinton administration's first secretary of transportation.

Soon after Peña became mayor of Denver in 1983, the oil boom went bust and the city's economy went into a tailspin. The downtown vacancy rate soared to 31 percent, the highest of any major city in America. In one year, more people moved out of Colorado than moved in. Locally, a suburban high-technology employment center was pulling workers out of downtown, while competition from suburban malls was draining downtown's retail sector. "I felt that if we couldn't keep the downtown vibrant, the city was basically going to implode," Peña said.

"We looked at other cities that had preserved their historic structures and saw how they had become economic engines. History is what makes one place different from another," the former mayor explained, "and I didn't want our downtown to be developed to look like every other in America."

Denver had just gone through a building boom, Peña noted, "and some people had criticized our buildings downtown. They said they looked like Houston."

Pointing Denver's development in a new direction, Peña led the city to capitalize on its past and its historic "ambience"—for economic development and as a boost to local morale. Looking at the unique historic assets of the city, Peña said, "we saw Lower Downtown as the best opportunity to kick off the revitalization of downtown Denver."

In 1988, the city council finally agreed and declared Lower Downtown a local historic district, with the condition that the economic impact of the designation be evaluated every two years. During the seven years it took to get the district designated, one-fifth of its historic structures had been demolished.

As it turned out, the landmark ordinance did not depress or inflate Lower Downtown's real estate market. It stabilized it, giving investors certainty and confidence to go ahead with plans, signaling what buildings would be saved and what buildings could be demolished, and reassuring every investor that neighboring properties would have to be developed to equally high standards. The oil bust turned out to be a savior, too, allowing the district to evolve slowly, in incremental steps. The relatively small historic buildings on small lots offered entrepreneurs manageable rehabilitation projects to undertake. The depressed market kept rents down, attracting a variety of professional office tenants and specialty retailers, especially art galleries. However, the unorthodox projects made conservative lenders nervous, especially proposals that combined commercial and residential space in a single building, presenting too many variables for their rigidly simplistic accounting formulas. After the crash of the oil boom, followed by the crash of the savings and loan industry, Denver's lenders were in no mood for risks.

"In Colorado, there were more bank examiners around than bankers," Crawford said over breakfast in her restored Oxford Hotel. "But bad times present a great opportunity to get things going, because the best friend of preservation is poverty. Preservation in Savannah and Charleston would not have happened without bad times."

To jump-start investment in the district, the Downtown Denver Partnership established a Lower Downtown Business Support Office. The office marketed the area to potential investors and managed a loan fund, capitalized by money from the city, downtown business interests, Historic Denver, and the National Trust for Historic Preservation. The loans covered gap financing, facade improvements, and upgrades required by building codes. On top of federal rehabilitation tax credits, Colorado offered state tax credits for reinvestment in historic properties, even residences. Colorado also offered credits for investments that led to job creation in state-designated enterprise zones.

One of the first adaptive reuse projects after the district's designation, John Hickenlooper's conversion of the 1899 J. S. Brown Mercantile Building on Wynkoop Street into a brew pub and restaurant, and apartments upstairs, "was done with seven layers of financing," said Bill Mosher, president of the Downtown Denver Partnership, the business lobby whose staff administered the fund. Dana Crawford's early successful conversion of a warehouse into loft condominiums, partially financed by a $948,000 bridge loan from city Community Development Block Grants, inspired other lofts to follow. "I always knew there was a market here" for lofts, she said, "because when I was doing Larimer Square, people were always coming up to me saying, 'Do you have any place to live?' " Lofts in the district turned out to be so popular that every unit in her next project was spoken for before construction began. "The values just continue to increase," she said in 1996. "The success of the projects assured the lending community that this was not a crapshoot, not a fly-by-night kind of thing, and that the market was adequate to sustain it," said Diane Blackman, an accountant who owned property in the district and served as the first president of Lower Downtown District Incorporated, the nonprofit association of district property owners and residents.

When the city reviewed the economic impact of the historic district designation in 1990, Lower Downtown had prospered better than downtown Denver as a whole. The study reported a "significant" increase in building renovations and "substantial" increases in new businesses and new housing units. Preservationists who had pushed for the designation felt vindicated. All through the 1980s, "we waited for the market to come to Lower Downtown and it never came," said Lisa Purdy. "It wouldn't have happened without the regulations to protect" the historic structures, she said. After more good economic news in 1992, the city council decided that the economic review every two years was no longer necessary. Even Dana Crawford, who had vigorously opposed the designation, called it a beneficial decision at a public forum in subsequent years.

Diane Blackman, the accountant who watched the value of her buildings in the protected district rise, said, "No one can call preservation here a 'taking' of private property. If anything, preservation has been a giving." From the designation in 1988 through 1995, vacancy rates fell from 40 percent to 10 percent, as $75 million in private investment poured into Lower Downtown. Jerry Glick, the one prominent property owner who supported the designation in public hearings, said he knew the district would eventually improve, but he admitted, "I never believed for a second that it would happen as quickly as it did."

Accelerating trends was the 1995 opening of Coors Field, Denver's new baseball park built at the district's edge for the Colorado Rockies, the expansion team awarded the city in 1991. Instead of building the park in a remote location along an interstate highway, Denver put the park downtown, at the very edge of Lower Downtown, within walking distance of offices and other cultural attractions on an accessible site with plenty of adjacent space for parking.

When architects from the firm of Hellmuth, Obata, and Kassabaum of Kansas City presented Denver with their initial design for the new stadium, citizens objected. The firm had given Denver a model similar to Chicago's new Comiskey Park, a white stadium that sits like an island in a sea of parking lots. Denver pleaded for a ballpark more like the firm's design for Oriole Park at Camden Yards in Baltimore, where a redbrick exterior complements surrounding historic brick buildings. Kathleen Brooker, president of Historic Denver, said, "Talented local architects gave very compelling suggestions, and, fortunately, they took the input pretty well." Similar to the park in Baltimore, Denver's Coors Field is a gem tucked inside a four-story brick box exterior that evokes Lower Downtown's industrial era. In a guide to the historic district, resident Barbara Gibson pointed out features of the ballpark that mimic details found on other Denver landmarks. A prominent clock above the stadium's entrance behind home plate is similar to a clock on Union Station down the street, as well as another clock atop downtown's signature landmark, the 1909 Daniels and Fisher Tower. Gibson also noted that bricks to build the park were supplied by Robinson Brick & Tile, a local firm in business since the silver boom of the nineteenth century.[11]

Had Coors Field opened before Lower Downtown's landmark protections were put in place, it could have had devastating consequences for the district, encouraging owners of neighboring properties to demolish their old brick buildings for lucrative parking lots. Instead, the new $215 million stadium stimulated more adaptive reuses of the district's historic buildings. With a seating capacity of fifty thousand, Coors Field drew into Lower Downtown thousands of people who had yet to see the changes that had taken place, the new art galleries, restaurants, and loft apartments, all in an inviting location in the process of becoming restored, renovated, and inhabited.

With the ballpark at one end and Larimer Square at the other, Lower Downtown was poised to benefit from activity in both locations. It also benefited from millions in public improvements. The city redid the district's streetscape, installing new street crossings, sidewalks, curbsides, street lighting, benches, signs, even new manhole covers stamped "Lower Downtown Historic District" with an artistic flair. Old viaducts, elevated streets that carried auto traffic over the rail yards and into the district on the way downtown, were removed, flooding streets with light for the first time in decades. City and state funds helped to restore prominent landmarks such as Union Station, where tourists during ski season board trains en route to ski towns to the west. Lower Downtown was no longer the dusty, empty district of a decade before. It had become "LoDo," an abbreviated nickname tagged on the trendy area by Dick Kreck, a columnist at the *Denver Post.*

Gritty survivors from the industrial era have become fashionable reminders of the district's past: cobblestone alleys and rail tracks between buildings; outdoor loading docks now used as porches; and second-story doorways that once opened onto the elevated streets. One elaborate second-story doorway survives above the street-level entrance to the new Tattered Cover Bookstore at 1628 Sixteenth Street, in the 1888 C. S. Morey Mercantile Company Building.

The bookstore is part of a $20 million multiproperty project called Mercantile Square. In addition to the bookstore, the place will hold a restaurant as well as ninety-four housing units, seventy-six of which are set aside for low-to-moderate-income residents. The project was financed by a range of local, state, and federal incentives, including a grant from the public share of Colorado gambling revenues. Casinos in historic Colorado mining towns contribute a portion of their profits to a state-administered fund that provides $7.5 million annually, up to $100,000 per grant, to worthy historic preservation projects. Towns that once mined silver for currency now employ slot machines to mine coins in their finished form. "Another extraction industry," quipped Kathleen Brooker.

Mercantile Square also received tax increment financing from the Denver Urban Renewal Authority, the city's redevelopment agency, created in 1958 to clear the city of run-down structures. The agency that once robbed Denver of its history now leads in the preservation of historic structures that remain. The agency's 1996 promotional brochure, for instance, highlights eight major projects in the city; all but two of them involve the rehabilitation of historic buildings. As of 1996, the agency had played a critical role in thirteen major rehabilitations that totaled $174 million.

DURA's experience with preservation began in 1988, when the May Company department store chain of St. Louis abandoned the six-story redbrick Denver Dry Goods Building that had stood in the heart of downtown's retail district for a century. Covered with thirty coats of paint that masked its elegant exterior, the building was still an important, if much neglected, landmark. To rescue the building from demolition, the authority assumed ownership and rehabilitated it in separate phases for new stores, offices, and apartments. In 1994, the authority moved into the fourth floor of the building from its former offices on the twenty-seventh floor of a modern high-rise office tower. Now, the city agency uses a detail from the landmark as its logo, symbolizing DURA's new preservation focus under Executive Director Susan Powers and its chairman, Jerry Glick, the property owner who pushed for the designation of the Lower Downtown district.

In many cities, urban redevelopment authorities have yet to see the preservation of historic places as part of their mission. If the Denver authority had not found itself trying to solve the dilemma of the Dry Goods vacancy, Glick said, "I'm not sure we wouldn't be where other cities' renewal authorities are today." Glick said the agency had to endure public criticism when it initially took over the Dry Goods Building. "People were asking us, 'How come the city took this turkey of a building?' " In time, however, the city not only restored an eyesore, it also brought new life to a declining section of the downtown retail district. After the experience, Glick said the agency decided, "This makes sense. There are some wonderful buildings downtown, and that's where we ought to be."

The preservation of historic Denver is enjoying momentum not felt since the years that followed Dana Crawford's creation of Larimer Square. Downtown office buildings from the early twentieth century are being converted to housing and hotels. In LoDo, so many landmarks are already restored or renovated that public attention has shifted from preserving individual structures to preserving the unique and fragile identity of the district as a whole.

With over fifty bars and restaurants, LoDo has become Denver's largest entertainment district. But it also remains a residential neighborhood. The number of apartments and condominiums in the district has grown to four hundred, with another three hundred planned. Lofts have sold well. Only 5 percent of Denver's downtown workforce lives downtown, well below the national average of 20 percent, so LoDo should gain more housing. But the proliferation of nightclubs, especially sports bars at the end of the district adjacent to Coors Field, has led to growing pains. Residents complain about noise levels when nightclubs shut down. A new stadium for football and other venues planned for a nearby site could generate even more crowds for entertainment, as could a reconstructed sixty-eight-acre amusement park, Elitch Gardens, behind Lower Downtown in the Central Platte Valley. Entrepreneurs are capitalizing on the potential. Actor Arnold Schwarzenegger, who owns a block of buildings in Lower Downtown near the ballpark, has plans to fill them with a Planet Hollywood restaurant and bar and an "eatertainment" marketplace.

Some fear that the balance between housing and entertainment in LoDo will be thrown off if nightclubs intrude too heavily on residential life. "As the quality of residential life declines, the ability to market residential space will decline," said Kathleen Brooker. Arguing for a "Good Neighbor Policy" as a balance between interests, Diane Blackman, past president of the district association, said newcomers "knew this was a mixed-use district when they came here. People are going to have to tolerate a level of noise. The question is, what is that level of noise?" Debates over liquor licenses have kept some retail space in the district empty, as property owners wait for chances to lease space to higher-profit establishments. Residents, on the other hand, want more tenants like dry cleaners and grocers who will cater to residential needs. What could be even trickier to balance, however, is LoDo's retail variety, including the more than two dozen art galleries. "Traditionally, the galleries pioneer in less developed areas, and as the area is developed, they get squeezed by rising rents because their margin is so low," Blackman said. So far, only one national retail chain, an upscale casual clothier, has opened an outlet in the district, but more could be on the way as the district's rising popularity increases demand for its limited space.

The increase in residents has also increased objections about high volumes of traffic running through the district between downtown and outlying neighborhoods. The city's road improvements not only enhanced the appearance of the district, they invited more traffic, as they were designed to do. Conflicts have arisen between traffic engineers, who want cars and trucks to move unimpeded through the district, and district advocates, who want to make streets more hospitable to pedestrians.

Another important issue for LoDo's future is how to ensure that new buildings complement the district's distinctive character. A quarter of the district's land is currently used as surface parking; another quarter of the district comprises buildings unworthy of historic district protections. Thus, fully half of the district's real estate—more than half of all highly visible corner lots—is potentially developable. While the historic district protections require new structures to be compatible with existing historic buildings, most of which are two to six stories tall and none of which is over 85 feet high, zoning laws allow new buildings up to 130 feet high, or about thirteen stories tall. Many people in the district are concerned that tall buildings would intrude on LoDo's traditional scale.

If Denver has a history of booms and busts, it also has a history of "height fights." In 1909, when Denver businessman William Daniels began to build a downtown department store based on St. Mark's Palace in Venice, complete with a bell tower 330 feet tall, not everyone in the city was pleased. "I am not a sentimentalist at all," said William "Buffalo Bill" Cody, the western showman born in 1846, but "every time I see the new massive steel frames of skyscrapers springing into the air, I cannot but think of the time when a view of the foothills could have been obtained—and a good one, too—from any point in the city."[12] The Daniels and Fisher Tower was Denver's tallest building until 1953. Modernism and the oil boom took the fight to new heights.

"The subsequent hodge-podge of heights culminating in the 56-story Public Plaza (1983) overshadows much of the downtown, creates wind tunnels, and blocks the mountain view from residential areas," wrote Noel and Norgren.[13] With the tall towers came growing concerns about their effect on the downtown at ground level. Though the high-rises lit up the city's skyline at night, one critic said they made people on the sidewalk feel inconsequential. Early skyscrapers, such as the Daniels and Fisher Tower, had followed traditional design principles: a base at ground level defined the sidewalk for pedestrians, a middle section defined the street wall, and an ornamental top defined the skyline. In place of traditional bases, new towers withdrew from the sidewalks, recessed into empty plazas, and had no ornamental caps, just blank walls from top to bottom. When the city's housing authority built three apartment towers in this style, detractors called them the "three ugly sisters." Like the oil-boom office towers built on a speculative basis, the three buildings stood half empty when the boom went bust, monuments to overbuilding, not to mention just plain poor buildings to begin with.

The new poverty of Denver's public built environment stemmed not from a poverty of investment but a poverty of general will. As Noel and Norgen wrote in their 1987 book, "In our own less ambitious age, when cities struggle to maintain their 'infrastructures' and even to survive, it is remarkable that a much smaller, poorer city of fifty years ago could not only keep up with urban needs, but also build with an eye to aesthetics."[14]

"In previous years, we let the private sector develop the quality of the downtown," said Jennifer Moulton, who went from posts with the Downtown Denver Partnership and Historic Denver to become director of the city planning department. Downtown landlords, she said, were not as concerned with the quality of downtown as much as the quality of their rents. "We said, 'Y'all come down here and build what you want, this is free-enterprise land.' We were not very sophisticated about it." After getting poor results from that process, Moulton said Denver learned that "we needed to take charge of our own lives and not look to others. We realized that our destiny is in our hands and nobody else's. . . .

"Coors Field looks as good as it does because of huge public participation," she said. "If we don't demand the quality of development of the public realm we want, we're going to get the kind of private development we deserve."

"Character is hard to build new," said preservationist Lisa Purdy over lunch in LoDo's Wazee Supper Club, a restaurant and bar operated by the Karagas family since 1954. "There is a scale here that people feel comfortable with. You don't sense that when you walk down a street of high-rise buildings or are out in the suburbs with its wide streets and parking lots. People's attitudes change when they spend time in a historic area like this one."

To set guidelines for future development in Lower Downtown and resolve outstanding controversies over sports bars, traffic, and height limits, the district association won a one-hundred-thousand-dollar grant from the state historic preservation office to formulate a long-range district plan that all interests could agree upon and the city council could approve. But the association repeated a mistake often made by public authorities. It hired planning consultants from out of town to draft the plans and then circulated a document for review. Jerry Glick, the property owner and chair of the city's urban renewal authority, called the draft a "planner's vision," not the vision of local interests brainstorming together. In trying to preserve the district, the neighborhood association had followed the same expert-driven kind of planning process that neighborhood preservationists had fought against for years. Starting over, the district association brought all major interests to the table and formed committees to handle certain issues. The committees and the consultants conducted interviews and focus groups, tested ideas, refined them, and tested them for feedback once again. The result was a district plan that incorporates a broad spectrum of viewpoints, one that achieved a remarkable amount of consensus. Crawford, who has rubbed elbows with district advocates in the past, called the experience "a wonderful process because it was so inclusive. In this case, developers were at the table. People who pay the taxes have to be consulted," she said. Glick, who along with Crawford opposed some elements in the planners' first draft, called the exercise a great lesson for everyone on how to work together. "Peña learned that the way to get people to agree on a direction is to bring everyone to the table, then make them talk ad nauseam until they reach a consensus. We'll still have people who won't agree, but today we have more diverse interests than we used to, and we have a lot more consensus."

The plan acknowledges that a balance of residential and entertainment uses is in LoDo's long-term interest. Diane Blackman sees room in the district for sports bars if they remain concentrated near Coors Field. "As long as it doesn't proliferate throughout the district, we'll be all right. We have to recognize that baseball is the gravy," even if it isn't the district's meat and potatoes. On the issue of height limits, the guidelines avoided a districtwide rule of one size fits all for a more flexible policy that respects existing height patterns block by block, allowing the tallest new buildings in three specific locations, while restricting heights in others. As for design regulations, the plan requires new construction to respect patterns set by surrounding significant structures. New buildings must follow the traditional pattern of a distinctive base at street level and a definable middle section capped by a well-defined top that includes a cornice, a common element of LoDo's historic structures. Building materials must be consistent with existing patterns:

masonry exteriors, with other materials allowed for details. New buildings must respect the street rhythm of facades, prominent centered entryways, and vertical window placement, recessed at least one brick deep. Street wall composition should enhance the attractiveness of streets. Retail activity is encouraged at ground level, as is the district's pattern of storefront windows instead of blank walls. The interplay of light and shadows on building facades is emphasized by encouraging traditional details such as arches over doors and cornices. Rather than call for repetition of historic architecture, the guidelines ask for sensitive and compatible new designs.[15]

At one edge of the district, a new parking garage built on Market Street behind Larimer Square lives up to the kinds of standards included in the district plan. The four-level garage is cleverly disguised behind a restaurant on the ground floor and a brick-and-concrete facade that plays off the district's early-twentieth-century industrial look and feel.

Lower Downtown should eventually benefit even more from one of Denver's greatest planning innovations, the Sixteenth Street Mall. After clearing automobile traffic from one mile of the busiest retail street downtown, Denver redesigned Sixteenth Street as an outdoor mall where custom-built buses pick up and drop off passengers at every corner for free. By concentrating pedestrian traffic along Sixteenth Street, the shuttle service encourages sidewalk traffic necessary to sustain retail establishments along the street. With shuttle buses stopping every seventy seconds or less, waits are short. Passengers hop on and off frequently. Denver calls the popular system a "horizontal elevator," inverting the original nineteenth-century description of the elevator as a "vertical railway." The shuttle carries passengers from the state capitol district at one end of the mall down Sixteenth Street into Lower Downtown at the other. Diane Blackman said that on days when the Rockies play at home, many baseball fans drive into downtown, where they can park for little or no money, take the shuttle down Sixteenth Street, and walk through Lower Downtown on the way to Coors Field. They consider the trip "part of the experience of getting to a game." To integrate the historic district more with the rest of downtown, the city plans to expand shuttle service three more blocks down the Sixteenth Street Mall to its natural terminus at LoDo's Union Station. The historic railroad depot will also soon provide rail service to Denver International Airport, twenty-five miles away.

On the site of former rail yards behind the station, in the Central Platte Valley, Denver is trying to decide how best to develop 4,500 acres of open land in the city's downtown. Few cities have Denver's opportunity to build a new downtown district entirely from scratch. Denver Urban Renewal Authority chairman Jerry Glick said that when the city gauged public reactions to photographs of other places, the most preferred model for development of the site was Lower Downtown. The least preferred model was Denver's High Tech Center, a low-density suburban employment center so dependent on automobiles that traffic there is the most congested in the region. "That's exactly what we don't want in downtown," Glick said.

The rediscovery of Lower Downtown has taught Denver lessons about the kind of environment necessary to make cities work. As a sign that this community takes its built environment seriously, the neighborhood news-paper carried an article by Joslyn Green, managing broker of City Life Real Estate, entitled "Does LoDo Have Great Streets?" The piece was a review of a book, *Great Streets*, by Allan Jacobs, a professor of city planning at the University of California and a former planner in San Francisco and Pitts-burgh. After outlining the author's criteria for "great streets," the reviewer concluded that, with more work, LoDo could have them.[16]

Jennifer Moulton, director of the city's Department of Planning and De-velopment, said that as a result of Lower Downtown's revival, "We have be-gun to look at downtown as more than one place." Denver now sees its downtown as a collection of subdistricts with distinct concentrations of activ-ities: shopping, cultural institutions, government, or private offices. When looking at Lower Downtown, Moulton said, "You know where it begins and where it ends. It's four blocks deep and six blocks long." Pulling out a map of downtown Denver in her office, she said that before the subdistricts were recognized downtown, "the only city that had as large an undistinguished [downtown] area was Atlanta." Learning from downtowns in Milwaukee and Cincinnati, Denver set guidelines for subdistrict heights and densities, hop-ing to densify the empty areas and create the kind of sidewalk traffic neces-sary for a safe and vibrant atmosphere.

With a population of just over 2 million, metropolitan Denver ranks twenty-second in the nation in size, but eleventh in terms of its downtown workforce, about 110,000 employees. With 93 percent of job growth hap-pening outside of downtown, however, downtown's share of the metropolitan workforce is "eroding as the suburbs get bigger," said the Downtown Denver Partnership's Bill Mosher. As the suburbs grow, most new retail space is go-ing into suburban shopping malls. Because of decentralizing trends, down-town Denver must look to specialty retailers, nightlife entertainment, and new housing to fill its empty spaces. In Denver, as in cities across the coun-try, from Wall Street in Manhattan to Main Street in Memphis, Tennessee, office space is giving way to living space as historic buildings are converted and marketed as fashionable addresses.

The Downtown Denver Partnership maintains its office in the 1890 Kit-tredge Building, a stone structure with large Romanesque arched windows overlooking the Sixteenth Street Mall. Historic photos of downtown Denver line the office walls. The group's logo is the 1909 Daniels and Fisher Tower. All the emphasis on downtown Denver's historic fabric is not accidental, Mosher says. "Downtowns need to be unique and different from the suburbs," he said. "The importance of that is difficult to get across to business interests who feel they have to be *more* like the suburbs. But if part of your advantage is being unique and different, that means capitalizing on your historic heritage."

"A lot of communities are realizing that the characteristics of their built environment are important," Dana Crawford said. "They give a community its own attraction, which is important to tourism and the community itself in a transient society. . . .

"A man came up from Houston recently and said, 'We've torn down our history. What are we going to do?' "

Lower Downtown, Crawford said, has given Denver "a destination and a sense of history," exactly what she gave Denver at Larimer Square, which she sold in 1986. Ten years later, Larimer Square's one-block-long marketplace has continued to mature. The buildings look impeccable. Sidewalks are spotless. Shops are lit brightly at night. Restaurants are full, serving diners on sidewalk tables. Street performers entertain people passing by. Christmas lights in trees lend the place a festive aura, along with banners and planted baskets hanging from the period-stylized lampposts. Music is broadcast throughout the block via outdoor speakers. Walking through Larimer Square is almost like walking inside a mall. The artificiality of the environment is a constant reminder that it exists, above all, to sell something. It's fun. But it's a stage set, unreal.

Judging from Larimer Square, the greatest question for LoDo's future is whether the neighborhood can remain a neighborhood, whether it can remain attractive to residents even as it becomes more of an attraction for visitors. Denver, with its gold rush entrepreneurialism, could wind up extracting every penny of profit from the district until it discovers the place has become too exhausted to give up any more.

"LoDo has all the makings of a great city within a city," wrote David Gottlieb in the *LoDo News* after stepping down as executive director of the district association in 1996.[17] As Gottlieb returned to his hometown of Chicago, he offered a parting warning about the district's future. Lower Downtown will change, he predicted. It will become even more of an "urban watering hole," especially for sports fans, and, as the Platte Valley fills up with new development, "LoDo will find itself more of a walled city than a downtown neighborhood. . . .

"Battles over design and new construction will get more heated," he wrote. "The mall shuttle will go through, so there will be more people on the street. More chain restaurants and retailers will come to cash in on the good times. More than half will fold when the market experiences a sharp downturn in about four years. Then, when the sun comes out again, Mom & Pop shops, homegrown theater companies and small cafes will take over the spaces, and the cycle will start all over again.

"What you'll be left with," said Gottlieb, is "a real live city, and a great one at that."

■ ■ ■

Minneapolis and St. Paul, the Twin Cities of Minnesota, are not identical twins. St. Paul, the smaller of the two and older by ten years, looks much more elderly than Minneapolis. In downtown St. Paul, the blocks are smaller, the buildings are closer together, and the skyline is still dominated by early to mid-twentieth-century structures faced with brick and stone. Among them stand dozens of historic commercial buildings and stunning civic landmarks, the Minnesota state capitol, built in 1903, and the 1915 Cathedral of St. Paul, easily one of the most beautiful churches in the world.

While St. Paul drew inspiration from the East, Minneapolis, on the west bank of the Mississippi River, drew its energy from the West, from the plains that supply the grain that still feeds the city's corporate fortunes. "Minneapolis is the beginning of the West, St. Paul the last outpost of the East," wrote one observer sixty years ago in a statement just as true today.[18] Minneapolis has historic landmarks too, but ever since the 775-foot-high IDS Center went up in 1973, the city's skyline has been dominated by shiny towers with smooth glass surfaces. Where St. Paul's landmarks display Old World extravagance, the new landmarks in Minneapolis display no-nonsense Scandinavian simplicity. As Minnesotan Garrison Keillor once described the Twin Cities, "Minneapolis is Wonder bread, St. Paul is pumpernickel."

During the Great Depression, St. Paul's rich flavor went stale. In 1936, a writer for *Fortune* magazine called the city "cramped, hilly and stagnant. . . . Its streets [are] narrow and its buildings small. . . . Its slums are among the worst in the land. . . . Above all, there is the atmosphere of a city grown old. . . . St. Paul is what Minneapolis has been fighting not to become: a city economically obsolete."[19] The insult sent St. Paul scurrying to hide its age. Civic shame over old buildings would not evolve into respect for another thirty years.

In 1945, industrial designer Raymond Loewy, a native of France who launched his career designing clothes, told St. Paul that its old downtown storefronts drove consumers to shop on better-looking streets in Minneapolis. "For decades St. Paul had prided itself on the architectural splendor of its

Queen Anne, Richardsonian, and various historic revival buildings," write Jeffery A. Hess and Paul Larsen in a history of St. Paul architecture. "In Loewy's eyes, however, this old-fashioned mixture of styles and ornamentation was a major stumbling block to a modern marketable downtown." As traditionally ornamented buildings gave way to the sleek and clean designs of the International Style, Loewy advised St. Paul merchants to hide their elaborate facades and remove all "ugly and superfluous architectural detail, such as cornices, pediments and rococo ornaments." The designer also promoted that "staple of post-war American retailing, the windowless department store," Hess and Larsen note. "Playing on the phrase of the great French architect Le Corbusier that a house was a 'machine for living,' Loewy contended that a department store was a 'machine for selling.'" By the 1950s, St. Paul's merchants were transforming Victorian wedding cakes into modern selling machines, hiding traditional storefronts behind "aluminum-framed display windows . . . polished granite . . . and porcelain enamel panels."[20]

In spite of Loewy-inspired modernizations, downtown's share of retail sales eroded. By the mid-1950s, after sales had slipped and property values had declined, planners called downtown "old . . . drab . . . depressing." The number of pedestrians on downtown sidewalks was down, hurt by the St. Paul Housing Renewal Authority's clearance of urban neighborhoods as well as migration of traffic to suburban markets. After the first fully enclosed, climate-controlled shopping mall opened on the outskirts of the Twin Cities in 1956, the mall's architect, Victor Gruen, worked on plans to redesign St. Paul's downtown retail district to make it more competitive with suburban outlets. The lesson of the mall for urban retail districts, Gruen believed, was to separate vehicular and pedestrian traffic. Inspired by the restriction of vehicles from the central precinct of his native Vienna, Gruen advocated pedestrian-only precincts in American cities. In fact, in the 1950s he designed the first urban pedestrian mall in America in Kalamazoo, Michigan. In St. Paul, the Dayton department store chain had Gruen design what Hess and Larsen call a "giant windowless box, as inward as any suburban shopping mall," complete with a parking garage served by a spiral ramp. As Hess and Larsen recall, "To drive into the Dayton's ramp was to drive out of the city."[21]

To encourage shoppers to drive into the city, Loewy had promoted the construction of parking garages equipped with bridges to carry pedestrians over streets into the second floors of stores, a concept brought to life in renewal plans of the 1960s. Inspired by Gruen's climate-controlled mall and Loewy's call for second-story, open-air pedestrian ramps, a team of St. Paul architects working in the mid-1960s designed what came to be called the city's system of "skyways," the fully enclosed, climate-controlled pedestrian bridges that link the second floors of downtown buildings. The skyways were just one element of a nine-structure urban renewal plan of the 1960s called Capital Centre, a plan to clear twelve blocks, 108 buildings, and 371 businesses, all for new construction.

One developer at the time predicted: "When the skyway program is completed, St. Paul will be one of the biggest shopping centers in the world—all under one roof."[22] But the plans failed to work as intended. In 1963, before skyways were built, downtown was home to 400 stores. By 1975, skyways enabled pedestrians to walk for two and a half miles without ever touching a sidewalk, but the number of stores downtown had fallen to 160. With the extreme climate driving pedestrians inside and skyways inviting them upstairs, office workers vanished from the sidewalks, denying small retailers the pedestrian traffic they needed to survive. A few streets spared skyways remained active, even in Minnesota's notorious winter months. But Wabash Street, a main artery of the downtown retail district, was transformed into the paralyzed spine of the Capital Centre renewal area. Downtown was damaged by its own devices.

When Minneapolis demolished its Romanesque 1890 Metropolitan Building in 1962, the loss of that treasured landmark energized preservationists in the region, particularly in St. Paul. One of them, Georgia Ray DeCoster, a member of the St. Paul planning board, warned that "American cities are threatened by a steady dilution of historic character and architectural personality." The issue was not simply the loss of landmarks, but the destruction of traditional urban form, the street walls and sidewalk life under assault from modernist designers and urban renewal authorities. "Today almost everybody agrees that landmarks must be preserved," DeCoster wrote in 1966, "but it is not generally recognized that the more ordinary older structures have a useful role to play in revitalized urban centers."[23]

St. Paul lost a couple of major landmarks before preservationists managed to rescue the threatened Federal Courts Building. It was downtown's most distinctive landmark, a Romanesque limestone building with a tall clock tower and copper-clad turrets, fronting the downtown city square, Rice Park. The General Services Administration, the federal agency in charge of federal property, wanted to demolish the grand structure for a parking lot to accommodate workers in a new federal building. After neighborhood activists at Irvine Park in the West Seventh Street neighborhood fought off a housing authority clearance program, St. Paul established its preservation commission in 1976—finally bringing to a halt the forty-year-long assault on the city's heritage.

That same year, St. Paul elected a new mayor, labor lawyer George Latimer, who inherited a city in desperate need of new life. When Latimer took office, St. Paul was losing both jobs and people. The city had lost 10,000 jobs in the early 1970s. The population was in the midst of dropping by 13 percent, from over 300,000 in 1970 to under 270,000 by 1980. Many stores on downtown streets had disappeared. Whole blocks of downtown buildings were demolished for urban renewal, only to be left unfilled. One spot seemed so impossible to fill that citizens called it the "Superhole." By the time he became mayor, Latimer said, "the holes in downtown St. Paul had been there so long they were competing for historic designations." Dick Broeker, Latimer's top assistant at city hall, recalled how "St. Paul was groping for its identity. People were distressed about the condition of the city. A few old-style urban renewal projects had leveled portions of the city for new construction, and yet, the city was still losing its vitality."

Until then, the conventional concept of urban redevelopment was for a city to seize control of a blighted spot on the map, level it to the ground, and then seek a developer willing to build on vacant land. But the era for that approach was over. The gush of federal money had slowed to a trickle; rising interest rates made new construction hard to justify. St. Paul had to settle for reasonable expectations about its future. A skyline of glass towers was not in the cards. The new interest in St. Paul's historic buildings, meanwhile, called out for the adaptation of old structures to meet new needs. "We realized that we were never going to be a Minneapolis," Broeker said. "Our destiny lay elsewhere."

Elsewhere, it turned out, was Lowertown, "a hodge-podge of warehouses, parking lots, railroad yards and rundown historic buildings" that edged up against the city center and the Mississippi River. Originally known as the "Lower Landing" for riverboat trade in the nineteenth century, Lowertown was the oldest section of St. Paul, a onetime frontier trading post that became Minnesota's capital in 1849. As St. Paul grew into a thriving timber town and distribution center for the Northwest, government offices, along with finance and retail trade, moved to their current downtown location. The old riverfront landing became an industrial zone. Lowertown saw a building boom from 1880 to 1920, as wealthy industrialists such as James J. Hill, magnate of the Great Northern Railway, erected massive warehouses out of stone and brick, cast iron and steel. More than merely functional, these warehouses were highly ornamented displays of wealth and power, built to last far beyond the lifetimes of their owners. Most of the warehouses were about six stories high, giving the district of individualized warehouses unity as a whole.

Founded in the age of steamboats and expanded in the age of rail, Lowertown declined in the age of the automobile. Its fortunes faded until Lowertown was but a poor man's extension of more valuable downtown real estate. By the end of the 1960s, Lowertown was home to little more than a few active industrial sites, low-value businesses, and vacancies. "It was eerily dead,"

Dick Broeker remembered. Few people worked there. Virtually no one lived there, save for the derelicts who roamed the empty streets. A park in the district's center "was largely unused," Broeker said. "There were no street activities, and the depot was closed," Amtrak having discontinued service to the landmark station in 1971. Though the district abutted the Mississippi River, "Lowertown had no relation to the waterfront. The area was just dead," Broeker said, "but it did not take a genius to appreciate the historic quality to it that made St. Paul a great place."

Though Lowertown's north quadrant had been leveled for I-94, the warehouse district's eleven-block core had been left virtually untouched by the urban renewal bulldozer. Seeing potential in Lowertown's undisturbed turn-of-the-century ambience, St. Paul philanthropist Norman Mears proposed a multimillion-dollar plan for its redevelopment in the early 1970s, but he died in 1974 before his vision could be realized. By the mid-1970s, however, artists had begun to discover the area, attracted to cheap rents in the large industrial buildings, where large floor areas, good lighting, wide doors, and freight elevators made perfect spaces for their studios. Setting up residences in their studios, nearly 250 artists moved into the district, a violation of city regulations, but evidence that Lowertown had potential to become an attractive place to live and work.

The Latimer administration, having formed no strong ties with the city's business leadership in the previous election campaign, looked at Lowertown with an open eye and saw the potential, too, inspired by the adaptive reuse of industrial waterfront districts such as Seattle's Pioneer Square and Georgetown's Chesapeake and Ohio Canal district, in Washington, D.C. In Lowertown, St. Paul officials envisioned an "urban village" for residents, office workers, shoppers, and diners, in addition to workers already employed at the district's existing industrial sites. Plans for the district's rehabilitation placed the greatest emphasis on the creation of new housing, with the belief that it would be easier to attract new residents to the district before attracting customers to patronize businesses in an uninhabited location. Market research, moreover, showed a demand for downtown apartments for couples without children, single professionals, and retirees.

St. Paul's private sector, however, was skeptical of the new city administration's plans. "We were swimming against the current," Dick Broeker recalled. "The private sector then only believed that you either built new—and up—or you were stuck in the dark ages. They didn't understand that historic preservation could be profitable and intriguing and could shape an environment that would offer a city vitality."

Though Lowertown represented a quarter of the downtown area, it held only 10 percent of the downtown tax base. The area had attracted $22 million in new investment over the previous ten years, but 75 percent of that had gone into a single manufacturing plant for Gillette. The district was not a location where additional investors were willing to risk large amounts of capital. After studying Lowertown's situation, Latimer's team decided that without some form of coordinated effort to stimulate investment in the area's historic structures, the rebirth of Lowertown would never occur in their lifetimes, certainly not during their time in office. They sought a creative way for city hall to leverage large amounts of private investment using limited public dollars.

The critical early believer in the vision turned out to be the McKnight Foundation, established by the family behind the 3M Corporation, the St. Paul–based manufacturer of Scotch tape and Post-it notes. Until then, the McKnight Foundation's mission had focused narrowly on human services. "It had never been a bricks-and-mortar organization," Broeker said, "but we knew they were looking for projects large enough to make a dramatic difference in the community." After a year in office, the new mayor went to the foundation with a proposal requesting $10 million for Lowertown's revitalization, claiming the money would attract $100 million more from private investors and public sources. Latimer told the foundation's directors, "Anything less than ten million dollars wouldn't be worth doing because it wouldn't be enough to transform the whole area." After weeks of negotiations, the foundation awarded the full $10 million request as seed capital to launch the Lowertown Redevelopment Corporation, a nonprofit, tax-exempt agency independent of city hall. The award stipulated that $1 million could fund administrative expenses, while the rest would finance Lowertown redevelopment projects.

Two decades later, Lowertown has evolved from a fading urban industrial area to one of St. Paul's fastest growing neighborhoods. Warehouses have been converted to offices and loft apartments. Ground-floor spaces have sprouted restaurants and specialty retailers. In creating new activity alongside downtown's central business district and the riverfront, the rebirth of Lowertown has allowed the city to plan redevelopment of the riverfront itself. Since 1978, Lowertown has captured $428 million in new investment, more than any comparable-sized area of St. Paul over the same period—nearly $43 in new investment for every dollar granted by the McKnight Foundation. Two-thirds of the district's historic structures, many of them vacant and crumbling before the effort began, have been revitalized and put to productive use. By 1994, some seventy-three projects involving renovation, rehabilitation, and new construction had created approximately 3,000 new construction jobs and an estimated 4,600 additional permanent jobs in the Lowertown area. Property taxes climbed from less than $900,000 to almost

$4 million in the first seven years alone. In 1994, Lowertown retailers, from art galleries to fast-food vendors to upscale restaurants, reported sales of $30 million, contributing $1.5 million in annual sales taxes to the city treasury. The McKnight Foundation's limited funding for administrative expenses has kept the Lowertown Redevelopment Corporation small. In fact, since 1982, the agency has been run by one urban planning professional aided by a full-time office assistant and specialists hired for specific tasks.

Weiming Lu, the LRC's executive director, came to St. Paul in 1979 with two decades of urban planning experience in Minneapolis and Dallas, where he helped to install that city's landmark commission. The LRC is also guided by corporate executives who serve on its board of directors, giving the agency public credibility as well as private clout. Though the LRC holds no regulatory powers and owns no real estate, Lu said that his nimble organization serves as Lowertown's development catalyst in three ways: as a marketing agency, a development bank, and an advocate for compatible urban design in the historic warehouse district.

When Lu first tried to attract entrepreneurs to the district, he said, "I went back to Dallas to see if I could get some old friends to invest in Lowertown. They came up here one night in their jet and I was here to greet them. It was dark. The place was still. Looking around, we saw there was nobody else in sight—no cars and no people on the street but those six tall Texans and me." In spite of the empty scene, Lu said, "I showed them the area and told them it was a great place to invest." After the tour, he said, the potential investors from Dallas promptly "went home and never came back."

Lu laughs about the experience now, because in the years since, he has successfully helped to attract investors to Lowertown from as far away as Los Angeles, Philadelphia, Chicago, and Montreal. Without an organization like his to market Lowertown's advantages, Lu said fewer investors would have found their way to the district on their own. "These warehouses mean nothing to the investor but risk, danger, and the unknown."

To the pioneering artists, however, Lowertown was home. A year after Latimer launched the city's effort, the Minneapolis Arts Commission founded a nonprofit agency to be a clearinghouse for artists who wanted to move into that city's own warehouse district. Over the next decade, the organization, Artspace Projects, Incorporated, evolved into a development agency that has consulted on the creation of affordable housing for artists in over a hundred communities nationwide, including St. Louis, Galveston, Texas, Shreveport, Louisiana, and Salt Lake City. According to Cheryl Kartes, a former Artspace Projects director, St. Paul officials decided that the cost of rehabilitating industrial buildings for studios and galleries was a good return for the city's relatively small contribution. With a $210,000 loan from the Lowertown Redevelopment Corporation and $540,000 from the city of St. Paul, Artspace Projects helped Lowertown artists convert a building for $1.7 million into a limited equity cooperative. The organization then converted two other structures, the 1908 Northern Warehouse and the 1894 Tilsner Building, into living and working spaces, assuring permanent enclaves for artists who might otherwise be pushed out by real estate speculators and rising rents.

When artists discovered Lowertown, "others didn't think the place could ever be used again without being leveled," said L. Kelley Lindquist, Artspace Projects' president. During the 1980s, however, Lowertown was one of the city's few neighborhoods that saw a rise in population. The district's 1,500 new residential units provide housing for a mix of incomes. Roughly 70 percent of the housing is market rate, including some luxury condominiums. The remaining 30 percent is reserved for moderate- and low-income residents. About 200 units serve as living and working space for artists, giving Lowertown one of the highest concentrations of artists of any location in the country. Throughout Lowertown, no single class or age group dominates, and the demographic variety helps make the area more vibrant. The social diversity was intended from the beginning, Latimer said, because the city realized "there is a deadening quality to monocultural developments." As a populist, Latimer wanted the preservation of the district to benefit the city as whole, not a narrow, yuppies-only segment of the population. The former mayor recalled that when his administration converted an abandoned seventy-five-acre rail yard into an energy-efficient industrial park that created five thousand jobs, "It wasn't just the rich who came to look at the converted historic rail barns. It was the kids of guys who had their first job in the rail yards. Preservation touches everybody," he said. "It's not elitist, and it doesn't have to be."

As a development bank, the LRC offers gap financing to worthy projects that wouldn't go forward without it, generally up to $200,000, or no more than 10 percent of a project's total cost, to jump-start proposals that it judges to be economically viable as well as compatible with the historic area. In one case, a loan of $120,000 from the LRC, along with the same amount from the city, helped to make possible the $3 million conversion of a warehouse into sixty units of subsidized housing for elderly tenants. By charging borrowers interest on loans at market rates, the LRC is able to recoup its administrative expenses without draining its principal endowment.

To capitalize on Lowertown's distinctive historic character, the LRC helped to get the district listed on the National Register of Historic Places in 1983. The designation gives national recognition to the area's history and makes owners of the designated properties eligible for investment tax credits when they restore their buildings to federal standards. Until tax credits were

diluted by tax-law changes in 1986, they were a valuable incentive for investors in the critical initial years of Lowertown's rehabilitation. "One of the
problems with cities is it's so much easier to get money to build than to maintain what has been built already," said Lowertown developer John Manillo,
who converted a century-old warehouse into offices. "But if you maintain
your quality, you'll have something over the long run. You'll have something
worth keeping."

To protect the district's historic character from adverse impacts, the LRC
in 1984 encouraged the city to create the Lowertown Heritage Preservation
District, which sets development guidelines for a seventeen-block area of
forty-four buildings, all but five of which are judged historically significant.
Though the LRC has no official powers to control development in the district, the organization's director and board have not been shy about using
their powers of persuasion at city hall. While some in the private sector re-
sent any interference in the development process by public-spirited citizens,
John Manillo, who has chaired the city's landmark commission, said that protecting the quality of the district is critical to its ultimate success. "I'm convinced that preservation adds value," he said.

St. Paul has also added value to the district by improving its public spaces,
right down to the smallest details, by investing in street improvements, new
sidewalks, and period street furniture, lampposts, bus stops, and benches. In
the center of the district, Mears Park, Lowertown's "village common," under-
went a five-year, $1.5 million redesign that transformed a cold brick plaza into
a more inviting space of soft green grass and trees. The renovated park even
has a stream of running water, the product of a design process that allowed for
considerable input from residents of the surrounding neighborhood.

The Lowertown district designation also provides a process for public input on new buildings, setting guidelines that protect the district's traditional
urban scale from the whims of out-of-town developers. For instance, when a
national hotel chain wanted to construct a new hotel in Lowertown next to a
ramp off I-94, the hotel's plans clashed with the district's existing building
patterns. The chain wanted a suburban hotel, set back from the sidewalk in
the middle of its parcel, surrounded by a lagoon of parking, as if it were isolated on some lonely suburban highway. Rather than chase the hotel chain
away, however, the LRC appealed to its representatives to build the structure
in a corner of the parcel, flush along the sidewalk similar to historic buildings
in the district, moving parking spaces to the side and rear and reserving unused land on the site for potential development later. The LRC also persuaded the hotel chain to alter its exterior design to make the building more
compatible with the district's historic structures. Weiming Lu said the most
important aspect of new construction in the district is not architectural styles

but whether new additions are compatible with the district and complementary to surrounding structures. "I am not a design czar dictating to everyone," he said. "Postmodern, modern, I don't care. If they relate to what's here, that's what counts. Design is not just a building, but the streetscape. How we put things together in the public realm is important."

While the LRC's quasi-public status created some friction with city bureaucrats who felt responsible for Lowertown's future, the LRC's independence has allowed the agency to focus its energy and resources on a well-defined location, outlasting the Latimer administration as well as others that have followed it. "I wanted to be sure that this had legs and would outrun my time in office and would be less subject to the pressures of politics," Latimer said. In an era of diminished federal support for urban redevelopment, Latimer also succeeded in kick-starting private action years before others recited the mantra of public/private partnerships.[24] Latimer, who served as an assistant to Secretary Henry Cisneros at the U.S. Department of Housing and Urban Development and now teaches urban studies at Macalester College in St. Paul, argues that mayors need to be catalysts, but they also need to step back and allow efforts to grow on their own. "I think mayors make a mistake when they feel they need to have their grubby little thumbprint on everything," he said.

The Lowertown effort's staying power stems also from a long-range plan that takes years to execute, managed diligently by the LRC's executive director of fourteen years, Weiming Lu. "You have to know a city; it's only after staying awhile that you can make a contribution and have some impact, be effective and be useful," Lu said. Lowertown developer John Manillo credited Lu's long-term outlook as a vital contribution to the district's revitalization. "He's concerned with the long term and not next month or next year," Manillo said. "Developers are always worried about whether they will be able to pay their bills—what's the least they have to put into a project to make money on it quickly?" That kind of thinking, Manillo said, "goes against the goals of preserving a district, because the district needs to be there ten years from now or else it will be a flash in the pan. Lowertown hasn't been that."

Urban analyst Neil Peirce made that very point when he visited St. Paul in 1988 on the occasion of the LRC's tenth anniversary. Peirce recalled how ten years before, when the LRC was formed, state and local governments in Pennsylvania coughed up $88 million in low-interest loans, tax incentives, and transportation improvements to lure a Volkswagen plant to Westmoreland. Less than ten years later, however, the auto plant closed and the jobs disappeared. "There's egg all over the face of the Pennsylvania officials who landed the deal, except that almost all of them are retired and off enjoying their pensions now," he noted. "All economic-development deals, no matter how glamorous, involve risk. But diversifying risk, forming multiple partnerships and shared responsibilities, husbanding one's resources, looking to indigenous resources for growth—those seem to be wiser policies. And they are precisely what the Lowertown venture has been about."

If the Lowertown effort has ever encountered trouble, it was in breaking from that formula for sustainable growth to construct Galtier Plaza, a pair of high-rise apartment and office towers set on top of a three-story indoor shopping mall in the heart of the historic district. Originally conceived by the Latimer administration as a means to create a critical mass of new development downtown, Galtier Plaza suffered financially from construction delays and cost overruns. In 1989, when Chemical Bank of New York sold the property, the city of St. Paul lost $9 million on the deal, an amount nearly equivalent to the McKnight Foundation's grant for the entire Lowertown revitalization effort.

Galtier Plaza created too much new space in one place at one time. The shopping mall, moreover, was poorly planned. When the initial retail tenants proved to be too upscale to attract enough customers, the mall had to be redesigned for stores, restaurant chains, and other tenants more tailored to local needs. A YMCA in the complex has proven to be a popular, successful addition to the district, but it has taken time for Galtier Plaza to recover from its losses. Time, however, cannot heal Galtier Plaza's disruption of Lowertown's historic environment. The structure's tall towers, one of which is forty-six stories high, are completely out of scale in a district of medium-rise warehouse buildings, and the exterior, which reuses bricks of a demolished warehouse at ground level to partially hide the suburban-style mall inside, is an example of bad facadism, a sorry compromise between historic integrity and new design, with the true benefits of neither.

Galtier Plaza was not inspired by indigenous Lowertown resources, but instead by a similar project in Minneapolis called Riverplace as well as another, much criticized project in downtown St. Paul called Town Square, a two-block complex where towers rise out of a three-level indoor shopping mall. Championed by Mayor Latimer as a device to fill the "Superhole" left empty by urban renewal, Town Square was built to boost the city's psyche, its retail sector, and the downtown real estate market, all of which needed stimulation in the mid-1970s. After a decade and a half, however, it is Town Square's shopping mall that needs help most of all, a victim of suburban competition as well as poor urban design. Though Town Square provided St. Paul with an innovative year-round garden under a glass roof, the mall below the garden has proven less successful. "From the sidewalk it has the appearance of a gray-walled fortress," a team of critics wrote. "No storefronts enliven the street, and the most prominent openings are driveways to the hotel entrance and underground garage. Only a few small doors lead from the sidewalk to the shopping area."[25] Because of its inward orientation, the mall drew fewer shoppers off the sidewalk than intended. According to urban scholars Bernard J. Frieden and Lynne B. Sagalyn, surveys showed that the majority of shoppers at Town Square actually drove from the suburbs to park in the mall's underground garage, but "most people who were interviewed said they preferred suburban malls because they were more convenient and because they offered a larger selection of items to buy."[26] The brutalistic complex was a choice made in economic desperation, in a time when "commerce was leaking out of cities and cities were willing to take the first developer to come along with any project at all," Dick Broeker said. Latimer now describes the structure as "that big, ugly gray building," and candidly calls its design his biggest regret, confessing that he "didn't have the stomach" to send the "aggressive" developers, Oxford Properties of Canada, back to the drawing board. As for Galtier Plaza several blocks away, Latimer readily admits that it "is way too out of scale for Lowertown, which has flourished in spite of it."

Lowertown flourishes most where St. Paul has capitalized on the traditional urbanism that was always there, the city's one-of-a-kind environment. Compared to the Capital Centre renewal area, with its high-rise towers recessed at ground level, its blank walls and windswept plazas, the twelve blocks around Lowertown's Mears Park are lively, a distinctive twenty-four-hour district in a nine-to-five downtown.

If downtown St. Paul has come far in the last twenty years, it still has some distance to go. Locals are the first to say so. Garrison Keillor, who broadcasts *A Prairie Home Companion* over Minnesota Public Radio each Saturday from St. Paul's 1910 Fitzgerald Theater, tells visitors to the city, "We won't be hurt or alarmed if you are underwhelmed. Most of our European ancestors came here expecting to find Eden, which turned out to be false advertising, and if there had been cheap airfare in the nineteenth century, they would have gone right back home."

Lowertown shows no pretensions of striving to become an Eden, just a pleasant "new urban village," as Weiming Lu describes it, a place in the city where people choose to work and live. "It's not finished yet," George Latimer said nearly twenty years after launching the effort to revive the district, "but it has come a long way.

"We've preserved our history. We won that battle. We've lost some little battles and some beautiful buildings along the way, but the historic infrastructure is here for another hundred years."

■ ■ ■

San Francisco, Seattle and Portland are likened to three sisters, says Portland historian Terence O'Donnell. "Seattle is the tart, San Francisco the debutante, and Portland is the spinster." Seattle and San Francisco grew thanks to prospectors drunk with gold rush greed. Portland, on the other hand, grew soberly. The pious Yankee families who settled Oregon's Willamette Valley in the mid-nineteenth century brought with them from New England a moralistic culture more concerned with protecting the commonwealth than accumulating personal wealth.[27] To this day, that legacy sets Portland apart in the libertarian West.

If San Francisco is the Manhattan of the West, a place of bewildering density and diversity, then Portland is more like Boston, smaller and more manageable, with a culture more proper than libertine and a compact urban environment remarkably well preserved. Boston, in fact, almost became the city's name. In 1845, pioneers Asa Lovejoy of Boston and Francis Pettygrove of Portland, Maine, each wanted to name the new settlement for his hometown back east. To resolve the matter, they tossed a penny. Pettygrove won two out of three.

As a river city, seventy-eight miles inland from the Pacific Ocean, where the Columbia and Willamette Rivers converge, Portland's topography has less in common with San Francisco by the Bay or Seattle by the Sound than with the river cities of the Ohio Valley: Pittsburgh, Cincinnati, Louisville, and St. Louis.[28] Topographically, Portland most resembles Pittsburgh, with its three-river junction and its bevy of bridges. Like Pittsburgh, downtown Portland is kept from sprawling by a natural barrier of western hills. And like Pittsburgh, Portland never built an outer beltway, a circumferential highway around its suburbs. If both cities have been contained by topography and transportation, Pittsburgh has done it more by accident, Portland more by design. Portlanders are protective of their region's postcard-perfect scenery. To the east lie Mount Hood, the Columbia River gorge, and the Cascade Range. To the west are the Coast Range and the Pacific shore. To the south is the fertile farmland of the Willamette Valley, the Garden of Eden that awaited eighty thousand pioneers at the end of the Oregon Trail. And for the last quarter century, Portlanders have protected their very traditional downtown, a compact web of tiny blocks only two hundred feet in length. Portland's city fathers mapped out small blocks in order to sell more valuable corner lots. But the numerous interesting corner properties and the short distance between intersections created one of the nation's most walkable downtowns, where the average building is only nine to twelve stories high. Some of them are small Victorian relics; others date from a construction boom after Portland's Lewis and Clark Centennial Exposition of 1905 attracted publicity for the city and new prosperity that lasted until the Great Depression.

Portland's traditional built environment and pedestrian-friendly scale then became a victim of postwar redevelopment. Before World War II had ended, city officials sent for Robert Moses to draw up a plan for Portland's future. Moses arrived with his aides and closed himself inside a room, where he pored over maps and plotted highways, hacking his way through the historic city with his meat axe. When the mayor called on Moses to check on progress, the mighty planner drove him away. "When I want to see the mayor, I'll send for him," Moses said. He emerged from the room with a number of ideas, including one for Harbor Drive, an expressway for fast-moving traffic through the heart of town.

"The Harbor Drive improvements wiped out scores of the handsomest buildings ever constructed in the city," wrote William J. Hawkins III, a Portland architect and great-grandson of pioneer San Francisco foundryman Jonathan Kittredge, whose firm supplied cast iron for some of the structures leveled for Harbor Drive.[29] The expressway removed for all time most of Portland's oldest surviving district, Old Town, the original downtown. Old Town had been in decline since the turn of the century, when downtown businesses moved west with the new streetcar traffic. Although dissenters objected to the demolition of Old Town, few in the city fully appreciated what they were tearing down, the largest collection of cast-iron buildings outside of SoHo in New York, another historic district once targeted by a Moses transportation scheme.

"It is ironic that in 1942 a group of London firemen brought to Portland an appeal for funds to help save and rebuild London's historic buildings," Hawkins noted. "A display of the war-damaged structures was set up in the Meier & Frank auditorium, attended by many concerned citizens. The Londoners would surely have been stunned to learn that the same Portlanders were in the course of destroying the best of their historic structures along the river—with less speed, perhaps, but with the same effect as the blitz."[30] Down the buildings came, block by block. Of some two hundred cast-iron structures that graced the Willamette River at the turn of the century, 90 percent of them disappeared. Only years later, when some of the demolished structures yielded nothing but parking lots, did the city's mood toward the structures shift from one of neglect to nostalgia.

More demolitions would occur before Portlanders realized they were being robbed. The Portland Hotel, the hub of the city's social scene for sixty years, came down in 1951 for a parking lot at the busiest intersection in town. South Portland, a turn-of-the-century neighborhood of 110 acres and forty-four blocks inhabited by low-income Italians and Jews, was cleared for a modern superblock of high-rise housing that increased property values as well as the city's tax base but stole the city's traditional street and sidewalk grid patterns. The more the demolitions continued, however, the more outraged the public became. As Portland planned a new ramp for Harbor Drive, intending to clear away the last survivors in the old cast-iron district, citizens learned of the plan. "This was in the old days before open government, when plans could get to a city council meeting for approval without anyone knowing about it, but somebody did find out, and the whole thing was stopped," said Portland architect George McMath, grandson of architect Albert E. Doyle, whose firm designed many of the city's landmarks during the first three decades of the century.

In 1965, as urban renewal activity moved into downtown from the former South Portland area, the city's urban renewal authority decided to spare a grand old cast-iron structure in its path and slated it for restoration. The *Oregonian,* the city's daily newspaper, published a rendering of the landmark as it would look after restoration. "But that was premature," McMath recalled, "because within two weeks the owner tore it down." Portland was outraged. "If there was a single trigger to spur our preservation program, that was it," McMath said. By 1968, Portland had one of the few historic landmark ordinances in the West.

Because so few cities had landmark protections at the time, McMath said no opponents rallied to defeat the measure. "It was remarkably easy" to pass, he said. "I don't think the city council at the time saw the impact. They saw it as a little old ladies' let's-save-the-nice-old-house kind of thing, and we didn't see it that way at all." Though the ordinance provided ways to review impending demolitions, its greatest value was in freeing preservationists from reacting to every crisis. Instead, it allowed them to identify areas of the city worth saving and to work their priorities into the city planning department's broader agenda. Over the next three decades, the preservation agenda was woven so thoroughly into the city's planning process that McMath could not recall the loss of more than two significant historic structures since the ordinance was passed. "Now, it has become so routine that it doesn't generate any passion anymore. It's just part of the process."

If the first challenge for the defenders of traditional Portland was to protect their city from demolition, the next was to defend its human scale from superhuman schemes, from Le Corbusier's vision of high-rise towers and high-speed lanes.

When Portland's famed architect Pietro Belluschi graced the city with its first modern office building, the thirteen-story aluminum-and-glass-paneled Equitable Building, in 1948, his innovative design still showed respect for downtown's traditional pattern of short buildings built flush to the sidewalks. Belluschi managed to challenge the old order without overthrowing it altogether. Within fifteen years, however, such respect was antiquated. High-rises of the 1960s, beginning with Standard Plaza and the Hilton Hotel in 1963, became monuments to corporate egos instead of emblems of civic pride. The new generation of buildings towered above their neighbors and blocked Portlanders' treasured views of the mountaintops in the distance. At ground level, their blank walls and empty elevated or sunken plazas showed contempt for pedestrians on the sidewalks. Sold as a symbol of urban vitality, the new fortress architecture did not enliven the city as much as deaden it, discouraging street life while proliferating parking lots on surrounding blocks. Portlanders tolerated the intrusions for a decade until the construction of the forty-story First Interstate Tower in 1972 sent them storming the fortress walls. The skyscraper was three times the height of a typical downtown building, a corporate complex built on two adjacent blocks—an office tower and squat box joined by a second-story skyway bridge that did even more to discourage pedestrians on the street below. Promoted as "a symbol of the new Portland and the new America, . . . a towering challenge to Mt. Hood," the structure was attacked by critics as a "disaster," a "travesty," a "monstrosity," and an "alien." "The dramatic clutch of new Portland skyscrapers is killing the life of the street with parking garages in 'podium' bases beloved by Establishment architects who successfully isolate their corporate totems from the urban fabric and the city's essential humanity," declared Ada Louise Huxtable, architectural critic for the *New York Times*. Portland, she said, "was a city in the act of destroying itself."

If the outrages of demolition and dubious design did anything for Portland, it was to help its citizens look carefully at their surroundings. Their downtown had been surrendered to the car, to freeways and parking lots. The high-rise towers and their empty plazas reinforced downtown's new hostility to people on the street. Urban renewal had cleared away low-income residents, making downtown empty in the evening, a habitat that invited only the occupants of skid row hotels. In the city's neighborhoods, middle-class residents began fleeing to suburbia, leaving behind once stable communities and a shrinking tax base. Downtown storefronts were increasingly vacant or occupied by pawnshops. In spite of the convenience created for the automobile, trips downtown were decreasing. Portland was fulfilling Lewis Mumford's warning that Americans will have every means of getting about their cities and absolutely no reason for going there. Portland's private sector felt it, too. In the words of Gideon Bosker and Lena Lencek, authors of a book on Portland architecture, "Developers found themselves in the tragicomic position of hosts who had cleared their home for a party to which no one came."[31]

Alarmed by the visible symbols of decay, those with an interest in downtown Portland—public officials, business leaders, neighborhood activists, and other civic boosters—coalesced behind an effort to draw up a long-term plan to guide economic development. With considerable grassroots input and advice from corporate boardrooms, the city cobbled together a broad package of proposed improvements in transportation and urban design and adopted the plan in 1972. Like the old urban renewal schemes, the new plan declared that a revitalized downtown would also infuse nearby neighborhoods, but in a break with the dogma of previous decades, the plan stressed preservation over demolition, transit over traffic congestion, and the improvement of public space over the maximization of profit. Unlike plans drawn on maps two-dimensionally, the plan viewed the city as its citizens would experience it, from the sidewalk. Among its stated goals, the plan sought to "create in downtown an urban setting with a definite sense of place and identity by developing strong boundaries, emphatic focal points, unique physical designs for identifiable areas and by enhancing special views such as the waterfront and historic or architecturally significant buildings."[32]

The new ideas were pushed by a gang of allies, among them a young city councillor, Neil Goldschmidt, who became mayor four days after the adoption of the plan, at the age of thirty-two. With a mandate to preserve the city's neighborhoods and reinvigorate its downtown, Goldschmidt was at the front of a generational change in city leadership. The city's postwar leaders, according to Portland historian Carl Abbott, had been stodgy, cautious, and stingy.[33] The new team was creative, bold, and eager to invest in the city's future. Looking back on that era in 1996, Goldschmidt called it "a revolution of rising expectations" against the ideology "of throwaway cities. A lot of people rose up and said, 'Quit destroying the neighborhoods in this city. If you don't treat your city as having something of value, nobody else will.'

"What happened here starting in 1970, with the elections that sent in a new city government, was a group of young Oregonians, many of us born and raised here, came home from school, home from military service, home from working in other places with the feeling that there was something really quite special about Oregon and that it ought to be taken care of." The preservation movement had already taken hold in Portland, and the environmental movement, which celebrated the first Earth Day in 1971, had plenty of supporters in this coastal state of old-growth forests and fertile farmland. Some of the younger generation of leaders had been in college for the initial publication of influential books by Rachel Carson and Jane Jacobs, on ecology and the ecology of cities. "We also came home with a real appreciation for the best things other people were doing in their communities," Goldschmidt said. "Our goal was to make the city of Portland as terrific as the state of Oregon."

Oregon, with all of its natural wonders, was also attracting a new wave of pioneers, most of whom were abandoning smog in the Golden State for the Great Northwest. Once in Oregon, however, the refugees of urbanization re-created the very urbanization they had left behind. From Portland, sprawling development crept outward into the Willamette Valley, where nut groves, wheat fields, and turkey farms gave way to strip malls, gas stations, and fast-food franchises.

Visit Oregon, but please don't stay was the blunt advice to newcomers from Oregon's Republican governor Tom McCall, one of the most outspoken voices against what critics called the "Californication" of the Oregon land-scape. "There is a shameless threat to our environment and to the whole quality of life—the unfettered despoiling of the land," McCall said in 1972. "Sagebrush subdivisions, coastal condomania, and the ravenous rampage of suburbia in the Willamette Valley all threaten to mock Oregon's status as the environmental model for the nation." Pleading for the legislature to manage mindless growth, McCall declared that the "interests of Oregon for today and for the future must be protected from the grasping wastrels of the land."

Just as Portland completed a plan to guide downtown development, Mc-Call signed into law a plan to guide growth statewide. Among the original sponsors was Republican legislator Hector McPherson, a dairy farmer who drove to Portland one day from his place in the Willamette Valley and spotted heavy earthmoving equipment plowing up the ground by the road. Curious about how the farmland was to be used, McPherson got out of his car, walked up to one of the workers, and reportedly asked, "What are you going to grow here?" "Houses," was the reply. McPherson felt that farmland in the valley was too fertile, too rare, and too valuable a resource to waste on subdivisions that could go anywhere. The legislature agreed and passed a landmark mea-sure that remains the most visionary growth-management tool in the nation. Adopted in 1973, it established a state Land Conservation and Development Commission with a mandate to preserve farmland, timber resources, and other undeveloped landscapes by encouraging orderly, efficient, and afford-able development in or close to the state's existing communities. The LCDC requires all cities and counties in Oregon to draw up their own growth-management plans as well as an urban growth boundary to contain the spread of sprawl.

In Kentucky, a growth boundary has preserved the bluegrass countryside around Lexington since 1958. In Oregon, growth boundaries around every incorporated municipality have preserved 25 million acres of farmland and forests, an area four times the size of New Jersey. The boundary "is not a de-vice to stop growth or even to slow growth," but a tool to demarcate where urbanization will occur, said Henry Richmond, a public-interest lawyer, who, with Governor McCall, in 1975 founded the nonprofit advocacy group 1,000 Friends of Oregon. Created as a watchdog to guard the land-use laws Mc-Call put in place, the organization has cultivated a broad coalition of allies to support growth-management initiatives, teaming up at times with the Oregon Farm Bureau, the Oregon Industries Council, even the home builders' lobby in Portland, which recognize the predictability that growth management has brought to their operations. "Land is the biggest capital input in agriculture," Richmond said. A farmer who leases land year to year within reach of creeping urbanization "does not have a predictable operation," he said, but with growth measures in place, farmers and timber companies gain assurance that long-term capital improvements to their property will not be lost to the "ravenous rampage of suburbia." Home builders benefit from greater certainty, too. Under Oregon's law, any development application within an urban growth boundary must be acted upon within 120 days, freeing developers from costly delays. "Now, developers are not usually happy to see twenty-five million acres of land ruled off limits to development and they are not real wild about the concept of an urban growth boundary," said Richmond, "but they know that without it, with the sort of anything-goes posture of the land-use decision-making process in the past, every project that they put forward is subject to opposition." To reduce opposition to development within the boundaries, Richmond's group allied itself with home builders to take on suburban snob zoning. "It was basically illegal to build housing that was more affordable and was being demanded in the marketplace," Richmond said, so Oregon quadrupled the small amount of land zoned for multi-family housing and tightened by a third the average size of new single-family lots, lowering costs for developers and home buyers as well as preserving open space. "Any strategy to deal with sprawl has to increase housing choice in the suburbs," Richmond said. Because Oregon's law is responsive to private as well as public needs, and because it allows for considerable public participation in the planning process, it has survived repeated challenges by property rights advocates.

Without a statewide growth-management mechanism, land-use planning remains a fractured process that breeds competition among neighboring localities instead of cooperation. In Portland, residents of the metropolitan area also realized that without additional management of development on a *regional* basis, growth at the urban periphery threatened to pave their open spaces, flood their roads with traffic, and drain investment from their urban core, wasting millions of tax dollars to duplicate existing public infrastructure. Voters in metropolitan Portland took a giant step toward solving that problem in 1978, when they approved the nation's first directly elected metropolitan government, which coordinates the growth-management plans of three counties and twenty-four municipalities in the Portland metropolitan region. The following year, the region drew its official urban growth boundary, encompassing an area of 234,000 acres or 362 square miles, enough land to accommodate new development for the next twenty years. "The boundary has been tested for years. It has stood the test of political will," said Mike Burton, who was elected head of the metropolitan government (nicknamed "Metro" by Portlanders) in 1994. Burton said private sector interests "may have some problems with it, but they've seen the benefits of it over time." John Chandler, an attorney for the state's home builders lobby, told a reporter from Florida, "I speak around the country, and I haven't seen a system I'd swap for. We're treated as partners. I'm not sure we would switch to an unregulated market. I just came back from Houston and it's just horrible."[34]

Conceived initially to preserve Oregon's natural environment from sprawl, the state's growth-management system also enjoys support from urban interests because it prevents investments from leaking beyond the urban edge. In Portland, the measure has helped to direct growth inward, preserving the city's traditional downtown as the hub of the metropolitan region. "The recent history of Portland shows that core city revitalization, neighborhood conservation, and suburban growth management are not separable options," writes Portland historian Carl Abbott. "A metropolis that works, in short, is one that has given equal attention to all of its pieces."[35]

A national leader in regional planning for over a decade, Portland has led the way in downtown redevelopment for an even longer period. Under Mayor Goldschmidt in the mid-1970s, Portland vetoed several highway projects, the most celebrated being the 1975 rejection of the Mount Hood Freeway, intended to give residents of eastern suburbs an easy commute into the city after the demolition of half a dozen Portland neighborhoods. The proposal struck Portlanders as unsensible, not just because of the demolition it would have required, but because the freeway was projected to be congested during rush hours from the day it opened and would require the construction of a new and expensive bridge. The proposal was rejected as bad for the city as well as bad transportation planning. "If the vision here is to buy the kind of mobility that you assume freeways will give you the day they open, then evidence shows that they don't work that way," was Goldschmidt's line of argument.

Goldschmidt went on to become U.S. secretary of transportation at the end of the 1970s, an experience that gave him a unique perspective for sizing up the impact of the interstate highway system on America's cities. "When the interstate was done, it promised something for everybody, and, sure as hell, everybody expected to get it," he said. "Some of that had to be built. I'm not arguing that we don't need any urban freeway systems." But in the rush to grab federal highway funds, cities built highways indiscrimi- nately, against their long-term interests, paving the way toward decentraliza- tion, disinvestment, and ultimate decay. "They were basically driving these daggers right into their own hearts. There is so much money involved that the political forces just overwhelm the city." Today, the former mayor and transportation secretary, who went on to serve a term as governor of Ore- gon, does not see how federal highway planners could have foreseen the full impact of the interstate system on America's cities, "but what was surprising to me," he said, "was how late the cities figured it out." By the time Portland did, "we were having a bloodbath trying to convince this bureaucracy that one formula doesn't fit all cities." When Portland wanted to do things differ- ently with funds allocated for the Mount Hood Freeway, the bureaucracy felt threatened.

"History is going to decide who made the right decision here," Gold- schmidt said about the choices Portland made. "It's way too early for anybody to be running around saying they got this thing all figured out, but this com- munity cast its lot with a vision which is very unusual for the West, and that was basically: Save everything of value that's worth saving. Quit devaluing everything that's old just because you can build new in the suburbs. Besides, the things you are going to build in the suburbs aren't affordable to a lot of the people you want to wipe out to convenience yourself. And the invisible net- work of interrelationships is really what a community stands for; it isn't just the buildings or the streets or the utility poles; it's this connectivity of people looking out for one another. That is the real value in neighborhoods."

During the postwar decades, Goldschmidt said, Portland devalued its neighborhoods until "it had gotten to the point where everybody assumed that anybody's neighborhood is fair game for a speeding car. So we decided to build a community that isn't quite so susceptible to being run over by an automobile. A centerpiece of this entire agenda was not to let the auto- mobile take over Portland."

A year before Portland rejected the Mount Hood Freeway, the city began to reclaim itself from the side effects of auto dependence when it tore up the Harbor Drive expressway and replaced the six-lane expressway with a river- front park. Portland named the park in honor of Governor McCall, who had urged the city to eliminate the expressway when an interstate highway on the opposite bank of the river made the road unnecessary. For the first time in decades, downtown Portland was reconnected with its riverfront, and dor- mant districts near the river began to spring to life. "It took downtown Port- land almost thirty years to shake off the shadow of Robert Moses," Carl Abbott noted in his history of the city.[36] The Moses-inspired expressway had demolished the city's history and blighted neighboring districts, but the new park stimulated interest in restoring the century-old cast-iron buildings that remained and catalyzed additional redevelopment downtown. Portland's latest riverfront proposal surrounds the Victorian Union Station, a landmark railroad depot with a 150-foot-high clock tower. The city improved the station and its environs for $3 million to prepare the site for new housing, nearly fifty years after Robert Moses called for the station's demolition. Moses had said any funds spent to improve the familiar landmark "would be wasted and an entirely new station should be built."[37] In the years since Portland rejected his advice, the city has gained a more mature respect for its existing resources as well as a healthy respect for public participation in the planning process, a process that has produced better results than dogmatic planners acting alone.

When Harbor Drive disappeared, a group of citizens calling themselves the Portland Friends of Cast Iron Architecture, led by architect Bill Hawkins and inspired by SoHo's activists in New York, persuaded the city to establish its first official local historic district near the riverfront around the 1888 cast-iron Skidmore Fountain. Property owners who wanted to rescue its rotting structures saw their costs reduced when the state legislature in 1975 passed a fifteen-year property tax assessment freeze on rehabilitated historic buildings. That financial incentive, along with others from a city-sponsored urban conservation fund as well as federal tax credits for historic preservation created in 1976, attracted investors to the district as well as other aging neighborhoods.

"Good citizens are the riches of a city," reads the inscription at the base of Skidmore Fountain, named for Stephen Skidmore, one of Portland's early benefactors. If Skidmore was the nineteenth-century citizen responsible for the Skidmore Fountain/Old Town district's development, then Bill Naito, a property owner and developer, was his twentieth-century counterpart. For decades, Naito invested his energy and money in old Portland's preservation. Bing Sheldon, president of the local architectural firm that worked on many of Naito's properties, described him as "a hard-nosed businessman who came up the hard way and didn't believe in throwing things away. He wasn't part of the throwaway society.

"When you throw away your history, you throw away who you are. It's important for your emotional placement to have a sense of where you've been," Sheldon said. Naito, the son of Japanese immigrants, began buying properties in Old Town during its down-and-out years, when the district was home to Portland's Japanese community, adjacent to the city's Chinatown. "Being Japanese after World War II meant that you had to go to a place where nobody else wanted you, and Old Town was a place where nobody else cared about," Sheldon said. Old Town's buildings at the time were cheap, but Naito foresaw their value, picking them up and patching them up one by one. To help bring the district to life, Naito donated space to create Saturday Market, a weekend crafts exhibit that showcases the work of artisans, a popular attraction since 1974. By drawing crowds each weekend, Saturday Market helped to reacquaint Portlanders to the historic district within walking distance of downtown's office buildings. In time, Naito's collection of cast-iron-covered landmarks gradually blossomed into an entertainment district of restaurants, bars, and theaters.

Less visionary owners used to demolish such structures for parking lots. Goldschmidt, the former mayor, said that one of his worst memories was of the city being unable to prevent one of those demolitions from taking place. But from that experience, Portland learned that if it couldn't ban a demolition, it could ban the spread of parking lots that encouraged demolitions. "That way you can make sure people don't tear down their buildings until they're ready to put something back up," Goldschmidt said. There is a saying in the real estate business that more buildings are torn down than fall down. Perhaps fewer of them would succumb to the wrecking ball if city officials understood that on average it takes a generation or more to replace a demolished building.

To prevent the surrender of the downtown to parking lots, Portland placed a cap on downtown parking at roughly forty-five thousand spaces. "That actually got a few guys' attention," Goldschmidt said. "They began to wonder if they could beat us legally or just wait until we were gone. But we said, 'You can't beat us legally, and you can't outlast us. We have a downtown plan, an economic study, that says don't have these little, small postage-stamp lots. They're bad for circulation. They're bad for air quality. And they frustrate the parkers who expect to find parking when they get to these lots, but there isn't any there.' "

To ease circulation in the downtown core, the city cleared auto traffic from two of three lanes on two parallel streets running the length of downtown. Rather than turn the streets into pedestrian malls, the city left them open as uncongested one-way routes for buses. This cut bus-trip lengths significantly, and now the buses carry passengers swiftly through the downtown zone—for free. As Goldschmidt described the strategy, "We were pushing in the direction of trying to get people out of their cars—the ones who rode downtown to an office building, parked their car all day, and then left at five o'clock—so we could allocate that street space to people who would come in and use the services that office building provided, or the retail store, or the hotel." Bing Sheldon, who chaired the city's planning bureau in the early 1970s, said, "The development community thought this was communism." Without new parking, the developers said, their new buildings would fail economically. "They said it'll never work," Sheldon said, "but now they will

privately tell you that it was the best thing that ever happened to them."
What Portland's planners did, as urban analysts Neil Peirce and Robert
Guskind noted, was "to reconceptualize the problem from one of *parking* to
one of *access*."[38] As long as people could get downtown, and get around
downtown easily, the city believed downtown Portland would thrive.

After rejecting the Mount Hood Freeway, which would have flooded the
city with cars, Portland instead used federal funds to build a fifteen-mile
light-rail line to the eastern suburbs in the 1980s. Like buses on the downtown transit mall, the light-rail is free for riders in the downtown zone, where
the private sector ponied up funds to improve the sidewalks and the
streetscapes along the route. The downtown route even carries streetcars re-
produced from vintage models brought back to Portland from Portugal,
where they were hunted down by Bill Naito. Within fifteen years after opening, the new bus and rail lines carried almost a third of commuters into
downtown Portland, where employment rose from under sixty thousand in
1970 to over one hundred thousand in 1995, while the cap on new parking
spaces remained in effect. In terms of size, Portland's downtown workforce is
comparable to the one in Minneapolis, where one of America's healthier urban retail districts thrives along the Nicollet Mall, a street designated for
pedestrians and buses, the original inspiration for the transit mall in Portland.

When Portland adopted its downtown plan in 1972, downtown held 90
percent of the region's top-quality office space, but retailers there soon began to feel the pinch of competition from suburban malls. "By having to figure out a strategy for parking," Goldschmidt said, "we were able to allocate
our attention to the people who were most vulnerable without it, the retailers." The city worked to convince the retail sector that it could indeed survive downtown, even as malls were going up in surrounding suburban areas.
"On one of the breakthrough days I can remember," Goldschmidt recalled,
"I was having a conversation with somebody from one of the retail stores. He
said, 'I just sent two of my managers down to look at the Saturday Market.
These people are just packing this place in—on Saturday! If they can do it,
why doesn't our store have more traffic?' " Confident that downtown could
still draw shoppers, Goldschmidt used the city's parking strategy and transit
plans to persuade the Nordstrom department store chain to build a store at
the city's busiest intersection, then occupied by a historic theater. "We hadn't
had a new store built downtown in fifty years," Goldschmidt said, but Nordstrom executives looked at the city's plans and realized "they would be at the
center of the retail universe downtown, which is still a bigger core than any
mall in the region."

Since adopting the downtown plan in 1972, Portland has added half a million square feet of retail space, most of it successful. Yamhill Marketplace, a

festival market in historic buildings near the river, failed to draw enough customers to a location without anchor tenants. It was also disturbed by surrounding construction projects at the worst possible time and was eventually overshadowed by a new urban shopping mall, Pioneer Place, the 1990 product of a partnership between the city and the Rouse development company of Baltimore. Spanning two downtown blocks connected by an underground food court and a second-story skyway (one of the city's concessions to the developers), Pioneer Place includes a Saks Fifth Avenue store on one block and a four-level mall surrounding an atrium on the other. To integrate the new structure with the surrounding historic retail district, city planners requested traditional storefront windows on exterior walls. In an era when malls are designed inward to hold shoppers hostage in order to capture sales, Pioneer Place succeeds with a traditional outward orientation aimed at luring pedestrians off the sidewalk. Riding an escalator, shoppers can even gaze through the glass roof to admire the 1912 Meier & Frank Company department store building (rival retail space!) across the street.

"We had a goal in mind of trying to create a very pedestrian-friendly downtown core with a strong belief that if you didn't increase the number of people moving around on the streets, the feeling of public safety wouldn't get better, it would get worse," Goldschmidt said. To make downtown more appealing to pedestrians, the city effectively outlawed the kind of modernist buildings that went up in the 1960s and rewrote the zoning code to emphasize traditional urban principles—no more setbacks away from the sidewalks, no more empty plazas at street level, no more blank facades. New structures are required to come flush against the sidewalk. In the downtown retail district, new buildings must leave ground-floor space for retail tenants. Instead of blank walls, new buildings must include storefront windows of traditional dimensions. And the city discourages the spread of Minnesota-style skyways, a fad of the 1960s that Goldschmidt called "a way to keep people off the streets." Instead, he said, "we wanted street life." Superblocks that gobble the city's traditional grid pattern are banned, as are any buildings over 430 feet high. Height limits are set even lower in most spots to respect the city's traditional scale. Views of Mount Hood to the east and Mount St. Helens to the north are preserved by special height limits within the view corridors. The tallest buildings are allowed along the transit mall, with height limits getting lower as building sites approach the riverfront. "The idea of stepping down to the river was controversial, because in theory you're depriving guys of the idea like they do in Chicago, where they build a wall of tall buildings right across the lakefront," Goldschmidt said, "but we wanted a step down in part because we wanted high density along the transit mall to build the heaviest trip demand close to transit."

One of the greatest improvements to the downtown was the conversion of a low-level parking garage in the heart of the city into a public square. Since the demolition of the old Portland Hotel in 1951, the Meier & Frank department store's ownership had coveted the spot for a multilevel parking garage. But the downtown plan had higher aims for the block. Since its transformation into a park in the 1980s, Pioneer Courthouse Square, as it is called, has been Portland's busiest public gathering place, fulfilling architect Willard Martin's vision to build a "living room" for the city. Built of bricks stamped with the names of donors who contributed money to the cause, the square serves as downtown's amphitheater, with rows of seats for spectators, space for street performers, even clean and safe public rest rooms beneath a coffeehouse. What was once the hub of social activity for the city's elite in the days of the Portland Hotel is now a hub of activity for anyone who chooses to be there.

Fronting the public square is the Pioneer Courthouse, a three-story stone landmark topped by a wooden cupola. Beginning in the early twentieth century, federal bureaucrats tried repeatedly to tear the 1869 building down, but it was saved by the Great Depression, then by a need for work space during World War II, and finally by the bureaucracy itself, when government employees learned the difficulty of getting the General Services Administration, the manager of federal property, to label a building surplus. When a new federal building revived calls for demolition in the 1960s, federal appeals court judge John Kilkenny and district court judge Gus Solomon intervened to preserve the structure. "If anyone can push the GSA, it's the judges," said George McMath, whose firm did restoration work on the building in the early 1970s. "Oh, it was a glorious time," McMath recalled as he walked around the building. "I remember dealing with the GSA's regional office in Seattle. They said, if you keep Judge Kilkenny happy, we'll be happy."

Along another side of the square, in the 1926 Pacific Building, is the Association for Portland Progress, established in 1979 as the lobbying arm for downtown business interests. Ruth Scott, the association's president, looked out a tenth-floor window onto the public square, around which historic buildings faced with cream-colored terra-cotta blocks gleamed in the midday sun. Portland's "historic fabric is important to our identity," Scott said, but she conceded that this importance is not fully appreciated by all of the city's business interests. "I'm not sure how clearly a few other than [the late] Bill Naito really understand the economic value of historic preservation." Scott did, however, mention a downtown parking magnate who has reconstructed an ornate glazed terra-cotta storefront that was stripped from one of his commercial buildings years before. He's not doing it because he's a preservationist, she said, "he's doing it because it's good business."

A revitalized central business district has attracted new residents to the city's neighborhoods, even residents in income levels that were leaving the city before the downtown plan was formalized. Neighborhoods on Portland's east side, the long-neglected stepchildren to the central business district on the Willamette's west bank, have benefited greatly. North of the downtown, the Northwest Triangle, a string of brick warehouses along Thirteenth Avenue in a neighborhood called the Pearl, is fast becoming home to loft apartments for empty nesters who want to live closer to work and friends, among new art galleries and new restaurants, as well as two of Portland institutions on the district's edge: Jake's, a fish restaurant that still maintains its 1892 ambience, and Powell's City of Books, reputed to stock more volumes than any other independent bookstore in America. Farther northwest from downtown, Twenty-third Avenue, the main commercial street in a turn-of-the-century streetcar neighborhood, has become such a trendy spot for restaurants that locals have nicknamed it "Trendy Third." The popularity of these areas, however, has created swarms of traffic that is unable to move through the narrow streets easily. Rather than surrender the neighborhoods to the automobile, Portland intends to build a new streetcar line running from the Portland State University campus in the southwest section of the city, through the downtown and the warehouse district, into the northwest neighborhoods. To keep these neighborhoods functioning as they did in the days of the streetcar, Portland, with help from federal funding obtained by Republican U.S. senator Mark Hatfield, is reviving the streetcar itself. Carl Abbott, the historian of urban planning, calls Portland "the streetcar city in the age of the automobile." In his book on Portland's streetcar era, John Labbe reminds readers that when bicycles became so popular in the 1890s, the city's rail service had to add special cars just to accommodate all the new two-wheeled vehicles.

Improvement in Portland's neighborhoods is not limited to upscale white areas only. Albina, a northeast section that is home to the city's greatest racial and income diversity, as well as a disproportionate share of crime and vacant lots, has improved, too. In the late 1980s, the city developed a plan for the area that called for the rehabilitation of existing houses and new home construction to match the old. Efforts to strengthen the neighborhood shopping district along Martin Luther King Boulevard have produced spotty results, but after seven years, property values in Albina have increased by 350 percent, leading some to worry that longtime low-income residents of the neighborhood could be priced out of their community by Portland's escalating housing market. In 1996, metropolitan Portland was growing at the rate of fifty thousand new residents a year.

"It's pretty easy to live here," said Rob DeGraff, the downtown association's vice president for policy. "I'm a refugee from the New York metropolitan area, and as a kid I never could have had access to the kinds of recreational activities here without a three-hour drive." DeGraff arrived in the mid-1970s and worked for the city on the Main Street revitalization of Hawthorne Boulevard, now a trendy area of southeast Portland near Reed College. DeGraff said he has seen downtown "evolve from a quiet, small town" into an exciting urban environment, especially after light-rail service was completed in the 1980s.

After two decades of saying no to more parking spaces and freeway lanes, Portland benefits from one of the country's lowest downtown retail vacancy rates (3.5 percent) and one of the lowest vacancy rates for top-quality office space (7 percent). But downtown interests remain concerned about the suburbanization of the metropolitan region. When the downtown plan was adopted, the city held 90 percent of the region's top office space and 70 percent of its jobs. As suburbs have spread, downtown's share of class A office space in the region has shrunk to just over half, while its share of the region's jobs has fallen to 14 percent, a reflection of both urban deindustrialization and the emergence of postindustrial suburban employers. As Portland's economy has diversified beyond shipping products from western forests and farms, high-technology firms have located in the suburbs, particularly around Beaverton and Hillsboro to the west, a region nicknamed the "Silicon Forest." So many jobs have sprung up in suburban locations that some residents of Portland have begun to make reverse commutes. Newcomers drawn to the new jobs have brought with them suburban preferences. They prefer newly carved subdivisions over Portland's time-tested streetcar neighborhoods. They shop in strip malls instead of Main Street commercial districts. They drive large sport utility vehicles instead of walking or riding mass transit. Living and working in low-density, auto-dependent environments, they drive considerably more than Oregonians drove in the past. Between 1970 and 1990, when Oregon's population grew by 38 percent, the amount of vehicle miles traveled by the state's residents increased by 97 percent. Oregon's growth-management laws may have prevented urbanization from creeping beyond the urban growth boundaries, but they have not prevented sprawl within them.

"There is sprawl inside of our urban growth boundary," Mike Burton, the regional metropolitan government's directly elected executive officer, said candidly. Drive south of Portland on State Highway 99, a designated scenic route through the Willamette Valley, and you will pass a junkscape of plastic signs and asphalt lots, the kind of visual pollution found on every commercialized strip in the United States. Such development is typical in suburbs like Tigard, Wilsonville, and Beaverton. Tigard, in the 1980s, "in desperation to get jobs, said, 'Come on down, we'll give you anything,'" Burton said. Today,

Tigard's Main Street is a highway. "They formulated their economy around people driving through it, but they forgot people have to get around downtown, so now they have a moratorium on building." Beyond the regional urban growth boundary, the formerly walkable Main Streets of historically small rural places such as Sandy, Canby, and Newberg have fast dissolved into sprawling strips of roadside development, leapfrog sprawl brought on by people willing to commute great distances to live in places where they perceive the quality of life to be high, where working farms are carved into farmettes of fifteen acres or five-acre mini-estates dotted by McMansions.

To accommodate new residents and new businesses in the region, "we're doing the easy development, California-style growth. But because it was all happening within this ring, nobody cared much about it," said Association for Portland Progress president Ruth Scott. Now, "we're afraid they're going to get gridlocked around us, and that they won't be able to get in." Downtown interests aren't the only ones worried. Suburbanites worry, too. Metropolitan Portland is projected to grow by half a million people by 2010. Metropolitan Seattle and Tacoma grew by that amount in the 1980s alone, resulting in square mile after square mile of the kind of urban sprawl that most Portlanders want to prevent.[39] As traffic grows more congested, as more open land is developed and scenic landscapes disappear, a majority of people in the metropolitan region believe their quality of life to be in jeopardy.

On one extreme of public opinion are the "no growth" advocates who want to close Oregon's gates to new arrivals. They have no desire to pay taxes to build infrastructure to accommodate people who don't yet live here. But if California and Texas can hardly stem the flow of illegal immigrants across their borders, Oregon will never stop the flow of legal immigrants across its own. At the other extreme are "no growth management" advocates who prefer laissez-faire development to Oregon's system of public order. But if development trends were allowed to continue, Portland's metropolitan region would grow at the edges, draining the downtown, leading to more sprawl, less open space, and more congestion all the way to the coast. Portlanders have seen the sprawl scenario play out in so many other cities, and it is not an option most of them are willing to accept. Between the extremes of "no growth" and "no growth management" is a majority of people willing to accept additional growth but eager to protect what the region has carefully preserved. They want to hold the urban growth boundary in place as tightly as possible and find acceptable ways of making room for hundreds of thousands more people inside it. "There is a strong public concern about not destroying natural resources and a concern about density," said Mike Burton, Metro's executive officer. "Nobody wants us to become like Tokyo, but nobody has a vision of this place becoming like Santa Barbara, either." For decades, Americans have run from one extreme to the other, from the congested vertical metropolis of skyscrapers to the empty horizontal metropolis of sprawl. Today, Portlanders are demanding an alternative to either extreme.

In 1988, a group called Sensible Transportation Options for People (STOP) objected to plans for a new Western Bypass highway, proposed to link the rapidly growing western suburbs with Interstate 5, Oregon's main north-south artery. The bypass quickly raised the ire of environmentalists because it would have bisected Portland's Forest Park, a 4,683-acre wilderness set aside by landscape architect John Olmsted for the exposition of 1905. But the plan eventually captured the attention of a broader audience because of its potential impact on the region as a whole. "We built a bypass on the east side in the 1960s and it produced all kinds of sprawl," said Keith Bartholomew, an attorney with 1,000 Friends of Oregon. According to Bartholomew, the proposed Western Bypass would have run outside of Portland's urban growth boundary for two-thirds of its length, paving the way for the development of protected open space into low-density, auto-dependent environments.

"We said this is crazy," Bartholomew recalled. "We've already committed to spend half a billion dollars on a western light-rail system running through enough land to accommodate two-thirds of new households and three-quarters of new jobs projected in the region over the next twenty years, all of it within walking distance of the transit line." When the Oregon Department of Transportation challenged Bartholomew's organization to come up with another plan, 1,000 Friends of Oregon raised $1.5 million to study alternatives and present them to the public. Some funds for the project came from the Federal Highway Administration, which was happy not to fund a new highway if it didn't have to, and some funds even came from oil companies. "We knew they had it, so we decided to ask," Bartholomew said with a grin.

The result, a study entitled *Land Use, Transportation and Air Quality* (called LUTRAQ for short), showed that new highways are not the solution to suburban gridlock but instead its very cause, leading to auto-dependent development patterns that make people prisoners of their cars. With models of alternative development patterns supplied by the San Francisco–based firm headed by community planner Peter Calthorpe, the study showed how to rearrange suburbia in ways that make people less dependent on private vehicles by offering them more walkable environments. If the expected growth could be redirected closer to the planned western light-rail line, light-rail stops could serve as nodes for clusters of offices, services, shopping centers, and apartments, all arranged into new town centers with walkable streets, a contemporary version of the traditional American small town. Beyond the town centers, neighborhoods could sprout within walking distance of those transit stops and within walking distance of parks, schools, and neighborhood stores, contemporary versions of the streetcar suburbs built in the earliest decades of the century. "Too often, neighbors assume new development has to have the negative characteristics of sprawl, more traffic, more asphalt, and more environmental blight," writes Calthorpe in his book, *The Next American Metropolis.* An architect by training, Calthorpe is the most articulate spokesman for the contemporary urban design movement called "New Urbanism," which encourages development based on the old planning wisdom in traditional towns and neighborhoods. "This is not just about going back to our beautiful old villages and towns," Calthorpe insists. "It is actually about how we fashion the next generation of growth."[40]

Calthorpe argues that the expansion of metropolitan highway systems should give way to the expansion of transit, in order to achieve a more compact urban form. He says, "Our ubiquitous single-use zoning should be replaced with standards for mixed-use, walkable neighborhoods." And he urges his peers to design places for people instead of cars, in ways that improve "the public domain."[41] In place of isolated office complexes surrounded by parking lots, we might one day see a village green surrounded by a complex of offices. In Sacramento, for example, at a new, mixed-use, transit-oriented community for ten thousand residents designed by Calthorpe's firm, the Apple Computer Company has already constructed a large facility in what Calthorpe calls "a major shift in the suburban status quo."[42] Such ideas represent a challenge to orthodox suburban zoning, but they are hardly revolutionary. "The village green is just as much an American tradition as the libertarian 'I'll do what I please on my plot,'" says Calthorpe, who calls these kinds of plans convenient and affordable, "simple and appropriate for our times, not utopian and not necessarily the product of some strong-armed regulating transformation." Though new, the early examples of this type of development should encourage, Calthorpe says. "The private sector really seems to be leaning in this direction, and if we can just get the regulations and the financing infrastructure to stop frustrating it, I think you would see an explosion of better environments, both in the city and in the suburbs."

Calthorpe's firm has already written "transit-oriented development" guidelines to shape the expansion of Sacramento and San Diego. Jurisdictions in metropolitan Portland are in the process of writing their own. In 1992, Oregon's voters showed yet more confidence in their ability to manage growth when they amended their state constitution to give Portland's metropolitan government even greater authority over these issues. Two-thirds of voters in the metropolitan region then gave the green light to the compilation of a new fifty-year regional growth plan. The "Region 2040" measure, to be adopted officially by the end of 1997, will expand the growth boundary only slightly. To make room for another 720,000 residents inside the boundary, Metro's planners are taking aim at sprawl's worst culprits. To cut down on the paving of land for surface parking that stays empty most of the day, especially around isolated office complexes and stand-alone roadside businesses, Metro will encourage the development of regional town centers at light-rail stops, places where jobs and services can be maintained in better balance, in closer proximity, reducing the length of trips between home and work. By allowing developers to build a mix of housing types for an increasingly diverse housing market, the size of the average new single-family lot will drop to less than half of what it was three decades ago. The creation of more compact and walkable mixed-use environments that allow both residential and commercial development could further reduce traffic congestion, as could the replacement of suburban cul-de-sac and arterial road systems with more traditional through-street grids. With a goal of constructing new homes in the suburbs at an average of six units per acre (roughly one-third of the minimum density of fifteen units to the acre required for urban living), metropolitan Portland has a long way to grow before becoming too dense for suburban preferences. In fact, the city of Portland actually has a lower population density than San Diego and almost half as many people per square mile as San Jose, in Santa Clara County's Silicon Valley.[43]

Is greater Portland truly ready to accept such alterations to deeply entrenched autocentric development patterns? Voters have already approved a $472 million bond issue to fund the new $900 million light-rail line that will give the western suburbs an opportunity to grow in more compact ways. Beaverton, for instance, a formless home of newly built office complexes, will try to use a light-rail stop to develop the kind of compact town center it never had. And rail service to Hillsboro farther west can only reinforce the railroad-era town center that remains there. Mike Burton, Metro's elected executive officer, said these ideas have already won the support of suburban-based corporate executives such as Intel's vice president, Keith Thompson. "He doesn't know about land use," Burton said, "but what he does know is that Santa Clara failed." At Intel's offices in California, Burton said, young employees fresh out of college can't find affordable housing within an easy commute "unless they're millionaires." Employers in the Portland region, he said, don't want to see such failures repeated here. "None of them will tell you we need to move the urban growth boundary. They live here, too. They don't want to screw it up."

"Right now, the suburbs here don't look any different from suburbs elsewhere in America, but we're on the cusp of the challenge of taking the success we've had downtown and following that in the suburbs," said 1,000

Friends of Oregon's Keith Bartholomew. "We have a nice downtown, but it didn't used to be nice. It became nice through policy and investment, not by magic or the silver bullet. Going for the silver bullet often leads to failure, and failures breed cynicism. Success comes from consistent efforts that use a variety of approaches." In downtown Portland, civic leaders combined a number of approaches to add variety and vitality to places where it was lacking, to fill holes that were empty, and to give Portlanders a city worthy of their pride. What Oregonians are attempting to do in Portland's suburbs today is every bit as bold.

Some downtown advocates, however, worry that while the suburbs strive to become more urbane, Portland's hard-earned urbanity is eroding. The downtown parking cap was lifted after heavy lobbying by business interests, and the city has approved a parking garage on a downtown block that was identified for park space in revisions to the downtown plan. The site originally belonged to Portland's "park blocks," a street of park space that dates to the city's founding years. Neil Goldschmidt was one who voiced strong opposition to the parking garage proposal. "We have these lots that can just about go anywhere, and this one is going someplace where I don't think it needs to be above-ground parking," he said. "It could be a park, or it could be an office building, or it could be retailing," with parking underground.

"I was in Omaha a month ago," Goldschmidt said in his Portland office in 1996. "I had never spent any time there. Warren Buffett's got his offices in a building in downtown Omaha. Union Pacific Railroad is there. They have more Fortune 500 people in downtown than we do, I'll betcha, and there is no 'there' there. The only place anybody goes to is their old town area, which has some wonderful buildings, but that's all." Goldschmidt said downtown Omaha has benefited from the renovation of a prominent historic building into a new hotel, "but you wouldn't walk on those streets. They're doing what we're doing with this damned garage. They got all the garages God would ever want, all the flat parking lots you'd ever want, and it looks like Berlin after World War II, which is just about the way we looked. I used to have pictures of Portland taken from the air, and it looked like a bombed-out area."

Today, times are good in Portland, and when times are good, "people get lazy and sloppy," Goldschmidt said. The generation that raised Portland's capital beginning with the plan of 1972 is now retired, Goldschmidt noted, "and the question is whether those who are spending the capital that has been built have any real understanding of what it will take to add to it. You don't have a choice of staying where you are. Things will either get better, or they will get worse. There is nothing in between."

Goldschmidt believes that, ultimately, downtown Portland will get better. Others are not so certain. "I don't think we have really visionary leaders," said Rob DeGraff, vice president of the Association for Portland Progress. "We continue to live off the vision of the Goldschmidt era." If the current leaders seem less imaginative, perhaps it is because there is less to imagine today than there was three decades ago. On one hand, Portland is lucky to be free of the outrages, the demolitions and bad designs that inspired activism in the 1960s and 1970s. On the other hand, downtown Portland could indeed be witnessing the almost invisible effects of slow erosion.

The question for other places is "Can Portland's success of the last quarter century be followed elsewhere?" A number of factors make Portland unique. Topography in Portland, as in Pittsburgh, has helped to prevent the rampant decentralization that has drained other cities. And like Pittsburgh, Portland has yet to build a highway system of outer beltways that displace central business districts, preferring a hub-and-spoke system, in which most routes lead into the city, rather than around it. From its inception, Portland has benefited from a cultural tradition that places a high value on the public realm, and since the Progressive-era presidency of Teddy Roosevelt, Oregon's state government has valued direct public participation in decision making. Racially, Portland is 85 percent white, the highest percentage of white residents of any large city in the United States. In a city with few distressed neighborhoods, where 90 percent of the city's children attend public schools, Portland suffers from none of the white flight that has decimated cities in the Great Lakes region and along the eastern seaboard. Because of all these factors, downtown Portland has remained politically strong, while its suburbs have remained politically weak.[44] Until now, Portland's economy has been sustained largely by newcomers seeking the very quality of life that Oregon has worked hard to preserve, expanding the constituency for livable places. In fact, quality of life has become such an important ingredient in the region's economic health that is doubtful that regional business interests would seek to destroy it. In 1991, William B. Conerly, a vice president and economist at First Interstate Bank, said, "Portland's growth defies the stereotypes about regional economies." While the region's large industries, such as timber, shrink and large regional employers engage in downsizing, the number of jobs in the region continues to rise. "Right now in Portland, the jobs are following the people who are moving here," he said, adding, "Portland's growth will continue as long as the quality of life is perceived to be better than elsewhere."[45]

The quality of this region has excited travelers and pioneers for almost two centuries. One of them, Lewis Mumford, addressed civic leaders at the Portland City Club in 1938. "I have seen a lot of scenery in my life, but I have seen nothing so tempting as a home . . . than this Oregon country," Mumford told them. "You have the basis here for civilization on its highest scale." Challenging them, he asked, "Are you good enough to have this country in your possession? Have you enough intelligence, imagination and cooperation among you to make the best use of these opportunities? Rebuilding our cities will be one of the major tasks of the next generation. You have an opportunity here to do a job of city planning like nowhere else in the world." By that account, Portland would seem to be unique, a city unlike any other city in the United States. But another account, offered a generation later, is worth repeating.

In 1965, John Painter Jr., a writer for the *Oregonian,* said Portland was then "a city that's going somewhere—but its urban destination is unclear." Although Portland had potential, it suffered from weak civic leadership and unimaginative city commissioners. It had failed to capitalize on amenities such as the riverfront and the empty block in front of the courthouse. Worse than anything, it had failed to prepare a plan to guide the city's future. "If Portland looks at its future needs and plans for them, if it ignores the commercial blandishments of city-destroying speculators and promoters; if it considers people instead of cars and freeways; if it carefully plots its residential, commercial and industrial sprawl; if it puts greenery before parking lots, its future could be unreservedly brilliant," he said. But the writer also offered a warning. "If Portland blunders on until it is clogged with cars and slashed by freeways; until its residential areas are overrun by garish apartment houses; until its parks are hopelessly overcrowded; until its people flee further and further into exurbia; until its back is against the wall of urban disaster, it will have fulfilled the destiny of its Eastern counterparts: to serve as a testament to the frailty of man's will and the weakness of his imagination."[46]

■　■　■

Downtowns across America are undergoing tremendous transformations, many of them for the worse, some for the better. But it would be a mistake to judge today's downtowns against what they used to be instead of what they might become.

Industrial flight from urban cores has been followed in the information age by the flight of professional service firms dispersed from downtowns by automobiles, fax machines, and computer networks that send offices across the horizon. Few sectors need to be centrally located anymore, with the exception of government, and, in some cases, financial services. A downtown center that cannot hold even these sectors is unlikely to enjoy a prosperous future. Yet any sectors that remain will continue to serve as downtown magnets that hold other uses together.

One powerful magnet will continue to be housing within an easy commute to downtown for urban residents at the high end of the residential market.

These are the executive-level individuals who make decisions about where their companies will locate, and those decisions are determined largely by the length of the executives' commute. If they live near downtown, chances are their offices will remain there. If they live in a new large houses fronting suburban golf courses, chances are that their offices will not be far away.

In the past, the housing that has served this category near downtown has typically been the best-preserved historic residential districts in a city. These are the places that sprang up early nearest the downtown core and have retained their timeless appeal to buyers who are willing to pay extra to live in such a location. The supply of such districts is finite, but cities across America are beginning to see apartments and condominiums created in downtown structures originally built for other purposes: loft apartments in brick warehouse buildings, condominiums in converted historic hotels and even in skyscrapers abandoned by Wall Street firms. Nationwide, demographic changes are driving the trend. Late-middle-aged couples, so called empty nesters, whose children have grown and moved away from home, find themselves with little need or time to maintain large houses and lawns. Some of them also are in search of proximity to vibrant urban nightlife, restaurants, and cultural attractions, and closeness to neighbors who share a similar lifestyle.

For the foreseeable future, entertainment appears to be one of the biggest growth sectors in American downtowns. People still seek exciting places to spend their time, and people continue to be drawn to places occupied by other people.

Reston, Virginia, one of the successful so-called new towns of the 1960s, appeared to have everything: residential structures of all kinds, diversity among its citizens, and plenty of open space and recreational facilities. But it had no downtown, and thus it had no heart. Now, Reston is building one.

Just a few miles away from Reston, the town of Rockville, Maryland, had a traditional downtown—bulldozed in the early 1970s to make room for the Rockville Mall. The mall has been a disaster, both economically and visually. Soon, it, too, will be torn down. The plan is to replace it, according to Rockville's announcement, with something "more closely resembling a city center of yesteryear"—in other words, a traditional downtown—"designed to look and feel pretty much like the bustling village Rockville once was." Hundreds of other communities made the same costly mistake in the 1960s and 1970s and learned the same hard lesson: a mall is not a downtown, and you can't substitute it for one.

An environment that sustains a variety of activities at various hours of the day needs to offer people a variety of ways to get around. A generation ago, architect Victor Gruen, inspired by the downtown pedestrian district in his native Vienna, wanted to strengthen downtown Fort Worth, Texas, by turning its streets into a giant pedestrian district surrounded at the perimeter by highways and parking garages for commuters. His plan never got off the ground. In the ensuing years, the people of Fort Worth largely abandoned their historic downtown for urban sprawl that spread unchecked across the flatlands for hundreds of square miles. Until a few years ago, there was little in downtown Fort Worth that was worth walking to, but the situation has recently begun to change.

Thanks to large investments by the locally based Bass family, downtown Fort Worth is witnessing a resurrection. Historic buildings have been rehabilitated into apartments or condominiums for professionals who work in downtown offices. New movie theaters and new restaurants and bars in a collection of formerly vacant historic buildings called Sundance Square are giving downtown the nightlife it hasn't had in years. A new concert center will soon fill a prominent but empty downtown block. Downtown Fort Worth is beginning to feel like Fort Worth again, instead of the empty center of just another sprawling metropolis.

Most dramatic is Fort Worth's decision to relocate an elevated highway that divided the downtown, isolating an Art Deco–era government office building and a massive neoclassical post office—two of downtown's most defining landmarks. Like Fort Worth, smart cities are swapping the meat axe of highwayman Robert Moses for a needle that can stitch pieces of the city back into the larger urban fabric. San Francisco has chosen not to rebuild the earthquake-damaged Embarcadero, its waterfront highway along the Bay. Now, the downtown will be reconnected with the water for the first time in decades. Similarly, in Boston, the elevated Central Artery expressway is being buried underground, after divorcing downtown from Boston Harbor for nearly half a century.

Le Corbusier's modernist City of Tomorrow—the city of high-rise towers and high-speed highways—is giving way to a postmodern city more sympathetic to traditional ideas. Instead of finding modernist ways to separate soaring towers and massive complexes, as well as pedestrians and automobiles, the postmodern urban planners are searching for connections. The problem facing most cities today is not congestion, but emptiness—how to fill in the empty holes.

From a transportation standpoint, less room for cars leaves more room for things that attract people. Places where people want to be are generally short on parking, so a shortage of parking is not necessarily a bad thing if people are still eager to get to a location in other ways. Portland, Oregon, for example, added thousands of new jobs to its downtown over two decades without adding a single parking space.

The change from an industrial economy to an information-dependent, service-dominated economy presents older cities with unique advantages and opportunities. The deindustrialization of historic warehouse districts in St. Paul and Denver is also taking place in cities such as Chattanooga and Richmond.

Waterfronts, too, are enjoying new life where heavy industry has left. Land values drop when former economic uses decline, freeing up relatively cheap property for new functions to replace the old ones. "The sight, sound, and feel of water naturally attract people, which is why waterfront developments often prosper," argues Kent A. Robertson of Minnesota's St. Cloud State University. As far back as the 1920s, San Antonio realized how a polluted waterway could become a great local amenity. Today, its Riverwalk is the second most visited attraction in town after the Alamo. Lately, Pittsburgh has discovered postindustrial vibrancy as a river city.

Scholars of urban history have argued that the transformation of aging industrial downtowns into postindustrial service centers and cultural attractions is analogous to the renaissance experienced in European cities from the fifteenth to the nineteenth centuries, when medieval workshops for the production of wealth gave way to the baroque era's "places of display and consumption."

"The central city is no longer a central business district based on maximum accessibility, but rather a center of display based on maximum visibility," writes Larry Ford of the University of San Diego. "Similarly, the inner city—at least in those cities going through this postindustrial transformation—is no longer a place for teeming masses laboring in the workaday world, but rather a place to promenade and seek a style of living."[47] Downtowns are changing from a place where things are made to a place where things are seen, purchased, and experienced.

In the postindustrial economy, a downtown's public realm, its built environment—the public face of buildings and surrounding streets—will take on greater importance as structures become valued as much for how they look as for what takes place inside them. Distinctive places will continue to attract people drawn for the experience of that particular place. Historic districts will only become more vital, both for the city's identity as well as for its economic advantage. Suburbs, after all, cannot manufacture history. Tragically, Omaha, Nebraska, only recently demolished its underutilized historic warehouse district for a new corporate headquarters for ConAgra, the agribusiness giant. The history of a place is a great asset that downtowns cannot afford to waste. Cities that destroy it will have less to offer.

In our impatient age, it is hard to have the patience or vision to remember or imagine how downtowns mature over time and generations. America's downtowns need time to develop—not time measured in decades, but time measured in lifetimes. And they also need guidance on the best ways to develop. Great places are not created by chance but by choice.

There will always be a need for downtowns as a place for people, a destination, a focal point for community life. That need may be difficult for some of us to imagine today in the age of sprawl, but in moments of doubt about the future of downtowns it is helpful to remember that the Renaissance was preceded by the black plague. Ruins, after all, are what give way to rehabilitation.

During the Renaissance, city walls and slow methods of transportation contained urban development tightly in the urban core, forcing people to think carefully each time their city grew. The walls protected the people inside from enemies outside, but the by-products were a cohesive, well-developed core as well as a cohesive and well-preserved surrounding natural environment, a great amenity for the urban population as well as its vital source of food. Think of the walls around the medieval city as a precursor to the urban growth boundaries around Portland, Oregon, and places that choose to follow Portland's lead. Watch these places carefully. As they mature, they will fill in their empty holes and fill their observers with optimism about the future of downtowns.

PRESERVATION IN THE AGE OF SPRAWL

> The preservation movement has one great curiosity. There is
> never retrospective controversy or regret. Preservationists are the
> only people in the world who are invariably confirmed in their
> wisdom after the fact.
>
> —John Kenneth Galbraith,
> "The Economic and Social Returns of Preservation"

New and exciting things are happening in traditional communities nationwide. Neighborhoods left for dead are being revitalized by self-motivated residents. Small-town merchants are reinvigorating their Main Street business districts. Entrepreneurs and enlightened public officials are turning dreary downtowns into places where people want to be. Because their achievements occur in bits and pieces, however, they often tend to go unnoticed. Most changes in a community happen slowly. Only after they reach a cumulative mass do they attract notice.

Places such as Pittsburgh, Portland, Oregon, and Chippewa Falls, Wisconsin, are beginning to attract notice because of the work of preservationists. Yet, the accomplishments of preservationists frequently collide with public perceptions of what "historic preservation" means. In some places, it still carries the stigma of elitism and indifference to the concerns of average citizens. In the 1850s, when a woman named Ann Pamela Cunningham rallied the nation to save Mount Vernon as a shrine to George Washington, preservation was defined for a century. Preservation became a nationwide effort to restore and refurnish historic houses where Americans could pay homage to their past. That is still what many people think of today when they hear the term "preservation."

Saving, interpreting, and promoting an appreciation of historic and architecturally significant landmarks will always be at the core of the preservation movement's mission, but the work of preservation is evolving and has become much more than that. It is still firmly rooted in an appreciation for the value of history, but it is no longer concerned primarily with the past. Preservation is the business of saving special places and the quality of life they support. It has to do with more than bricks, balustrades, columns, and cobblestones. It has to do with the way individuals, families, and communities come together in good environments.

"If the preservation movement is to be successful, it must go beyond saving bricks and mortar. It must go beyond saving occasional historic houses and opening museums. It must be more than a cult of antiquarians. It must do more than revere a few precious national shrines. It must attempt to give a sense of orientation to our society, using structures and objects of the past to establish values of time and place." So urged the special committee of the U.S. Conference of Mayors that drafted *With Heritage So Rich,* a landmark 1966 book that defined the preservation movement in the era of urban renewal.[1]

Today, the work of thousands of preservationists, both professionals and volunteers, is guided by a vision of the future in which communities make historic places a vital part of daily life. In the course of doing so, they have made preservation one of the most effective tools for revitalizing communities of all kinds and sizes.

Arthur Bergeron, a lawyer in Marlborough, Massachusetts, reflects the new energy and direction of the movement. Several years ago, he became president of Historic Massachusetts, a statewide nonprofit organization, and with his board, he decided to broaden his preservation group's perspective. Inspired by Stanley Lowe in Pittsburgh, Bergeron and his colleagues launched neighborhood revitalization projects in the working-class communities of Lawrence, a mill city near the New Hampshire border; Chelsea, a depressed nineteenth-century suburb of Boston; and New Bedford, a coastal port. The strategy was to provide financial and technical assistance to one strategically selected project in each place, with the idea that each project would become a catalyst for others nearby.

When presented with Bergeron's plans, however, a few traditional New England preservationists told him that the architecture in those places lacked merit to make them worthy of attention and that community redevelopment is not what preservation is about. In some places, the preservation movement has yet to evolve from a concern for isolated landmarks to concern for the communities that surround them. In fact, some preservationists are guilty of the very myopia they accused modernist architects of having for years: they have failed to consider buildings in the context of their locales; they are thinking about buildings and not people, the people who must confront the buildings on a daily basis. On the other hand, Bergeron, like many others, has seen the connection between buildings and their setting, and a setting and its inhabitants. Preservation is not just about buildings. Its about what buildings mean to people. Saying that a particular place matters is a way of saying that its people matter, too. "The merit of a project lies in whether or not it builds pride in a neighborhood," Bergeron replies to his critics. "Historic preservation is important to the extent that it's building America. If it's not doing that, it's not important."[2]

Bergeron's path was actually blazed decades ago by pioneering preservationists, people like Arthur Ziegler in Pittsburgh and Dana Crawford in Denver, as well as Frances Edmunds in Charleston, Carl Westmoreland in Cincinnati, Lee Adler in Savannah, Antoinette Downing in Providence, and their counterparts in Philadelphia, Seattle, and a dozen other cities. These early practitioners have inspired many others, among them, Stanley Lowe in Pittsburgh, Maryell Batin in Macon, Georgia, Mtominika Youngblood in the Martin Luther King Historic District of Atlanta, Clark Schoettle in Providence, Patty Gay in New Orleans, and Kathleen Crowther in Cleveland. To help replicate the efforts of these determined activists, the National Trust in 1994 established Community Partners for Revitalization, a neighborhood counterpart to its Main Street commercial district revitalization program. If the preservation movement is to realize its full potential in any place, it will require the emergence of energetic leadership determined to transform older, decaying communities into newly livable ones.

More must join them if preservation is to become an ethic, a value, accepted by all Americans. Eighty percent of Americans regard themselves as environmentalists, according to public opinion polls. They mean different things by that term, but all see stewardship of the natural environment in some form as a belief with which they want to be associated. That must become the goal of the preservation movement—to instill in the American people an ethic, a belief that shaping and caring for the built environment is every bit as important to human health and happiness as caring for the natural environment. If the preservation movement is to grow even further and evolve to become an ethic accepted by all Americans, it must become more relevant to their lives.

Three decades ago, the publication of *With Heritage So Rich* gave attention to the cause of preservation. But the manifesto looked mainly to government to carry it out through regulations—particularly the federal government, then a leading destroyer of the nation's historic built environment through its highway and urban renewal programs. The preservation of historic districts with rules and regulation in the United States really became necessary when the informal, unwritten norms that preserve a community had broken down, when property owners and government officials began to ignore the preservation of local customs. Regulations helped to stop the destruction of America's historic places, but the act of revitalization cannot be done by regulation. It is not enough for preservationists just to prevent bad development from happening. For good development to occur, the preservationist's toolbox must include the carrot—not just the stick. It is not enough to be mere stewards of our inheritance, for we have too many places in need of fixing. We must be the agents of regeneration and the architects of our own renewal.

The work of preservation today cannot be done by government alone, or even largely by government. It requires the active participation of the private market. For that to happen, preservationists have to understand buildings and places in an economic context. As real estate consultant Donovan Rypkema, a specialist in the economics of historic preservation, argues, "Historic preservation will not take place in the private sector on a sustained basis unless it makes economic sense."[3]

Historic buildings rise in economic value when they are scarce, useful, and desired by buyers who are willing to pay for them. But the *relative* economic value of real estate is determined largely by its location. That's why the most effective preservation efforts focus on locations. By focusing on a district and not simply a single property, preservationists can do what market-driven developers cannot or will not do, and that is to reduce the economic risk to investors in a location. Most investors are unwilling to take risks in locations with uncertain futures. Preservationists have to take those risks if they want to be successful, whether they are individual homeowners or non-profit organizations.

When preserving a district, preservationists cannot neglect the hard fact that they must compete for limited amounts of investment in a real estate market that transcends the boundaries of their district. "Capital moves to where there is money to be made," Rypkema reminds them.[4] Anyone can open a Sunday newspaper real estate section, look at the promotions of new developments, and see what competition really means. As entrepreneurial preservationists in New Orleans have demonstrated, they must learn to promote their locations or nobody else will.

Smart local governments will assist them whenever possible. Why? "People care where they live and economic activity tends to follow them," argues Thomas Michael Power, chair of the Department of Economics at the University of Montana. Preserving the special qualities of an appealing environment must be part of any local economic development strategy, he says. "They are not just social or aesthetic concerns."[5]

In the past, places thrived or died because of industries that were there. Mill towns were mill towns. Port towns were fishing towns. And rural towns depended on farming to stay alive. That's still true in many places, but the lesson of Portland, Oregon, or Franklin, Tennessee, is that localities that protect the high quality of their environment will ultimately attract skilled workers seeking high qualities of life. Just as low-wage industries chase pools of low-cost labor, high-wage employers are drawn to places with highly skilled workers.[6] Over the long term, places "with strong, distinctive identities" are more likely to prosper than places without them. Every place "must identify its strongest and most distinctive features and develop them or run the risk of being all things to all persons and nothing special to any."[7] Nobel Prize–winning economist Robert Solow puts it this way: "Livability is not some middle-class luxury. It is an economic imperative."

No place can afford to ignore the importance of preservation to its long-term economic interests or even its short-term economic needs. "Dollar for dollar, historic preservation is one of the highest job-generating economic development options available," Rypkema points out.[8] A labor-intensive activity, preserving historic buildings creates more jobs dollar for dollar than new construction—or many basic industries, for that matter. In fact, $1 million invested in building rehabilitation creates twelve more jobs than $1 million worth of manufacturing cars in Michigan; twenty more jobs than $1 million of coal mining in West Virginia; twenty-nine more jobs than $1 million of pumping oil in Oklahoma; even more jobs than similar amounts spent on manufacturing electronic equipment in California, agriculture in South Dakota, or textiles in South Carolina.[9]

Investments in a local built environment are investments that stay in a local economy, paying for themselves many times over. For every dollar appropriated by the Rhode Island General Assembly for historic preservation over a recent twenty-year period, Rhode Island got back $1.69 in state revenue. Measuring multiplier effects, Edward F. Sanderson, Rhode Island's historic preservation officer, explained that for every dollar Rhode Island invested in historic preservation, the state's economy benefited from $29 more in related spending.[10]

Governments at all levels have recognized that preservation often requires financial incentives to get things started. In the late 1970s, the federal government began offering tax incentives for the restoration of income-producing structures (hotels, stores, offices, and apartments) that were eligible for listing in the National Register of Historic Places, the nation's official inventory of places worth saving. The incentives worked. By 1995, they had attracted more than $17 billion in private capital to twenty-six thousand separate preservation projects, most of them affordable housing. The historic-rehabilitation tax credit stimulated the largest infusion of dollars into the preservation of America's past that the country has ever seen. There is hardly a city anywhere whose downtown or neighborhoods do not reflect the effects.

In 1986, however, Congress, in the name of tax reform, largely vitiated the tax credit, allowing it to remain on the books but making it much more difficult to obtain. The number of tax-credit projects has dropped by more than 80 percent since the mid-1980s. Ironically, as others have already observed, now that America finally knows how to repair what ails our aging neighborhoods, business districts, and downtowns, there are few incentives from Washington to help.

Preservationists have begun to promote a new kind of tax credit, one less expensive to the federal treasury and more carefully targeted to the needs of America's older communities. It is called the Historic Homeowner Assistance Act, now before Congress and picking up strong bipartisan support because it would extend credits to homeowners who rehabilitate their homes. It would save homes listed in the National Register, regardless of their purchase price or value; give residents of older and often disinvested neighborhoods incentives to stay in place and invest in their community's future; and provide an incentive for others to move back into older neighborhoods.

Some states and localities have already offered their own incentives. As St. Paul mayor George Latimer's administration demonstrated in a time of diminishing federal assistance, limited amounts of public money, if managed wisely, can leverage much larger amounts of private investment. The state of New Mexico now allows property owners to take a state income tax credit on up to half of certain rehabilitation expenses. Wisconsin offers a tax credit for up to 25 percent of home improvements. Some states, such as Florida, Georgia, and Illinois, allow a freeze on the tax assessments of rehabilitated properties. Without the freeze, property owners are penalized for reinvesting in declining properties. In the state of Washington, when officials studied the impact of their rehabilitation tax credit on the state and local tax bases, the credit proved to be a net gain for the public treasuries. They also found that almost two-thirds of the rehabilitation projects occurred in run-down neighborhoods and that 70 percent of them stimulated other rehabilitation projects nearby.[11]

Not every unit of government will choose to employ such incentives to jump-start the revitalization of decaying places, but none should be allowed to cause harm or stand in the way. One sure way to lure reinvestment into locations that need it is to remove regulatory barriers and cut red tape. For many places, it means exempting owners of historic buildings from rigid compliance with building codes written with the design of new structures in mind. In Chippewa Falls, it meant getting a state waiver to redevelop a historic mill built in a floodplain restricted by a more recent law. For the town of Eureka, California, it meant rezoning the upper floors of historic commercial buildings to permit the creation of living spaces for artists. California made special allowances for code compliance of historic properties, an act that helped revive San Diego's historic Gas Lamp District.[12] Similarly, the state of Minnesota and the federal Environmental Protection Agency have applied more flexibility and common sense to the rules governing liability at redeveloped, polluted industrial sites called "brownfields."

Preservation strategies can repair pieces of our urban fabric, but they cannot fill in all the empty holes. Because of America's abundant supply of easily developed land, we can never fully heal a disinvested core until we contain sprawl at its periphery. Sprawl is as big a threat to the cause of preservation today as urban renewal was a generation ago. Urban renewal was the crucible in which a generation of preservationists was tested. In fact, the threat of urban renewal to America's historic places shaped and mobilized the movement more than anything. For decades, the greatest threat to America's historic landmarks and historic districts was urban redevelopment: slum clearances and the construction of new highways and inhumane public housing. The National Trust for Historic Preservation was created by Congress and President Harry Truman in 1949—the same year they enacted urban renewal legislation. Since then, historic preservation has proved to be more beneficial than urban renewal, but, a half century later, the greatest threat to historic places is not urban redevelopment but urban disinvestment—wherever graveyards of past communities lie buried by urban sprawl.

■   ■   ■

On the eve of the twenty-first century, Americans once again find themselves confronting the ills of urbanization. A century ago, the problem was urban congestion, the city of tenements, industrial pollution, and poor sanitation. Today, the problem is urban sprawl, urbanization that creeps unchecked across the landscape, siphoning the life out of historic centers while turning countryside into clutter. After decades of sprawl, Americans are beginning to realize that places are developing in ways that are not good for them. People feel it instinctively whenever they are stuck in traffic, losing time as prisoners to the automobile. They know something must be wrong when their taxes rise higher and higher even as "growth" spreads farther and farther. And they see that things are obviously wrong just by looking around. Eighty percent of everything built in the United States has been built in the last fifty years, writes author James Howard Kunstler, "and most of it is depressing, brutal, ugly, unhealthy and spiritually degrading."[13]

"Americans moved to the suburbs largely for privacy, mobility, security and ownership," writes California-based architect and community planner Peter Calthorpe. "Increasingly they now have isolation, congestion, rising crime and overwhelming costs."[14]

The real costs of urban sprawl, long a concern of urban planners and environmentalists, are only now seeping into public consciousness. In December of 1995, the *Kansas City Star* ran a six-part series of articles on the causes and effects of sprawl in the metropolitan region. From 1960 to 1990, Kansas City's population grew by less than a third while the flight of people from the urban core expanded its land area by 110 percent. "Like most American cities, Kansas City has been seduced by all things new," wrote reporters Chris Lester and Jeffrey Spivak. "The resulting sprawl has left in its wake a chronic rot, eroding our region from the inside out. Now, even the suburbs grapple with its ill effects. Is this really what we want? Not to growing numbers of people who realize our dilemma: We cannot afford the continuing chaos of sprawl."[15]

Current patterns of urbanization are unsustainable. In 1995, the Bank of America dissented from the gospel of unmanaged growth to cosponsor a report that announced, "As we approach the 21st century, it is clear that sprawl has created enormous costs that California can no longer afford."[16] Across California, as in other states, the decentralization of employment centers, housing developments, and increased dependence on the automobile have "surfaced enormous social, environmental and economic costs, which until now have been hidden, ignored, or quietly borne by society." Sprawl has trapped the unemployed in places without jobs while more mobile residents relocate in the hinterlands, some pulled by the only supply of safe, affordable housing, others pushed there by the declining quality of life in badly built environments they leave behind.

In few places are the consequences felt more sharply than in California's Central Valley, the most productive agricultural area in the United States. Because of climatic conditions unique to the region, eleven counties there produce 250 crops (from almonds to zucchini), with a 1994 market value of $13.3 billion. That's 8 percent of U.S. agricultural sales that year. But this remarkable farmland is being devoured by sprawl at an alarming rate.

The Central Valley's population is expected to triple by the year 2040. Even now, residential and commercial sprawl gobbles an estimated 15,000 acres of farmland there each year. In the next forty-five years, according to a study undertaken by the American Farmland Trust, sprawl will consume or indirectly affect more than 3.6 million acres, or more than half of the valley's irrigated farmland. By 2040, such a loss would reduce the value of farm products grown in the area by $2.1 billion annually—the equivalent of the entire agricultural production of the state of Oregon. According to the study, this would mean the loss of more than forty thousand farm-related jobs. It also projects that the cost of providing the current level of public services and infrastructure to the new housing tracts, shopping malls, and office parks to be built on former farmland will exceed the expected tax revenues of Central Valley cities to pay for them, by about a billion dollars annually. This means that those communities will have no choice but to reduce services or increase taxes, or both. Cities requiring state or federal bailouts today are the imploding cities, ones that suffer from a massive loss of population and a disinvested core. In the twenty-first century, the cities requiring public bailouts will be the explosively growing places that failed to contain the costs and consequences of unmanaged sprawl.

Because of urban regions that grew inefficiently, Californians face a shortage of affordable housing, inaccessible jobs, and horrendous commutes, as well as unhealthy air and other environmental damage. Businesses are burdened with higher costs, loss in worker productivity, and underutilized investments in older communities. In the 1980s, more than 300,000 Californians sought a better, more affordable quality of life in other states, draining California of capital, both money and brainpower. Echoing the findings of California's Growth Management Council, created by Governor Pete Wilson, the Bank of America's "Beyond Sprawl" report said California continues to grow in ways that no longer work in a state of 32 million people, 80 percent of whom live in urbanized areas of 1 million people or more. Sprawl "cannot be sustained forever," the report declared. "We can no longer afford the luxury of sprawl."

Feeling threatened, industries that have prospered from sprawl have issued their own report in defense of business as usual—instead of spending time and effort learning how to develop new places in better ways. The California Building Industry Association, Wells Fargo Bank, and the Building Industry Institute have joined to say that consumers love sprawl.

Yes, buyers flock to affordable private homes, but many of them hate the sprawl that spreads around them. The most vociferous opponents of sprawl, in fact, are homeowners who realize they will soon have to live surrounded by it. Like Frank Lloyd Wright in the Arizona desert, they love their own private home, its interior spaces, and, best of all, the surrounding natural landscape. But as others seek the same things and sprawl creeps around them, they grow irate. Similarly, consumers love the prices and inventory of choices inside a Wal-Mart, but outside the store, they hate the environment it creates. It's the public realm outside the buildings that leaves them wishing they were someplace else. Indeed, as sprawl matures and ages poorly, people flee it, only to build more sprawl down the road. Fifty years after World War II, we are confronted with not only the burdens of abandoned urban neighborhoods and downtowns, but the fiscal, social, and environmental problems of abandoned first-generation sprawl, including the equivalent of four thousand abandoned shopping centers.

The suburban antigrowth movement is just one of the more vocal signals of "democracy's discontent." Philosopher and author Michael J. Sandel has argued that two issues "lie at the heart of democracy's discontent. One is the fear that, individually and collectively, we are losing control of the forces that govern our lives. The other is the sense that, from family to neighborhood to nation, the moral fabric of community is unraveling around us. These two fears—for the loss of self-government and the erosion of community—together define the anxiety of our age."[17]

Americans are confused by the status of their communities in large part because the places they inhabit do not function as communities at all. "If the word community is to mean or amount to anything," writes Wendell Berry, America's most eloquent essayist on the topic of community, "it must refer to a place and its people" who share "a common knowledge of themselves and of their place."[18] The closer the community, the more intimate that knowledge becomes. Face-to-face communication ensures accountability to others in ways that mediated communication (such as "flaming" on the Internet or toxic talk radio) do not. Without knowledge of and accountability to our neighbors, a place is little more than a postal address for transient residents. The less we know a place and the people with whom we share it, the less we will ever care for either.[19]

We must not interpret the flight from places burdened by crime and bad schools as an endorsement of sprawl or even a rejection of traditional urbanism. More than anything, it is an indictment of bad urban conditions, of crime and bad schools. Many people prefer to live closer to work in safe, appealing, walkable neighborhoods where they exist. Yet, for decades, experts and the building industries have dictated only a choice between hyperdensity high-rise housing on the one hand or the emptiness of sprawl on the other. Now, the experts are beginning to listen more carefully to consumers, asking Americans what *they* want. Architect Tony Nelessen, a professor at Rutgers University, shows audiences 240 slides of places and has them rank the scenes according to their ideal places in which to live and work. Contradicting the claim that Americans love sprawl, Nelessen's respondents overwhelmingly shun sprawl. Instead, they give high marks to traditional places such as Main Street business districts and turn-of-the-century streetcar neighborhoods, places that are attractive, safe, and walkable—not monolithic, single-use developments. One of the great limitations of sprawl is how its appeal is linked to its newness. The more it ages, the more it generally fades and loses its original appeal, driving people to move on to greener pastures. By contrast, traditional places, if well maintained, can retain a timeless appeal.

Recognizing that sprawl has left a good number of Americans unsatisfied and yearning for "the architecture of community," visionary contemporary

architects and planners in the movement for New Urbanism are trying to improve development patterns. They are striving to create new places, such as
Seaside, on Florida's Gulf Coast, based on the wisdom contained in historic
places where people love to be.

If Celebration, the Disney Company's neotraditional community in Florida,
succeeds as a model, it could help New Urbanists crack the rigid suburban
zoning codes that dictate sprawl. But until New Urbanism demonstrates that it
is serious about repairing the old urbanism rather than simply finding more
ways to develop open land, the movement will only operate—quite literally—
on the periphery of the problems of bad urbanization. Aware of the movement's suburban emphasis to date, professor of architecture Vincent Scully,
who taught some prominent young New Urbanists at Yale University and who
promotes their efforts in general, wonders if "the New Suburbanism might be
a truer label" for their work.

Clearly, the placelessness of sprawl needs to be addressed; yet, the conditions of our aging cities and aging suburbs cry out for the gifted hand of the
most talented designers practicing today. Acknowledging this need, the Congress for New Urbanism adopted a charter in 1996 that "views disinvestment
in central cities, the spread of placeless sprawl, increasing separation by race
and income, environmental deterioration, loss of agricultural lands and
wilderness, and the erosion of society's built heritage as one interrelated
community-building challenge." Peter Calthorpe, one of the most articulate
practitioners in the movement, has set an admirable example by putting the
expertise of his firm into the repair of existing places and the development of
regional plans for metropolitan areas. More New Urbanists need to follow
his lead.

In a time more optimistic than our own, Henry Ford said, "We shall solve
the city problem by leaving the city." Such escapist sentiments have since
proven to be nothing less than a costly denial of problems grown worse.
America did not and cannot solve the problem of the city by leaving it. The
abandoned slums have not become appealing green parks, as Rex Tugwell,
the New Deal developer of New Towns, once imagined, and Americans have
not migrated to the prairie as Frank Lloyd Wright foresaw. Most Americans
live in a metropolis and will continue to do so because of the centripetal pull
of metropolitan economies.

For over half a century, America has largely ignored the fact that metropolitan growth demands some form of metropolitan governance. In some
large metropolitan areas, competing jurisdictions number in the hundreds.
The six-county area of metropolitan Chicago, for example, contains more
than 1,300 local governments, including 260 separate cities and villages. In
the American system, states have the power to govern how land is used and

most delegate that power to localities with few strings attached. That system worked in the nineteenth century and into part of the twentieth, but in our own time it has left us with dysfunctional and dispiriting urban regions. It has become the foremost anachronism of our governmental system.

Thomas Jefferson, who approved the Louisiana Purchase and expanded the American frontier, predicted the new land would provide enough room for all foreseeable future generations of frontier families. Jefferson could never have imagined the impact of industry and immigrants on the pace or shape of American urban settlements. Only eight generations later, most Americans live in metropolitan regions—there is no frontier. We have long ceased to be a nation of independent yeomen and have become a nation of interdependent neighbors, citizens of the town or the metropolis, whether we choose to admit it or not. Some Americans will continue to make themselves at home in remote locations, but to live with an eighteenth-century frontier mentality in the twenty-first-century metropolis is folly.

"As our cause is new, so must we think anew and act anew," Abraham Lincoln once said. To deal effectively with sprawl we must insist on new and more effective means of land-use planning. For some reason we have an aversion to the term "land-use planning," but it's a concept we must come to terms with because it goes to the very heart of the issue. Otherwise we're just dealing with the symptoms of the problem rather than its root cause. The land we have now will have to serve us forever, and decisions made now will have enormously important consequences for our future.

The first step is to recognize that the way we zone and design our communities either opens up or forecloses alternatives to the automobile. Communities need to scrap provisions in their land-use policies that mandate auto-oriented sprawl and doom efforts to provide cost-effective public transit or to make communities more walkable. They also need to promote downtown housing and mixed-use zoning that reduces the distances people must travel between home and work and shopping. The goal should be an integrated system of planning decisions that knit communities together instead of tear them apart.

Some enlightened communities are beginning to take steps in pursuit of that goal. Santa Monica, California, has instituted a proactive policy that encourages the development of downtown housing, and it is beginning to pay off in encouraging ways. Because there is now a downtown market for its products, Toys "R" Us decided to locate a new store there instead of on the city's periphery. The presence of a major national toy chain on a downtown street corner doesn't seem very significant in itself, but replicated often enough, it could represent the reversal of a trend that has seen major retailers abandon downtowns in droves.

Calvert County, Maryland, stands almost directly across the Washington, D.C., metropolitan area from Prince William County, Virginia, and in some ways, the two counties are mirror images of each other. Both are traditionally rural, second-ring counties now experiencing extremely rapid growth, but they are dealing with that growth in starkly different ways. Whereas Prince William County reflects an "almost anything goes" approach and has the ugly strip malls to prove it, Calvert County decided in 1983 to contain future commercial development in existing "town centers." There is commercial clutter within the towns, to be sure, but the county has largely achieved its goal of retaining its rural character. For the same reason, the county requires clustered arrangements for new residential development. It is also proposing more mixed-use development to reduce automobile dependency, architectural and site-design standards to help preserve the attractiveness of the local environment, and a limit on the size of single retail stores to thirty thousand square feet. Calvert is not a wealthy county nor does it have many wealthy residents. Rather, it is populated by farmers, Chesapeake Bay watermen, and working men and women who commute to the Washington metropolis. What distinguishes the place is that it knows what it wants to be. County-sponsored surveys reflect an overwhelming desire on the part of residents to keep its rural character and the quality of life that goes with it. Enlightened public and private leaders in the county recognized that they had choices: they could do nothing and be overwhelmed by sprawl as several of their neighboring counties have been; or they could try to manage growth in a way that served their larger goals. They chose the latter course, and it is working.

On election day in November 1996, the voters in four communities in Sonoma County, California, approved the creation of Oregon-style urban growth boundaries around their hometowns as well as a countywide measure to restrict development in unincorporated areas adjacent to the new boundaries. San Jose soon thereafter adopted its own urban growth boundary. This marks the first time that California communities have embraced the concept.

As important as it is for communities to make the kinds of decisions that the city of Santa Monica and Calvert and Sonoma Counties have made, it is beyond the ability of many limited jurisdictions with boundaries arbitrarily established sometimes centuries ago to deal effectively with the modern problems of growth. The size of the problem is usually so great and the competition for new sources of tax revenue so intense that many municipalities feel that they have little choice but to let the developers have their way.

That is why regional or statewide planning mechanisms are needed in many cases to provide a broader perspective that will allow comprehensive and coordinated decision making on new development. Oregon's landmark legislation mandating urban growth boundaries stands head and shoulders over other attempts to manage growth. Whereas the state had been losing thirty thousand acres of farmland a year, now it is losing only two thousand acres a year (compared with Colorado, which is losing fifty thousand acres a year). The urban growth boundary works in Portland because it is mandated by the state, governed by an elected regional council, and is enforceable. A 1991 study showed that Portland's growth boundary had expanded by only 2 percent in the preceding seventeen years—but that it had absorbed 95 percent of the area's residential growth. Developers are now building single-family houses on smaller lots and constructing more of the multifamily housing that constitutes about half of the market demand. This concentration of development has made mass transit feasible and has stimulated the renovation and rescue of downtown buildings. In just two decades the number of jobs in downtown Portland has doubled—without the city adding a single new parking space. No other city in America can make that kind of claim. Portland is likely to sustain its financial viability and its much valued quality of life well into the twenty-first century when other cities—particularly other high-growth western cities like Denver, Phoenix, Salt Lake City, and especially Las Vegas—are struggling to maintain the infrastructure and public services that sprawl requires of them.

Some argue that Oregon is unique, that the combination of its culture, racial demographics, and politics allow the growth boundary to work there, but that it wouldn't work as well in places where those factors were different. There is also no question that the stars were aligned perfectly a quarter of a century ago when a popular and visionary Republican governor, Tom McCall, was willing to invest his political capital in the concept. But that doesn't mean that some variation of Oregon's approach, or a different approach with the same goal in mind, can't work in places blessed to have bold and visionary leaders.

Washington State is one of the few that has attempted to build on the Oregon experience by requiring its fastest-growing communities—twenty-nine of the state's thirty-nine counties—to plan for future growth and establish "urban service areas," similar in most respects to urban growth boundaries.

A few states have taken entirely different approaches. For example, Vermont requires reviews of major development projects to evaluate whether they will create "scattered development" and whether they will unreasonably burden a municipality's ability to provide government services. Rhode Island and Delaware require localities to plan for future growth. In Georgia, localities that don't plan for growth cannot apply for state water and sewer grants and other growth-related state funding.

Only state governments can address some growth issues effectively. The federal government can't mandate solutions, and local governments are for the most part hopelessly overwhelmed by the issue. States alone have the ability to see the regional picture and have the legal reach to sort out complicated political and economic issues. Only states can require local governments to develop rational strategies for using already developed land more efficiently, to make thoughtful choices about where new development should and should not go, and to set up land-use mechanisms that transcend local political boundaries. Most important, only states have the financial leverage to get results. Yet relatively few states have anything resembling growth-management legislation on their books. The rest, including some of the largest and fastest growing, have no plans to address an issue that is affecting them more than any other. Clinging to such an agnostic approach by leaving counties and municipalities to cope with growth on their own might have worked thirty or forty years ago, but it won't work in most places today, and it certainly won't work anywhere in the future.

Smart state governors know this, and a few are trying to do something about it. Roy Romer of Colorado, where growth is the number one issue in public opinion polls, has undertaken a "smart growth" initiative to prevent the entire Front Range of the Rockies from being turned into one giant megalopolis stretching from Fort Collins to Colorado Springs. Governor Michael O. Leavitt of Utah has convened a "growth summit" to heighten awareness of the problem and, if possible, to seek a consensus as to how to deal with it. Governor Tom Carper of Delaware has formed a cabinet committee on state planning matters as well as a citizens council to advise him on growth issues. These and similar initiatives are steps in the right direction.

One of the most ambitious state efforts to contain sprawl is under way in Maryland, where Governor Parris N. Glendening has won legislative approval of a "smart growth" initiative. With the state's population expected to grow by 1.1 million by 2020 and with 500,000 current residents expected to leave older neighborhoods for new developments in the same period, Glendening is determined to focus state spending on existing communities while protecting rapidly disappearing farmland and open space. He maintains that urban sprawl is draining the life out of the state's urban areas, particularly Baltimore, and threatening to bankrupt state government by wasting money on new roads, schools, and other facilities while older ones are abandoned or underused. If the governor's initiative works as intended, Maryland will no longer help pay for sprawl development.

Any measures designed to deal effectively with sprawl require state legislation, and legislation that limits sprawl creates difficult and contentious politics. A legislature is usually fraught with urban-suburban-rural tensions, and these tensions are compounded by the often fierce competition between fast-growing suburbs for new development that will add to the local tax base.

Not least, self-proclaimed "property rights" advocates often look askance at land-use control measures on the grounds that they infringe on an individual's right to do what he pleases with his land, even though such rights in the United States have never been unconditional. Rights carry responsibilities. No property owner has the absolute right to abuse the rights of neighbors or unreasonably diminish the value of a neighbor's property. Yet, property rights advocates have persuaded lawmakers in forty-one states to introduce so-called takings bills, which usually require more layers of government to thwart government action. Or, worse, they require government to pay property owners when government action prevents them from capitalizing on moneymaking endeavors and developing the most lucrative use of land. Such bills, for example, would require government to pay a property owner for not putting a toxic waste dump in a residential neighborhood. Wisely, voters in the states of Arizona and Washington have defeated such measures by wide margins.

Managing growth is not an easy task, but it is one that governments must undertake if they are to fulfill their responsibilities to their citizens. Each place is different in its history, its culture, its politics, and its growth patterns, and therefore each place needs to find the solution that fits the locale. There is no one-size-fits-all answer to growth management. But failing to find the right answer, or, worse, failing to *try* to find the right answer will almost certainly lead to unwanted answers down the road—fiscal bankruptcies, abandoned older communities, unnecessary loss of open space, and chaos.

A Rutgers University study put all this in perspective a few years ago when it concluded that New Jersey's growth-management plan, which was by no means a no-growth plan, would not adversely affect job and business creation. Over a twenty-year period, the plan would, however, preserve 36,500 acres of "frail" natural areas and 108,000 acres of productive farmland—while saving the state $1.3 billion in capital infrastructure costs, $400 million in operating costs for public school districts and municipalities, $740 million in road construction costs, and $440 million in water and sewer construction costs. While growth management makes sense from many perspectives, it unarguably makes economic sense.

Economist Thomas Michael Power explains that "the objectives of a community are more complex than those of a business operating in a commercial market. A business focuses on the bottom line." Ask members of a community what *they* want, however, and "it quickly becomes apparent that most of their wishes are qualitative"—a good place to live and work and raise a family. These are subjective goals. It is hard to put a price tag on them.[20] But reaching public agreement on what they mean is part of the process that brings people in a community together. Urban planner and author Jonathan

Barnett puts it another way: the first goal of any public growth policy should be "to make the creation of communities the primary objective."[21]

Consider how much better our communities would be if preservationists no longer had to prove why saving a community is in the community's best interest. Imagine what would happen if developers were the ones who had to prove why their proposals would not harm a community.[22] To shift the burden of proof, communities should make sprawl developers pay the full costs of their projects. If sprawl were tested by a truly "free" market, far less sprawl would occur on private financing alone. But too often, sprawl developers capture benefits for themselves while everyone else in a community bears the costs. As mentioned, in Terrell, Texas, a retail developer told the town, "I don't care how you get the money, but this is what we need to make this a viable site." The town responded by providing $3 million worth of incentives in the form of new roads, utilities, and water and sewer lines, and even $125,000 annually for seven years for marketing.

Seeking these kinds of inducements has become an integral part of most developers' strategies, primarily because they know how hungry so many communities are for new projects and because they know how to play them off against each other. "Inducement packages are a significant part of the development of every one of our centers, averaging well into seven figures per project," boasted the CEO of one development firm whose portfolio included seventeen retail outlet centers throughout the country. He estimated that his company has received a total of more than $50 million of inducements from local, county, and state governments, occasions when the developer's costs were shifted to the taxpayers.

Communities in every corner of the country allow themselves to be whipsawed in this fashion. They accept a developer's idea of how their community should be shaped, because they have few ideas of their own. How much better off they would be if they would step back from immediate development pressures, allow the community to decide what it wants to be, and then proceed to make it happen. Some communities, however, can't seem to find the wisdom to restrain themselves from making short-term decisions with long-term implications. The fact is, places everywhere subsidize sprawl because of imagined gains. Few of them ever pause to measure the true costs of such development proposals.

Most small communities are so concerned with bringing dollars in, they rarely consider the prospect of dollars leaking out. "The bait that has opened communities to exploitation and destruction has always been cash for local people," writes Wendell Berry. But "the supply of ready cash has tended to be undependable or temporary, and it has usually come as a substitute for things more permanent and dearer than cash, and harder to replace once lost." The only cure, Berry suggests, "is for people to choose one another and their place" over illusory promises of prosperity. "The local community must understand itself finally as a community of interest—a common dependence on a common life and a common ground. And because a community is, by definition, *placed,* its success cannot be divided from the success of its place."[23]

When Wal-Mart came to town, the people of Greenfield, Massachusetts, had the corporation pay the costs of an economic impact study. It revealed that the proposed discount store would displace almost 60 percent of the locality's existing businesses. With that information in hand, Greenfield turned the proposal down.

Unfortunately for localities, many public subsidies for sprawl made at their expense are provided by higher authorities. In Chicago, when Sears Roebuck and Company left its Sears Tower downtown for Hoffman Estates, thirty-seven miles away near O'Hare Airport, the move was supported by some $186 million in government subsidies under a new Illinois tax increment financing law.[24] If we ever decide to curb sprawl and become serious about revitalizing cities, towns, and neighborhoods, governments at all levels will have to reevaluate and alter economic development and transportation policies that work against these goals.

The consequences stemming from unrestrained sprawl are devastating. Why we accept them is one question, why we pay for them another. Those who insist that sprawl is merely the natural result of market forces ignore the fact that government at every level is riddled with policies that encourage, mandate, or even subsidize sprawl. Sprawl development is played on anything but a level playing field.

For years federal housing and lending policies have encouraged sprawl, but road building is undoubtedly the biggest current offender. Transportation policy should be based on principles that reward rational planning and efficiency. Too often it is just the reverse: policy is rooted in principles that reward sprawl. New highways, especially new multilane highways expanding the perimeter of metropolitan areas, rank among the greatest stimulants of sprawl.

Many states have standards for new roads that systematically destroy the pedestrian-friendly layout of small-town Main Streets and big-city downtowns and neighborhoods. By mandating excessively wide streets and roads, state highway departments outlaw the creation of traditional walkable environments. They invite fast-moving traffic on excessively wide streets in quiet residential areas, which then requires the installation of speed bumps to correct the mistake. And they mandate the kind of sprawl that turns Americans into slaves to the automobile. Eighty-two percent of all trips in the United

States are taken by car, costing the average American household 18 percent of its budget in transportation expenses, more than it spends on food. When people have nothing to walk to, driving is the only option.

What do we get for this enormous investment of our resources? Congested roads. And the Federal Highway Administration expects that over the next twenty years congestion will grow fourfold on our freeways and twofold on other roads. What makes this even worse is the fact that the money to fuel this comes out of our own pockets. A recent study concluded that drivers traveling alone to work pay only a quarter of the actual cost of their commutes. We subsidize the rest.

The subsidies underpinning residential sprawl are less obvious and direct, but they exist in a very big way. 1,000 Friends of Oregon, a nonprofit group formed to monitor the state's growth-management law, found that the cost of providing facilities and services to new residential subdivisions in the state averages $25,000 per home, but that developers are asked to pay only a fraction of the costs, typically between $2,000 and $6,000. Similarly, a study in Tallahassee, Florida, concluded that the cost of providing sewer hookups ranged from about $4,000 per house in the inner-city neighborhoods to about $11,000 in outlying subdivisions. Nonetheless, everyone was charged the same fee, approximately $6,000, meaning that the high-cost users in the newer areas were getting a subsidy financed by the low-cost users in the inner city.

Phil Burgess, president of the Center for the New West, a research organization based in Denver, argues that if developers were made to pay the full costs of the schools, roads, sewers, and other facilities that new communities require, many of them would build—or rebuild—within existing urban areas. "You make them pay the full costs," he says, "and all of a sudden that $130,000 home in the far suburbs is $230,000."[25]

If states are serious about containing sprawl and redirecting development to existing communities, the first thing they should do is eliminate the direct and indirect subsidies that have given residential and commercial sprawl their momentum. These subsidies do violence to free-market economics, to concepts of taxpayer fairness, and to sound land-use planning. Halting subsidies won't stop sprawl in its tracks, but it would probably do more than any other single thing to slow it down so that states could deal with the issue more comprehensively.

America can no longer afford the profligacy of the throwaway culture. The costs to maintain all the sprawl already built is now coming due. "The initial capital costs for infrastructure are the cheap part," notes Donovan Rypkema. "Maintaining the infrastructure for 30 or 40 or 50 years is the biggest expense."[26]

Government can begin to stem the tide of sprawl by building facilities and infrastructure in ways that do no harm. Chippewa County, Wisconsin, did this when it built its new office on the Main Street of downtown Chippewa Falls. At the federal level, the Clinton administration in 1996 ordered federal agencies to locate their facilities in places where they will reinforce the economic health and physical stability of existing communities: in historic buildings and historic downtowns.

New fiscal realities demand that we end the throwaway culture written into our tax codes and subsidized by taxpayers. Our tax laws penalize property owners who maintain or raise the value of their property and reward demolition by neglect. Even worse, depreciation allowances treat a building as a "wasting asset," with a productive economic life span that ends after 31.5 years. "Buildings are torn down not because their physical life is over but because their remaining economic life is deemed to be limited," Rypkema explains, adding that the "rebirth of economic life is reinvestment, not demolition." If property owners could not deduct such losses, they would do more to preserve the value of their property—as well as the value of the surrounding locations that determine the value of their property.[27]

Showing little concern for the preservation of existing buildings, the tax code shows even less for new ones. Tax code recognition of "real estate as Kleenex," as Rypkema says, "also reduces the quality of new buildings being built. Why spend the time and money to design and erect a structure to enable it to last 100 years, when its anticipated life is 31 ('and anyway, my accountant says I should sell it seven years from now')?"

Years ago, in 1922, Jesse Clyde Nichols, a visionary real estate developer who founded the Urban Land Institute, came back from a tour of Europe worried about America's stewardship of its built environment. "We have been thoughtless, carefree opportunists, outgrowing our cities [and] the houses of our fathers," he said. "Either we tear down and rebuild or we move away from the old centers. This is not 'progress' but an enormous destruction of property values."[28] We owe it to ourselves and our children to decide whether we really prefer living in a society in which, to paraphrase Joan Didion, the only thing constant is the rate at which it disappears.

Americans do not have the wherewithal to save every place or building, nor should we try. But the time is ripe for Americans to apply the concept of "sustainable development" (currently in vogue with environmentalists) to the built environment. Sustainable development is growth that meets the economic needs of living generations without spoiling assets for the generations that follow. In the natural environment, exhausting resources such as water, soils, forests, and fisheries for short-term economic gain ultimately leads to economic ruin. When forests are cut clear, work for loggers disappears, and when fish stocks disappear, fishing industries disappear with them. Because of our abundance of resources and developable land, Americans have been poor at balancing new development with the capacity of a location to support additional development. If cycles of regeneration are to occur, however, new investment in a location must keep pace with the rate of its depreciation. We will always need new buildings to meet new needs, but rampant overbuilding leads to waste and ruin. And the ruin of a community's built environment ultimately ruins its economic potential, its civic confidence, and the quality of community life itself. Habitats for civilized life are as necessary as habitats for wildlife.

As a nation, we also need to confront the dilemma posed by the condition of older communities, particularly the troubled neighborhoods of our inner cities. We have huge investments in the physical resources of such places, in the infrastructure and the buildings themselves. We can't afford to waste them as we used to do. More important, we can't afford to waste the people in those places, whose lives are too often plagued by the absence of opportunity, by hopelessness, drugs, and crime. Historic preservation can't address all of those concerns, but it can play a role in making places more habitable when other problems are addressed. As neighborhoods in Pittsburgh have shown, preservation of a place builds pride and pride builds hope.

The real question is whether America can muster the will and resources, public and private, to address the needs of decaying places, in poverty-ridden rural regions as well as cities. Most Americans know that what is happening in our cities is one of the most serious crises of our time. Yet there is nothing resembling a national commitment let alone a national strategy to do anything about it. With declining populations and declining resources, our cities are essentially left to fend for themselves against growing odds.

We can run from these problems, but we can't hide, at least not for long. We can keep moving farther and farther away from them, but they are creeping toward us steadily. Gated housing complexes are a symptom, not a solution.

No reasonable person would suggest massive new public spending programs for cities similar to failed programs of the past. But no reasonable person could reject carefully targeted incentives for job creation and training, industrial-site cleanup, the rehabilitation of residential areas, and whatever it takes to provide Americans with safe streets and schools that educate our children.

America's troubled places are a matter of enormous urgency. The consequences of neglect are growing worse. The longer we ignore them, the harder and more expensive it will be to solve them. We can become a nation ever more divided by economics, race, and geography, with all the serious ills those divisions bring. Or we can become a nation of healthy communities, growing healthier by growing together.

Such an effort will depend primarily on the people in those communities themselves, but state and federal leadership as well as private sector participation are vital. Citizens must mobilize for the task, but leaders of vision and courage and ability must lead the way.

"The earth belongs in usufruct to the living," was one of Thomas Jefferson's favorite phrases. He believed that the living should never be enslaved to the past. But he also knew that it is unwise for the living to ruin the best of what previous generations have left in their care. And he considered it a crime for the living to leave their debts behind for successive generations to pay.

To gain respect for history is to recognize the finite span of a single human life, that an individual belongs to something larger than the self. Without that awareness, without anchors, existence leaves us adrift, rootless, and disoriented. But gaining respect for the work of others who came before and those who will come after us helps us to respect who we are, where we are, and those who live around us. Only when we know our place and share a respect for it with others does a place change from a private residence to a community of neighbors, to a place worthy of our affection and demanding of our citizenship to sustain it.

We are living in a time of market-driven mentalities. To succeed, preservationists must adapt to the ways in which the market works. But the value of landmarks cannot be tabulated like cash flow. If America ever reaches the point where the preservation of its historic places can only be justified by economics alone, America will have sold its soul.

The built environment is our collective memory. As David McCullough has said, it "isn't just the work of an architect"; rather, it is "the work of a civilization." Places orient our lives in ways that other things do not. "We need stories," he says. "And in the loud, tawdry, throwaway culture of modern television, we need stories of a quieter kind, a longer lasting kind, a kind with character. And communities have stories. Without a story, who are we? Destroy the past, abuse the past, turn your backs on the past and you're turning your backs on and destroying all we have. We haven't got the future. The present is very uncertain. Somebody once said the world got along fine before Beethoven, but once we had Beethoven, we can't get along *without* Beethoven." Historic places affect our lives in similar ways. After learning to appreciate them, it is hard to get along without them.

In saving our heritage of older buildings and neighborhoods, we strengthen a partnership that makes for orderly growth and change in our communities: the perpetual partnership among the past, the present, and the future. This partnership recognizes that we cannot afford to live in the past, so it encourages each generation to build in its own style, to meet its own needs by taking advantage of the best contemporary thought and technology. But it also recognizes that we can't afford to reject the history, the culture, the traditions and values on which our lives and our futures are built.

When this partnership falls apart, when the connections between successive generations of Americans are removed, gaps interrupt our understanding of who we are. History dissolves into myth and ceases to be useful or even relevant. Timeless values erode. But when this bond works as it is supposed to, that partnership produces a healthy society with confidence and an enduring concept of community.

"How can we live without our lives?" cry the women of the Joad family in a passage from John Steinbeck's *The Grapes of Wrath*. "How will we know it's us without our past?"

Like individuals, a community can fall victim to amnesia, can lose the memory of what it was, and thereby lose touch with what it is and what it was meant to be. The loss of community memory happens most frequently and most dramatically in the destruction of familiar landmarks that are themselves familiar reminders of who we were, what we believed, and where we were headed.

Bricks and boards of old buildings, and the buildings that together compose a place, are tangible expressions of people long gone, an entryway into a community's collective memory. By saving places where memory resides, we become part of an infinite continuum, immersed in a perpetual stream in which past and future are inseparable parts. In that way, preservation helps us satisfy the need for continuity that art historian Sigfried Gideon says is "part of the very backbone of human dignity."

Day-to-day contact with evidence of our past gives us confidence because it enables us to know where we came from as well as where we are. It gives us a standard against which to measure ourselves and our accomplishments. And it confronts us with the realization—sometimes exhilarating, sometimes disturbing—that we, too, will be remembered and held accountable. Future generations will look at our work as the standard against which to measure their own performance. Will we be remembered for what we have allowed to disappear? Or will we be remembered for what we have left behind? The answer is ours to decide.

NOTES

PREFACE

1. Jane Jacobs, *The Death and Life of Great American Cities* (New York: Modern Library, 1993).

2. James Howard Kunstler, *The Geography of Nowhere: The Rise and Decline of America's Man-made Landscape* (New York: Simon & Schuster, 1994).

3. Lewis Mumford, *The Culture of Cities* (Orlando, Fla.: Harcourt Brace, 1970).

CHAPTER 1

1. Isaac Taylor in Richard Moe, *The Last Full Measure: The Life and Death of the First Minnesota Volunteers* (New York: Avon Books, 1993), 86, 250.

2. Bill McKelway, "Virginia's Disney Thrill Race," *Richmond Times-Dispatch,* 12 November 1993.

3. John Pulley, "PW: 'Magic Kingdom,' " *Journal Messenger,* 12 November 1993.

4. "PW Eyed for Disney Park," *Journal Messenger,* 10 November 1993.

5. John Pulley, "Disney Worked Quietly and Long before Unveiling Plan," *Journal Messenger,* 13 November 1993.

6. Bruce Potter and Peter Hardin, "Disney Planning State Theme Park," *Richmond Times Dispatch,* 10 November 1993.

7. Greg Schneider, "Disney Theme Park Won't Be Trip to Fantasy Land," *Virginian-Pilot,* 12 November 1993.

8. Preservation Alliance of Virginia, *Virginia's Economy & Historic Preservation* (1995), 9.

9. Michelle Singletary and Spencer Hsu, "Disney Says Va. Park Will Be Serious Fun; America's Exhibits Won't Sugarcoat History," *Washington Post,* 12 November 1993.

10. John Pulley, "Disney Seeks Making Civil War Important," *Journal Messenger,* 12 November 1993.

11. Richard Turner, "Disney Retreats from Battle over 'America' Theme Park," *Wall Street Journal,* 30 September 1994.

12. Peter Carlson, "Mickey Mouse History," *Washington Post Magazine,* May 15, 1994.

13. Bruce Potter, "Disney Bringing America to State," *Richmond Times Dispatch,* 12 November 1993.

14. Matthew Cox, "Manassas a Top 20 City," *Journal Messenger,* 7 September 1994.

15. Senate Subcommittee on Public Lands, National Parks and Forests of the Committee on Energy and Natural Resources, 1994.

16. Senate Subcommittee on Public Lands, National Parks and Forests of the Committee on Energy and Natural Resources, 100th Cong., 2d sess., September 8, 1988, 116–19.

17. Spencer S. Hsu, and Stephen C. Fehr, "Disney Dollars, Jobs Tempt County," *Washington Post,* 3 July 1994.

18. Charles Ashby, "Officials Map Park Strategy," *Potomac News,* 12 November 1993.

19. Will Jones, "New Routes Will Pave the Way to Park," *Potomac News,* 12 November 1993.

20. Scott Achelpohl, "Disney Is Buzz Word at Economic Confab," *Journal Messenger,* 18 November 1993.

21. Charles Ashby, "Disney Yes," *Potomac News,* 11 November 1993.

22. Thomas Hylton, *Save Our Land, Save Our Towns: A Plan for Pennsylvania* (Harrisburg, Pa.: RB Books, 1995), 16.

23. Spencer S. Hsu and Maria E. Odum, "Residents Fear Park Will Overwhelm Rural Area," *Washington Post,* 13 November 1993.

24. John Pulley, "Shop Owners Polling Public About Disney," *Potomac News,* 16 November 1993.

25. Harold H. Dutton Jr., "Be Aware, Disney Co. Has Followed Development Script," *Potomac News,* 11 September 1994.

26. William Powers, "Disney Ties Va. Park to Road Money, Eisner Warns Company May Consider Prince William Site," *Washington Post,* 19 December 1993.

27. Singletary and Hsu.

28. Charles Ashby, "Disney Lured with $137 Million Carrot," *Potomac News,* 21 January 1994.

29. Richard Squires, "Disney's Trojan Horse," *Washington Post,* 23 January 1994.

30. Neal R. Peirce, "Governors Giving Away the Store," *Rochester (Minnesota) Post-Bulletin,* 12 February 1994.

31. Joe Spivey Jr., "Learn from Florida's Experience with Disney," *Potomac News,* 4 September 1994.

32. "Summary, Fiscal Revenue Impacts, Disney's America, Prince William County, Virginia," prepared by Kotin, Regan & Moulchy, December 1993.

33. Jonathan Yardley, "The Mouse Springs Its Trap," *Washington Post,* 10 January 1994.

34. John Beardsley, "Disney in the Old Dominion," *Landscape Architecture,* July 1994, 36.

35. William Powers, "Hail to the Mouse," *Washington Post,* 25 April 1994.

36. Carl P. Leubsdorf, "In Dixie Land, We'll Take Our Stand," *Dallas Morning News,* 17 July 1994.

37. Benjamin Forgey, "Disneyopolis," *Washington Post,* 7 May 1994.

38. "Misdirected Fire," *Prince William Journal,* 23 June 1994.

39. "Be Aware, Disney Co. Has Followed Development Script," *Potomac News,* 11 September 1994.

40. William Powers, "Eisner Says Disney Won't Back Down," *Washington Post,* 14 June 1994.

41. "Disney's America, Impact on National Resources." Fairfax, Va.: Synergy Planning, 1994.

42. Ibid.

43. "Virginia, Say No to the Mouse," *New York Times,* 24 February 1994.

44. Georgie Boge and Margie Holder Boge, *Paving Over the Past: A History and Guide to Civil War Battlefield Preservation* (Washington, D.C.: Island Press, 1993), 100.

45. Senate Subcommittee on Public Lands, National Parks and Forests of the Committee on Energy and Natural Resources, 100th Cong., 2d sess., September 8, 1988, 49.

46. James M. McPherson, ed., *The Atlas of the Civil War* (New York: MacMillan, 1994), 68.

47. David W. Dunlap, "Reviving a True Classic on West 42d Street," *New York Times,* 14 August 1994.

48. "The Report of the Partnership for Regional Excellence" (Washington, D.C.: Metropolitan Washington Council of Governments, 1993). For warnings of the impact of sprawl on the region's future see also "A Legacy of Excellence for the Washington Region: Task Force Report on Growth and Transportation" (Washington, D.C.: Metropolitan Washington Council of Governments, 1991).

49. Powers, "Hail to the Mouse."

50. Joel Garreau, "What's in It for Us to Help Disney Build a Competitor Edge City?" *Edge City News,* February 1994, 6.

51. Powers, "Hail to the Mouse."

52. Russ Rymer, "Back to the Future: Disney Reinvents the Company Town," *Harper's,* October 1996, 70.

53. Linda Feldman, "Disney Theme Park Sparks New Civil War in Virginia," *Christian Science Monitor,* June 28, 1994.

54. Rudy Abramson, *Hallowed Ground: Preserving America's Heritage* (Charlottesville, Va.: Thomasson–Grant and Lickle, 1996), 151.

55. Forgey, "Disneyopolis."

56. Paul Bradley, "Disney Shows Old Tactics Won't Do," *Richmond Times-Dispatch,* 1 October 1994.

57. Rymer, "Back to the Future: Disney Reinvents the Company Town."

58. Lecture at the National Building Museum, Washington, D.C., December 4, 1996.

59. William H. Whyte, *The Last Landscape* (Garden City, N.Y.: Doubleday & Co., 1968), 234.

CHAPTER 2

1. Mel Scott, *American City Planning Since 1890* (Berkeley: University of California Press, 1969), 45.

2. Robert L. Wrigley, "The Plan of Chicago," in Donald A. Krueckeberg, ed., *Introduction to Planning History in the United States* (New Brunswick, N.J.: Center for Urban Policy Research, 1983), 58.

3. Ibid., 71.

4. Scott, 33.

5. Robert Fishman, *Urban Utopias in the Twentieth Century: Ebenezer Howard, Frank Lloyd Wright, Le Corbusier* (Cambridge, Mass.: The MIT Press, 1982), 38.

6. Stanley Buder, *Visionaries and Planners: The Garden City Movement and the Modern Community* (New York: Oxford University Press, 1990), ix.

7. Jonathan Barnett, *The Elusive City: Five Centuries of Design, Ambition and Miscalculation* (New York: Harper & Row, 1986), 76.

8. Peter Hall, *Cities of Tomorrow: An Intellectual History of Urban Planning and Design in the Twentieth Century* (Oxford, England: Basil Blackwell, 1988), 100.

9. Ibid., 97.

10. John Nolen, *Madison: A Model City,* excerpt reprinted in *Nolen in the '90s: A Symposium Examining the Modern-day Relevance of John Nolen's Classic Urban Designs* (Madison, Wis.: Isthmus Publishing Co., Inc., 1995), 6.

11. Frederick L. Ackerman, "Where Goes the City-Planning Movement?" *Journal of the American Institute of Architects* 7 (December 1919), 519–20.

12. Gwendolyn Wright, *Building the Dream: A Social History of Housing in America* (New York: Pantheon, 1981), 208.

13. Kenneth T. Jackson, *Crabgrass Frontier: The Suburbanization of the United States* (New York: Oxford University Press, 1985), 162.

14. Peter G. Rowe, *Making a Middle Landscape* (Cambridge, Mass.: MIT Press, 1991), 184.

15. Jackson, 170.

16. Hall, 126.

17. Ibid., 123.

18. Jackson, 162.

19. Scott, 260.

20. Rowe, 211.

21. Le Corbusier, "The City of To-morrow and Its Planning," in Richard T. Le Gates and Frederic Stout, eds., *The City Reader* (New York: Routledge, 1996), 368–75.

22. Ibid., 373–74.

23. Hall, 205.

24. Ibid., 207.

25. Fishman, 190.

26. Le Corbusier, 368.

27. Hall, 207.

28. Vincent Scully, "Back to the Future, with a Detour through Miami," *New York Times,* 27 January 1991.

29. Vincent Scully, "The Civilizing Force of Architecture," *Humanities* 16, no. 3 (May–June 1995), 10.

30. Vincent Scully, "The Architecture of Community," in Peter Katz, *The New Urbanism: Toward an Architecture of Community* (New York: McGraw-Hill, 1994), 223.

31. Scully, "Back to the Future, with a Detour through Miami."

32. Frank Lloyd Wright, *The Disappearing City* (New York: W. F. Payson, 1932), 38.

33. Ibid., 43.

34. Ibid., 61.

35. Ibid., 77.

36. Ibid., 38.

37. Robert A. M. Stern, *Pride of Place: Building the American Dream* (Boston: Houghton Mifflin Co., 1986), 150.

38. F. L. Wright, *Disappearing City,* 71.

39. Catherine Bauer, "Review of *The Disappearing City,*" *The Nation* 136 (January 1933), 99–100.

40. Hall, 151.

41. Ibid., 146.

42. David Myhra, "Rexford Guy Tugwell: Initiator of America's Greenbelt New Towns, 1935 to 1936," *Journal of the American Institute of Planners* 40, no. 3 (May 1974), 181.

43. Hall, 132.

44. Gwendolyn Wright, 199.

45. Jackson, 205.

46. Ibid., 207.

47. Federal Housing Administration, Technical Bulletin #7, 1938, in Keller Easterling, *American Town Plans: A Comparative Time Line* (New York: Princeton Architectural Press, 1993), 63.

48. Lewis Mumford, *The City in History: Its Origins and Transformations and Its Prospects* (New York: Harcourt, Brace and World, 1961), 505.

49. Jackson, 214.

50. Ibid., 209.

51. Thomas O'Connor, *Building a New Boston: Politics and Urban Renewal 1950 to 1970* (Boston: Northeastern University Press, 1993), 66.

52. Ashley A. Foard and Hilbert Fefferman, "Federal Urban Renewal Legislation," in James Q. Wilson, ed., *Urban Renewal: The Record and the Controversy* (Cambridge, Mass.: MIT Press, 1966), 78.

53. *Waverly: A Study in Neighborhood Conservation* (Washington, D.C.: Federal Home Loan Bank Board, 1940).

54. Fishman, 148.

55. Harry K. Schwartz, "A Federal Historic Rehabilitation Tax Credit for Home Ownership: Proposing a New Way to Revive Our Communities," *Historic Preservation News*, October/November 1994, 14–17.

56. Harry K. Schwartz, "Why Provide Tax Incentives?" in Constance Beaumont, *Smart States, Better Communities: How State Governments Can Help Preserve Their Communities* (Washington, D.C.: National Trust for Historic Preservation, 1996), 94.

57. Federal Housing Administration, Technical Bulletin #2, "Modern Design," March 1, 1941.

58. Carl Feiss, "Taking Stock: A Resume of Planning Accomplishments in the United States," in William R. Ewald Jr., ed., *Environment and Change: The Next Fifty Years* (Bloomington, Ind.: Indiana University Press, 1968), 223.

59. Jackson, 240.

60. David Halberstam, *The Fifties* (New York: Villard Books, 1993), 140.

61. Jackson, 233.

62. Easterling, 7.

63. Gwendolyn Wright, 240.

64. Jackson, 239.

65. Halberstam, 140.

66. Ray Oldenburg, *The Great Good Place: Cafes, Coffee Shops, Community Centers, Beauty Parlors, General Stores, Bars, Hangouts, and How They Get You through the Day* (New York: Paragon House, 1989), 267–69.

67. Jon C. Teaford, *The Rough Road to Renaissance: Urban Revitalization in America, 1940–1985* (Baltimore: Johns Hopkins University Press, 1990), 10.

68. John F. Bauman, "Visions of a Post-war City: A Perspective on Urban Planning in Philadelphia and the Nation, 1942–1945," in Donald A. Krueckeberg, ed., *Introduction to Planning History in the United States* (New Brunswick, N.J.: Center for Urban Policy Research, 1983), 172.

69. O'Connor, 67.

70. Teaford, 10.

71. Frank Lloyd Wright, *When Democracy Builds* (Chicago: University of Chicago Press, 1945) 130.

72. Bauman, 182.

73. Foard and Fefferman, 77.

74. Scott, 476.

75. Gwendolyn Wright, 246.

76. Scott, 498.

77. Ibid., 499.

78. Ibid., 503.

79. William L. Slayton, "The Operation and Achievements of the Urban Renewal Program," in James Q. Wilson, ed., *Urban Renewal: The Record and the Controversy* (Cambridge, Mass.: MIT Press, 1966), 214.

80. Scott, 186.

81. Stephen B. Goddard, *Getting There: The Epic Struggle between Road and Rail in the Twentieth Century* (New York: Basic Books, 1994), 170.

82. Ibid., 164.

83. Daniel P. Moynihan, "New Roads and Urban Chaos," *The Reporter,* 14 April 1960, 13.

84. Ian McHarg, *Design with Nature* (Garden City, N.Y.: Natural History Press, 1969), 31.

85. Rowe, 185–90.

86. Ibid., 191.

87. Goddard, 170.

88. James Howard Kunstler, *The Geography of Nowhere: The Rise and Decline of America's Man-made Landscape* (New York: Simon & Schuster, 1994), 100.

89. Robert Caro, *The Power Broker: Robert Moses and the Fall of New York* (New York: Alfred A. Knopf, 1974), 19.

90. Ibid., 878.

91. Carl Feiss in *With Heritage So Rich* (reprint; Washington, D.C.: Preservation Press, 1983), 229.

92. Robert Caro noted this irony in his biography of Moses.

93. Goddard, 182.

94. Ed Weiner, *Urban Transportation Planning in the United States: An Historical Overview* (Washington, D.C.: U.S. Department of Transportation, 1992).

95. Scott, 449.

96. Moynihan, 14.

97. Weiner, 97.

98. Caro, 11.

99. Goddard, 182.

100. Scott, 538.

101. Lewis Mumford, *The Highway and the City* (New York: Mentor Books, 1963), 244.

102. Mumford, *The City in History,* 430.

103. Rowe, 120.

104. Ibid., 121.

105. Ibid., 120.

106. Philip Langdon, *A Better Place to Live: Reshaping the American Suburb* (Amherst: The University of Massachusetts Press, 1994), 197.

107. Herbert Muschamp, *Man About Town: Frank Lloyd Wright in New York City* (Cambridge, Mass.: MIT Press, 1983), 185. The authors acknowledge Peter Hall, *Cities of Tomorrow: An Intellectual History of Urban Planning and Design in the Twentieth Century* (Oxford, England: Basil Blackwell, 1988), for calling attention to this story in Muschamp's book.

108. Rowe, 127.

109. William Severini Kowinski, *The Malling of America: An Inside Look at the Great Consumer Paradise* (New York: William Morrow and Company, Inc., 1985).

110. Rowe, 128.

111. Ibid., 134.

112. Ibid., 140.

113. Kowinski, 109.

114. Jane Jacobs, *The Death and Life of Great American Cities* (New York: Modern Library, 1993), 440.

115. *With Heritage So Rich,* 191.

116. Ibid., 118.

117. James Marston Fitch, *Historic Preservation: Curatorial Management of the Built World* (New York: McGraw-Hill, 1982), 35.

118. Vincent Scully, "The Civilizing Force of Architecture," 10.

119. O'Connor, 139.

120. Martin Anderson, "Fiasco of Urban Renewal," in James Q. Wilson, ed., *Urban Renewal: The Record and the Controversy* (Cambridge, Mass.: MIT Press, 1966), 492.

121. Hall, 204.

122. Kenneth T. Jackson, "America's Rush to Suburbia," *New York Times,* 9 June 1996.

123. Peter Calthorpe, *The Next American Metropolis: Ecology, Community, and the American Dream* (New York: Simon & Schuster, 1993), 19.

124. Ibid.

125. Joel Garreau, *Edge City: Life on the New Frontier* (New York: Anchor Books, 1991).

126. Henry L. Diamond and Patrick F. Noonan, *Land Use in America* (Washington, D.C.: Island Press, 1996), 4.

127. Thomas Hylton, *Save Our Land, Save Our Towns: A Plan for Pennsylvania* (Harrisburg, Pa.: RB Books, 1995), 17.

128. Janet Whitemore, "Sprawl Towns," *Architecture Minnesota* 21, no. 5 (September–October 1995), Vol. 40.

129. Thomas Bier and Ivan Maric, "Cuyahoga County Outmigration," research paper, Housing Policy Research Program at the Urban Center, Levin College of Urban Affairs, Cleveland State University, Cleveland, Ohio, March 1993.

130. William Lucy and David Phillips, "Why Some Suburbs Thrive," *Planning* 61, no. 6, 20.

131. Richard Voith, "Do Suburbs Need Cities?" Working Paper Number 93-27/R, Federal Reserve Bank of Philadelphia, November 1994.

132. George F. Will, "Can Happy Mayor Save Hartford?" *Boston Globe,* 1 December 1996.

133. Rodger Doyle, *Atlas of Contemporary America: A Portrait of the Nation* (New York: Facts on File, 1994), 162.

134. Will, "Can Happy Mayor Save Hartford?"

135. Robert D. Putnam, "Tuning In, Tuning Out: The Strange Disappearance of Social Capital in America," *PS: Political Science and Politics* 28, no. 4 (December 1995), 681.

136. Michael Young and Peter Willmott, " 'Kinship and Community' and 'Keeping Themselves to Themselves,' " in Richard T. Le Gates and Frederic Stout, eds., *The City Reader* (New York: Routledge, 1996), 207.

137. Ibid., 214.

138. Putnam, 678.

139. Oldenburg, 285.

140. Ibid., 208.

141. Ibid., xi.

142. Ibid., 203.

143. Ibid., 210.

144. Christopher Lasch, *The Revolt of the Elites and the Betrayal of Democracy* (New York: W. W. Norton, 1995), 8.

145. Stern, 154–55.

146. Lasch, 47.

CHAPTER 3

1. John E. Harkins, *Metropolis of the American Nile: An Illustrated History of Memphis and Shelby County*, Pyramid Edition (Oxford, Miss.: The Guild Bindery Press, 1991), 34.

2. Ibid.

3. Turner Catledge, *My Life and the Times* (New York: Harper & Row, 1971), 37.

4. David M. Tucker, *Memphis Since Crump: Bossisim, Blacks, and Civic Reformers 1948–1968* (Knoxville: University of Tennessee Press, 1980), 22.

5. Ibid., 44.

6. Eugene J. Johnson and Robert D. Russell, *Memphis: An Architectural Guide* (Knoxville: University of Tennessee Press, 1990), 62.

7. Ibid., 7.

8. Robert A. Sigafoos, *Cotton Row to Beale Street: A Business History of Memphis* (Memphis, Tenn.: Memphis State University Press, 1979), 93.

9. Johnson and Russell, 48.

10. Harkins, 134.

11. Johnson and Russell, 34.

12. Ibid., 45–46.

13. Ibid., 58.

14. Sigafoos, 150.

15. Larry R. Ford, *Cities and Buildings: Skyscrapers, Skid Rows, and Suburbs* (Baltimore: Johns Hopkins University Press, 1994), 7.

16. Sigafoos, 221.

17. Ibid., 223.

18. Joel Garreau, *Edge City: Life on the New Frontier* (New York: Anchor Books, 1991), 32.

19. Sigafoos, 147.

20. Ibid., 285.

21. Ibid., 334.

22. Ibid., 337.

23. Harkins, 148.

24. Sigafoos, 286.

25. George W. Lee, *Beale Street: Where the Blues Began* (New York: R. O. Ballou, 1934), 13.

26. Charles Reagan Wilson and William Ferris, eds., *Encyclopedia of Southern Culture* (Chapel Hill, N.C.: University of North Carolina Press, 1989), 1044.

27. Johnson and Russell, 133.

28. Ibid., 134.

29. Ford, 89.

30. Sigafoos, 278.

31. Harkins, 152.

32. Johnson and Russell, 8.

33. Tucker, 167.

34. Johnson and Russell, 9.

35. Sigafoos, 288.

36. Harkins, 151.

37. Johnson and Russell, 78.

38. Jackson, 271.

39. *With Heritage So Rich* (reprint; Washington, D.C.: Preservation Press, 1983), 159.

40. Peter Calthorpe, *The Next American Metropolis: Ecology, Community, and the American Dream* (New York: Simon & Schuster, 1993), 33.

41. Garreau, 9.

42. Henry L. Diamond and Patrick F. Noonan, *Land Use in America* (Washington, D.C.: Island Press, 1996), 208.

43. Jackson, 276.

44. Editorial, "A Defeat for the Bulldozer," *New York Times*, 25 March 1971.

45. Johnson and Russell, 51.

46. Jackson, 271.

47. Harkins, 150.

CHAPTER 4

1. David Rusk, "Thinking Regionally: Stretching Cities," in *The State of the American Community,* ed. Robert McNulty (Washington, D.C.: Partners for Livable Communities, 1994), 45–46.

2. Witold Rybczynski, *City Life: Urban Expectations in a New World* (New York: Scribner's, 1995), 227.

3. Jane Jacobs, *The Death and Life of Great American Cities* (New York: Modern Library, 1993), 354.

4. Winifred Gallagher, *The Power of Place: How Our Surroundings Shape Our Thoughts, Emotions and Actions* (New York: HarperCollins, 1993), 191.

5. Henry G. Cisneros, "Defensible Space: Deterring Crime and Building Community" (Washington, D.C.: U.S. Department of Housing and Urban Development, 1995), 14.

6. Ibid., 22–24.

7. Jacobs, 354.

8. John William Reps, *Making of Urban America: A History of City Planning in the United States* (Princeton, N.J.: Princeton University Press, 1965), 294.

9. Kenneth Severans, *Southern Architecture: 350 Years of Distinctive Buildings* (New York: E. P. Dutton, 1981), 25.

10. Rybczynski, 63.

11. Roberta Brandes Gratz, *The Living City: How Urban Residents Are Revitalizing America's Neighborhoods and Downtown Shopping Districts by Thinking Small in a Big Way* (New York: Simon & Schuster, 1989), 43.

12. Series of articles entitled "The Disappearing City, Abandoned Houses, Abandoned Hope," *New Orleans Times-Picayune,* 12–15 January 1992.

13. Christopher Cooper, "Success Is a Matter of Style," *New Orleans Times-Picayune,* 14 January 1992.

14. Alexander Garvin, *The American City: What Works, What Doesn't* (New York: McGraw-Hill, 1996), xi.

15. Patricia H. Gay, "The Urgency of Urban Preservation," in *Past Meets Future: Saving America's Historic Environments,* ed. Antoinette J. Lee (Washington, D.C.: Preservation Press, 1992), 107.

16. Patricia H. Gay, "Urbs and Burbs," *Preservation in Print* (newsletter of the Preservation Resource Center of New Orleans), September 1995, 6.

17. Lynne Lewicki, "Introducing Joe Canizaro," *Urban Land,* October 1995, 77.

18. Franklin Toker, *Pittsburgh: An Urban Portrait* (Pittsburgh, Pa.: University of Pittsburgh Press, 1986), 11.

19. Ibid., 66.

20. Ibid., 10.

21. Lewis Mumford, *The Culture of Cities* (New York: Harcourt Brace Jovanovich, 1970), 191–93.

22. Roy Lubove, "City Beautiful, City Banal: Design Advocacy and Historic Preservation in Pittsburgh," an essay reprinted by the Pittsburgh History and Landmarks Foundation from *Pittsburgh History,* spring 1992, a publication of the Historical Society of Western Pennsylvania.

23. Walter C. Kidney, *Pittsburgh in Your Pocket: A Guide to Pittsburgh-Area Architecture* (Pittsburgh, Pa.: Pittsburgh History and Landmarks Foundation), 225–34.

24. Toker, 13.

25. Kidney, 90.

26. Roy Lubove, *Twentieth-Century Pittsburgh* (Pittsburgh, Pa.: University of Pittsburgh Press, 1996), 107.

27. Kidney, 174.

28. James D. Van Trump, *Life and Architecture in Pittsburgh* (Pittsburgh, Pa.: Pittsburgh History and Landmarks Foundation, 1983), 11.

29. Lubove, "City Beautiful, City Banal."

30. Stefan Lorant, *Pittsburgh: The Story of an American City* (New York: Garden City, 1964), 373.

31. Lubove, "City Beautiful, City Banal."

32. For an earlier explanation of this point, see Joseph B. Rose, "Landmarks Preservation in New York," in *The Public Face of Architecture: Civic Culture and Public Spaces,* eds. Nathan Glazer and Mark Lilla (New York: Free Press, 1987), 428.

33. "Legal Techniques in Historic Preservation," National Trust for Historic Preservation, 1972, reprinted in Norman Williams Jr., Edmund H. Kellogg, and Frank B. Gilbert, eds., *Readings in Historic Preservation: Why? What? How?* (New Brunswick, N.J.: Center for Urban Policy Research, 1983), 308.

34. In 1995, the city of Boston, under Mayor Thomas M. Menino, joined with the National Trust for Historic Preservation to launch the first citywide, multidistrict Main Streets program in the United States. A decade before, Menino had represented Boston's Roslindale neighborhood as a city councillor when that district joined Pittsburgh's East Carson Street as part of the first group of urban Main Street programs.

35. Rebecca L. Flora, "South Side Local Development Company," *Historic Preservation Forum,* National Trust for Historic Preservation, spring 1995, 26.

36. Gratz, 72–73.

37. Arthur P. Zeigler Jr., Leopold Adler II, and Walter C. Kidney, *Revolving Funds for Historic Preservation: A Manual of Practice* (Pittsburgh, Pa.: Ober Park Associates, 1975), 107.

38. Toker, 17.

39. Jay Farbstein and Richard Wener, *Rebuilding Communities: Re-creating Urban Excellence* (New York: The Bruner Foundation, 1993), 45.

40. Rochelle L. Stanfield, *National Journal,* September 14, 1996, 1,948.

41. Gallagher, 200.

42. Ibid., 192.

43. Stanfield, 1,950.

CHAPTER 5

1. Witold Rybczynski, *City Life* (New York: Scribner's, 1995), 216.

2. Kenneth E. Stone, *Competing with the Retail Giants: How to Survive in the New Retail Landscape* (New York: John Wiley & Sons, 1995), 61.

3. Ibid., 67.

4. Christopher Gunn and Hazel Dayton Gunn, *Reclaiming Capital: Democratic Initiatives and Community Development* (Ithaca, N.Y.: Cornell University Press, 1991), 28.

5. Urban Land Institute.

6. Kennedy Lawson Smith, "Main Street at 15," *Historic Preservation Forum*, National Trust for Historic Preservation, spring 1995, 55.

7. Robert Berner, "Retailers Keep Expanding amid a Glut of Stores," *Wall Street Journal*, 28 May 1996.

8. Susan Warner, "Remaking a Mall," *Urban Land*, October 1995, 71.

9. Jennifer Steinhauer, "Malls Hope Make-overs Will Attract the Affluent," *New York Times*, 3 November 1995.

10. For more on the evolution of the Main Street program philosophy, see Kennedy Lawson Smith, 49–64.

11. Richard Critchfield, *Trees, Why Do You Wait? America's Changing Rural Culture* (Washington, D.C.: Island Press, 1991), 208.

12. Mike Gunn explained Bonaparte's story in "Bonaparte, Iowa: Rebirth of a Small Town," in *Main Street News*, National Main Street Network, National Main Street Center, National Trust for Historic Preservation, November 1990.

13. Kelley Flury, "City to Play Bigger Role in Future Ads," Leinenkugel's 125th Anniversary section, *Chippewa Herald Telegram*, 3 September 1992.

14. William A. Galston and Karen J. Baehler, *Rural Development in the United States: Connecting Theory, Practice and Possibilities* (Washington, D.C.: Island Press, 1995).

15. Allen Freeman, "A Perfect Alliance," *Preservation News*, National Trust for Historic Preservation, April–May 1994.

16. "Historic Preservation and Tourism," *Preservation Forum*, fall 1988, 10.

17. Chinitz and Horan, "Communications Technology and Settlement Patterns," *Landlines*, Lincoln Institute of Land Policy, September 1996.

18. Ray Oldenburg, *The Great Good Place: Cafes, Coffee Shops, Community Centers, Beauty Parlors, General Stores, Bars, Hangouts, and How They Get You Through the Day* (New York: Paragon House, 1989), 3.

CHAPTER 6

1. Lewis Mumford, *The Culture of Cities* (Orlando, Fla.: Harcourt Brace, 1970), 17.

2. Thomas J. Noel and Barbara S. Norgren, *Denver: The City Beautiful and Its Architects, 1893–1941* (Denver: Historic Denver, 1987), 8.

3. Ibid., 15.

4. Ibid., 14.

5. Mayor Wellington Webb would utter a similar line after highly publicized cost overruns, alterations, and construction delays plagued the new Denver International Airport, a multibillion-dollar facility that in 1995 replaced an airport named for the spendthrift Mayor Stapleton.

6. Thomas J. Noel, *Denver's Larimer Street: Main Street, Skid Row, and Urban Renaissance* (Denver: Historic Denver, 1981), 123.

7. Barbara Gibson, *The Lower Downtown Historic District* (Denver: Historic Denver in cooperation with the Denver Museum of Natural History, 1995), 6.

8. Noel and Norgren, 102.

9. Sandra Widener, "Is She the Most Powerful Woman in Denver?" *Empire Magazine, Denver Post*, 2 January 1983, 9.

10. Joanne Ditmer, "Queen Sized Ruling," *Denver Post*, 13 March 1988.

11. Gibson, 84.

12. Noel, *Denver's Larimer Street*, 123.

13. Ibid., 123–24.

14. Noel and Norgren, 183.

15. Lower Downtown Neighborhood Plan, prepared for the Lower Downtown District, Inc., draft dated July 26, 1996.

16. Joslyn Green, "Does LoDo Have Great Streets?," *LoDo News*, June 1996, 24.

17. David Gottlieb, "Lookin' at LoDo, Final Thoughts, 'Bye . . .'," *LoDo News* 3, no. 2 (June 1996), 23.

18. "A Practical Guide to the Twin Cities," *Fortune*, April 1936, 13.

19. Jeffrey A. Hess and Paul Larsen, "From Modern to Postmodern in St. Paul, 1940–1985," unpublished manuscript prepared for the St. Paul Heritage Preservation Commission, 1996.

20. Hess and Larsen, 12, 13, 14, 17.

21. Ibid., 64.

22. Ibid., 70.

23. Ibid., 86.

24. David Osborne, "Government That Means Business," *New York Times Magazine*, 1 March 1992, 26.

25. Bernard J. Friedan and Lynne B. Sagalyn, *Downtown, Inc.: How America Rebuilds Cities* (Cambridge, Mass.: MIT Press, 1989), 18.

26. Ibid. 190.

27. Political scientist Daniel Elazar, quoted in Philip Langdon, "How Portland Does It," *The Atlantic*, November 1992, 136.

28. Carl Abbott, *Portland: Planning, Politics, and Growth in a Twentieth-century City* (Lincoln, Nebr.: University of Nebraska Press, 1983), 3.

29. William John Hawkins III, *The Grand Era of Cast-iron Architecture in Portland* (Portland, Ore.: Binford and Mort, 1976), 162.

30. Ibid.

31. Gideon Bosker and Lena Lencek, *Frozen Music: A History of Portland Architecture* (Portland, Ore.: Western Imprints/The Oregon Historical Society, 1985), 209.

32. Virginia Guest Ferriday, *Last of the Handmade Buildings: Glazed Terra Cotta in Downtown Portland* (Portland, Ore.: Mark Publishing Co., 1984), 61.

33. Carl Abbott, "The Capital of Good Planning: Metropolitan Portland since 1970," paper prepared for the American Studies Program of the Smithsonian Institution, Washington, D.C., 1995, 8.

34. Martin Wisckol, "Stopping the Sprawl," *Jacksonville Times-Union*, June 16, 1996.

35. Abbott, "The Capital of Good Planning," 25.

36. Abbott, *Portland*, 207.

37. Bosker and Lencek, 220.

38. Neal R. Peirce and Robert Guskind, *Breakthroughs: Re-creating the American City* (New Brunswick, N.J.: Center for Urban Policy Research, 1995), 59.

39. Philip Langdon, *A Better Place to Live* (Amherst: The University of Massachusetts Press, 1994), 136.

40. Remarks made by Peter Calthorpe at a conference entitled "Alternatives to Sprawl," held at The Brookings Institution, Washington, D.C. March 22, 1995.

41. Peter Calthorpe, *The Next American Metropolis: Ecology, Community, and the American Dream* (New York: Simon & Schuster, 1993), 41.

42. Ibid., 147.

43. "Pedestrian and Cycling Friendly Cities," *Urban Quality Indicators* 1, no. 2 (summer 1996), 10–11.

44. Abbott, "The Capital of Good Planning," 9.

45. Quoted in Elaine S. Friedman, *The Facts on Life in Portland, Oregon* (Portland, Ore.: Portland Possibilities, Inc., 1994), 341.

46. John Painter Jr., "Architecturally, Portland Short On Innovations," *Portland Oregonian,* 13 June 1965.

47. Larry R. Ford, "A Metatheory of Urban Structure," in *Our Changing Cities,* ed. John Fraser Hart (Baltimore, Md.: Johns Hopkins University Press, 1991), 17.

CHAPTER 7

1. *With Heritage So Rich* (New York: Random House, 1966), 207.

2. Constance Beaumont, *Smart States, Better Communities: How State Governments Can Help Citizens Preserve Their Communities* (Washington, D.C.: National Trust for Historic Preservation, 1996), 10.

3. Antoinette J. Lee, ed., *Past Meets Future: Saving America's Historic Environments* (Washington, D.C.: National Trust for Historic Preservation), 205.

4. Ibid.

5. Thomas Michael Power, *Lost Landscapes and Failed Economies: The Search for a Value of Place* (Washington, D.C.: Island Press, 1996), 238.

6. Ibid., 15.

7. Robert H. McNulty, Dorothy R. Jacobson, and R. Leo Penne, "The Economics of Amenity: Community Future and Quality of Life: A Policy Guide to Urban Economic Development" (Washington, D.C.: Partners for Livable Places, 1985). Quoted in Roy Lubove, *Twentieth-Century Pittsburgh* (Pittsburgh, Pa.: University of Pittsburgh Press, 1996), 357.

8. Donovan D. Rypkema, *The Economics of Historic Preservation: A Community Leader's Guide* (Washington, D.C.: National Trust for Historic Preservation, 1994), 13.

9. Ibid.

10. Edward F. Sanderson, "Economic Effects of Historic Preservation in Rhode Island," *Historic Preservation Forum,* fall 1994, 25–26.

11. Beaumont, 97–105.

12. Ibid., 147.

13. James Howard Kunstler, *The Geography of Nowhere: The Rise and Decline of America's Man-made Landscape* (New York: Simon & Schuster, 1993), 10.

14. Peter Calthorpe, *The Next American Metropolis: Ecology, Community, and the American Dream* (New York: Princeton Architectural Press, 1993), 18.

15. Chris Lester and Jeffrey Spivak, "The Test of Success: Teamwork," *Kansas City Star,* 22 December 1995.

16. "Beyond Sprawl: New Patterns of Growth to Fit the New California," a report sponsored by the Bank of America, the California Resources Agency, the Greenbelt Alliance, and the Low-Income Housing Fund. San Francisco, California, February 1995.

17. Michael J. Sandel, *Democracy's Discontent* (Cambridge, Mass.: The Belknap Press of Harvard University Press, 1996), 3.

18. Wendell Berry, *Sex, Economy, Freedom and Community* (New York: Pantheon Books, 1993), 168.

19. Ibid., 4–5.

20. Power, 247.

21. Quoted in Robert Campbell, "Eco Chambers: Sustainable Architecture, the Movement to Design Buildings for a Better Environment, Is About Changing How We Live, Not Just How We Build," *Boston Sunday Globe,* Focus section, 25 July 1993.

22. Robert E. Stipe and Antoinette J. Lee, eds., *The American Mosaic: Preserving a Nation's Heritage* (Washington, D.C.: The United States Committee of the International Council on Monuments and Sites, 1987), 286.

23. Wendell Berry, *Home Economics* (New York: North Point Press, 1993), 191–92.

24. Jonathan Barnett, "Rebuilding America's Cities," *Architecture,* April 1995, 55–56.

25. Timothy Egan, "Drawing a Hard Line Against Urban Sprawl," *New York Times,* 30 December 1996.

26. Rypkema, *The Economics of Historic Preservation: A Community Leader's Guide,* 40.

27. Rypkema, "Rethinking Economic Values," in Antoinette J. Lee, ed., *Past Meets Future: Saving America's Historic Environments,* 210.

28. Lester and Spivak.

INDEX